This *Companion to Victorian Poetry* provides an up-to-date introduction to many of the pressing issues that absorbed the attention of poets from the 1830s to the 1890s. It introduces readers to a range of topics – including historicism, patriotism, prosody, and religious belief. The thirteen specially-commissioned chapters offer fresh insights into the works of well-known figures such as Matthew Arnold, Robert Browning, and Alfred Tennyson and the writings of women poets – like Michael Field, Amy Levy, and Augusta Webster – whose contribution to Victorian culture has only recently been acknowledged by modern scholars. Revealing the breadth of the Victorians' experiments with poetic form, this Companion also discloses the extent to which their writings addressed the prominent intellectual and social questions of the day. The volume, which will be of interest to scholars and students alike, features a detailed chronology of the Victorian period and a comprehensive guide to further reading.

THE CAMBRIDGE
COMPANION TO
VICTORIAN
POETRY

CAMBRIDGE COMPANIONS TO LITERATURE

THE CAMBRIDGE
COMPANION TO
VICTORIAN
POETRY

EDITED BY
JOSEPH BRISTOW

CAMBRIDGE
UNIVERSITY PRESS

PUBLISHED BY THE PRESS SYNDICATE OF THE UNIVERSITY OF CAMBRIDGE
The Pitt Building, Trumpington Street, Cambridge CB2 1RP, United Kingdom

CAMBRIDGE UNIVERSITY PRESS
The Edinburgh Building, Cambridge CB2 2RU, United Kingdom
http://www.cup.cam.ac.uk
40 West 20th Street, New York, NY 10011–4211, USA
http://www.cup.org
10 Stamford Road, Oakleigh, Melbourne 3166, Australia

© Cambridge University Press 2000

First published 2000

Printed in the United Kingdom at the University Press, Cambridge

Typeset in Sabon 10/13 pt. System 3B2   [CE]

A catalogue record for this book is available from the British Library

Library of Congress cataloging in publication data
The Cambridge companion to Victorian poetry / edited by
Joseph Bristow.
p.   cm. – (Cambridge companions to literature)
Includes bibliographical references and index.
ISBN 0 521 64115 2 (hardback)   0 521 64680 4 (paperback)
1. English poetry– 19th century – History and criticism.   2. Bristow,
Joseph. II. Series.
PR591.C36   2000
821'.309 – dc21   00–020013   CIP

ISBN 0 521 64115 2 hardback
ISBN 0 521 64680 4 paperback

CONTENTS

    THAïS E. MORGAN

11 Aesthetic and Decadent poetry   228
    KAREN ALKALAY-GUT

12 Victorian poetry and patriotism   255
    TRICIA LOOTENS

13 Voices of authority, voices of subversion: poetry in the late nineteenth   280
    century
    JOHN LUCAS

    Glossary   302
    Guide to Further Reading   304
    Index   312

NOTES ON CONTRIBUTORS

KAREN ALKALAY-GUT, Senior Lecturer in the Department of English at Tel-Aviv University, is the author of *Alone in the Dawn: The Life of Adelaide Crapsey* (University of Georgia Press, 1988) and many books of poetry in English and Hebrew. Her essays on Dowson, Swinburne, and Wilde have appeared in such journals as *Criticism, Journal of Pre-Raphaelite Studies, Victorians Institute Journal*, and *Victorian Poetry*. She is now at work on a study to be titled "The Logic of Late-Victorian Poetry."

JOSEPH BRISTOW is Professor of English at the University of California, Los Angeles. His books include *Effeminate England: Homoerotic Writing after 1885* (Columbia University Press, 1995) and *Sexuality* (Routledge, 1997). In addition, he has edited (with Isobel Armstrong and Cath Sharrock) *Victorian Women Poets: An Oxford Anthology* (Oxford University Press, 1996). He is completing a full-length study of Victorian poetry and sexual desire.

DANIEL BROWN teaches English at the University of Western Australia. In 1997, he published *Hopkins's Idealism: Philosophy, Physics, Poetry* (Oxford University Press) and (with Hilary Fraser) *English Prose of the Nineteenth Century* (Addison Wesley Longman).

SUSAN BROWN teaches English at the University of Guelph, Canada. Her work in Victorian poetry seeks to understand its relationship to diverse social fields including feminism, imperialism, and economics. Her current research is concentrated in the Orlando Project, a collaborative electronic history of British women's writing.

HILARY FRASER, Professor of English at the University of Western Australia, is the author of *The Victorians and Renaissance Italy* (Basil Blackwell, 1992) and (with Daniel Brown) *English Prose of the Nineteenth Century* (Addison Wesley Longman, 1997). She is currently working on women writing art history in nineteenth-century Britain, and is also engaged in a collaborative project on women, gender, and the nineteenth-century British periodical press.

TRICIA LOOTENS, Associate Professor of English at the University of Georgia, is the author of *Lost Saints: Silence, Gender, and Victorian Literary Canonization* (University Press of Virginia, 1996).

JOHN LUCAS, Professor of English at Nottingham Trent University, has published extensively on nineteenth- and twentieth-century British literature. His many books include *England and Englishness* (Hogarth Press, 1990) and *The Radical Twenties: Writing, Politics, and Culture* (Rutgers University Press, 1999).

THAÏS E. MORGAN, Associate Professor of English at Arizona State University (Tempe), writes in the fields of Victorian poetry and nonfiction prose, Aestheticism, the history of criticism, and contemporary critical theory. Her books include *Victorian Sages and Cultural Discourse: Renegotiating Gender and Power* (Rutgers University Press, 1990) and *Men Writing the Feminine: Literature, Theory, and the Question of Genders* (SUNY Press, 1990).

CORNELIA D.J. PEARSALL teaches English at Smith College, Northampton, MA. She is currently completing two books. One, "Transforming Tennyson: Victorian Culture and the Performance of the Poet," explores the poet's complex relation to his age through the form of the dramatic monologue. The other, "Loved Remains: The Materialization of Mourning in Victorian Britain," is an interdisciplinary investigation of the monuments, both literary and sculptural, that Victorians raised to their dead.

YOPIE PRINS, Associate Professor of English and Comparative Literature at the University of Michigan, is the author of *Victorian Sappho* (Princeton University Press, 1999) and co-editor of *Dwelling in Possibility: Women Poets and Critics on Poetry* (Ithaca, NY: Cornell University Press, 1999). She has published articles on Victorian poetry, Classical literature, and nineteenth-century Hellenism, and is currently writing a series of essays on meter.

KATHY ALEXIS PSOMIADES is Associate Professor of English at the University of Notre Dame, Indiana. She is the author of *Beauty's Body: Femininity and Representation in British Aestheticism* (Stanford University Press, 1997) and co-editor (with Talia S. Schaffer) of *Women and British Aestheticism* (University Press of Virginia, 1999). She is currently working on a project on late-Victorian novels and anthropology.

CYNTHIA SCHEINBERG is Associate Professor of English at Mills College, California. She has edited a special issue of *Victorian Literature and Culture* on Anglo-Jewish literary history. Her essays on Victorian women poets and theology have appeared in several places, including *Victorian Studies* and

Victorian Poetry. During 1996–97, she was Visiting Fellow at Harvard Divinity School's program in Women's Studies and Religion.

E. WARWICK SLINN is Associate Professor of English at Massey University, New Zealand. He has studied in Canada and England and has been a Fulbright Scholar at the University of Virginia and Duke University. He is the author of *Browning and the Fictions of Identity* (University Press of Virginia, 1982) and *The Discourse of Self in Victorian Poetry* (Macmillan, 1991).

PREFACE

The Cambridge Companion to Victorian Poetry presents some of the most exciting critical developments in an area of inquiry that has undergone remarkable changes during the past twenty years. Featuring thirteen chapters that address broad topics that came to public attention during Her Majesty Queen Victoria's long reign (1837–1901), this volume introduces readers to the dynamic – and, on occasion, contentious – roles that poetry played in a period covering some eight decades. Throughout this era poetry addressed issues such as patriotism, religious faith, science, sexuality, and social reform that often aroused polemical debate. At the same time, the poets whom we classify as Victorian frequently devised experiments that expanded the possibilities of the genre, creating innovative forms and types of prosody that enabled new kinds of poetic voices to emerge in print. The period saw the rise of a decidedly innovative kind of poem in the dramatic monologue, together with the emergence of other ambitious forms such as the bildungsroman-in-verse. Beginning with poems written in light of the Great Reform Bill of 1832 and ending with the election of Poet Laureate after Alfred Tennyson's death in 1892, this *Companion* offers detailed studies that deepen our understanding of the many different literary, historical, and political contexts in which Victorian poems were produced and consumed. Some of the chapters concentrate attention on the linguistic, metrical, and stylistic features that came to prominence during this epoch, while others explore the complex ways in which Victorian poets intervened in the controversies of the time. Taken together the chapters of this volume disclose how writers of miscellaneous temperaments – conservatives, liberals, and radicals, among many others – could express their conflicting perspectives on a society in which poetry commanded cultural authority.

Critics, however, have not always viewed the poetry of this era as such a rich resource, partly because of the rather negative connotations tradition-ally attached to the word Victorian: a term that only came into wide circulation some forty years after the Queen ascended the throne. And when it was eventually embedded in modern consciousness, the label Victorian more often than not conjured a rather dreary and forbidding vision of the world. At its most extreme, the adjective Victorian characterized those austere values to which Margaret Thatcher (British Prime Minister from 1979 to 1990) attempted to espouse her Tory government. On this view, Victorian invoked an unremitting lower-middle-class morality, one based on values of decency, self-help, and thrift, not to say knowing one's place in a class-stratified society. To pay respect to one's betters, to pull oneself up by the bootstraps, to remain firmly independent of support from the state: all of these actions formed part of a stereotypical – and thus misleading – image of the codes of conduct by which all good citizens from the 1830s to the 1890s were purported to have lived. And even when modern intellectuals expressed profound criticism of these unforgiving Victorian principles, they frequently concurred that the culture that developed during this long period adhered mainly to these strictures and little else. The Modernists – who came to public attention from the time of the Great War (1914–18) onward – adopted this perspective on their Victorian forebears. Some of the most notable Modernist criticisms of Victorian narrow-mindedness emerge in the writings of the Bloomsbury Group, the London-based coterie whose distinguished members included the novelists E.M. Forster and Virginia Woolf. One of its noted intellectuals, Lytton Strachey, wittily mocked various types of imperial zeal, philanthropic patronage, and Christian piety in his four famous studies of eminent Victorians. In an iconoclastic spirit, Strachey refused to elevate a figure such as Florence Nightingale as a "saintly, self-sacrificing woman": he presented her instead as someone who brought order to the military hospitals of the Crimea "by strict method, by stern discipline, by rigid attention to detail, by ceaseless labour, by the fixed determination of an indomitable will" (*Eminent Victorians: Cardinal Manning, Florence Nightingale, Dr. Arnold, General Gordon* [London: Chatto and Windus, 1918], 119, 137). It was from this unappealing inheritance that Modernists such as Strachey sought to emancipate themselves.

Given the Modernists unfavorable outlook on the mid- and late-nineteenth century, one might be led to believe that all things Victorian were morally fierce, socially restrictive, and sexually repressive. Certainly some of the most widely anthologized Victorian poems articulate a defiant self-determination, one that upholds imperial and patriotic ideals. In this respect, W.E. Henley's "Invictus" (1875) remains perhaps the ultimate example of the Victorian spirit that remains valiantly prepared to endure the trials of adversity, whatever the cost. "I am the master of my fate," the speaker memorably declares, "I am the captain of my soul": a sentiment that may well sound to some ears as quintessentially of its time. But by the mid-twentieth century Jerome H. Buckley began a critical trend that looked more closely at the ways in which the kind of "Victorianism" that we might find in "Invictus" "persisted" as "a shield for the conservative and a target for the modernist" (4). In *The Victorian Temper: A Study in Literary Culture* (Cambridge, MA: Harvard University Press, 1951), Buckley contends that to understand "Victorianism" critics need to distance themselves from this rhetoric of "praise and blame" (7). Better, he thinks, to acknowledge that the "Victorians were quite unable to view their long era as a static entity, a unique whole to be described by a single sweeping formula." In Buckley's view the Victorian temper – even though marked by a definite article – belonged to an era whose "tensions . . . militated against complete spontaneity and singleness of purpose" (12), given the scope and breadth of British culture during this long period of history.

This *Companion* follows Buckley's lead in showing how and why it remains difficult to summarize what it might mean to be characteristically Victorian – either in relation to poetry in particular or to the culture in general. Indeed, the danger in using any broad term like Victorian lies in how it may appear an all-encompassing concept, as if the adjective could reasonably draw together the multiple elements of an amorphous society into a coherent and stable order. None of the chapters in this volume assumes that a unitary set of values accords with the term Victorian. Nor do these studies propose that there is a specific type of poetry that stands for the age. Instead, the word has a different usage. It defines an epoch – an expanse of time so the long that it often remains hard to see clear cultural, political, and indeed poetic continuities from beginning to end. If, then, we admit that scholars employ the term Victorian to designate a period of literary history that has no unchanging core, we may as well ask why we keep using the word at all.

This question is an important one. But it has, of course, an obvious answer. The main reason for currently holding on to the term Victorian relates to matters of scholarly convention and syllabus design. It goes without saying that readers will consult this volume because they wish to know more about a field of study designated as Victorian poetry. Yet, as with all periods of literary history, this field does not have entirely fixed boundaries, especially with regard to the specific poets whom critics have come to value most highly. The value attributed to the many different poetical works that fall within this field has transformed considerably over time. Correspondingly, the kinds of poetry that have been deemed worthy of analysis have changed as well.

It is fair to assert that until the 1980s critical volumes devoted to

Victorian poetry often focused on a triumvirate – Alfred Tennyson, Robert Browning, and Matthew Arnold, with each poet ranked in that descending order. There were good reasons why researchers and teachers concentrated much of their attention on such a small – if undeniably eminent – group of poets. In the early part of the twentieth century when the discipline of English literature sometimes struggled to establish itself as a legitimate area of inquiry, many scholars followed Arnold's influential lead to underline the distinctions between major and minor talents (see Arnold, "Heinrich Heine" [1863]). Much has been written on how the imperative to discriminate between greater and lesser authors fuelled a powerful current in literary studies as a whole. The effort to preserve and study the best poetry resulted in the analysis of a rather constricted – though by no means static – canon of "major" poets (namely Tennyson, Robert Browning, and Arnold), even while modest amounts of research on many semi-canonical or "minor" figures thrived at the same time.

Two imposing studies from Cambridge University Press show this process at work. In *The Cambridge History of English Literature* – a compendious fifteen-volume series published between 1907 and 1927 – the chapters give pride of place to the exalted Victorian triumvirate, somewhat more selective treatment of their less noted contemporaries, and accounts of numerous other writers who receive the briefest mention. The editors assign one chapter each to the Tennyson brothers (much to Alfred, far less to Charles) and another to Robert Browning and Elizabeth Barrett Browning. They combine Arnold's poetic writings with those of his close friend Arthur Hugh Clough and the Republican writer James Thomson ("B.V."). The Pre-Raphaelites – William Morris, Christina Rossetti, Dante Gabriel Rossetti, Algernon Charles Swinburne, and Arthur O'Shaughnessey – feature together. The remaining writers, who appear abundant in comparison, populate the longest discussion titled "Lesser Poets of the Middle and Later Nineteenth Century." Equally noteworthy in this respect is *The New Cambridge Bibliography of English Literature* (1969–77) whose five volumes provide an indispensable tool of research for literary scholars. In its comprehensive listings, this bibliography separates major from minor writers. But it would be mistaken to see the persistence of canon-formation in these two books, published some seventy years apart, as a wholly exclusive enterprise. In fact, both of these excellent works of reference offer reliable access to an astonishing range of so-called lesser writings whose value can be understood in terms markedly different from those that elevate Tennyson, Robert Browning, and Arnold into the Pantheon.

In the *Cambridge History* George Saintsbury's long and detailed chapters on "lesser" poets of the nineteenth century give a fair indication of some of the difficulties facing scholars when it comes to comprehending the comparative merits of the vast quantities of poetry with which they are acquainted. At times, Saintsbury – an immensely knowledgeable critic – views the question of a poet's value as a matter of critical consensus, though it remains obvious from his metaphors that it has not always been easy to agree on who should rise above the others. Discussing "Lesser Poets, 1790–1837" (the period usually categorized as Romantic), he remarks: "[Robert] Southey, indeed, may have been 'knocked out' in the competition on one side, on the general opinion, and [Walter] Scott and [George] Crabbe, on the other, may hold their ground, though with considerably fewer points to their credit than [William] Wordsworth and [Samuel Taylor] Coleridge" (XII, 95). And for those writers who have not even managed to jump into the ring and fight to the last, Saintsbury finds other measures to disclose their weakness. Among the band of late-Romantic poets who came to public attention in the 1820s and 1830s – such as Thomas Lovell Beddoes, Thomas Hood, Winthrop Mackworth Praed, and Henry Taylor – he declares "there is still something about them is indigested and incomplete." Unable to show their physical strength, women poets unsurprisingly fare worse. Although there is one lesser late-Victorian figure, M.E. Coleridge, who impresses Saintsbury, he remarks that the huge popularity of L.E.L. (Letitia Elizabeth Landon) much earlier in the century "set a most unfortunate precedent . . . for women verse-writers" (XII, 126) – because their poetry, we might assume, enfeebled their already frail constitutions.

Saintsbury's commentary too readily lends itself to mockery, and it remains easy for modern critics to poke fun at the seemingly outdated condition of his scholarship. To be sure, in his inexhaustible enumeration of various lesser poets, it is amusing to find Saintsbury wondering why he might be discussing them at all. Turning his attention to Martin Farquar Tupper's *Proverbial Philosophy* (1838–76) – originally sold at a farthing to reach a growing lower middle-class readership – he remarks that "at times, the dullness ferments itself into sheer silliness" (XIII, 150). But he nevertheless finds himself obliged to declare that since Tupper's work was so popular "it can never wholly lose its position" (XIII, 150). Indeed, he produces another – more compelling – reason for reviewing all of the expressly lesser materials drawn from his wide reading. No matter what misgivings he may have about these inferior writers, he remains convinced about the ultimate value that dwells within this eclectic body of minor work:

There is, beyond all question, in this long period and among the crowd of lesser singers, an amount of diffused poetry which cannot be paralleled in any other age or country except perhaps, perhaps, in our own land and language between 1580 and 1674. At no period, not even then, has the standard of technical craftsmanship been so high; at none has there been anything like such variety of subject and, to a rather lesser extent, of tone. (XIII, 221–22)

For all their minority status, therefore, those poets congregating in the lower ranks of literature have nonetheless produced work that in its attention to form and its diversity of subject matter stands as a tribute to the nation. On these terms, the lesser writers appear sufficiently great that one could (like Saintsbury) almost begin to question why they should have been devalued in the first place.

Based on different ideas of literary value, *The Cambridge Companion to Victorian Poetry* does not subscribe to the canon-bolstering assumptions that underpin (albeit uncomfortably) Saintsbury's influential essays in *The Cambridge History of English Literature*. Rather than spend time discriminating between major and minor authors, all but one of the chapters in the present volume look instead at a large topic that preoccupied a range of writers. And the study that takes as its subject the most canonical of all Victorian poets – Alfred Tennyson – does so to contemplate the kinds of value that successive generations of critics have staked upon one of his most celebrated poems, "The Lady of Shalott." Each discussion in turn adopts a range of modern critical approaches – drawn from sources as diverse as gender studies, materialist critique, post-structuralist thought, and cultural historicism – to analyze a much wider span of writers than proponents of the major canon were for decades willing to take seriously. Tennyson, Robert Browning, and Arnold assuredly maintain a prominent position in these pages, not least because their works absorbed an immense amount of critical attention during their lifetimes. But so too do Elizabeth Barrett Browning, Morris, Christina Rossetti, Dante Gabriel Rossetti, and Swinburne – writers who made a profound impression on their age but who were often pushed to the sidelines when the modern discipline of English literature became somewhat selective in the objects that it felt were suitable for study.

Women poets in particular occupy a more noticeable place in this *Companion* than they do in the anthologies and works of criticism that circulated in colleges and universities during the mid-twentieth century. Consider, for example, *Poetry of the Victorian Period*, first published in 1930, and subsequently revised and expanded in various editions until 1965. This weighty volume, with its thorough annotations and generous selections from some forty-seven poets, includes in its 1965 imprint only five women writers. Similar limitations appear in *The Oxford Book of Nineteenth-Century English Verse* (1964), which – in the course of some nine-hundred pages – features no more than eleven women poets. It would take until 1978 when The Women's Press issued Cora Kaplan's impressive edition of Barrett Browning's *Aurora Leigh* (1856) – a poem of epic proportions that dramatizes one woman's poetic career – before scholars began to reassess how and why the reputation of a writer whom a mid-Victorian readership often held in very high regard should have gone into serious decline toward the close of the nineteenth century. Not long after Barrett Browning's *magnum opus* drew the praise of a new generation of readers, R.W. Crump's magnificent variorum edition of Christina Rossetti's poetry was published, helping to establish this poet's imposing oeuvre on syllabi. Ever since the late 1970s many Victorianists have devoted energies to unearthing, reevaluating, and then reprinting selections from the inspiring works of writers as different as Michael Field (Katherine Bradley and Edith Cooper), Amy Levy, and Augusta Webster: all of whom speak powerfully to a new generation of readers who want to know more about women's distinctive contributions to nineteenth-century culture.

Appearing almost a century after the Victorian period officially came to an end, this *Companion* shows that this era comes very much to life when we embrace an inclusive range of poetry by many different poets whose work need no longer be categorized in terms of major or minor talents. In the coming decades, it is more than likely that research into varieties of working-class poetry, poetry for children, dialect poetry, and poems that appeared in a very broad range of print media (such as regional news-papers) will further broaden our knowledge of different aspects of British culture as it unfolded from the 1830s to the 1890s. It seems more than probable that as the twenty-first century runs its course, scholars will reconfigure how we think about the many works brought together under the heading Victorian poetry. In all probability they will suggest alternative frameworks for comprehending the poems that passed into print while the Queen presided over the nation. Such critics will no doubt rise to the challenge of redefining the label Victorian – perhaps to the point of devising terms that will eventually displace it.

ACKNOWLEDGMENTS

The Cambridge Companion to Victorian Poetry began to take shape when I held a Senior External Research Fellowship at the Stanford Humanities Center in 1995–96. My thanks go to the Director of Center, Keith Michael Baker, and his friendly staff for their hospitality. Two fellow Victorianists, Regenia Gagnier and Yopie Prins, offered helpful advice during the early stages of editing. At the University of California, Los Angeles, Ronald Lear and Thomas Wortham generously shared their editorial wisdom. In the UCLA English Department, Jeanette Gilkison undertook countless tasks that eased communication between California and England. During 1997–99, Matthew Titolo, Laura Franey, and James Walter Caufield in turn provided excellent research assistance. At the other end of the UCLA campus, the surgical skills of Donald Becker and the medical support of Jerome Greenberg enabled me to continue with my life. The staffs of the Young Research Library (UCLA), the William Andrews Clark Memorial Library (UCLA), and the London Library (St James's Square, London) guided me toward resources that I would otherwise have missed. At Cambridge University Press, Josie Dixon's encouragement and patience proved inspiring. Likewise, Linda Bree's painstaking editorial feedback strengthened the volume as a whole. Finally, I must express my gratitude to all of the contributors – without whom, of course, this *Companion* would not have been possible.

"O What a Silence in this Wilderness" appears by permission of Oxford University Press and is taken from Gerard Manley Hopkins, *The Poetical Works*, ed. Norman H. MacKenzie (Oxford: Clarendon Press, 1990).

Joseph Bristow

ABBREVIATIONS

ACS   Algernon Charles Swinburne, *The Poems of Algernon Charles Swinburne*, 6 vols. (London: Chatto and Windus, 1904); volume and page references appear in parentheses

AHC   Arthur Hugh Clough, *Amours de Voyage*, ed. Patrick Scott (Brisbane: University of Queensland Press, 1974); line references appear in parentheses

AL   Amy Levy, *The Complete Novels and Selected Writings of Amy Levy 1861–1889*, ed. Melvyn New (Gainesville, FL: University Press of Florida, 1993); line references appear in parentheses

AS   Arthur Symons, *Collected Works*, 9 vols. (London: Martin Secker, 1924); volume and page references appear in parentheses

AT   Alfred Tennyson, *The Poems of Tennyson*, Second Edition, ed. Christopher Ricks, 3 vols. (Harlow: Longman, 1987); line references appear in parentheses

CR   Christina Rossetti, *The Complete Poems of Christina Rossetti*, ed. R.W. Crump, 3 vols. (Baton Rouge, LA: Louisiana State University Press, 1979–90); line references appear in parentheses

DGR   Dante Gabriel Rossetti, *The Works of Dante Gabriel Rossetti*, revised and enlarged edition, ed. William M. Rossetti (London: Ellis, 1911); page references appear in parentheses

EBB   Elizabeth Barrett Browning, *The Complete Works of Elizabeth Barrett Browning*, ed. Charlotte Porter and Helen A. Clarke, 6 vols. (New York: Thomas Y. Crowell, 1900); line references appear in parentheses.

EBBAL   Elizabeth Barrett Browning, *Aurora Leigh*, ed. Margaret Reynolds (Athens, OH: Ohio University Press, 1992); line references appear in parentheses

ED   Ernest Dowson, *Poems*, ed. Mark Longaker (Philadelphia, PA, University of Pennsylvania Press, 1962); page references appear in parentheses

FH   Felicia Hemans, *The Works of Mrs. Hemans; with a Memoir of her Life, by Her Sister*, 7 vols. (Edinburgh: William Blackwood, 1839); volume and page references appear in parentheses

GM   George Meredith, *The Poems of George Meredith*, ed. Phyllis B. Bartlett, 2 vols. (New Haven, CT: Yale University Press, 1978); line numbers appear in parentheses.

GMH   Gerard Manley Hopkins, *The Poetical Works*, ed. Norman H. MacKenzie (Oxford: Clarendon Press, 1990); line references appear in parentheses

LEL   Letitia Elizabeth Landon [L.E.L.], *Poetical Works*, ed. F. J. Sypher (Delmar, NY: Scholars' Facsimiles and Reprints, 1990); page references appear in parentheses

MA   Matthew Arnold, *The Poems of Matthew Arnold*, second edition, ed. Kenneth Allott and Miriam Allott (London: Longman, 1979); line references appear in parentheses

OW   Oscar Wilde, *Complete Poems*, ed. Isobel Murray, The World's Classics (Oxford: Oxford University Press, 1997); line references appear in parentheses

RB   Robert Browning, *The Poems*, ed. John Pettigrew and Thomas J. Collins, 2 vols. (Harmondsworth: Penguin Books); line references appear in parentheses

RBRB   Robert Browning, *The Ring and the Book*, ed. Richard D. Altick (Harmondsworth: Penguin Books, 1969); line references appear in parentheses

RK   Rudyard Kipling, *Verse*, definitive edition (New York: Doran and Doran, 1940); page references appear in parentheses

TH   Thomas Hardy, *The Complete Poetical Works*, ed. Samuel Hynes, 5 vols. (Oxford: Clarendon Press, 1982–95); line references appear in parentheses

WBY   W.B. Yeats, *The Poems*, revised edition, ed. Richard Finneran (New York: Macmillan, 1989); line references appear in parentheses

WEH   W.E. Henley, *Poems* (London: Macmillan, 1926); page numbers appear in parentheses

WM   *The Collected Works of William Morris*, ed. May Morris, 24 vols. (London: Longmans Green and Company, 1910); volume and page references appear in parentheses

NOTE ON THE TEXTS

For the sake of consistency, all of the contributors to this volume quote from the same editions of poetry. To help minimize the number of endnotes, abbreviations are used sparingly in the main text to indicate the editions from which quotations have been taken. These editions have been selected on the basis of their reliability. In several cases, however, these texts remain unfortunately out of print. Readers will note that it is still the case that scholars must use authoritative editions of Elizabeth Barrett Browning's, Dante Gabriel Rossetti's, and Algernon Charles Swinburne's poetical works that were originally published in 1901, 1911, and 1904 respectively. Given the considerable revival of scholarly interest in each of these poets, one can only hope that publishers will seize on the opportunity to issue new much-needed annotated editions of these authors' works.

Since some readers may be unfamiliar with a number of critical terms relating to such issues as prosody, I have provided a succinct glossary at the end of the volume. For more detailed accounts of each of the terms listed, see M.H. Abrams, *A Glossary of Literary Terms*, seventh edition (Fort Worth, TX: Harcourt Brace, 1999) and Alex Preminger and T.V.F. Brogan et al., eds., *The New Princeton Encyclopedia of Poetry and Poetics* (Princeton: N.J.: Princeton University Press, 1993). Finally, this *Companion* contains a "Guide to Further Reading" that presents a selection of critical works, dating from the 1960s to the present, that reflect recent developments in the study of Victorian poetry. References to many influential earlier critical works in the field can be located both in the endnotes to each chapter and in Frederick F. Faverty, *The Victorian Poets: A Guide to Research*, second edition (Cambridge, MA: Harvard University Press, 1968).

In Victorian studies it is the convention to identify wherever possible the names of writers who contributed unsigned articles to the periodicals of the day. These names appear in square parentheses in the endnotes.

JEB

CHRONOLOGY OF PUBLICATIONS AND EVENTS

1820   Elizabeth Barrett, *The Battle of Marathon*

1824   L.E.L. [Letitia Elizabeth Landon], *The Improvisatrice*

1826   Elizabeth Barrett, *An Essay on Mind, with Other Poems*

1827   John Clare, *The Shepherd's Calendar*
        John Keble, *The Christian Year*

1828   Felicia Hemans, *Records of Woman and Other Poems*
        L.E.L., *The Venetian Bracelet*
        Repeal of Test and Corporation Acts; Nonconformists admitted
        to parliament

1829   Thomas Carlyle, "Signs of the Times"
        Alfred Tennyson and Charles Tennyson, *Poems by Two Brothers*
        Catholic Emancipation Act
        Metropolitan Police Act (London)

1830   Felicia Hemans, *Songs of the Affections*
        Charles Lyell, *Principles of Geology* (completed 1833)
        (June) Death of George IV; accession of William IV
        (September) Liverpool and Manchester Railway
        (November) Grey administration

1831   Arthur Henry Hallam, "On Some Characteristics of Modern
        Poetry"
        Ebenezer Elliott, *Corn-Law Rhymes*
        Tennyson, *Poems, Chiefly Lyrical*
        (March) Lord John Russell introduces First Reform Bill into

House of Commons
(October) House of Lords rejects Reform Bill; riots in
Nottingham, Derby, Bristol

1832   Tennyson, *Poems*
(June) First Reform Bill given royal assent

1833   Robert Browning, *Pauline; a Fragment of a Confession*
John Stuart Mill, "What Is Poetry?" and "The Two Kinds of
Poetry"
Oxford Movement begins; *Tracts for the Times* (until 1841)
Bridgewater Treatises (until 1837)
(August) Abolition of slavery in British Empire

1834   Hemans, *National Lyrics and Song for Music*
Hemans, *Scenes and Hymns of Life*
(July) Poor Law Amendment Act ("New Poor Law")
(December) Peel administration

1835   Robert Browning, *Paracelsus*
(April) Second Melbourne administration

1836   A.W.G. Pugin, *Contrasts: or a Parallel between the Noble
Edifices of the Fourteenth and Fifteenth Centuries and Similar
Buildings of the Present Day, Shewing the Decay of Taste*

1837   (June) Death of William IV; accession of Victoria

1838   Elizabeth Barrett, *The Seraphim and Other Poems*
(May) People's Charter published
(September) John Bright and Richard Cobden form Anti-Corn
Law League

1839   L.E.L., *The Zenana and Minor Poems*
(May) "Opium War" against China begins
(June) Chartist petition presented to parliament; rejected the
following month

1840   Robert Browning, *Sordello*
Caroline Norton, *The Dream and Other Poems*
Jewish Reform Movement founded

1841   Carlyle, *On Heroes, Hero-Worship, and the Heroic in History*
        (August) Second Peel administration

1842   Robert Browning, *Dramatic Lyrics*
        Tennyson, *Poems*
        (August) Treaty of Nanking ends "Opium War"
        Income Tax (abolished in 1816) reintroduced at 7*d.* in the £

1843   Carlyle, *Past and Present*
        John Ruskin, *Modern Painters* (completed 1860)

1844   Elizabeth Barrett, *Poems*
        Robert Chambers, *Vestiges of the Natural History of Creation*
        Coventry Patmore, *Poems*

1845   Robert Browning, *Dramatic Romances and Lyrics*
        Edward Lear, *A Book of Nonsense*
        John Henry Newman converts to Rome
        (October) Irish famine (until 1850)
        Evangelical Alliance formed

1846   George Eliot's English translation of David Friedrich Strauss, *The
        Life of Jesus, Critically Examined* (the "Higher Criticism")
        (June) Repeal of the Corn Laws
        (June) Russell administration

1847   Tennyson, *The Princess*
        (April) Chartist demonstration at Kennington Common, London

1848   Arthur Hugh Clough, *The Bothie of Toper-na-fuosich*

1849   Matthew Arnold, *The Strayed Reveller and Other Poems*
        Clough (with Thomas Burbidge), *Ambarvalia*

1850   Elizabeth Barrett Browning, *Sonnets from the Portuguese*
        Robert Browning, *Christmas-Eve and Easter-Day*
        Tennyson, *In Memoriam, A.H.H.*
        (September) Roman Catholic hierarchy reestablished in England

1851   Elizabeth Barrett Browning, *Casa Guidi Windows*
        George Meredith, *Poems*

Ruskin, *The Stones of Venice* (completed 1853)
Census of Religious Worship in England and Wales
(May) Great Exhibition in Hyde Park, London

1852   Arnold, *Empedocles on Etna and Other Poems*
(February) Edward Stanley, 14th Earl of Derby's administration

1853   Arnold, *Poems: A New Edition* (with "Preface" explaining
exclusion of "Empedocles on Etna")
Patmore, *Tamerton Church-Tower and Other Poems*
(December) Aberdeen administration

1854   *The Angel in the House* (completed 1856; revised editions until
1885)
(March) Crimean War begins

1855   Arnold, *Poems: Second Series*
Robert Browning, *Men and Women*
Tennyson, *Maud and Other Poems*
(February) Palmerston administration

1856   (December) Elizabeth Barrett Browning, *Aurora Leigh*
(March) Treaty of Paris ends Crimean War

1857   (May) Indian Mutiny
Matrimonial Causes Act ("Divorce Act")

1858   Arnold, *Merope: A Tragedy*
Arthur Hugh Clough, *Amours de Voyages*
William Morris, *The Defence of Guenevere and Other Poems*
Adelaide Anne Procter, *Legends and Lyrics*
(February) Second Derby administration

1859   Charles Darwin, *On the Origin of Species by Means of Natural
Selection*
Edward FitzGerald, *The Rubáiyát of Omar Khayyám* (revised
editions in 1869, 1872, 1879, and 1889)
Tennyson, *Idylls of the King* (completed 1885)
John Stuart Mill, *On Liberty*
(June) Second Palmerston administration

1868 Robert Browning, *The Ring and the Book* (completed 1869)
Morris, *The Earthly Paradise* (completed 1870)
First Trades Union Congress
(October) Suez Canal opens
(December) Liberal Government; Gladstone (Prime Minister and Chancellor of the Exchequer)

1869 Arnold, *Culture and Anarchy*
John Stuart Mill, *The Subjection of Women*

1870 Alfred Austin, *The Poetry of the Period*
Dante Gabriel Rossetti, *Poems*
Webster, *Portraits*
(August) Forster's Elementary Education Act

1871 Robert Browning, *Balaustion's Adventure*
Robert Browning, *Prince Hohenstiel-Schwangau: Saviour of Society*
Robert Buchanan, "The Fleshly School of Poetry: Dante Gabriel Rossetti"
Darwin, *The Descent of Man, and Selection in Relation to Sex*
Swinburne, *Songs before Sunrise*
Newnham College, Cambridge, founded
(June) Religious tests abolished at the Universities of Oxford and Cambridge.
(June) Trade Union Act

1872 Robert Browning, *Fifine at the Fair*
Buchanan, *The Fleshly School of Poetry and Other Phenomena of the Day*
Christina Rossetti, *Sing-Song: A Nursery Rhyme-Book*
(August) Licensing Act restricts sale of alcoholic beverages

1873 Robert Browning, *Red-Cotton Night-Cap Country: or Turf and Towers*
Mill, *Autobiography*
Pater, *Studies in the History of the Renaissance* (later known as *The Renaissance*)
(June) Ashanti War begins in Gold Coast

1874 James Thomson ("B.V."), "The City of Dreadful Night"

1875   Robert Browning, *The Inn Album*
Christina Rossetti, *Goblin Market, The Prince's Progress, and Other Poems*
(February) Conservative government; Disraeli (Prime Minister)

1876   Robert Browning, *Pacchiarotto and How He Worked in Distemper; with Other Poems*
Swinburne, *Erechtheus*

1877   Morris, *The Story of Sigurd the Volsung and the Fall of the Niblungs*
Patmore, *The Unknown Eros and Other Odes*
(January) Victoria proclaimed Empress of India

1878   Robert Browning, *La Saisiaz, and The Two Poets of Croisic*
Swinburne, *Poems and Ballads: Second Series*
(January) Zulu War (until 1879)

1879   Robert Browning, *Dramatic Idyls*

1880   Arnold, "The Study of Poetry"
Robert Browning, *Dramatic Idyls: Second Series*
Dante Gabriel Rossetti, *Ballads and Sonnets*
Swinburne, *Songs of the Springtides*
Tennyson, *Ballads and Other Poems*
(April) Liberal government; Gladstone (Prime Minister)
(December) Boers declare independence in South Africa; First Anglo-Boer War (until 1881)

1881   Christina Rossetti, *A Pageant and Other Poems*
Oscar Wilde, *Poems*
Married Women's Property Act (ownership of property)

1882   Swinburne, *Tristram of Lyonesse and Other Poems*

1883   Robert Browning, *Jocoseria*

1884   Robert Browning, *Ferishtah's Fancies*
Amy Levy, *A Minor Poet and Oher Verse*
Married Women's Property Act (legal status as independent person)

(May) Franchise Bill (Third Reform Bill) introduced into House of Commons

(November) Third Reform Act given royal assent

1885   Tennyson, *Tiresias and Other Poems*

Criminal Law Amendment Act (age of consent for male–female sexual relations raised to 16; sexual relations between men classed as "gross indecency")

(June) Conservative government; Robert Gascoyne-Cecil, 5th Marquess of Salisbury (Prime Minister)

1886   Rudyard Kipling, *Departmental Ditties and Other Verses*

Morris, *The Pilgrims of Hope: A Poem in Thirteen Books*

Tennyson, *Locksley Hall Sixty Years After, Etc.*

W.B. Yeats, *Mosada: A Dramatic Poem*

(February) Liberal government; Gladstone (Prime Minister)

(April) Gladstone introduces Irish Home Rule Bill into House of Commons

(June) Defeat of Irish Home Rule Bill

(July) Conservative government; Marquess of Salisbury (Prime Minister)

1887   Robert Browning, *Parleyings with Certain People of Importance in Their Day*

Meredith, *Ballads and Poems of the Tragic Life*

Robert Louis Stevenson, *Underwoods*

(June) Victoria's Golden Jubilee

(November) Police and troops break up Social Democratic Federation meeting at Trafalgar Square, London ("Bloody Sunday")

1888   Meredith, *A Reading of Earth*

1889   Robert Browning, *Asolando: Fancies and Facts*

Michael Field, *Long Ago*

Levy, *A London-Plane Tree and Other Verse*

Swinburne, *Poems and Ballads: Third Series*

Arthur Symons, *Days and Nights*

Tennyson, *Demeter and Other Poems*

Yeats, *The Wandering of Oisin and Other Poems*

(August–September) London dock strike

1890   Christina Rossetti, *Poems*
        First British mosque, Woking, Surrey

1891   Morris, *Chants for Socialists*
        Morris, *Poems by the Way*

1892   Michael Field, *Sight and Song*
        W.E. Henley, *The Song of the Sword and Other Verses*
        Kipling, *Barrack-Room Ballads and Other Verses*
        Meredith, *Poems: The Empty Purse, with Odes to the Comic
        Spirit, to Youth in Memory, and Verses*
        Symons, *Silhouettes*
        Tennyson, *The Death of Oenone, Akbar's Dream and Other Poems*
        (August) Liberal government; Gladstone (Prime Minister)

1893   Michael Field, *Underneath the Bough*
        Henley, *London Voluntaries and Other Verses*
        Christina Rossetti, *Verses*
        Independent Labour Party established
        (September) Gladstone introduces Second Irish Home Rule Bill
        into House of Commons
        (September) Second Irish Home Rule Bill defeated in House of
        Lords

1894   Swinburne, *Astrophel and Other Poems*
        Symons, *London Nights*
        Wilde, *The Sphinx*
        (March) Gladstone resigns; Archibald Primrose, 5th Earl of
        Rosebery (Prime Minister)

1895   Lionel Johnson, *Poems*
        Yeats, *Poems* (revised 1899 and 1901)
        (April) Imprisonment of Wilde
        (July) Conservative–Liberal Unionist government; Marquess of
        Salisbury (Prime Minister)
        (December) Jameson Raid, South Africa

1896   Ernest Dowson, *Verses*

1897   Lionel Johnson, *Ireland, with Other Poems*
        Symons, *Amoris Victima*

National Union of Women's Suffrage Societies founded; Millicent Fawcett (President)

(June) Victoria's Diamond Jubilee

1898   Thomas Hardy, *Wessex Poems and Other Verses*

Wilde, *The Ballad of Reading Gaol*

(September) British and French military forces conflict at Fashoda ("Fashoda Crisis")

1899   Dowson, *Decorations in Verse and Prose*

Symons, *Images of Good and Evil*

Yeats, *The Wind among the Reeds*

(October) Second Anglo-Boer War begins

1900   (October) Conservative–Liberal Unionist government ("Khaki Election"); Marquess of Salisbury (Prime Minister)

A Reading of Life with Other Poems

(January) Death of Victoria; accession of Edward VII

1902   Hardy, *Poems of the Past and the Present*

(May) Second Anglo-Boer War ends

(December) Education Act (Local Education Authorities provide secondary education)

1918   Gerard Manley Hopkins, *Poems*

Ebenezer Elliott (1781–1849)
R.H. Barham (1788–1845)
John Keble (1792–1866)
John Clare (1793–1864)
Felicia Hemans (1793–1835)
Thomas Hood (1799–1845)
Mary Howitt (1799–1888)
William Barnes (1801–1886)
Caroline Clive ("V.") (1801–1873)
John Henry Newman (1801–1890)
Sara Coleridge (1802–1852)
L.E.L. (Letitia Elizabeth Landon)
  (1802–1838)
Winthrop Mackworth Praed
  (1802–1839)
Thomas Lovell Beddoes
  (1803–1849)
R.S. Hawker (1803–1875)
Elizabeth Barrett Browning
  (1806–1861)
Caroline Norton (1808–1877)
Charles Tennyson (later Turner)
  (1808–1879)
Edward FitzGerald (1809–1883)
Frances Kemble (1809–1893)
Alfred Tennyson (1809–1892)
Martin Farquhar Tupper
  (1810–1889)
Robert Browning (1812–1889)
Edward Lear (1812–1875)

W.J. Linton (1812–1898)
Aubrey de Vere (1814–1902)
Frederick William Faber
  (1814–1863)
Grace Aguilar (1816–1855)
Philip James Bailey (1816–1902)
Charlotte Brontë (1816–1855)
Emily Brontë (1818–1848)
Eliza Cook (1818–1889)
Arthur Hugh Clough (1819–1861)
George Eliot (1819–1880)
Ernest Jones (1819–1869)
Charles Kingsley (1819–1875)
Jean Ingelow (1820–1897)
Ebenezer Jones (1820–1860)
Matthew Arnold (1821–1888)
Dora Greenwell (1821–1882)
Jane Francesca Wilde ("Speranza")
  (1821–1896)
Coventry Patmore (1823–1896)
Dante Gabriel Rossetti
  (1823–1882)
William Allingham (1824–1889)
Louisa Shore (1824–1895)
Adelaide Anne Procter
  (1825–1864)
Emily Pfeiffer (1827–1890)
Gerald Massey (1828–1911)
Bessie Rayner Parkes (later Belloc)
  (1829–1925)

Alexander Smith (1829–1867)
T.E. Brown (1830–1897)
Christina Rossetti (1830–1894)
Charles Stuart Calverley
 (1831–1884)
Isa Craig (later Craig-Knox)
 (1831–1903)
Edwin Arnold (1832–1904)
Charles Lutwidge Dodgson ("Lewis
 Carroll") (1832–1898)
Richard Watson Dixon
 (1833–1900)
Lewis Morris (1833–1907)
William Morris (1834–1896)
James Thomson ("B.V.")
 (1834–1882)
Alfred Austin (1835–1913)
Frances Ridley Havergal
 (1836–1879)
Algernon Charles Swinburne
 (1837–1909)
Augusta Webster (1837–1894)
Wilfrid Scawen Blunt (1840–1922)
Thomas Hardy (1840–1928)
Harriet Eleanor Hamilton King
 (1840–1920)
John Addington Symonds
 (1840–1893)
Mathilde Blind (1841–1896)
Robert Buchanan (1841–1901)
"Violet Fane" (Mary Montgomerie
 Lamb, later Singleton, later Lady
 Currie) (1843–1905)

Edward Carpenter (1844–1929)
Gerard Manley Hopkins
 (1844–1889)
Katherine Bradley (Michael Field)
 (1846–1914)
Alice Meynell (1847–1922)
W.E. Henley (1849–1903)
Robert Louis Stevenson
 (1850–1894)
Oscar Wilde (1854–1900)
John Davidson (1857–1909)
A. Mary F. Robinson (later
 Darmesteter, later Duclaux)
 (1857–1944)
Constance Naden (1858–1935)
William Watson (1858–1935)
A.E. Housman (1859–1936)
Rosamund Marriott Watson
 ("Graham R. Tomson")
 (1860–1911)
M.E. Coleridge (1861–1907)
May Kendall (1861–1942)
Amy Levy (1861–1889)
Katherine Tynan (1861–1931)
Edith Cooper (Michael Field)
 (1862–1913)
Henry Newbolt (1862–1938)
Rudyard Kipling (1865–1936)
Arthur Symons (1865–1945)
W.B. Yeats (1865–1939)
Ernest Dowson (1867–1900)
Lionel Johnson (1867–1902)
Alfred Douglas (1870–1945)

I

JOSEPH BRISTOW

Reforming Victorian poetry: poetics after 1832

I

Historians of nineteenth-century British writing sometimes claim that the Victorian period properly begins some five years before Her Majesty the Queen ascended the throne. There are good reasons to justify why 1832, rather than 1837, should open the Victorian age. To be sure, the obligation within the discipline of English literature to compartmentalize historical periods often imposes barriers that can obscure important continuities between what precedes and follows a supposedly defining moment. Delimiting fields of study according to hard-and-fast distinctions looks all the more incoherent when we consider that some epochs such as the Romantic characterize a dynamic intellectual movement, while others like the Victorian remain subject to the presiding authority of a monarch. But whatever disputes we may have with the peculiar manner in which we find ourselves dividing one period from the next, 1832 designates a decisive turn of events.

The year 1832 witnessed the passing of the Great Reform Bill. This parliamentary act acknowledged a massive transformation that the nation had been undergoing for almost two decades – one whose repercussions would resonate long after Her Majesty expired in 1901. Once the Battle of Waterloo terminated the Napoleonic Wars in 1815, Tory-governed Britain moved into a phase of political unrest. In this respect, the most famous conflict occurred at St Peter's Fields, Manchester, in 1819 when some 80,000 people demonstrated for annual parliaments, universal suffrage, and the lifting of the Corn Laws (which made bread, the staple diet of the poor, costly). Mown down by a troop of hussars, eleven people were killed and some four hundred seriously injured. Occurring in the year before his premature death, Peterloo impelled radical poet Percy Bysshe Shelley to denounce Britain's ruling elite. In "The Mask of Anarchy" (1819) – a poem censored until 1832 – he personified the Prime Minister, Robert Stewart

(Viscount Castlereagh), as "Murder."[1] And in the famous sonnet "England in 1819" he condemned "An old, mad, blind, despised, and dying King" (George III) for siring a disreputable family of future "Rulers" whose "leechlike" behavior was sucking the blood out of a "people starved and stabb'd in th' untilled field."[2]

More than ten years would pass before a newly elected Whig government embarked on its eighteen-month campaign to lead the Bill through parliament. Unquestionably, this legislation opened up deep social rifts. The conservative William Wordsworth, for example, bewailed the Bill in early 1832, fearing an imminent "popular commotion."[3] In his view, both the insurrection in Paris that overthrew Charles X's reactionary Polignac ministry in July 1830 and the riots that set Bristol ablaze in October 1830 "prove[d] what mischief may be done by a mere rabble." Not surprisingly, the Tory press expressed similar fears. Just before the Bill (in the first of its three versions) entered parliament in January 1831, the *Quarterly Review* declared that it was dangerous to "dignify" as *"public opinion,"* such widespread disturbances as "burnings and machine-breakings."[4] If "democratic influence," it contended, "should be increased" in the House of Commons, then "successive stages of vote by ballot" would inevitably lead to "the extinction of the aristocracy and the monarchy, and to the entire prostration of rank and property at the feet of a Jacobin faction" (256). By contrast, left-leaning journals such the *Westminster Review* advanced Utilitarian arguments about the urgency of reform. Even though it felt that the Bill remained "full of anomalies," the *Westminster* approved the Whig ministry for having "wisely judged the signs of the times," "prudently" following "the onward march of events."[5] Public feeling could not have been more divided.

Eventually passed in June 1832, the Great Reform Bill for the first time acknowledged an electorate whose class and political affiliations were more diverse than the Tories had been willing to countenance. Even though the Bill managed to double the size of the voting public, only one in six men had the suffrage. Harold Perkin observes that this parliamentary act gave "little direct power to the urban, emancipated middle class."[6] "The radical change produced by the Reform Act," he wryly remarks, "was from aristocratic rule by prescription to aristocratic rule by consent."[7] But the passing of the Bill nonetheless admitted that political influence would increasingly emerge from a growing bourgeoisie whose interests often lay in a commercial, industrial, and urban world that contrasted sharply with the conservative values upheld by the superannuated gentry. Since the Bill slightly redrew the electoral map, expanding cities such as Birmingham, Manchester, and Preston could now send Members to the Commons, though the majority of seats still lay in the counties and smaller boroughs. Thereafter, as the middle class gained ascendancy in many spheres of Victorian culture, the later Reform Bills of 1867 and 1884 would turn their attention to another – eminently vocal – group: the laboring men whose earliest trades unions flourished after the founding of the London Working Men's Association in 1834. Such events remind us that if the Victorian period begins on a resounding note, then it concerns structural changes in class relations – ones that have somewhat minor relevance to a young, inexperienced, and (in the early years of her career) uninfluential queen.

1832, to the historian of literature, stands as a significant year for poetry as well. During the months leading up to the passing of the Bill, the earliest work of Alfred Tennyson came to public attention. In 1832, he published his third collection titled *Poems*, whose contents featured "The Lady of Shalott," "The Lotos-Eaters," and "The Palace of Art." These famous poems, along with several others, would undergo extensive revision for republication in the first of the two volumes of Tennyson's next major work, once again named *Poems* (1842). His 1842 volumes so solidly established his reputation that eight years later he was appointed Poet Laureate: the official state position that won him considerable favor with Her Majesty. Since he held the position until his death in 1892, Tennyson's career looks almost synonymous with the Victorian period itself. Certainly, in the annals of literary history Tennyson ranks – both in stature and precedence – as the first Victorian poet.

But Tennyson's fame was far from immediate. At the start of the 1830s, Tennyson's writings formed part of a heated debate about the state of poetry in general. Modern critics often claim that pointed criticism of his writings forced the sensitive Tennyson into a monastic "ten years' silence." It is fair to say that at the start of his career the first Victorian poet met with a measure of unsuccess. According to some prominent contemporaries, Tennyson's poetry seemed to embody the widespread deficiencies of his age. Reviewing *Poems, Chiefly Lyrical* in *Blackwood's Edinburgh Magazine*, the conservative John Wilson declared that "England ought to be producing some young poets now, that there may be no dull interregnum when the old shall have passed away."[8] "It is thought by many," he added, that "all the poetical genius which has worked such wonders in our day, was brought into power . . . by the French Revolution." The present time, Wilson argues, bears comparison with the events of 1789: "Europe, long ere bright heads are grey, will see blood poured out like water; and there will be the noise of many old establishments quaking to their foundations, or rent asunder, or overthrown" (724). Is Tennyson equipped to meet the impending revolution? The answer is flatly no. Especially depressing in

Wilson's view are Tennyson's patriotic lyrics such as "National Song" ("There is no land like England" [*AT* 1]): "It would not be safe to recite them by the sea-shore, on invasion of the French" because they are "dismal drivel" (726). There is indubitably "fine music" in Tennyson's work; indeed, the young writer's "fine faculties" are such that Wilson can confidently assert "that Alfred Tennyson is a poet" (740). But "he has much to learn . . . before his genius can achieve its destined triumphs."

Only by returning to the fraught discussion of poetry in the early 1830s can we see why the first Victorian poet on occasion failed to convince his readership that his talents were suitably robust for the age. In fact, when we look at some of the more decisive statements on poetics from that decade, Tennyson's work provides a key reference-point in a debate that rarely reaches consensus on the function and purpose of poetry. This chapter examines how early and mid-Victorian intellectuals explored the competing demands made upon the poet either to participate in or retire from the turbulence of modern society. Was the time ripe for poetry to embrace politics in the name of social change? Or should poetry repudiate social discontent and fix its attention instead on spiritual ideals? Whatever answers to such questions were forthcoming, one thing was for sure: The language of poetics remained inextricable from reform – a word that certainly dramatized the uneasy relations between the poet and the people.

II

During the months when Tennyson's early collections were faring unevenly in the press, another – now largely forgotten – writer attracted much more positive attention, not least because of the topicality of his work. In 1831, the fifty-year-old Ebenezer Elliott published an anonymous pamphlet titled *Corn-Law Rhymes*, a series of mostly short lyrics protesting the ban that the Tories imposed on imported wheat at the end of the wars against France. In one exuberant poem after another, Elliott deplores an agricultural system in which inflated rents support idle landowners whose exploitative tenants keep the price of bread beyond the reach of the laboring poor. "England!" exclaims Elliott, "what for mine and me, / What hath bread-tax done for thee?" (I, 73).[9] If only there were free trade, Elliott declares, then bread would be affordable once more. In the meantime, working people remain the victims of nothing less than robbery: "What is bad government, thou slave, / Whom robbers represent?" (I, 63). The answer, we learn, is "the deadly *Will*, that takes, / What labour ought to keep" (I, 64). Indeed, it is the "deadly *Power*, that makes / Bread dear, and labour cheap."

The sources of Elliott's polemic were well known. These sentiments derived from T. Perronet Thompson's frequently reprinted *Catechism on the Corn Laws* (1827). Thompson, who owned *Westminster Review* from 1829 to 1836, analyzed the severe shortcomings of the Corn Laws from a Utilitarian perspective: "The attempt to prevent one man from buying what another is willing to sell to him, and oblige him to buy from a third person with the avowed object of making him pay that third person a greater price, is so manifestly of the nature of robbery, that nothing can make it tolerable in a country where ideas of justice and civil liberty have made any considerable progress."[10] Elliott dedicated *Corn-Law Rhymes* to "all who revere the Memory of OUR SECOND LOCKE, JEREMY BENTHAM, and Advocate" who espoused the doctrine of "the greatest happiness of the greatest number" (I, 45) – the slogan that encapsulated Utilitarian thought. A radical writer hailing from industrial Sheffield, the working-class Elliott articulated the kind of oppositional voice whose political authority progressive campaigners such as Thompson wanted to secure in the public domain.

But if committed to repealing the Corn Laws, Elliott nonetheless knew that he was on less secure ground when using poetry to contest injustice. Though the *Athenaeum* applauded Elliott's "bold, *sculptured*, and correct versification," it nevertheless stated that his "mere twopenny pamphlet" gave the impression "that the Sheffield Mechanic consider[ed] poetry a mere vehicle for politics."[11] "If politics are to continue the burden of his song," it added, the poet's "coarse invective, technical allusions, and fierce denunciations, will mar his claim to the title of poet." To those readers who felt that his work presented a conflict between poetic expression and political principles, Elliott offered the following defense:

> The utilitarians say, that poets are generally servile fools, and that poetry, when it is not nonsense, is almost sure to be something worse; while the more elegant critics complain that the union of poetry with politics, is always hurtful to the politics and fatal to the poetry. But the utilitarians can hardly be right, and the gentlemen critics must be wrong, if Homer, Dante, Milton, Cowper, and Burns were poets. Why should the sensitive bard take less interest than other men, in those things which most nearly concern mankind? The contrary ought to be, and is, true. All genuine poets are fervid politicians.
>
> (I, 49)

While aligning himself with Bentham politically, however, Elliott understood that he was at odds with him poetically. In *The Rationale of Reward* (1825), Bentham had made some crushing remarks on the utility of poetry in relation to the quality of pleasure that it might generate. "Prejudice apart," Bentham states dryly, "the game of push-pin is of equal value with the arts and sciences of music and poetry. If the game of push-pin furnish more pleasure, it is more valuable than either."[12] Further, "push-pin" – a children's game – gives pleasure to a much larger number of people than poetry: "Everybody can play at push-pin: poetry and music are relished only by a few." On this account, the value of poetry can only go from bad to worse. "Push-pin," we learn, "is always innocent: it were well that could the same be said of poetry." As Bentham sees it, poetry wrongly maintains a "natural opposition" with truth. Bound by its "false morals" and "fictitious nature," the poet devotes his art to "stimulating our passions, and exciting our prejudices." Given that poetry builds an elaborate "super-structure" of "ornaments," it follows that "[t]ruth, exactitude of any kind, is fatal to poetry." Little wonder that its pleasures appear dubious: "If poetry and music deserve to be preferred before a game of push-pin, it must be because they are calculated to gratify those individuals who are most difficult to be pleased" (207). In fairness, Bentham admits that poetry might produce satisfaction, even if it does so mischievously. But throughout his discussion he stresses that the genre appeals to the "few" (not the many), the "false" (not the true), and the "difficult" (not the simple). In sum, "push-pin" emerges as a more honest and indeed democratic source of pleasure.

Keenly aware of Bentham's reservations, Elliott pursues his belief that "genuine poets are fervid politicians" by turning the Utilitarian philoso-pher's thinking on its head. Emphasizing the fervor that "the sensitive bard" like Dante or Milton takes in "those things which most nearly concern mankind," he asks rhetorically: "What *is* poetry but impassioned truth – philosophy in its *essence* – the *spirit* of that bright consummate flower, whose root is in our bosoms?" (I, 49). On this model, poetry appears everywhere in British culture, all the way from *Macbeth* ("a sublime political treatise") to the "fine . . . illustrative poetry" in the contemporary prose of Bentham himself. But Elliott boldly contends that it is not the just the political and philosophical aspects of poetry that command our attention. Poetry matters because its roots reach deep into our understanding of historical experience. "Where," he wonders, "will our children look for the *living* character of the year 1793" – which marked the beginning of the French wars (I, 50)? Certainly not to the conservative Edmund Burke whose writings – denouncing such decisive events as the French Revolution – would hardly concur with the laboring poet Robert Burns who stated that hereditary "titles are but the *guinea's stamp*."[13] Instead, future generations will learn from "the writings of Burns, and *from his life*, that, during a certain crusade for ignominy, it was necessary, yet perilous, and in his case, fatal, to say, 'the man's the goud for a' that.'" By quoting from one of Burns's finest lyrics, Elliott presents *Corn-Law Rhymes* as "the earnest product of experience," one that embodies the "signs of the times" (I, 51).

As John Johnstone acknowledged in *Tait's Edinburgh Magazine* (a journal sympathetic to the Utilitarian cause), Elliott wrote poetry "entirely different from the sounding brass and tinkling cymbal of ordinary minstrelsy."[14] The "impassioned truth" of such writing, in Johnstone's view, made Elliott "an original writer in an imitative age" – "a time tending in literature to feebleness and effeminacy." On this point, even Wilson agreed. Although it was obvious that "on the question of the Corn Laws" his Toryism and Elliott's radicalism were necessarily "opposed,"[15] Wilson could not help but admire the poet's resilience. "Elliott," Wilson declared, "is a worker in iron" who "undertakes to instruct you and people like you – not in his craft . . . but in his condition – its vices, its virtues, it trials and temptations, its joys and its sorrows . . . in the causes that, as he opines, oppress it with affliction not inevitable to such lot, and cheat him when he has 'broken a ton,' out of half his own and his children's rightful claim to bread" (821).

In many ways, Elliott possessed those stalwart qualities that Wilson and other critics felt that Tennyson lacked in an era of reform. But the future Poet Laureate had several staunch defenders, including one in the Utilitarian camp. Reviewing *Poems, Chiefly Lyrical* in the *Westminster*, W.J. Fox upheld the Benthamite commitment to calculable progress by stating that the "machinery of a poem is not less susceptible of improvement than the machinery of a cotton-mill."[16] Noting that the "great principle of human improvement is at work in poetry as well as everywhere else" (74), Fox discovers in Tennyson's writing a highly advanced state of perception, one that enables him to "obtain entrance into a mind as he would make his way into a landscape" (76). In Fox's view, this astonishing capacity becomes most vivid in poems like "The Merman" where Tennyson "takes" the "senses, feelings, nerves, and brain" of a particular character, "along with their names and habitations," while retaining his own "self in them, modified but not absorbed by their peculiar constitution and mode of being" (77). Wilson characterized Fox's statement as "a perfect specimen of the super-hyperbolical ultra-extravagance of outrageous Cockney eulogistic foolishness" (728). (Here the moniker "Cockney" defines the radicalism that *Blackwood's* had for years disapproved in the work of poets such as John Keats.) As if such fulmination were not enough, Wilson poured scorn on another review, one that appeared in a short-lived periodical praising Tennyson in rather different terms. "The Englishman's Magazine," Wilson remarked, "ought not to have died" (724). "An Essay 'on the Genius of

Alfred Tennyson,'" however, "sent it to the grave." Published in early 1831, the review in question was by the poet's closest friend Arthur Henry Hallam. Even if it made Wilson "guffaw," Hallam's discussion advanced a powerful argument to rethink the relations between a particular type of poetic genius and the poet's frequently unappreciative audience.

A gifted critic, Hallam remains best known as the subject of Tennyson's lyric elegy *In Memoriam* (1850), which preoccupied the poet for some seventeen years after his friend's demise from a brain hemorrhage in September 1833. (At the time of his death, Hallam was twenty-two years old; he had also recently become engaged to Tennyson's sister Emily.) Repeatedly the elegiac voice of *In Memoriam* insists on Hallam's indisputable greatness: "He still outstript me in the race; / It was but unity of place / That made me dream I ranked with him" (*AT* XLII, 3–4). The "place" that they first shared was Trinity College, Cambridge, where Hallam emerged as one of the most talented members of the select debating society whose twelve members called themselves the Apostles. They had immediate experience of political struggle. During the long vacation of 1830, they traveled to the Pyrenees to supply Spanish rebels with funds and messages in support of their campaign against Ferdinand VII. (Eighteen months later, the rebel leader General Torrijos was captured and executed.) At the end of 1830, they witnessed rural Cambridgeshire blazing with the rick-burnings ignited by the "Captain Swing" riots. Writing to another Apostle in December that year, Hallam observed:

> The game is lost in Spain; but how much good remains to be done here! The country is in a more awful state that you can well conceive. While I write, Maddingley [*sic*], or some adjoining village, is in a state of conflagration, and the sky above is coloured flame-red. This is one of a thousand such actions committed daily throughout England. The laws are almost suspended; the money of foreign factions at work with a population exasperated into reckless fury.[17]

Even though Hallam does not "apprehend a revolution," it remains the case that England teeters on the brink of collapse. His distrust in the belief that reform will better all aspects of English culture informs his essay on *Poems, Chiefly Lyrical*. In Hallam's view, Tennyson's poetry possesses special qualities that contest the belief that "the diffusion of poetry must be in the direct ratio of the diffusion of machinery"[18] – phrasing that echoes, only to refute, Fox's commentary. Rather than subscribe to the idea that poetry should form part of an "*objective* amelioration," Hallam contends that the genre must resist the "continual absorption of the higher feelings into the palpable interests of ordinary life" (190). In other words, if and when poetry becomes a mere instrument of social improvement, then "*subjective* power" will be inevitably diminished. As he sees it, the great virtue of Tennyson's volume lies in its refusal to succumb to the "prevalence of social activity."

Hallam establishes this opinion by recalling Wordsworth's remarks toward the end of the "Essay, Supplementary to the Preface" (1815). "Mr Wordsworth," Hallam observes, "asserted that immediate or rapid popularity was not the test of poetry" (183). In his "Essay," Wordsworth insists that one should banish "the senseless iteration of the word, *popular*, applied to new works of poetry."[19] According to Hallam, Wordsworth's comments presented a "truth" that "prevailed" against both "that hydra, the reading Public" and "the Wordsworthians themselves" (184). But just at the point where Hallam appears to make Wordsworth's doctrine his own, he resists ventriloquizing the Romantic poet's voice. Observing that "even the genius cannot expand itself to the full periphery of art," Hallam finds fault with both Wordsworth and his followers for claiming that "the highest species of poetry is the reflective." By "reflective," Hallam loosely means philosophical: "much has been said by [Wordsworth] which is good as philosophy, powerful as rhetoric, but false as poetry" (185).

Yet, as Eric Griffiths suggests, both here and elsewhere in Hallam's writings it proves somewhat difficult to prize poetry and philosophy apart. On the one hand, Hallam claims that "false art" results from "[w]henever the mind of artist suffers itself to be occupied . . . by any other predominant motive than the desire of beauty" (184). On the other hand, he concedes that "beauty" may be found "in those moods of emotion, which arise from the combinations of reflective thought." Then again, it seems more likely to Hallam that "a man whose reveries take a reasoning turn" will ultimately "pile his thoughts in a rhetorical battery" that aims to "convince" an audience (184–85). Griffiths observes that underneath this rather unstable opposition between poetry and philosophy lies a "conceptual distinction between emotion and intellect," which "come[s] to Hallam from Kant, more generally from that Kantianism diffused in England principally by Coleridge."[20] In *The Critique of Pure Reason* (1781), Kant makes a distinction between *Anschauung* ("intuition") and *Begriff* ("concept"). For Kant, neither one can subsist without the other. Hallam, however, wishes to place particular emphasis on the role that *Anschauung* plays in shaping the poetic imagination. He believes that the highest poetry gathers its energy from intuition.

At this juncture, Hallam praises "a new school of reformers" (185) whose works contest the Wordsworthian "reflective mode." But the poems of these so-called "reformers" manifest decisive poetic changes rather than political ones. He maintains that these poets' works "contain . . . more genuine inspiration . . . than any *form* of art that has existed in this country since the days of Milton." In this regard, the leading lights are Keats and Shelley: writers "of opposite genius" who nevertheless share "a ground-work of similarity sufficient for the purposes of classification." "They are," Hallam insists, "both poets of sensation rather than reflection" (186). Having elevated this type of writer to such heights, he explains the immense distance that necessarily exists between the poet of sensation and his readership. "The public," he remarks, "very naturally derided" Keats and Shelley "as visionaries, and gibbeted *in terrorem* those inaccuracies of diction occasioned sometimes by the speed of their conceptions." As a consequence, such writing may at times prove unintelligible. Is it really the case, then, that "we must be themselves before we can understand them in the least?" The only way to resolve this problem lies in placing a new responsibility upon the reader. "Every bosom," Hallam writes, "contains the elements of those complex emotions which the artist feels" (186–87). Yet the ability to "understand his expressions and sympathize with his state" involves "some degree of exertion" (188). Assuming that "those writers will be most popular who require the least degree of exertion," Hallam argues that the finest poetry "is likely to have little authority over public opinion" (190).

Tennyson remained divided on this issue, as *Poems, Chiefly Lyrical* shows. Two inclusions in this volume adopt antithetical positions for the writer of poetry. In "The Poet," he depicts an idealistic image of one "born" "in a golden clime" (*AT* 1) whose "thoughts" like "viewless arrows" (11) traveled across Europe, filling the "winds which bore / Them" (17–18) with "light" (16). "[L]ike the arrow-seeds of the field flower" (19), the poet's "fruitful wit" took root. In Romantic imagery familiar to readers of Keats and Shelley,[21] these poetic "seeds" grew into a "flower all gold" (24) whose "wingèd shafts of truth" (26) continued to propagate. "Thus," we learn, "truth was multiplied on truth" (33), eventually enabling a female icon of "Freedom" to emerge. Upon her hem, the word "Wisdom" (46) appeared. This "sacred name" (47) could "shake / All evil dreams of power" (46–47). "Her words" (49) rumbled with both "thunder" and "lightning" (50), "riving the spirit of man" (51). But her capacity to "riv[e]" the human spirit was in no respect violent: "No sword / Of wrath her right arm whirled " (53–54). Instead, she upheld "one poor poet's scroll" (55), shaking Europe with "*his* word" (55). "The Poet," therefore, advances the view that the male poet's truth can indeed fortify the world. Though taking flight upon "arrow-seeds," his truth actually relies upon another source of power: a "mother plant" that finally gives birth to a female icon of

"Freedom." For some reason, "The Poet" suggests that his truth must be mediated through forms of femininity because they more adequately represent his authority than he himself can. The male poet remains implicitly unable to influence a whole continent on the basis of his gender.

"The Poet's Mind" reverses the scene depicted in "The Poet." In this poem, the poet needs to be kept safe from any "[d]ark-browed sophist" (*AT* 8) who intrudes upon his sacrosanct "ground" (9). "Vex not thou," the speaker proclaims, "the poet's mind / With thy shallow wit" (1–2). The "sophist" threatens to bring "cruel cheer" (15) onto this "holy" (9) domain. For that reason, "holy water" (12) will be poured around this enclosed garden where "the merry bird chants" (22). "In the middle," we discover, "leaps a fountain" (24). Bright with "lightning" (25) and murmuring with "low melodious thunder" (27), its waters draw on those distinctly Romantic energies already noted in "The Poet." Indeed, the fountain "sings a song of undying love" (33). But should the "sophist" approach it, he "would never hear it" (35), for "It would shrink to the earth" (37) if that "dull" (35) person ventured in. Herbert F. Tucker claims that "[t]here is something mean-spirited about the claim of 'The Poet's Mind' . . . that nobody understands the message of the excluded, exclusive poet; but we may pardon him when we reflect on the way the poet is estranged from his very message."[22] The fountain, Tucker observes, derives its power from other sources: namely, the "brain of the purple mountain / That stands in the distance yonder" (29–30), which in turn receives its streams "from Heaven above" (32). To some degree, the secluded poet thrives on reserves that are not entirely his own. For all their differences of emphasis, both "The Poet" and "The Poet's Mind" appear to agree on one point. The poet – whether known throughout Europe or sequestered in his garden – requires other agencies to support him.

Tennyson's work played a significant role in the distinguished liberal philosopher John Stuart Mill's developing ideas about the role that poets should adopt in the contemporary age. In his generous 1835 review of Tennyson's early volumes, Mill identifies how the poet "luxuriate[s] in sensuous imagery."[23] But much as Mill would like to praise this aspect of Tennyson's work, he expresses some misgivings about the ways in which the poet's "nominal subject sometimes lies buried in a heap of it." Better, Mill argues, for Tennyson "to strengthen his intellect for the discrimination" of "truths" – the "exalted purpose" of poetry. He recommends Tennyson to "cultivate, and with no half devotion, philosophy as well as poetry." "[S]tates of emotion, embodied in sensuous imagery" need to advance to a higher condition so that they can symbolize "spiritual truths." Mill's advice, however, points as much to his own incertitude about the role of poetry as it does to any deficiency in Tennyson's art. In fact, his belief that Tennyson should aspire to "philosophy" runs somewhat against the grain of two earlier essays – "What Is Poetry?" and "The Two Kinds of Poetry" – that he published during his late twenties in 1833. To understand how these influential essays form a significant part in Mill's changing attitudes to how the poet might relate to the public in an era of reform, it is useful to turn momentarily to the personal and political struggle that he underwent as an emergent intellectual.

During this turbulent period of Mill's life, poetry began to provide the emotional sustenance that his strict Utilitarian upbringing had denied. In his *Autobiography* (1873), he recollects how the rigorous education that his father James Mill gave him insisted "that all mental and moral feelings and qualities, whether of a good of a bad kind, were the results of association."[24] Here "association" characterizes the psychological mechanism that induces feelings of pleasure or pain. (The terminology originally derives from David Hartley's *Observations on Man* [1749], a work that plays a vital role in Coleridge's *Biographia Literaria* [1817].) The young Mill grew up to believe "that the object of education should be to form the strongest possible associations of the salutary class; associations of pleasure with all things beneficial to the great whole, and of pain with all things hurtful to it." Yet by the time he turned twenty, doubts were stirring in the "old familiar instruments" to quantify pleasure and pain that he inherited from his father. Gradually he saw how "the habit of analysis has a tendency to wear away the feelings." In due course, the "cultivation of the feelings became one of the cardinal points in" Mill's "ethical and philosophical creed" (147). Suffering from depression, he turned to poetry. Wordsworth's 1802 "Preface" to *Lyrical Ballads* taught him "that there was real, permanent happiness in tranquil contemplation" (153). After meeting the poet in 1831, Mill informed a friend that although he had "differences" with Wordsworth (just as he would have with "any other philosophic Tory"), he remained overwhelmed by the "largeness & expansiveness of his feelings."[25] Two years later, Mill would declare that the "object of poetry is confessedly to act upon the emotions."[26] He invests so deeply in the emotional capacities of poetry that he removes it, in some ways like Hallam, from the world of public intercourse. The resulting version of the poet that we find in Mill's two significant 1833 essays provides the core of the cultivated individual – the one for whom "self-protection" stands paramount in the face of social dominance – that takes center stage in his *Of Liberty* (1859).[27]

First published in Fox's *Monthly Repository* (a Unitarian journal with strong Utilitarian sympathies), Mill's 1833 essays warrant attention because they count among the most strenuous attempts to theorize how, "in an age of revolutions, the cotemporary [*sic*] poets, if they are not before their age, are almost sure to be behind it" (364). Rather than view poets as figures who directly exert influence over historical events, he claims that they exist in "solitude" (348), unaware of an audience. "All poetry," he maintains, "is the nature of soliloquy" (349). In this respect, poetry must be distinguished from eloquence. Although Mill agrees with Elliott that "poetry is impassioned truth" (348), he points out that eloquence might also come under that rubric. To refine the argument, he states that where "eloquence is *heard*, poetry is *over*heard." "Eloquence," he adds, "supposes an audience; the peculiarity of poetry appears to us to lie in the poet's utter unconsciousness of a listener." At all costs, true poets refrain from any "desire of making an impression upon another mind" (349). Since this model precludes direct contact between author and reader, it seems obvious why poets cannot "head the movement" that "break[s] up old modes of belief" (365). Less clear is how "those who have any individuality of character" might stand "behind" – in the sense of supporting the mood of – the age. The answer seems to lie in the true poet's acutely sensitive constitution. Having lauded Wordsworth in 1831 for his capacity to feel, in these later essays Mill asserts that he "never seems *possessed* by any feeling; no emotion seems ever so strong as to have entire sway, for the time being, over the current of his thoughts" (359). Since Wordsworth proves too philosophical, Mill looks to Shelley as the figure for whom "voluntary mental discipline had done little," while "the vividness of his emotions and of his sensations had done all" (359). Yet Mill pays no attention to Shelley's support for political reform, characterizing him instead as a man whose responsiveness to the era lay in the "susceptibility of his nervous system, which made his emotions intense" (360).

III

Mill's 1833 essays promulgate a view that one influential contemporary could not withstand. "It is damnable heresy in criticism," wrote Thomas Carlyle in 1826, "to maintain either expressly or implicately that the ultimate object of Poetry is sensation."[28] In all probability, Mill rethought how and why "sensual imagery" ought to aspire to "spiritual truths" during the early 1830s when he developed a somewhat fragile friendship with Carlyle. Although Carlyle would for some time praise Mill "as one of the best, clearest-headed and clearest hearted young men now living in London,"[29] they would more or less part company within a matter of years. So great was the political chasm that eventually separated them that by the time of the Second Reform Bill they embodied two completely different sides of Victorian politics. In 1865, the Governor Eyre controversy – which involved the brutal massacre of protesting black workers at Morant Bay, Jamaica – split public opinion. On the one hand, the liberal Mill headed the Jamaica Committee that condemned Eyre's unhesitating use of excessive force to quell a minor public disturbance. (Eyre declared martial law. His officers shot or hanged 439 people.) On the other hand, Carlyle lent his support to the Eyre Defence Fund, which he followed up with "Shooting Niagara: And after?" (1867) – his well-known essay that berates "these ballot-boxing, Nigger-emancipating, empty, dirt-eclipsed days."[30] By the mid-1860s, Carlyle stood as one of the most outspoken critics of liberal democracy – whether such democracy involved abolishing slavery, extending the franchise, or promoting *laissez faire*.

Part of the reason for Mill's absorption in Carlyle's early essays, which began to appear in the mid-1820s, lay not so much in what they said but how they said it. To Mill, reading Carlyle's "haze of poetry and German metaphysics" proved one of the main "influences through which [Mill] enlarged [his] early narrow creed" (*Autobiography*, 181). "[T]he good his writing did me," Mill recalled, "was not as philosophy to instruct, but as poetry to animate" (182). Certainly, the very texture of Carlyle's prose, shaped by a hardly inconspicuous Calvinist heritage, seeks to enliven readers to do anything but philosophize. Instead of pursuing "moral goodness," he says, the Benthams of the world "inculcate" the belief that "our happiness depends on external circumstances" such as legislative reform ("Signs of the Times" [1829], XXVII, 67). Little wonder that Carlyle concludes "Signs of the Times" by insisting that "to reform a nation, no wise man will undertake" (XXVII, 82). Accordingly, "the only solid, though a far slower reformation, is what each begins and perfects on *himself*." Although Carlyle's phrasing often sounded like an "insane rhapsody" to Mill's ears (*Autobiography*, 169), he recognized that the man who would become the ultimate Victorian sage "was a poet" (183). "I," Mill adds, "was not."

Strictly speaking, Carlyle – for all the stamina of his writing – was no poet either. Nor do his private notebooks suggest that his enthusiasm for poetry ran deep. "What is poetry?" he queried. "Do I really love poetry? I sometimes fancy almost, not" (*Two Notebooks*, 151). But in his published essays he never ceases to invoke poetry as part of the cure-all to a culture where "*Mechanics*" (the attention to "external circumstances") have full reign. He deplores how modern society remains bereft of "*Dynamics*": "the primary, unmodified forces and energies of man, the mysterious springs of Love, and Fear, and Wonder, of Enthusiasm, Poetry, Religion" ("Signs of the Times," XXVII, 68). Unlike the "Mechanism" enshrined in such things as the "unspeakably wearisome Reform Bill,"[31] "Poetry" counted among those "primary . . . energies" that possessed a "truly vital and *infinite* character" (V, 68). Carlyle claims that in Victorian England those near-divine "energies" have waned. Return to earlier times like those of the "Roman Republic" and it becomes evident that "Society was what we name healthy" ("Characteristics" [1831], XXVIII, 14–15). "The individual man in himself," he observes in the same essay, "was a whole, or complete union." Given this marvelous state of completeness, "Opinion and Action had not yet become disunited." "[T]hus," he contends, "instead of Speculation, we had Poetry." And the "Poet" like the "Priest" stood as the "sign of vigour and well-being" (XXVIII, 16). The poet, however, embodies something more than an animating principle. Echoing Philip Sidney's famous disquisition on poetry, Carlyle elsewhere asserts that the poet "is a *vates*, a seer" ("Burns" [1828], XXVI, 272). The wellspring of true poetry, therefore, comes from prophecy.

Carlyle would endorse these prophetic capabilities throughout his lecture, "The Hero as Poet" (1841). Such heroism emerged from the "kind of inarticulate unfathomable speech, which leads us to the edge of Infinity" (V, 83). Once again, however, he stresses how the "*Vates* poet . . . seems to hold a poor rank among us" (V, 84). Only the likes of Dante and Shakespeare, as "Saints of Poetry" (V, 85), fulfill this hagiographic role. Yet in other writings Carlyle discerns at least two modern writers who in different ways incarnate vatic qualities. One is Burns: "He shows himself at least a Poet of Nature's own making" (XXVI, 272). Like Byron, Burns counts among those "sent forth as missionaries to their generation, to teach it a higher Doctrine, a purer Truth" (XXVI, 316). Carlyle, however, reserves some of his highest praise for Elliott: "a voice coming from the deep Cyclopean forges, where Labour, in real soot and sweat, beats with the thousand hammers 'the red son of the furnace'" ("Corn-Law Rhymes" [1831], XXVIII, 138). In every respect, Elliott manifests those capabilities that energize Carlyle's vision of the poet: "Here is an earnest truth-speaking man; no theoriser, sentimentaliser, but a practical man of work and endeavour, man of sufferance and endurance. He has used his eyes for seeing" (XXVIII, 145). Without question, Elliott is "a Reformer, at least a stern Complainer, radical to the core" (XXVIII, 145). But Carlyle asserts that Elliott's politics remain unimportant when we see how "under the disguises of the Radical, the Poet is still recognisable." Everywhere in the Corn-Law Rhymer's works, Carlyle detects "a certain music" that "breathes through all dissonances." Such discoveries encourage Carlyle to repeat once more that "all Reform except a moral one will prove unavailing" (XXVIII,

160). By looking to a poet such as Elliott – one who bears traces of "the antique spirit" – we discover a "true man."

Carlyle's emphasis on the "true man" was certainly gendered, as his notebooks reveal. Contemplating "the true relation of moral genius to poetic genius; of Religion to Poetry," he concluded that that "the *faculties*" for both "always go together" (*Two Note Books*, 188). On reflection, however, he realized that this "relation" was exclusively male. Undoubtedly, there were "female geniuses" whose "minds" both "admire[d] and receive[d]." But women, he felt, could "hardly create." One acclaimed writer would absorb Carlyle's ideas about the poet as prophet, only to contest the belief that "poetic genius" was a male preserve. Elizabeth Barrett Browning was in her forties – the time of her liberating marriage – before she staked a distinctly feminist claim upon the poet as *vates*. In some respects, her political outlook contrasted with Carlyle's. "The Bill has past [*sic*]," she declared in 1832. "We may be prouder of calling ourselves English, than we were before it past . . . & stand higher among nations, not only a freer people, but as a people worthy of being free."[32] There were, though, types of reform – especially those connected with "*Mechanics*" – that drove Barrett Browning in the 1850s to refashion Carlyle's ideas in ways that proved that "female geniuses" could not only "admire" and "receive" but also "create."

Barrett Browning's longest work, *Aurora Leigh* (1856), pits the poetic talents of her eponymous protagonist against those of her cousin, the social reformer Romney Leigh. Aurora and Romney (though ultimately destined for marriage) embody clashing ideologies. Aurora often champions her poetic vocation in near-Carlylean terms. Poets, she claims, stand as "the only truth-tellers now left to God" (*EBBAL* I. 859). But sometimes Aurora appears less confident than Carlyle when elaborating how poets can morally reform the nation; "Thus is Art," she argues later, "Self-magnified in magnifying a truth / Which, fully recognised, would change the world / And change its morals" (VII. 854–56). This statement noticeably remains in the tentative conditional tense. As her narrative proceeds, Aurora discloses that poets – figures whom she says maintain a "twofold life," "staggering 'neath the burden as mere men, / Being called to stand up straight as demi-gods" (V. 381, 383–84) – fail to transform humanity through lack of recognition. "If a man," she maintains, "could feel, / Not one day, in the artist's ecstasy, / But every day," then he would experience how "The spiritual significance burn[s] through / The hieroglyphic of material shows" (VII. 857–61). Structured like a syllogism, these lines articulate a disparity between the wished-for result and the actual state of affairs. Try as they might, poets cannot exert sufficient influence throughout a culture that needs interpretive help in reaching the "spirit" veiled by "material" signs.

Elsewhere, however, Aurora attributes considerable authority to poetry when she chooses to depart from Carlylean thought. In an important passage, she begins by restating "The Hero as Poet" when she claims that "every age / Appears to souls who live in't (ask Carlyle) / Most unheroic" (V. 155–56). But she then performs a most unCarlylean maneuver to uphold the idea that the inhabitants of any epoch cannot always perceive its glories. Rather than condemn the Victorian era outright, she urges poets to address "this live, throbbing age, / That brawls, cheats, maddens, calculates, aspires" (V. 203–04). Instantly, the very "life" pours forth in "the burning lava of a song," whose molten flows express "The full-veined, heaving, double-breasted Age" (V. 214–15), reminding future generations of "the paps we all have sucked" (V. 219). With its passionate lava and life-giving milk, this striking image stands among Barrett Browning's most memorable efforts to represent poetic eminence in an unapologetic female form.

Such imagery supports Aurora's frequent battles with Romney's condescending attitude toward her professional ambitions. Early in *Aurora Leigh*, Romney insists that "men, and still less women, happily, / Scarce need be poets" (II. 92–93). Better, he thinks, for Aurora to marry him and join in his plans to reform class relations through "phalansteries" (II. 756) that put into practice the type of collective living advocated by utopian thinker Charles Fourier. But rather than accept his offer, Aurora states that what he loves "Is not a woman . . . but a cause" (II. 401). In any case, she feels that he has "a wife already" – namely, his "social theory" (II. 409–10). Her polemic against his principles intensifies. "Ah, your Fouriers failed," she argues, "Because not poets enough to understand / That life develops from within" (II. 484–85). "[I]t takes a high-souled man," she tells him, "To move the masses" (II. 480–81). Although she admits that he could be correct in feeling that "a woman's soul / Aspires, and not creates" (II. 487–88), she wishes to prove him wrong. And so she does. Where Aurora gains in poetic celebrity, Romney's loses in reformist zeal. Stressing the mistaken nature of his political idealism, Aurora describes Romney's aborted wedding to the working-class Marian Erle in imagery that rivals the less palatable moments in Carlyle's prose. As she looks at the laborers attending the ill-fated celebration, Aurora observes how "They clogged the streets, they oozed into the church, / In a dark slow stream, like blood" (IV. 553–54). Even if such similes aim to dramatize the "peccant social wound" (IV. 542) that working people wrongly bear (since they appear "Lame, blind, and worse" [IV. 543]), their "finished generation" (IV. 548) induces more horror than compassion in Aurora. Such grotesque descriptions serve to legitimate how and why Marian must not marry Romney. By the end of the poem Romney's "phalanstery" has been razed to the ground, the flames leaving him blind. But this literal lack of sight converts him to Aurora's vatic perspective. "Fourier's void," he finally concedes (IX. 868). Such words give Aurora her cue to reiterate how "The man, most man, / Works best for men . . . / . . . gets his manhood plainest from his soul" (IX. 880). As a result, her poetic vocation turns out to be her romantic fulfillment, triumphant over his reformist designs.

Barrett Browning herself never endured such a tumultuous courtship. Early in her intense correspondence with Robert Browning (which led to their clandestine marriage in September 1846), she celebrated their shared respect for Carlyle: "the great teacher of the age . . . who is also yours & mine."[33] "He fills," she added, "the office of a poet – does he not?" Even though Robert Browning at times expressed misgivings about Carlyle's outbursts (he felt that "Shooting Niagara" resembled a "grin through a horse-collar" – in other words, a bad joke),[34] he reproduced the sage's teachings about poetry, most explicitly in his "Essay on Shelley" (1852). In his youth, he emulated Shelley to the point that he professed, like his idol, atheism. But soon afterward the adult Robert Browning recovered his faith to espouse a distinctly religious model of poetry. In his essay, he examines the relative merits – ones that Hallam and Mill analyzed twenty years before – between two types of poet. He begins by detailing the limited gifts of the "objective poet": "one whose endeavour has been to reproduce things external," and whose insights enhance the "average mind."[35] Altogether greater is the "subjective poet," the "seer" whose work stands not in reference to "the many below" but to "the supreme Intelligence which apprehends all things in their absolute truth" (I, 1002). The "subjective poet" "struggle[s]" toward "[n]ot what man sees, but what God sees – the *Ideas* of Plato, seeds of creation lying burningly on the Divine Hand." Such reasoning provides the basis of his belief that "had Shelley lived he would have finally ranged himself with the Christians" (I, 1009). Although Robert Browning does not say it, one imagines that reading Carlyle's essays would have finally disabused Shelley of "mistaking Churchdom for Christianity, and for marriage . . . the law of sexual oppression," ensuring that the radical poet focused his attention on "the Divine" (I, 1010) rather than the people.

IV

To conclude this chapter, I want to look briefly at two contrasting responses to the models that critics and writers put forward to secure a place for poetry in an era of reform. Born in 1821, Matthew Arnold presents the strongest extension and revision of Carlyle's thought. Where Carlyle set "*Dynamics*" above "*Mechanics*," Arnold eventually forged a vocabulary in the late 1860s that positioned "Culture" over "Anarchy." In the late 1840s, he echoed Carlyle when condemning the "damned times."[36] Yet while stating that the problems of the age lay in "the absence of great *natures*," no one – including the sage – proved free from scorn. He regretted "unavoidable contact with millions of small [natures], newspapers, cities, light profligate friends, moral desperadoes like Carlyle, our own selves." His frustrations did not diminish. "Carlyle," he observed eight years later, "is part man – of genius – part fanatic – and part tom-fool."[37] Unlike Carlyle, Arnold could not pledge faith in poetry to bring about moral and spiritual reform. He persistently disparaged "how deeply *unpoetical* the age & all one's surroundings" were.[38] In the late 1840s, he held Keats responsible for creating "harm . . . in English Poetry." Arnold contends that what he sees as Keats's restlessness manifests itself in Robert Browning whose poetry obtains "but a confused multitudinousness."[39] "They will not be patient," he observes. What they need to do is "begin with an Idea of the world in order not to be prevailed over by the world." Even in 1857 when Arnold admitted for once that the "*time*" proved "a first class one," he still felt that Victorian poetry appeared overwhelmed by and thus "not *adequate* to it."[40]

Arnold nevertheless produced remarkable poetry that grappled with its inadequacy to the age. "Resignation: To Fausta" (1849), for example, proposes that poetry should neither be caught in the impulsive passions nor remote from the bustling life of Victorian England. Opening with a list of historical events and rituals (from "pilgrims, bound for Mecca" [*MA* 3] to the "Goth, bound Rome-wards" [9]), the speaker looks skeptically on any such "struggle" (25) to reach "A goal" in the belief that once it has been "gained" it "may give repose" (17). Preferable by far is the Wordsworthian desire, stated in the 1802 "Preface" to *Lyrical Ballads*, to derive poetry from "emotion recollected in tranquillity"[41]: "an unblamed serenity / . . . freed from passions" (23–24). But if following Wordsworth in one direction, the speaker departs from him in another. He implicitly questions the poetic vision promoted in "Tintern Abbey" (1807) that states that "with an eye made quiet by the power / Of harmony, and the deep power of joy, / We see into the life of things."[42] Returning with Fausta to "the self-same road" (86) that they visited ten years earlier, he lends a different inflection to notions of harmony of mind and depth of insight while surveying the landscape around them.

Instead of actively seeing "into the life of things," the speaker claims that the poet – "to whose mighty heart / Heaven doth a quicker pulse impart"

(144–45) – carefully "Subdues" that divinely granted "energy" in order to "scan" the world before him in a mood of resignation. Though God-given, the poet's faculties are not so much those of a prophet as a witness to a world that in every way remains greater than his vision. Whether the poet "looks down, / At sunset, on a populous town" (164–65) or "mingle[s] with the crowd" (162), one thing is for certain – he "does not say: *I am alone*" (169). The negation is intriguing. In the process of situating the poet's role, the speaker reminds us of what it is not. The repudiation of what the poet might claim to be continues when the speaker "scan[s]" Fausta's responses to his musings. "*He leaves his kind*" (211), he imagines her thinking of the poet, "*And flees the common life of men*" (212), since this figure supposedly breathes "*immortal air*" (207). In the speaker's view, such exalted ideas only amplify what most of us might eventually grasp. Even if the poet's privileged vision is "*wide*" (216), such insights – no matter how much they broaden the "scope" (218) of human "affections" (219) – still leave individuals (poet and people alike) looking upon "Far regions of eternal change" (222): a world that endures as an "Eternal mundane spectacle" (228). Poetic vision, therefore, cannot bring about change, only recognize its paradoxical permanence. Significantly, Arnold arrived at this viewpoint by turning away from European sources – ones that may have only compounded his frustrations – to Eastern philosophy, particularly the spiritual wisdom expressed in the *Bhagavad-Gita*.

"Resignation" may be read in autobiographical terms, conflating the speaker with Arnold and Fausta with the poet's sister, Jane. But these persons and personae are not necessarily the same. After all, the speaker declares that "fate grudge[s]" both himself and Fausta the "poet's rapt security" (245–46). Yet such a "grudge" hardly works to their disadvantage. Suspicious of the claims that might be made upon the poet, the speaker sets a resigned distance between himself and that elevated identity. In the ensuing decades, Arnold struggled with the problem of how poetry might best serve society. By the 1870s, he had more or less given up writing poetry, advocating the critical study of it instead. Toward the end of his long career – most of it spent as an Inspector of Schools – he sought to restitute the genre by focusing on its educational use: "In poetry, as a criticism of life under the conditions fixed for such a criticism by the laws of poetic truth and poetic beauty, the spirit of our race will find . . . its consolation and stay."[43] On this view, it is not poets who will improve the world. Instead, better readers will make a better culture – though not, it seems, immediately.

In the early 1860s, Algernon Charles Swinburne made unsparing criticisms of the culture-saving graces of poetry that absorbed Arnold's attention. Throughout his groundbreaking review of Charles Baudelaire's *Les fleurs du mal* (the sexually risk-taking collection that the French state censored in 1857), the twenty-four-year-old Swinburne insisted upon the anti-Utilitarian, unprophetic, and amoral condition of poetry. Swinburne styled both his analysis and his praise on what Baudelaire wrote in his own 1857 *Notes nouvelles sur Edgar Poe*. There Baudelaire memorably denounces "the heresy . . . that the aim of poetry is a lesson of some sort, that it must now fortify the conscience, now perfect morals, now in short *prove* something or other which is useful."[44] (Such remarks resonate with many of Poe's observations in "The Poetic Principle" [1850] where he condemns "the heresy of *The Didactic*," claiming instead that the "poem is written solely for the poem's sake."[45]) Vindicating the French poet, Swinburne makes it clear why Baudelaire's "flowers of evil" impart a distinctly modern type of wisdom: namely, their refusal to "redeem the age and remould society."[46] "No other form of art," declares Swinburne of poetry in general, "is so pestered with this impotent appetite for meddling in quite extraneous matters." "[B]ut," he laments, "the mass of readers seem actually to think that a poem is the better for containing a moral lesson or assisting in a tangible and material good work." Disregarding the spirit of philanthropy, having no use for any "theory of progress," and disconnected from the "tangible and material" concerns of society, the best poetry in Swinburne's view exists purely for itself.

Rather than educate, moralize, or preach to a readership, the poems collected in *Les fleurs du mal* filled Swinburne with admiration because they gave precedence to "physical beauty and perfection of sound or scent" (999). Wary, however, that English readers might follow their French counterparts by laying charges of immorality against Baudelaire's work, Swinburne suggests that such thoughts are only the products of semi-educated, if not vulgar, minds. He argues that the persistent critical demand for a moral message necessarily degrades poetry like Baudelaire's. "If any reader," writes Swinburne, "could extract from any poem a positive spiritual medicine – if he could swallow a sonnet like a moral prescription – then clearly the poet supplying these intellectual drugs would be a bad artist." As a consequence, the moral-making poet is little better than a tradesman, "no real artist, but a huckster and vendor of miscellaneous wares."

Such commentary usurps the *vates*, toppling him from divine heights and throwing him into the streets. Swinburne's review stands as a forthright rejection of those Carlylean precepts that influenced much thinking about poetry in the decades that followed 1832. But in disentangling the genre from its supposed moral mission, and encouraging it to embrace previously unrecognized sensations, Swinburne occupies a position that has a certain familiarity. Swinburne's firm belief in "art for art's sake" – partly derived from Théophile Gautier's "Préface" to the sexually controversial novel *Mademoiselle de Maupin* (1835) – in some respects led poetry back into the Tennysonian garden where the poet's mind had to be protected from intruders. It would be left to later Victorian poets to figure out if it were possible – or even desirable – for their art to return to the people.

NOTES

My thanks to James Walter Caufield for casting his critical eye over this chapter.

1 Percy Bysshe Shelley, "The Mask of Anarchy," in *Shelley's Poetry and Prose*, ed. Donald H. Reiman and Sharon B. Powers (New York: W.W. Norton, 1977), 301.

2 Shelley, "England in 1819," in *Shelley's Poetry and Prose*, 311. This poem was first published in 1839.

3 William Wordsworth, "To Lord Lonsdale," 24 February 1832, in *The Letters of William and Dorothy Wordsworth*, second edition, ed. Chester L. Shaver et al., 8 vols. (Oxford: Clarendon Press, 1967–93), V, 499.

4 [John Fullarton,] "Reform in Parliament," *Quarterly Review* 45 (1831), 283; further page reference appears in parentheses.

5 [Anonymous,] "Parliamentary Reform Bill," *Westminster Review* 15 (1831), 150.

6 Harold Perkin, *The Origins of Modern English Society* (London: Routledge and Kegan Paul, 1969), 313.

7 Perkin, *The Origins of Modern English Society*, 315.

8 [John Wilson,] "Tennyson's Poems," *Blackwood's Edinburgh Magazine* 31 (1832), 723; further page references appear in parentheses.

9 Ebenezer Elliott, "The Black Hole of Calcutta," in Elliott, *The Splendid Village: Corn-Law Rhymes; and Other Poems*, first collected edition, 3 vols. (London: Benjamin Still, 1834); volume and page references appear in parentheses.

10 [T. Peronnet Thompson,] *A Catechism on the Corn Laws; with a List of Fallacies and the Answers*, third edition (London: James Ridgway, 1827), 22.

11 [Anonymous,] "Poetry by the People," *Athenaeum* (11 June 1831), 370.

12 Jeremy Bentham, *The Rationale of Reward* (London: John and H.L. Hunt, 1825), 206; further page number appears in parentheses.

13 Robert Burns, "Song – For a' that and a' that" (1795), in Burns, *The Poems and Songs of Robert Burns*, ed. James Kinsley, 3 vols. (Oxford: Clarendon Press, 1968), II, 762.

14 [John Johnstone,] "The Radical Poets," *Tait's Edinburgh Magazine* 1 (1832), 140; further page number appear in parentheses.

15 [John Wilson,] "Poetry of Ebenezer Elliott," *Blackwood's Edinburgh Magazine* 35 (1834), 821; further page reference appears in parentheses.

16 [W. J. Fox,] Review of Tennyson, *Poems, Chiefly Lyrical*, *Westminster Review* 14 (1831), 210–24, reprinted in Isobel Armstrong, *Victorian Scrutinies: Reviews of Poetry, 1830–1870* (London: Athlone, 1972), 71; further page references appear in parentheses.

17 Arthur Henry Hallam, "To Richard Chenevix Trench," December 2, 1830, in *The Letters of Arthur Henry Hallam*, ed. Jack Kolb (Columbus, OH: Ohio State University Press, 1981), 387. Three months later, Tennyson remarked that "the instigating spirit of reform" would "bring on the confiscation of church property and maybe the downfall of the church altogether"; he saw the "Sect of St Simonistes" as "a proof of the immense mass of evil" developing at the time: "To Elizabeth Russell," 18 March 1832, in *The Letters of Alfred Lord Tennyson*, ed. Cecil Y. Lang and Edgar F. Shannon, Jr., 3 vols. (Oxford: Clarendon Press, 1982), I, 69.

18 Arthur Henry Hallam, "On Some Characteristics of Modern Poetry," *Englishman's Magazine* 1 (1831), 616–28, reprinted in *The Writings of Arthur Hallam*, ed. T.H. Vail Motter (New York: MLA, 1943), 190; further page references appear in parentheses.

19 William Wordsworth, "Essay, Supplementary to the Preface," in *The Prose Works of William Wordsworth*, ed. W.J.B. Owen and Jane Worthington Smyser, 3 vols. (Oxford: Clarendon Press, 1974), III, 83.

20 Eric Griffiths, "Tennyson's Idle Tears," in *Tennyson: Seven Essays*, ed. Philip Collins (Basingstoke: Macmillan, 1992), 43. Hallam's categories may have other sources derived from Kant, including Friedrich Schiller, *On the Aesthetic Education of Man in a Series of Letters* (1793), trans. Elizabeth M. Wilkinson and L.A. Willougby (Oxford: Clarendon Press, 1967), 33–35; on this point, see Isobel Armstrong, *Victorian Poetry: Poetry, Poetics and Politics* (London: Routledge, 1993), 61.

21 Ricks notes many of the echoes in "The Poet" from Keats's and Shelley's poetry: *The Poems of Tennyson*, I, 243–44.

22 Herbert F. Tucker, *Tennyson and the Doom of Romanticism* (Cambridge, MA: Harvard University Press, 1988), 88.

23 John Stuart Mill, "Tennyson's Poems," *London Review* 1 (1835), 402–35, reprinted in Mill, *Autobiography and Literary Essays*, ed. John M. Robson et al., *The Collected Works of John Stuart Mill*, 33 vols. (Toronto: University of Toronto Press, 1963–91), I, 414.

24 John Stuart Mill, *Autobiography*, in *Autobiography and Literary Essays*, 141; further page references appear in parentheses.

25 John Stuart Mill, "To John Sterling," 21–22 October 1831, in *The Earlier Letters of John Stuart Mill*, ed. Francis E. Mineka (Toronto: University of Toronto Press, 1963), 81.

26 John Stuart Mill, "Thoughts on Poetry and Its Varieties" (1867), reprinted in *Autobiography and Literary Essays*, 344; further page references appear in parentheses. This essay combines and revises "What Is Poetry?" and "The Two Kinds of Poetry," *Monthly Repository* n.s. 7 (1833), 60–70, 714–24.

27 John Stuart Mill, *On Liberty*, in *The Collected Works of John Stuart Mill*, XVIII, 223.

28 Thomas Carlyle, "Notebook Entry," 3 December 1826, in *Two Note Books of Thomas Carlyle*, ed. Charles Eliot Norton (New York: Grolier Club, 1898), 71; further page number appears in parentheses.

29 Thomas Carlyle, "To Leigh Hunt," 20 November 1831, in *The Collected Letters of Thomas and Jane Welsh Carlyle*, ed. Charles Richard Sanders and

Kenneth J. Fielding et al., 26 vols. to date (Durham, NC: Duke University Press, 1970–), VI, 265.

30 Thomas Carlyle, "Shooting Niagara: And after?" in *The Works of Thomas Carlyle*, 30 vols. (London: Chapman and Hall, 1896–99), XXX, 24; further volume and page references to this edition appear in parentheses.

31 Thomas Carlyle, "To William Graham," 17 October 1831, in *The Collected Letters of Thomas and Jane Welsh Carlyle*, VI, 21.

32 Elizabeth Barrett, "To Hugh Stuart Boyd," 9 June 1832, in *The Brownings' Correspondence*, ed. Philip Kelley et al., 14 vols. to date (Winfield, KS: Wedgestone Press, 1984–), III, 25.

33 Elizabeth Barrett, "To Robert Browning," 27 February 1845, in *The Brownings' Correspondence*, X, 101.

34 Cited in Fred Kaplan, *Thomas Carlyle: A Biography* (Cambridge: Cambridge University Press, 1983), 494.

35 Robert Browning, "Introductory Essay" ["Essay on Shelley"], in Browning, *The Poems*, ed. John Pettigrew and Thomas J. Collins, 2 vols. (Harmondsworth: Penguin Books, 1981), I, 1001; further volume and page references appear in parentheses.

36 Matthew Arnold, "To Arthur Hugh Clough," 23 September 1849, in *The Letters of Matthew Arnold*, ed. Cecil Y. Lang, 3 vols. to date (Charlottesville, VA: University Press of Virginia, 1996–), I, 156.

37 Arnold, "To Thomas Arnold," 28 December 1857, in *The Letters of Matthew Arnold*, I, 370.

38 Arnold, "To Arthur Hugh Clough," early February, 1849, in *The Letters of Matthew Arnold*, I, 131.

39 Arnold, "To Arthur Hugh Clough," December 1848, in *The Letters of Matthew Arnold*, I, 128.

40 Arnold, "To Thomas Arnold," 28 December 1857, in *The Letters of Matthew Arnold*, I, 369.

41 Wordsworth, "Preface" to *Lyrical Ballads*, in *The Prose Works of William Wordsworth*, I, 148.

42 Wordsworth, "Lines Composed a Few Miles above Tintern Abbey, on Revisiting the Banks of the Wye during a Tour, 13th July 1798," in *Lyrical Ballads and Other Poems, 1797–1900*, ed. James Butler and Karen Green, The Cornell Wordsworth (Ithaca, NY: Cornell University Press, 1992), 117.

43 Matthew Arnold, "The Study of Poetry" (1880), in Arnold, *English Literature and Irish Politics*, ed. R.H. Super, *The Complete Prose Works Of Matthew Arnold*, 11 vols. (Ann Arbor, MI: University Of Michigan Press, 1960–77), IX, 163.

44 Charles Baudelaire. "New Notes on Edgar Poe," trans. Lois Hyslop and Francis Hyslop, in *The Recognition of Edgar Allan Poe: Selected Criticism since 1829*, ed. Eric W. Carlson, (Ann Arbor, MI: University of Michigan Press, 1966), 56.

45 Edgar Allan Poe, "The Poetic Principle," *Sartain's University Magazine*, October 1850, reprinted in Poe, *Essays and Reviews*, ed. G.R. Thomson (New York: The Library of America, 1984), 75–76.

46 [Algernon Charles Swinburne,] "Charles Baudelaire: Les Fleurs du Mal," *Spectator* 35 (1862), 998; further page reference appears in parentheses.

2

KATHY ALEXIS PSOMIADES

"The Lady of Shalott" and the critical fortunes of Victorian poetry

Introduction

The standard story about the critical fortunes of Victorian poetry in the twentieth century goes like this. During the early part of the century, particularly after 1914, modernist writers like T.S. Eliot and Virginia Woolf defined themselves against the Victorians, whom they saw as old-fashioned, somewhat hypocritical, and not particularly good writers. Eliot compared Alfred Tennyson and Robert Browning unfavorably to the seventeenth-century poet John Donne, arguing that the former "are poets, and they think; but they do not feel their thought . . . as immediately as the odor of a rose . . . A thought to Donne was an experience; it modified his sensibility."[1] In *A Room of One's Own* (1929), Woolf quoted love lyrics from Tennyson and Christina Rossetti to invoke "some feeling that one used to have (at luncheon parties before the war perhaps)," and believed this poetry was inspired by an "illusion." "Why," she asked, "not praise the catastrophe . . . that destroyed the illusion and put truth in its place?"[2] "The Angel in the House," the title of Coventry Patmore's famous mid-Victorian poem, became for Woolf the name for an oppressive Victorian model of femininity that modernist women writers needed to discard in order to write freely.[3]

Although the study of English Literature in schools and universities has its roots in the Victorian period (when it served as an alternative to the classics in the education of women, working-class men, and colonial administrators), it was in the 1920s and 1930s that literary criticism emerged as a professional scholarly discipline worthy of the attention of elite men.[4] As literary scholars both in the United Kingdom (I.A. Richards, F.R. Leavis) and the United States (Robert Penn Warren, Cleanth Brooks) developed a mode of literary criticism that valued poems as self-contained artifacts (the New Criticism), Victorian poetry became almost synonymous with bad poetry. In part, this orthodoxy arose because both high modernism and the New Criticism valued formal and technical "difficulty" in art. Unlike Tennyson, who wrote for a general audience, poets like Eliot sought to distinguish their work from easily consumable mass-cultural forms. A poem like Tennyson's *In Memoriam* (1850) could be bedtime reading for either workers or the Queen. But the successful interpretation of Eliot's "The Waste Land" (1922) requires a reader with a vast amount of literary and historical knowledge. The new profession of scholarly literary criticism depended on "difficulty" for its very existence: university students needed to be trained in techniques of close reading and analysis in order to be able to appreciate real poetry, and trained out of their uncultured tastes for sentimental and easily understood verse. Most of the examples of second-rate poetry in the notes to Richards's *Principles of Literary Criticism* (1924) and in the poems collected in *Understanding Poetry* (1938), Brooks and Warren's famous textbook, are Victorian.

After the Second World War, however, Victorian literature came into its own. New Critical modes of reading were still dominant but the renewed interest in the relationship between literature and society made the topicality of Victorian literature and poetry attractive. As the study of literature became more and more professionalized, Victorian poetry also became a field of specialization that grew rapidly through the 1950s and 1960s. During the late 1970s and early 1980s when post-structuralism (in the form of deconstruction and Lacanian psychoanalysis) provided new ways of reading Romantic poetry, literary theory hardly touched the work of Victorian poets. Yet the revival of interest in questions of culture, gender, history, and sexuality during the 1980s benefited the study of Victorian poetry considerably. Indeed, almost all versions of the standard story about the field in the twentieth century end with the invocation of some point in the recent past, or perhaps just now arising, or anticipated in the near future, when Victorian poetry receives its proper due at last.[5]

This story is historically useful in that it shows the unique position of Victorian poetry as that area of literary endeavor upon whose devaluation the profession of literary criticism was founded. It is also rhetorically satisfying: an account of the slow progress of a mistreated Cinderella of genres toward the inevitable encounter with the slipper-bearing theorist who will reveal her true worth. For these reasons, I join the critics who tell the standard story. But I also want to add to this story. Literary criticism may have been founded on Victorian poetry's devaluation but the central issues of literary criticism were first articulated as issues, with great sophistication, in Victorian poetry itself. What art is and what its relation to the rest of society might be, what literature is and how it changes over time, how language and representation work, what gender and sexuality mean – these are all questions that Victorian poetry poses long before literary criticism does. It is not just that Victorian poetry invents the categories of poetry and society, literature and other writing, representation and reality, masculine and feminine and sets these categories in opposition to each other. Victorian poetry also articulates these categories as *problems*, as the problems of modernity.

Tennyson's "The Lady of Shalott" directly engages with all of the issues that I have just outlined. One of the best known and most widely anthologized Victorian poems, it is frequently taken as representative of its age. First published in 1832 and substantially revised for publication in 1842, the poem tells the story of a Lady mysteriously consigned to an island tower from which the "whisper" (*AT* 39) of "a curse" (40) prevents her from looking out directly. Instead, she sees the world outside her window "through a mirror clear" (46) and weaves the reflected "shadows of the world" (48) into "a magic web with colours gay" (38). When the glittering figure of "bold Sir Lancelot" (77) flashes into her mirror, the Lady, grown "half sick of shadows" (71) and without her own "loyal knight and true" (62) leaves her weaving to look out of the window directly:

> She left the web, she left the loom,
> She made three paces through the room,
> She saw the water-lily bloom,
> She saw the helmet and the plume,
>   She looked down to Camelot.
> Out flew the web and floated wide;
> The mirror cracked from side to side;
> "The curse is come upon me," cried
>   The Lady of Shalott.   (109–17)

The Lady leaves her bower, finds a boat, writes her name on it, lies down in it, and floats down to Camelot, "singing her last song" (143) as she dies. When her dead body, "a gleaming shape" (156), appears in Camelot, it mystifies the assembled crowd. But Lancelot, in the 1842 version of the poem, comments on its beauty: "She has a lovely face; / God in his mercy lend her grace, / The Lady of Shalott" (169–71).[6]

Even from this brief synopsis, we can see how the poem opposes the Lady's private artistic activity to the real world outside her tower and constructs that opposition as a *problem*. Through the imagery of windows, mirrors, weaving, and writing, it figures the processes of representation and interpretation as difficult and complicated. By making Lancelot, the representative of the outside world, into a figure composed of fragments of other texts – Thomas Malory's *Morte Darthur* (composed 1470, published

1485), Edmund Spenser's *The Faerie Queene* (1590–96), and varieties of quest romance – it both courts and refuses the separation of writing and the real. And in allowing issues of gender and sexuality to turn a story about aesthetic production into a story about a woman who dies for love, the poem problematizes gender and sexuality as well. The present chapter traces the responses of critics in the twentieth century to the questions that both Tennyson's poem and Victorian poetry in general pose.

Poetry and society

The problem of the relationship between "poetry" and "society" can only emerge at a historical moment when aesthetic activity appears different in kind from economic and political activity. When the market replaces the patron as the source of economic gain and the means of distribution to an audience, poets paradoxically are both more and less independent. No longer subject to the whims of patrons or to the favor of a court, they are instead at the mercy of a larger, more distant audience whose purchasing power can make or break them. At the point, then, at which the artist becomes just another producer for the market, artists claim to be special people: autonomous geniuses who through their unique imaginative abilities have access to truths otherwise not available to the culture. As Marxist critic Raymond Williams points out, this ideology of imagination is not only a compensation for the poet but also "an emphasis on the embodiment in art of certain human values, capacities, energies, which the development of society towards an industrial civilization was felt to be threatening or even destroying."[7]

Art's separation from everyday life is a constant concern of Victorian poetry. In "The Lady of Shalott," aesthetic activity – singing, weaving, writing – is fundamentally shaped by the Lady's separation from the outside world both in that this separation is a necessary condition of production, and in that all of her activities aim at bridging the gap of that separation. Not only, then, does the poem suggest that poetry and society point toward different kinds of things but also toward things defined against each other, whose relationship must then inevitably be problematic.

Yet the problem of the relationship between poetry and society also implies some connection between these two categories. Just as the category of art is under construction in the nineteenth century, so too is the category of the social – that is to say, the way in which people imagine themselves as belonging to groups linked by common ideas about what it means to be fully human. Art's function as celebrant and preserver of private values makes it very useful in the project of defining the human. Lancelot, at the end of Tennyson's poem, may be an obtuse reader of the text that is the Lady. Yet that text is able to appeal to his private sensibilities – the appreciation of beauty, the ability to empathize, to desire. "She has a lovely face" may be an inadequate response to the Lady but it is not, for example, as inadequate as "Can I watch the autopsy?" or "Do you think I could have the boat after we bury her?" The notion that the Lady has something to offer the people of Camelot as a group, the way in which her mysteriousness to them links together the various elements of this society so that they are identifiable as a group with some commonality, is part of the way in which poetry represents but also helps to construct the social.

Both poetry and society, then, were ideas under construction during the nineteenth century. The problem of what the relationship between them should be is thus a particularly modern problem. In other words, it is a problem that emerges during the centuries in which bourgeois capitalism restructures social and political life in such a manner that art and society appear related and yet somehow unrelated kinds of things. To the modernists, it looked as if the Victorians were merely the producers of a bad solution to this problem: like the Lady, they seemed both to care too much about social intervention and to withdraw too much from the world. As Raymond Macdonald Alden, author of *Alfred Tennyson, How to Know Him* (1917), observes: "it sometimes seems to us as if the Victorians represented that uninteresting state of mankind before the fall, whereas we have eaten of the tree of knowledge."[8] At this time, Victorian poetry felt both out of touch with life's gritty realities and excessively topical and didactic.

The tendency to characterize Victorian poetry as too involved in Victorian society or too isolated from it began to shift after the Second World War when the question of art's relation to the social acquired new urgency in an era of cultural and economic reconstruction. Three important studies – Graham Hough's *The Last Romantics* (1947), John Heath-Stubbs's *The Darkling Plain* (1950), and E.D.H. Johnson's *The Alien Vision of Victorian Poetry* (1952) – argued for the continuing relevance of Victorian poetry in a world torn apart by the ravages of war. Hough and Heath-Stubbs reevaluated the later Victorian poets like Algernon Charles Swinburne and Dante Gabriel Rossetti as the precursors of the modernists, carving out a space for art in a hostile culture made more hostile by science. For Hough the poets usually seen as escapist were not just retreating from society but trying to create an alternative to it: a project for which there was even more necessity in a world in which modern science had produced nuclear bombs. Similarly, Heath-Stubbs values later Victorian poetry and its gesture of withdrawal as a response to the materialism of Victorian culture, by which he means its desire for money and commodities, its valorization of a scientific world view, and its loss of faith. For both critics, the later Victorian poets are preferable to Tennyson, Browning, and Arnold because these earlier writers tried to engage with and comment on a culture not worth engaging with. Heath-Stubbs asserts that a poem like "The Lady of Shalott" gives "the most complete artistic satisfaction" insofar as it is "purely decorative." By this he means that the poem gives "satisfaction" because it does not comment on contemporary society but creates a beautiful alternative to that ugly reality, like "paintings in words or pieces of lovely tapestry."[9] Yet when Tennyson tries to deal with social problems in his monodrama *Maud* (1855), featuring a crazed speaker betrayed in love and agitated by the tumult of the Crimean War, the poet's "reaction is scarcely adult, and his final refuge is in a hysterical jingoism."[10]

It is Johnson, however, who argues most strongly for the complexity of Victorian poetry, for the doubleness that results from poets like Tennyson, Browning, and Arnold being torn between private vision and public responsibility. Unlike earlier critics who saw these poets as merely surrendering to the demands of their readership, Johnson saw them combating the prevalent values of the age, concealing within public poems their true private insights. Johnson identifies a doubleness in Victorian poetry that critics interested in the relations between poetry and society still comment on today: "The expressed content has a dark companion, its imaginative counterpart, which accompanies and comments on apparent meaning in such a way as to suggest ulterior motives."[11] This doubleness springs from the Victorian poets' shared desire to be true to their own imaginative vision, and yet to engage a wide audience in such a way as to have an impact on social life. In Johnson's view, this remains an impossible project. From his perspective, what is valuable about art in modern society is its opposition to status quo, its "alien vision": the insights that come from its separation from popular values and ideas. Johnson reads "The Lady of Shalott" as a poem about how the life of the imagination can be destroyed by the desire to enter into a more public, actual life. The Lady's web and mirror stand as "metaphors for the creative imagination which has been shattered by the intrusion of direct experience."[12] In the private insights concealed in poems that on the surface might seem bland and complacent, Victorian poets take up thoroughly modern concerns.

With Robert Langbaum's *The Poetry of Experience* (1957), we move beyond the question of whether Victorian poets were too involved or too uninvolved with their society, and toward a more complex conception of the relationship between poetic form and historical events. The phrase "poetry of experience" describes poetry of the post-Enlightenment period –

Romantic, Victorian, and modern – that rather than merely reflecting the dissociation of fact and value, intellect and emotion, brought about by the scientific world view, is "an attempt to salvage on science's own empiric grounds the validity of individual perception against scientific abstractions."[13] For Langbaum, nineteenth- and twentieth-century poetry is linked by the idea "that the imaginative apprehension gained through immediate experience is primary and certain, whereas the analytic reflection that follows is secondary and problematical."[14] Thus poets from both centuries share a concern about the relations between subjects and objects, the ways that subjects can know objects, and the question of individual perception. According to Langbaum, these shared concerns mimic scientists' concerns with the collection of data through observation and the relation between that data and the scientific conclusions drawn from it. At the same time, poets oppose these scientific concerns. Langbaum is less concerned with a poem's "scientific" content than he is with the new poetic forms that emerge during the period to explore the new concern with perception. Such forms include the dramatic lyric and lyric drama in Romanticism, the Victorian dramatic monologue, and the modernist use of dramatic monologue and symbol. What makes Langbaum's work so interesting, even more than forty years later, is the way it connects poetic form to larger historical shifts.

Marxist criticism, however, supplied a critique of some of the liberal humanist notions underpinning Langbaum's emphasis on a "poetry of experience." In this regard, Alan Sinfield's *Alfred Tennyson* (1986) sees poetry not passively mirroring a historical situation but actively interpreting and intervening "from a specific position in the social order."[15] From his standpoint, Victorian poetry is political not only because the genre, at least through most of the century, had a political role. Sinfield also claims that "poetry which appears to be remote from political issues is in fact involved with the political life of its society: it disseminates ideas, images and narratives of the way the world is, and that is always a political activity" (11). In addition to reading the poetry in the context of historical events, Sinfield elucidates how Tennyson's poems help to produce the idea that poetry has a specific kind of self-contained language that creates the illusion of "a ground of truth and ultimate being beyond the unstable constructions of language" (87). He argues that poetry is not just an example of culture but also contributes to the construction of the idea of culture itself.

To undertake this task Sinfield makes use of theories about language and subjectivity derived from two types of post-structuralist theory: deconstruction and the psychoanalysis of Jacques Lacan. Associated with the philosophical inquiries of Jacques Derrida, deconstruction sees language as self-referential, rather than referring to an external world of objects. To a deconstructionist the word "boat" has meaning not because it refers to a hollow wooden structure but because it is not "coat" or "moat" or even "albatross." Language, in other words, is a system in which the component parts have meaning as part of a system: it does not refer to some external truth nor is it grounded in any external reality. Lacanian psychoanalysis in turn ties this unstable language to the question of identity: we only know ourselves as selves in language, and thus the notion of a stable self is just another illusion about the belief in a truth beyond language to which language refers. Read from this perspective, "The Lady of Shalott" becomes for Sinfield a poem about the construction of the bourgeois self and the anxieties attendant on this construction. The Lady's web fails to give her "a coherent sense of herself in the world" (68). When she acknowledges the web as illusion and sets out for Camelot with a sign bearing her name, she tries "to enter language and social identity." But her death shows the impossibility of her project.

We can see how literary criticism's conception of the political has widened here: no longer is the Lady of Shalott a merely decorative poem, or even a poem about the irreconcilability of poetry and politics. Rather the poem's political content lies in those areas – desire, subject formation, gender – formerly thought to lie outside of politics in the subject's personal life. This critical inquiry into the private/public split in part is a legacy of the influential claim of feminism in the 1960s and 1970s that "the personal is political." The net result is to allow critics to talk about even the most seemingly apolitical Victorian poetry in the context of politics and economics.

The culmination of this more historical approach to Victorian poetry is Isobel Armstrong's *Victorian Poetry: Poetry, Poetics and Politics* (1993), an imposing study that returns to the question of the relationship between Victorian poetry and the larger culture that critics of the 1950s found so pressing. Drawing on insights from Marxism, deconstruction, psychoanalysis, and feminist criticism, Armstrong seeks to develop "the political implications of Johnson's work and the epistemological implications of Langbaum."[16] Like Johnson and Langbaum, she sees the Victorian poets as responding to and intervening in the specificity of their historical moment: "post-revolutionary, post-industrial, post-teleological, post-Kantian" (4). Like Johnson, she sees *doubleness* as the defining characteristic of Victorian poetry, where a single poem may be thought almost always to contain two different and contradictory poems. Like Langbaum, Armstrong is interested in how poetic form evolves in response to cultural change. She sees

Victorian poetry as "a complex entity, defining and participating in an area of struggle" (10). In her view, part of what the Victorian poem struggles with is "the logic of its own contradictions" (15). What such poetry anticipates, indeed makes possible, is not just, as for Langbaum, modernist poetry but also, and perhaps most importantly, post-structuralist criticism. From Armstrong's perspective, the modes of reading that Victorian poetry invents ultimately lead to deconstruction, Lacanian psychoanalysis, and most other contemporary theories about representation. At the same time, Victorian poetry is deeply political, intensely engaged in political debates and invested in questions of social change.

One of the central features of Armstrong's work is its tendency to draw upon an eclectic mixture of methodologies and approaches to demonstrate the complexity of Victorian poems, rather than expecting them to yield their riches to one master narrative, however compelling. In a long essay on "The Lady of Shalott," she views the work as two poems: first, a poem in which the lady is caught between binary oppositions like rural/urban, labor/mercantilism, isolation/community, passivity/action and cannot mediate between them; and second, a critique of that poem in which these oppositions are almost revealed as ideological constructs and interrogated as such. Yet her analysis does not stop there. The Cambridge Apostles – the avant-garde group of conservative intellectuals to which Tennyson belonged in the 1830s – were very much concerned with the role of the intellectual in the regeneration of society. (The Apostles included among its members Arthur Hallam, whose death prompted *In Memoriam*, as well as R.C. Trench, the philologist.) Placing "The Lady of Shalott" in the context of the Cambridge Apostles' study of myth and early nineteenth-century theories about myth, Armstrong shows how the poem both attempts to use myth as a political tool and interrogates this use of myth. Moreover, she sees the poem in the context of the plight of industrial cotton weavers, noting how the Lady's weaving connects her to the other workers of the poem, the reapers in the field. The Lady's weaving allows contemporary industrial issues to be displaced on to her, so that the reapers can provide a Romantic organic version of what was a source of serious social unrest. Further still, Armstrong interprets the poem in the context of psycho-analytic theories of gender and language, demonstrating how the poem "is about binary opposition rather than being an expression of it."[17] Whereas a more traditional Marxist reading like Sinfield's locates the poem's politics primarily in its construction of the private realm of desire, subjectivity and gender, Armstrong's reading disturbs the distinctions between personal and political by showing how they provide different kinds of vocabulary for addressing the same issues.

Poetry and literary tradition

To some extent, of course, all criticism deals with the relationship between poetry and society: even formalist critics, who look at the poem as a self-contained unit, often engage with the social effects of their close readings. But poetry is also a specific kind of writing, different from magazine articles, nonfiction prose, and novels. Increasingly, as the nineteenth century progressed, part of the value placed on poetry lay in its difference from other types of writing, particularly writing produced for a mass audience. To understand Victorian poetry, we need to know how concepts like "literature" and "tradition" – concepts that announced the difference of poetry from other writing – both shaped and were shaped by Victorian poems.

The idea of tradition is perhaps most evident in the practice of allusion through which a poem announces its relation to previously written poems. In general terms, tradition means that succeeding generations of poets assert their dynamic engagement with the poetic past. In other words, since tradition represents the view that the great poems of great poets occupy positions of high artistic value, emergent poets must learn how to absorb and reproduce the cultural authority accorded to a venerated poetic canon. At the same time, emergent poets must not simply imitate the great works that have gone before them. Aspiring poets must instead assert their own distinctiveness and originality. Tradition, then, involves each new poet claiming his or her affiliation with and independence from the great poetic past. When Lancelot appears in Tennyson's poem, he, unlike the Lady, already has an extensive literary identity – Arthurian legend makes clear who he is, and what Camelot is, even if Shalott remains unknown to us. Through Lancelot, the poem claims some connection between the medieval and the Victorian, and through the presence of the knight and lady on his shield, it also recalls Spenser's epic poem on the virtues and the establishment of Britain. Yet by positioning him on the periphery, and making the Lady its central agent, the poem claims both a relation to and a difference from the traditions of Arthurian legend and epic poetry: it tells a story that these traditions cannot tell, at a new and different historical moment.

Perhaps the most important figure for thinking about poetic tradition in the second half of the twentieth century is Harold Bloom, whose work of the 1960s and 1970s revitalized the reading of influence in nineteenth- and twentieth-century poetry. Whereas Bloom's earlier criticism – *The Ringers in the Tower* (1971), for example – valued Romantic over Victorian poetry, he comes to value Victorian poetry much more highly in later work like *Poetry and Repression* (1976). Insisting that poems can only be made out of other poems, only have meaning in relation to other poems, Bloomian influence theory sees poets after Milton anxiously misreading and rewriting their predecessors to clear a space for themselves. This struggle proves, according to Bloom, increasingly difficult for the emergent poet since there are more and more poems against which to assert one's self. From Bloom's viewpoint, "The Lady of Shalott" only makes sense when we interpret it as a *mis*reading of and contention with what he calls the "strong" poems that precede it, particularly poems by Romantics like Shelley and Keats. Bloom claims: "Tennyson's transformation of Keats was the largest single factor in British and American Poetry from 1830 until about 1915."[18]

The idea that all poems are made up of other poems and only have meaning in relation to other poems both draws upon and reinforces the idea of "literature" as a recognizable category of writing, a category different from other kinds of writing, requiring certain special skills for its decipherment. As the Victorians made literature, and as twentieth-century intellectuals professionalized the study of literature, concepts such as tradition, source, and influence were key terms for expressing the special value of literary writings. As literary study in the 1980s readdressed links between poetry and society, a more critical approach to the idea of tradition and of influence prevailed. Intertextuality – when viewed as the relations between a much broader range of texts than those that have been labeled literature – seemed more suited to historicist study than theories dedicated purely to poetic influence. Critics began to explore how the idea of literature was implicated in the development of nationalist and imperialist projects, how it might be used as a tool for domination, and how the very notion of literature could act to mystify or obscure the connections between poetry and society. Yet "poetry," "literature," and "the aesthetic" are, as categories, real historical entities; Victorian poems do allude to other poems and put energy into setting themselves in relation to these poems; and it seems rather simplistic to reduce all this activity to a species of bad faith.

One of the most powerful and convincing arguments for the importance of continuing to think about poetic influence is made by Andrew Elfenbein in *Byron and the Victorians* (1995). Drawing upon sociologist Pierre Bourdieu's concept of symbolic capital – power that takes the form of status and prestige rather than money – Elfenbein sees struggles between poets and their predecessors as part of the way in which cultural producers assert themselves in the field of cultural production.[19] These struggles are not only a matter of relations between texts but also signally shaped by the apparatuses of cultural production and consumption in place at any given time – the material production of print texts, the education system, the structures of publishing, selling, reviewing, and so on. "Whereas Bloom sees the agonistic position of younger writers towards precursors as an inner psychological struggle," writes Elfenbein, "Bourdieu demystifies it as the structural result of a competition for symbolic capital."[20]

Elfenbein's analysis of influence in "The Lady of Shalott" thus begins in much the same way as a Bloomian reading would, by locating in Tennyson's poem echoes of a Romantic predecessor. Yet, unlike Bloom, he sees that predecessor not as Shelley or Keats but as Byron. He connects the "little isle" and "silkensailed" shallops "skimming down" to Camelot in the 1832 version of the poem, with the "little isle" and the boats with "whiter sails" that "go skimming down" that Byron's imprisoned Bonnivard sees out the window of his cell in *The Prisoner of Chillon* (1816).[21] Tennyson, Elfenbein argues, is replacing Byronic romance, which ends with a masculine hero's rejection of the world, with Tennysonian lyric, which ends (in the 1832 version) with the Lady's entry into the world where she figures as the dead author of a lyric poem. But rather than connect this argument to a personal psychological struggle with Byron as paternal predecessor, in which Tennyson admires Byron's strength but valiantly attempts to clear a space in which he can write, Elfenbein examines the early nineteenth-century culture industry. On the one hand, Byron provides a powerful model of poetic subjectivity as self-revelation that Tennyson imitates in his Lady's final "This is I." On the other hand, abandoning Byron is a way of asserting a value above popularity for literary texts, a way of identifying with a new high culture whose new form, the pure lyric, announces its highness through its separation from the everyday. This is a project embraced by Tennyson's circle, the Cambridge Apostles. By the 1842 version, a more established Tennyson does not need to use Byron to locate his poetry in the cultural field, and most of the Byronic references are excised.

Whether we call it tradition, influence, or intertextuality, the relations between texts and their declarations of their affinities with and differences from other texts is even more important for us today than it was for the Victorians, for even more than they, we live in a culture of texts – both written and visual – that constantly refer to one another. The increasing intermelding of computers, film, television, visual images, and writing, together with shifts in the production and marketing of books, and changes in the education system – all combine to create new literacies and new cultural forms. Today the challenges posed to the categories of "literature" and "art" by these technological and social innovations are as pressing as those challenges that the Victorians experienced. Thinking more about the complex ways in which Victorians formulated questions about "literature" and "cultural capital" at a time when these categories were emerging might help us to be more self-conscious about how we articulate the presence of these problems in our own culture.

Poetry and representation

"The Lady of Shalott" is only one among many Victorian poems concerned with the slipperiness of representation, the tendency of language and other signs to take on a life of their own. The Lady reproduces in her weaving what she sees in her magic mirror of the world outside but whether that mirror provides an accurate reflection is by no means clear. Lancelot, who seems to precipitate her desire for contact with the real, is himself the bearer of another representation (the knight kneeling to a lady), just as he is a dazzle of reflected light, and also a reflection in the river. As a mysterious decorative object, bearing the label of her name as she floats into Camelot, the Lady herself is a sign of which Lancelot's remark – "She has a lovely face" – is both an adequate and inadequate reading.

Modernist ideas about how poetry ought to work shaped the early criticism of Victorian poetry – the idea of the poem as a self-contained system, one conveying its meaning through language and imagery and yielding its truth only to the intelligent and persistent reader was foundational to the development of academic criticism. The ornateness of Victorian poetry and the diffuseness of its imagery seemed to the New Critics to militate against the virtues of ambiguity and paradox. It is for this reason that many of the examples of bad or second-rate poetry in the notes to Richards's *Principles of Literary Criticism* (1924) and in the poems collected in Brooks and Warren's *Understanding Poetry* (1938) happen to be Victorian. In *Understanding Poetry*, for example, a poem by the popular writer Adelaide Anne Procter is pronounced "stupid, trivial and not worthy of the subject,"[22] and the study question for Tennyson's "The Palace of Art" (1832, revised 1842) clearly expects a negative reply: "But does the imagery really bear a close and functional relation to the idea of the poem?"[23] Later, in *The Well-Wrought Urn*, Brooks praises Tennyson's lyric "Tears Idle Tears" (from *The Princess* [1847]) but finds it atypical of the poet: "perhaps the last English poet one would think of associating with the subtleties of paradox and ambiguity."[24]

The revaluation of Victorian poetry in the 1950s was primarily organized around questions of poetry's social role, rather than language or poetic technique. When critics return to social questions in the 1980s and 1990s, they do so with a renewed interest in issues of representation, and a new vocabulary for discussing these issues that comes out of deconstruction and post-structuralist psychoanalysis. In *Tennyson and the Text: The Weaver's*

Shuttle (1992), Gerhard Joseph claims that "The Lady of Shalott" is "*the* Victorian poem that has most readily lent itself to the insinuation of 'theory' – especially of the Derridean and Lacanian variety."[25] He shows how the poem can be read as a "parable concerning the problematics of mimesis" (106), as a fable about "the radically attenuated 'emergence' of the self, driven by a naïve belief in unmediated presence, into the world" (107), as "an allegory charting the signifier's drift though the abyss, isolated from its signified, its audience, and the intention of its sender" (108), and even as "a parable of recent literary history charting the drift from a New critical analysis of authored 'works' to a post-structuralist reading of authorially-unbounded 'texts'" (122). We can see how all of these readings refer directly to the poem's treatment of issues of representation. Mimesis is a problem because the Lady cannot see the world directly to imitate it in her tapestry. The idea that one *can* experience reality directly, rather than through the mediation of the mirror, proves illusory, since the Lady does not survive her journey. The Lady's body itself becomes a sign in death but what it means, who it is for, and what the Lady intended it to say remain unknowable. Finally, the Lady's tapestry stands as a work with an author but her dead body figures as a text cut loose from its author, a text placed in the hands of readers like Lancelot, whose appreciation of it as an aesthetic object depends on their not knowing its author's story.

Like Sinfield, Joseph draws upon the work of Geoffrey Hartman, perhaps the most famous deconstructive critic to discuss Tennyson's poem. In *Saving the Text: Literature / Derrida / Philosophy* (1981), Hartman mentions Tennyson's poem in passing in a chapter on Derrida and Lacan. He locates in the Lady's claim to be "half-sick of shadows" "the wish to put ourselves in an unmediated relation to whatever 'really' is, to know something absolutely . . . to be defined totally."[26] But of course to be fixed by a word in this way proves impossible: the Lady dies as she sails down the river labeled with her name. "She becomes in death what she was without knowing it in life: a floating signifier"[27] – a sign without any stable referent. The poem thus exposes the desire to own one's own name – that is, to have a fixed identity, or write a poem that is somehow connected to a stable ground of meaning – as an impossible desire. It does so with the doubleness associated with the fetish in psychoanalysis – it knows that completeness is an illusion but it produces that illusion all the same. Hartman's brief elliptical discussion of how representation works in "The Lady of Shalott" went a long way toward demonstrating how sophisticated Victorian poetry can be when it considers issues of representation.

Psychoanalytic criticism, too, places a special emphasis on intricate structures of language and representation. Matthew Rowlinson argues for the usefulness of psychoanalytic theory for reading Victorian poetry and provides a good example of how issues of gender and sexuality may be combined with issues about language and representation.[28] In his view, the Lady of Shalott's weaving connects to Freud's reading of weaving as a means by which women resist the gaze and conceal their castration: woven fabric is also a threshold, like the hymen, or like that dash that separates binary oppositions from one another. For the Lady, weaving is a defense against castratory lack, since she is visible as a body only as a sign of loss. So for Rowlinson Tennyson's poem allies the loss that constitutes textuality (when the Lady becomes a visible text to the outside world, you can no longer hear her voice – just as the poem goes forward on the printed page without the author's voice behind it) with the loss that makes women visible (castration, lack). Lancelot functions as a sort of phallus made out of poems – a sign of the poetic belatedness the Lady embodies and defends against. When he enters the poem, he brings sexual difference with him, breaking the intactness of the Lady's mirror and her weaving. The defense against castration is no longer possible, the Lady becomes visible as woman, as lack, and as text, and with that the poem can end.

Poetry, gender, and sexuality

That the Victorians played a central role in inventing gender and sexuality as we now know them is a critical commonplace. The work of Michel Foucault (notably his introductory volume to *The History of Sexuality* [1976]) and the research of countless feminist scholars of the 1980s demonstrated how the Victorians constructed the categories of normal and perverse, heterosexual and homosexual, masculine and feminine. As Nancy Armstrong has argued, during the nineteenth century gender and sexuality were particularly useful in providing an arena into which political material could be transferred and depoliticized.[29] Further, because of the way in which Victorian culture constructed public and private, economic production and cultural and sexual reproduction as gendered spheres, it followed that gender and sexuality became intricately intertwined with issues of art and artistry. When Tennyson portrays the artist in "The Lady of Shalott" as an enclosed *feminine* consciousness and figures her problems as both aesthetic and erotic, he inaugurates a century-long concern with the sex and gender of art and artistry, a concern that culminates in British aestheticism's use of the erotic in the 1870s and 1880s to mark out a space for an elite autonomous art.

To the immediate heirs of the Victorians, however, gender and sexuality were givens. Since the Victorians did not have the benefit of Freud and seemed consequently repressed, they appeared to the modernists to be absurdly ignorant of their own desires. From the perspective of the early twentieth century, the truth about sex had been newly revealed and Tennyson's passionate love for his friend Arthur Henry Hallam, Swinburne's alleged inability to understand that "biting's no use," and Christina Rossetti's repeated refusals of marriage offers could all be brought forth to bolster the notion that there was something wrong with the Victorians that made their poetry less than it could have been, a sexual block that also blocked the creative process.

In the 1960s and 1970s, an emergent feminist literary criticism began to examine gender and sexuality as cultural constructs, and the work of women poets like Christina Rossetti and Elizabeth Barrett Browning started to receive more attention. Sandra M. Gilbert and Susan Gubar's *The Madwoman in the Attic: The Woman Writer and the Nineteenth-Century Literary Imagination* (1979), a foundational text for feminist criticism, included extensive discussion of both poets and this work, along with Margaret Homans's *Women Writers and Poetic Identity* (1980), with its discussion of women's responses to Romanticism, brought Bloom's Freud-inflected theories of influence to texts by women. Bloom's use of Freudian models to talk about how influence operates for male poets made it impossible to think about poetry as gender neutral by making visible the ideologies of masculinity interlinked with ideologies of poetry and aesthetics. Feminist critics like Gilbert, Gubar, and Homans could then look at the ways in which these ideologies of masculinity acted to block women writers' creative imaginations, by making the categories of poet and woman mutually exclusive. Allied with mute silent nature, lacking phallic strength, having as a Miltonic model of rebellion Eve, rather than the heroic Satan, women poets had even more to contend with in the poetic tradition than their anxious brothers.

In this groundbreaking feminist criticism, there is a stress on women poets' responses to an oppressive patriarchal tradition, on the absence of women poets relative to women novelists, and on the difficulties that femininity poses for a sense of poetic identity. This type of feminist inquiry reacts against the way that women poets had hitherto been treated in literary criticism – as bad poets who wrote about their personal experience in an embarrassingly transparent manner, and who were merely pretty, or hysterical, or worth only biographical consideration. While early feminist critics focused on women poet's oppression, self-repression, and failure, they revealed how thoroughly masculinist the dominant ideologies of poetic identity were. Moving away from biography, Gilbert, Gubar, and Homans combined Bloom, Freud, and feminism to disclose how thoroughly gender was written into ideas about poetry, imagery, form, and intertextual reference, and thus how gendered poetry itself was.

Because feminist criticism has made use of all the major theories and methodologies, the concerns I have outlined in previous sections of this chapter – the poet's relation to society, tradition and influence, language and representation – have been concerns for feminist criticism of Victorian poetry as well, concerns inflected by gender and sexuality. Feminist historicist critics, for example, might read Christina Rossetti's "Goblin Market" (1862) not as a fairy tale for children but as a trenchant analysis of the workings of capitalism, as a contribution to and meditation on the discourses circulating around the "rescuing" of fallen women (particularly those produced around Magdalene Houses), and as yet another example of the way the figure of the sexually imperiled white woman could be called upon to justify imperial violence in India.[30] Just as critics generally have historicized ideas of tradition and influence, so have feminist critics sought women's traditions in the writing of poetry, and new ways of seeing women poets' relation to the canon. Just as psychoanalytic critics used Lacan and Derrida to bring together issues of representation and gender, so feminist psychoanalytic critics made use of Lacan, Derrida, and French feminist psychoanalytic critics like Hélène Cixous, Luce Irigaray, and Julia Kristeva to produce feminist readings of these issues. Homans, for example, in an essay on Rossetti and Emily Dickinson, draws on Irigaray and other psychoanalytic and deconstructive critics to distinguish between metaphor and metonymy in "Goblin Market" by showing the different relations these tropes have to the feminine body.[31]

Feminist criticism has changed the face of Victorian poetry in two central ways. First, by focusing on how Victorian poetry constructs gender and sexuality, it made visible how central ideas about gender and sexuality are to this poetry, not only as subject matter but also as kind of foundational structure. For instance, Joseph Chadwick, writing about "The Lady of Shalott" in 1986, pointed out how the Lady's femininity was central to the ideas about art she embodied, how the same split between public and private that confined women to domesticity also made culture itself – aesthetic activity – separate from the public world of money and politics, and thus allied it with femininity. Yet both women and artists are dependent on the public world from which they seem to be separated and safe, a world "which accords them no stable or certain value at all."[32] So the poem critiques both domestic ideology and the ideology of aesthetic autonomy as a kind of mystification of the true status of women and artists. Here the insights of feminist criticism are called into play to illuminate the old question of the poet's position in bourgeois culture. The presence of metaphors of gender and sexuality in Victorian critical works, the increasing association of the realm of culture with the realm of sexuality, the repeated attempt to produce accounts of the differences between the masculine and feminine imagination – all of these elements suggest that gender and sexuality operated as a discursive field in which battles about art and society, literature and tradition, language and representation, might be played out. The idea, put forward by Barbara Charlesworth Gelpi, Carol T. Christ, and Dorothy Mermin, among others, that Victorian poetry was somehow feminized, that even the male poet had a more complex relation to femininity than simple exploitation or oppression, inaugurated a new interest in what sexuality and gender had to say about art, and a new interest too in masculinity, particularly in dissident masculinities.[33]

As Foucault famously observed, it was also during the Victorian period that homosexuality and heterosexuality were first classified as sexual identities. Critics in the later 1980s began to be interested in the homoeroticism of *In Memoriam*, the figuring of "the perverse" in Swinburne, and the invocation of homophilia in Hopkins.[34] In 1990, Richard Dellamora treated the poetry of Tennyson, Hopkins, and Swinburne to show how desire between men and notions of poetic androgyny underwrite and indeed structure conceptions of art and poetry throughout the nineteenth century.[35] Thaïs E. Morgan and Yopie Prins have also explored the use of figures of same-sex desire by both male and female poets.[36]

The second way in which feminist criticism has changed the face of Victorian poetry is through the challenge made by the recovery of women poets' writings, since the reclamation of this large body of work encourages a radical rethinking of the poetic canon. The 1913 edition of *The Oxford Book of Victorian Verse*, edited by Arthur Quiller-Couch, contains a huge array of male and female authors, many more even than there are in the most inclusive anthologies available today. Yet from about 1930, when the first edition of George Woods's *Poetry of the Victorian Period* was published, to 1959, when Walter Houghton and G. Robert Stange's anthology *Victorian Poetry and Poetics* appeared, we can see a gradual process of narrowing down both the number of poets included and the amount of work from each. In the 1990s, however, research on women poets flourished, and several paperback anthologies made it possible to introduce the work of these women to a wider audience.[37] The recovery of poetry by women writers has implications for the study of more traditional writers as well. A poem like "The Lady of Shalott" can be read not only against Byron but also against the extremely popular women poets of the 1820s and 1830s Hemans and L.E.L., who made women's emotional experiences the ideal subject matter of poetry. But the full impact of the recovery of women poets on the canon of Victorian poetry is only now beginning to be felt in the anthologies that incorporate the work of both men and women poets. When they predominate, the idea that women poets are an extra, an interesting supplement to the study of "real" Victorian poetry for those who are interested in that sort of thing, will disappear.

This brings me to my final point. The Victorians posed the central questions of their time through the language of gender and sexuality. They structured gender and sexuality around binary oppositions – masculine/feminine, angel/whore, heterosexual/homosexual, normal/perverse – and they used these oppositions to pose the problem of binary thinking itself, in a variety of venues. To some extent, of course, we do the same thing today. And yet today these categories are coming to seem increasingly archaic: to call upon them is to call upon the past, to use them is to reinscribe a Victorian world on a contemporary one. Studying how the Victorians created a world structured by these categories might help us to imagine what it might mean to think beyond them.

NOTES

This essay is made possible in part by support from the Institute for Scholarship in the Liberal Arts, College of Arts and Letters, University of Notre Dame, Indiana. Thanks are also due to Joseph Bristow for his advice and suggestions.

1 T.S. Eliot, *Selected Essays* (1932), Third Edition (London: Faber and Faber, 1951), 287.

2 Virginia Woolf, *A Room of One's Own* (New York: Harcourt Brace, Jovanovich, 1929), 14–15.

3 "Killing the Angel in the House was part of the occupation of a woman writer," Virginia Woolf writes in "Professions for Women" (1931), in Woolf, *Collected Essays*, 4 vols. (London: Hogarth Press, 1966), II, 286.

4 For more on the development of English Studies in the United Kingdom and United States respectively, see Brian Doyle, *English and Englishness* (London: Routledge, 1989) and Gerald Graff, *Professing Literature: An Institutional History* (Chicago, IL: University of Chicago Press, 1987).

5 For various recent versions of this story see George Levine, "Victorian Studies," in *Redrawing the Boundaries: The Transformation of English and American Literary Studies*, eds. Steven Greenblatt and Giles Gunn (New York: MLA, 1992), 130–53, Gerhard Joseph, "Why Are They Saying Such Bad Things about Victorian Poetry? Recent Tennyson Criticism," *Victorian Studies* 38 (1995), 255–64, and Thaïs E. Morgan, "Theorizing Victorian Poetry: An Introduction," *Victorian Poetry* 29 (1991), 329–32.

6 In the 1832 version of the poem, Lancelot does not appear in the final stanza; instead the "well-fed wits" of Camelot gather around the boat to read the puzzling piece of parchment on the Lady's breast: "The web was woven

curiously, / The charm is broken utterly, / Draw near and fear not – This is I, / The Lady of Shalott."

7 Raymond Williams, *Culture and Society: 1780–1950* (New York: Columbia University Press, 1983), 36.

8 Raymond Macdonald Alden, *Alfred Tennyson: How to Know Him* (Indianapolis, IN: Bobbs-Merrill, 1917), 354.

9 John Heath-Stubbs, *The Darkling Plain: A Study of the Later Fortunes of Romanticism in English Poetry from George Darley to W.B. Yeats* (London: Eyre and Spottiswoode, 1950), 148.

10 Heath-Stubbs, *The Darkling Plain*, 99.

11 E.D.H. Johnson, *The Alien Vision of Victorian Poetry: Sources of the Poetic Imagination in Tennyson, Browning and Arnold* (Princeton, NJ: Princeton University Press, 1952), 217.

12 Johnson, *The Alien Vision of Victorian Poetry*, 9.

13 Robert Langbaum, *The Poetry of Experience: The Dramatic Monologue in Modern Literary Tradition* (New York: Random House, 1957), 27.

14 Langbaum, *The Poetry of Experience*, 35.

15 Alan Sinfield, *Alfred Tennyson* (Oxford: Basil Blackwell, 1986), 8; further page references appear in parentheses.

16 Isobel Armstrong, *Victorian Poetry: Poetry, Poetics and Politics* (London: Routledge, 1993), 15; further page references appear in parentheses.

17 Isobel Armstrong, "Tennyson's 'The Lady of Shalott': Victorian Mythography and the Politics of Narcissism," in *The Sun is God: Painting, Literature and Mythology in the Nineteenth Century*, ed. J. B. Bullen (Oxford: Clarendon Press, 1989), 71.

18 Harold Bloom, *Poetry and Repression: Revisionism from Blake to Stevens* (New Haven, CT: Yale University Press, 1976), 144–45. For an extended discussion of Bloom and Victorian poetry, see James R. Kincaid, "Antithetical Criticism, Harold Bloom, and Victorian Poetry," *Victorian Poetry* 14 (1976), 365–82.

19 See especially Pierre Bourdieu, *The Field of Cultural Production: Essays on Art and Literature*, ed. Randal Johnson (New York: Columbia University Press, 1993).

20 Andrew Elfenbein, *Byron and the Victorians* (Cambridge: Cambridge University Press, 1995), 6–7.

21 Elfenbein, *Byron and the Victorians*, 169–87.

22 Cleanth Brooks and Robert Penn Warren, *Understanding Poetry: An Anthology for College Students* (New York: Henry Holt, 1938), 334

23 Brooks and Warren, *Understanding Poetry*, 509.

24 Cleanth Brooks, *The Well-Wrought Urn: Studies in the Structure of Poetry* (New York: Harcourt Brace, 1947), 167.

25 Gerhard Joseph, *Tennyson and the Text: The Weaver's Shuttle* (Cambridge: Cambridge University Press, 1992), 104; further page references appear in parentheses.

26 Geoffrey H. Hartman, *Saving the Text: Literature/Derrida/Philosophy* (Baltimore, MD: Johns Hopkins University Press, 1981), 97.

27 Hartman, *Saving the Text*, 110.

28 Matthew Rowlinson, *Tennyson's Fixations: Psychoanalysis and the Topics of*

the Early Poetry (Charlottesville, VA: University Press of Virginia, 1994), 74–95.

29 Nancy Armstrong, *Desire and Domestic Fiction: A Political History of the Novel* (New York: Oxford University Press, 1987).

30 Elizabeth K. Helsinger, "Consumer Power and the Utopia of Desire: Christina Rossetti's 'Goblin Market,'" *ELH* 58 (1991), 903–33; Diane d'Amico, "'Equal Before God': Christina Rossetti and the Fallen Women of Highgate Penitentiary," in *Gender and Discourse in Victorian Literature and Art*, eds. Antony H. Harrison and Beverly Taylor (DeKalb, IL: Northern Illinois University Press, 1992), 67–83; and Mary Wilson Carpenter, "'Eat Me, Drink Me, Love Me': The Consumable Female Body in Christina Rossetti's *Goblin Market*," *Victorian Poetry* 29 (1991), 415–34.

31 Margaret Homans, "'Syllables of Velvet': Dickinson, Rossetti, and the Rhetorics of Sexuality," *Feminist Studies* 11 (1985), 569–93.

32 Joseph Chadwick, "A Blessing and a Curse: The Poetics of Privacy in Tennyson's 'The Lady of Shalott,'" *Victorian Poetry* 24 (1986), 25.

33 Barbara Charlesworth Gelpi, "The Feminization of D.G. Rossetti," in *The Victorian Experience: The Poets*, ed. Richard A. Levine (Columbus, OH: Ohio University Press, 1982), 94–114; Carol Christ, "The Feminine Subject in Victorian Poetry," *ELH* 54 (1987), 385–401; and Dorothy Mermin, "The Damsel, The Knight and the Victorian Woman Poet," *Critical Inquiry* 13 (1986), 64–80.

34 See Jeff Nunokawa, "*In Memoriam* and the Extinction of the Homosexual," *ELH* 58 (1991), 427–38; and Thaïs E. Morgan, "Violence, Creativity and the Feminine: Poetics and Gender Politics in Swinburne and Hopkins," in *Gender and Discourse in Victorian Literature and Art*, eds. Harrison and Taylor 84–107.

35 Richard Dellamora, *Masculine Desire: The Sexual Politics of Victorian Aestheticism* (Chapel Hill, NC: University of North Carolina Press, 1990).

36 See especially Morgan, "Male Lesbian Bodies: The Construction of Alternative Masculinities in Courbet, Baudelaire, and Swinburne," *Genders* 15 (1992), 37–57; and Prins, "Sappho Doubled: Michael Field," *Yale Journal of Criticism* 8 (1995), 165–86.

37 See for example *Victorian Women Poets: An Anthology*, eds. Angela Leighton and Margaret Reynolds (Oxford: Blackwell, 1995), *British Women Poets of the Nineteenth Century*, ed. Margaret Randolph Higonnet (New York: Penguin, 1996), *Nineteenth-Century Women Poets: An Oxford Anthology*, eds. Isobel Armstrong, Joseph Bristow, and Cath Sharrock (Oxford: Clarendon Press, 1996).

3

E. WARWICK SLINN

Experimental form in Victorian poetry

In 1844, Elizabeth Barrett Browning wanted to write "a poem of a new class," one that included "[c]onversations & events" and "philosophical dreaming & digression."[1] She also wanted to purify George Gordon Byron's sexually contentious poetry, to write "a Don Juan, without the mockery & impurity." But this moral aim, while acknowledging her wish to elude the precedents created by Byron, was less important than her larger formal purpose. This desire to compose a new poetic form, one that would adapt established styles to contemporary needs, and particularly one that would combine narrative and speculative commentary with the requirements of aesthetic unity, typifies many Victorian poets. It led to widespread poetic play that transgressed boundaries between the three classical genres identified by the Greeks – epic (or narrative), drama, and lyric. And in the twentieth century it led in turn to standard critical discussions of Victorian experiments with form.[2]

Established accounts of experimentation tend to work within a critical legacy that associates experimental writing with internal features of structure and style. More recent critical practice, however, directs our attention to broader cultural contexts and particularly to the potential for cultural critique. Robert Con Davis and Ronald Schleifer, for instance, distinguish two types of critique: *institutional critique*, which aims to expose the conditions and principles which govern existing institutions and cultural practices, and *transformative critique*, which aims not only to question the conditions which sustain existing institutions but to change cultural practice. Poetry, I suggest, is more likely to offer examples of institutional critique.[3] In other words, when genres are reshaped or recovered (like medieval ballads in the eighteenth century), they may test or expose paradigms of contemporary values (reason, orderliness, universality) as well as aesthetic norms (neoclassical decorum). Alternatively, when new forms are developed they tend to cohere culturally at the point where their characteristics become recognizable or even dominant within an emerging social system (such as the nineteenth-century novel of manners). The consequence of this approach is to broaden the cultural significance of experimental writing. It can involve testing cultural conventions and assumptions, where testing means checking the resilience and flexibility of received literary norms, seeing if shifts in cultural practices and beliefs require new cultural forms. Conversely, it may entail seeing whether new or revitalized forms might themselves provoke changed cultural perceptions. In this sense, literary experimentation functions as a form of social dynamism, breaking up the inertia of linguistic habits and, ambiguously, questioning or rehabilitating them.

By the time Victoria came to the throne in 1837, Romantic poets had already begun this kind of cultural testing. Generic categories had long been challenged and reshaped by several decades of shifting poetic structures, ones that adapted old forms (ballads, odes, and pastoral) and refashioned old hybrids (the lyrical ballads of William Wordsworth and Samuel Taylor Coleridge, or the lyrical drama of Byron and Percy Bysshe Shelley). Victorian poets certainly continued to employ a range of differing forms. But in this general cultural shift they tended to sustain further movements and variations rather than offer sudden innovation – Barrett Browning, for instance, had to acknowledge that Byron had in part anticipated her purpose. At the same time, the one generic exception is the dramatic monologue, and this innovative form helps us to understand what is at stake in other modes of poetic experimentation in the period. Critics generally concur that this type of poem stands as the main Victorian contribution to a distinctly modern, if not Modernist, literature. With its hybrid combination of lyric and drama, the dramatic monologue produced an intensive focus on the exigencies and processes of human subjectivity. This concentration on human agency – on the psychology and politics of individuation – draws attention to a consistent feature of Victorian poetic forms, as the title of Langbaum's famous 1957 study, *The Poetry of Experience*, suggests. Victorian forms emphasize a particular conceptual strand of experimentation: namely, that which overlaps with the modern category of experience.

The English word experiment derives from the Latin *experimentum* (proof or trial) and *experiri* (prove, test, try), which is also the source of *experientia* (experience).[4] If experience is that which is based on actual observation, on practical acquaintance with events considered as a source of knowledge, then the experimental is that which is based on experience only – on direct acquaintance or personal knowledge, not on separate or agreed authority. These close correlations between experience, experiment, and testing produce a sense of knowledge as incomplete, neither authoritative nor fixed. In an age of growing challenges to established knowledge, therefore, it is hardly surprising that poetic forms emphasize the experiencing, thinking and feeling, human subject. Growth in the sciences, particularly the physical sciences such as botany and geology, as well as in theological questioning (notably the Higher Criticism of the Bible), created an intensifying uncertainty in the face of fundamental change. Emergent ideas about evolution, for example, displaced earlier concepts of mutability where change involved cyclical repetition rather than radical transformation, so that in Tennyson's *In Memoriam* (1850) even solid lands "melt like mist" (*AT* CXXIII, 7).

In conjunction with this uncertainty, poetic forms shift in emphasis. Rather than discovering completed wholes, we find structures that stress movement toward an end but where the attainment of that end is shrouded in incertitude. In other words, speakers in Victorian poems rarely find the palpable end or closure that would ensure aesthetic order and cultural or personal meaningfulness. There is no attainable goal for the eponymous hero of Tennyson's dramatic monologue "Ulysses" (1842): for him the "margin fades / For ever and for ever" when he moves (*AT* 20–21). Similarly, the concluding vision of a New Jerusalem in Barrett Browning's epic *Aurora Leigh* (1856) remains rhetorically articulated yet tantalizingly remote: the "first foundations of that new, near Day" (*EBBAL* IX. 956) lie "faint and far. . . / Beyond the circle of the conscious hills" (IX. 952–54). In Arthur Hugh Clough's *Amours de Voyage* (1858), the protagonist's moment of conclusion is the debilitating paradox of an active passivity, a determination of will that is a capitulation of intent: "I will go where I am led" (*AHC* V. 179).[5] And for Robert Browning's speaker in "Childe Roland to the Dark Tower Came" (1855), the moment of discovering the dark tower, the object of his quest, is a moment of utter ambiguity where revelation and destruction are inseparable. Like a sailor at the mercy of a storm, he sees "the unseen shelf / He strikes on, only when the timbers start" (*RB* 185–86).

In many respects, "Childe Roland" might be considered the quintessential Victorian experiment. It was a poem that Browning felt compelled to write, despite his uncertainty about its purpose; it was written in a single day, in fulfillment of a New Year resolution to write a poem a day;[6] and its intensively figurative style has generally baffled anyone seeking allegorical solutions to its perplexing narrative. Roland, the presumed protagonist, has spent a lifetime searching for the dark tower, much in the manner of a Childe (a knight in training), who is on a mission to secure his identity as knight. But Roland has journeyed without success. At the beginning of the poem, he seeks only an end to his suffering. On glimpsing the prospect of an "end descried," he feels only "gladness that some end might be" (17–18). He has heard failure prophesied so often and stated so many times of those other knights who have preceded him, that now "just to fail as they, seemed best" (41). Hence the poem resembles a medieval quest, a journey of self-discovery, but one in which the ghastly wasteland imagery sends the speaker into an intensifyingly isolated confrontation with strange grotesque phenomena. Once he leaves the road, it disappears. The grass, he says, grew "as scant as hair / In leprosy" (73–74). He sees a "stiff blind horse" (76). He crosses a stream which might have been a "bath" (112) for the "fiend's glowing hoof" (113) or contain "a dead man's cheek" (122). And he finds inexplicable marks "trample[d]" in the soil (130). Unexpectedly, when about to give up again, he realizes he is at "the place!" (176) – the tower is discovered. At the same time, he is trapped among hills, and his peers seem arranged to view "the last" of him (200). Yet he concludes by dauntlessly blowing his "slug-horn" (203), apparently announcing his presence: "'*Childe Roland to the Dark Tower came*'" (204).

The poem's formal features close around a past-tense narrative whose effect is paradoxically one of present immediacy. While the poem grammatically relates a series of past events, the result is one of continuing action, as if the speaker were attempting to explain events as they happen: "grey plain all round: / Nothing but plain to the horizon's bound. / I might go on; naught else remained to do" (52–54). Momentary expostulations indicate present-tense outbursts: "For mark!" (49), "No!" (61), "Alive?" (79), "Not it!" (91). The exclamations also accentuate the attempt to make sense of his experience: "solve it, you!" (167). Hence, as the horrendous features multiply, the poem dramatizes the attempt to wrest, through narrative structure, accountability and understanding from confusion and uncertainty. It represents the search for a structural and thus structuring conclusion from the despair of continuing failure. The poem, therefore, is dominated by the desire for a structural principle that would ensure the homogeneity of completed form. In terms of content, this principle becomes embodied in the formalized object of the tower, which thus structures both quest and poem. But formal homogeneity is disrupted in two respects: first, by the gross condition of the tower once it appears (it is both "round" and "squat" [182]); and second, by the concluding location of the tower within a phrase, cited and italicized, from outside the poem ("'*Childe Roland to the Dark Tower came*'"). "Childe Roland," then, refuses to supply a seamless unified object, whether as narrative event or structured poem. Instead, this haunting work draws attention to the means by which the speaker attempts to make sense of his world. He confronts strange signs in the landscape: "What made those holes and rents . . . ?"

(69); "Who were the strugglers . . . ?" (129). And he offers grotesque answers: "'tis a brute must walk / Pashing their life out" (71–72); "Toads in a poisoned tank, / Or wild cats in a red-hot iron cage" (131–32). Through this very process of articulating his responses, the speaker enunciates the means by which experience is constructed and thereby given shape. The harrowing features of the landscape emerge generally from his own similes or speculations rather than from any external reality: the little river appeared "As unexpected as a serpent comes" (110), and its waters "might have been" (109) a "bath" for the "fiend's glowing hoof." If the writing of "Childe Roland" was Browning's experiment with disciplined creativity, then the poem itself enacts the speaker's experiment with his own life, where the metaphor of the quest figures the fusion of personal experience with the necessary experiment that constitutes a life seeking meaningfulness and identity.

Acclaimed Romantic poems such as Wordsworth's "Tintern Abbey" (1798) or "Intimations of Immortality" (1807) can be said to have anticipated this attention to the relationship between past perceptions and present understanding. But the disturbance of harmonious form through ironic discrepancies within self-conscious speakers becomes an increasingly Victorian phenomenon. Even when self-consciousness is not undercut by irony, the emphasis on formal experiment as formalized experience remains. In this regard, Barrett Browning's "The Runaway Slave at Pilgrim's Point" (1848) provides a good example. Spoken by an escaped female slave, the poem recounts the events that have led to the present moment of direct address to the slave-owning sons who have run her down. The monologue falls into three parts: an apostrophe to the Pilgrim Fathers; a narrative about the slave's infanticide; and a cursing of the slave-owners. The first two sections act as a prelude and grounding for the immediacy of the third, where the poem establishes the conditions of a performative speech act: a curse that enacts its own meaning and thus constitutes the agency and identity of the speaker (acting on her own behalf). The poem moves from contemplating the contradictory legacy of the Pilgrim Fathers (who built a supposedly free nation on slavery) and the ambivalence of blackness (black people are made to feel inhuman and yet animals and birds treat them as people) to an assertion of her blackness when the slave claims that the ghosts of the Pilgrim Fathers will no longer confront her: "My face is black, but it glares with a scorn / Which they dare not meet by day" (*EBB* 202–03). On one level, the poem offers a conclusion that promotes unity and closure: a climactic self-assertion that transforms the slave's initial doubt about her black identity. But on another level, the speaker's reflexive recounting of events introduces the insurgent dimension of an uncertain performativity, notably at the moment when her claimed identity has to be constructed in terms of the social context provided by the "hunter sons" who finally encircle her (204). At that moment, she neither stands alone nor speaks alone. The assertion of a single unified voice is disturbed by the intruding strands of class difference and racial threat: the voices of the "hunter sons" echo in her monologue as she accosts them with the marks on her wrist where she was tied for flogging, and she speaks for all slaves in their rebellion against oppression – "*We* are too heavy for our cross, / And fall and crush you" (244–45). Both "Childe Roland" and "The Runaway Slave," therefore, produce a similar formalist effect. In each monologue, formal properties of art are tied to the dramatization of human experience. This link means that the principle of aesthetic unity is enacted as a feature of personal desire while it is simultaneously subverted as an impossible ideal.

The concept of form as a homogeneous whole was promoted by Romantic aesthetics. In this concept, all parts cohere: they should, according to Coleridge, "mutually support and explain each other."[7] The model is an organic one, taken from nature – from plants that consist of distinct yet inseparable components (roots, stem, and leaves). Organic form, Coleridge writes, "shapes as it develops itself from within, and the fullness of its development is one and the same with the perfection of its outward form."[8] In this organicism, however, there remains a fundamental conflict between form as a fixed completed object and form as an ongoing process. Coleridge's formulation implies an inward essence that is represented by an outward shape. Yet the organic model also allows for growth: a dynamic movement toward wholeness. Does, then, the truth of the oak reside only in its fully grown shape? Or is it also present in the acorn from which the oak will grow? Presumably, the essence of the oak includes both acorn and tree. But wherein lies the whole? In the moment of completion? Or in the progress toward it? In other words, how far should a concern with form as innate being incorporate vigorous process and growth (temporality and movement) as well as fixed shape or architectural space (aestheticized truth)?[9]

This inquiry underscores the necessary materiality of all poetic form. Coleridge acknowledges the point when he says that the spirit of poetry "must embody in order to reveal itself."[10] But he nevertheless continues to privilege the truth of the spirit that precedes the embodiment, neglecting how the mode of revelation might affect the nature of what is revealed. The materiality of appearances leaves an inherent ambiguity between their function as representation and their function as constitution. The former gives rise to the sense of a reality or truth that is ahistorical or transcendent (the idealist emphases of Romantic aesthetics), whereas the latter suggests process and incompleteness (the gaps of Romantic irony). Fundamental to this organic concept of form, therefore, is a conflict – one that Romantic practice could not ultimately avoid – between form as embodied essence (complete product, unified perfection) and form as material process (sensible effects, dynamic shaping, empty ceremony). If Romantic poems accentuate the former, then Victorian poems strive to accommodate the latter.

The claims of idealist poetics about the innate truth of organic form tend to presuppose an essentialism that is inherent in the individual organism. It is as if the organism can be separated from its support systems or mediums of development and growth. This assumption informs the strong emphasis in Romantic poetry on lyrical modes – such as the ode, the hymn, pastoral, and the sonnet – which articulate the voices of solitary speakers. It also nurtured twentieth-century tendencies to treat poetic form as if it were self-enclosed, leading in the 1930s and 1940s to influential New Critical views of the poem as icon. According to this critical approach, poetry was to be viewed as a well-wrought urn whose imaginative success was demonstrated by its internal coherence, where all parts mutually support a homogenous whole.[11] For both Romantic poets and New Critics, organic form was also most successfully realized in shorter lyrics where the poetic artifact could more readily establish its formal unity. Longer forms, however, shift inevitably toward the urgency of temporal process, thus affecting their own structural components. Wordsworth's *The Prelude*, for instance, as an attempt to represent the growth of a poet's imagination, keeps changing its size from two books (in 1802) to thirteen (in 1805) and eventually to fourteen (in 1850). If idealist essentialism is more readily represented in shorter forms, then the move in Victorian poetry away from personalized and homogeneous lyrics toward dramatic–lyrical and epic–narrative–lyrical hybrids suggests a growing dissatisfaction with the essentialist assumptions of organic poetics. Such hybrids shift individual expressiveness away from isolated subjectivism toward social contexts and culturally produced discursive processes. Consequently, formal experimentation by Victorian poets continually suggests the inseparability of material reality from the sentient subject's experience.

As he does for so many Victorian poetic issues, Matthew Arnold epitomizes this disjunction between Romantic poetics and Victorian practice. In "The Study of Poetry" (1880), he claims that for poetry "the idea is everything."[12] Whereas religion attaches its emotion to fact, "poetry attaches its emotion to the idea; the idea *is* the fact." Thus Arnold articulates the idealist view that poetry gives shape to an abstract idea. In such a view poetry provides access to a metaphysical absolute, one free from material taint – including its embodiment in sign and print. But here Arnold, in the final decade of his career, attempts to make large claims for poetry as a cultural substitute for religion, while his own poetry (much of it written in the 1840s and 1850s) belies the theory. Whether exposed on darkling plains, wandering between worlds, or dying in craters, his fraught speakers show all too often the limitations of materialism or the failures of idealism. In particular, "The Scholar-Gipsy" (1852) exemplifies what we might call the Victorian formalist dilemma where a poet like Arnold not only seeks the conditions of aesthetic wholeness and transcendent truth but also wishes to incorporate the conflicting conditions of mid-nineteenth-century values.

"The Scholar-Gipsy" rests upon a conflict between the values of pastoral (the relaxed peacefulness and untainted idealism manifested in the simple life of shepherds) and modernity (the confused, aimless and mechanized life of Victorian England). The poem begins with the celebration of a pastoral setting wherein a shepherd is urged, once he has fed his "wistful flock" (*MA* 3), to begin again "the quest" (a "quest," we assume, for the Oxford scholar-gipsy of the title). The poet-speaker, however, remains separate. He sits and waits, "Screen'd" in a "nook" (21). Instead of actively joining the pastoral context, he reads again Joseph Glanvill's book – *The Vanity of Dogmatizing* (1661) – which Arnold purchased in 1844. In this seventeenth-century work, Glanvill recalls "lately a lad in the University of Oxford, who being of very pregnant and ready parts, and yet wanting the encouragement of preferment, was by his poverty forced to leave his studies there, and to cast himself upon the wide world for his livelihood . . . he was at last forced to join himself to a company of vagabond gypsies."[13] This "lad" enjoys the gypsy life for some time before he is discovered by some of his former university friends, who take him back in their company. Arnold's poet-speaker undertakes to reimagine the young scholar's extraordinary story, locating his adventures within the harmonious naturalness of the Oxfordshire countryside. After thirteen stanzas, however, the appeal to literary pastoralism is dismissed: "But what," the speaker exclaims, "I dream!" (131). With this abrupt turn, he introduces the contrasting realities that comprise "this strange disease of modern life" (203). The opening evocation of the fields near Oxford as a repetition of pastoral values transmutes, then, into the recognition that these values belong to an outmoded and idealized past – the dream provoked by "Glanvill's book" (31). Subsequently, the organicist detail of the opening description ("round green roots and yellowing stalks I see / Pale pink convolvulus in tendrils creep" [24–25]), repeating the specificity of Romantic – indeed Keatsian –

sensuality, gives way to the obvious conventionality of an abstract pastoral: "silver'd branches of the glade" (214), "forest-skirts" (215), "moonlit pales" (216), and "dark dingles" (220). Thus the formal structure of the poem articulates an opposition. This opposition is between the ideal (represented by the life of the gypsies and the scholar who left Oxford in order to join them) and the real (contemporary social conditions, character-ized by images of sickness and disease).

What becomes apparent in "The Scholar-Gipsy" is that the cultural basis for positing the conditions of aesthetic idealism was more and more in doubt. Although it was still possible amid the emerging industrialism of Victorian cities to walk in the woods and renew acquaintance with pastoral surroundings (such as the Cumnor Hills outside Oxford where Arnold's poet-speaker reads Glanvill's book), it was no longer possible to literalize the values of earlier neoclassical convention and establish the countryside as a referent for the pastoral. Instead, the pronounced imitation of Keatsian stanzas, notably those of "Ode to a Nightingale" (1820), implodes upon their structural division. Arnold also shifts the trimeter (surrounded by pentameters) to the sixth line, instead of Keats's eighth. This more central position of the short line within ten-line stanzas produces the formal condition for a turn, one that encourages antithesis ("But when the fields are still" [6]) and opposition ("Here will I sit and wait" [16]). Resolution in any organic sense proves difficult because the aesthetic and formal means of such unity (the literary conventions and metaphors of past ideals) remain unavailable: their cultural currency is no longer underwritten by what Arnold later claimed as the poetic gold standard – the guarantor of the "idea" as referent.

The speaker in "The Scholar-Gipsy" acknowledges this insufficiency of the idea when he reaches the emotive climax of the poem, instructing the scholar-gypsy to flee his "feverish contact" (221) – contact that would infect the disease-free scholar. The speaker is tied irrevocably to the contemporary social world, one whose mental life has been infected by the disease of "sick hurry" and "divided aims" (204). In order to sustain the scholar's contrasting unity of purpose ("*one* aim, *one* business, *one* desire"[152]), he must keep the scholar separate in a world of literary idealism located on "some mild pastoral slope" where the scholar may "listen with enchanted ears, / . . . to the nightingales!" (219–20). But the idea of the pastoral (the slope and the nightingales) refers to no contem-porary reality and therefore cannot exist for the poet-speaker in his modern world. Arnold's determination to attach poetic emotion to the idea requires the speaker in this poem to sustain a painful dichotomy between literary idea and historical truth. Any formal poetic construction of pastoral idealism must consequently surrender to the juxtaposition of irreconcilable opposites. The speaker, for instance, apostrophizes the gypsy ("O born in days when wits were fresh and clear" [201]), constructing a vision of untainted delight (when "life ran gaily as the sparkling Thames" [202]), only to shift immediately into its contemporary alternative: "this strange disease of modern life." Here Arnold implicitly admits the fundamental paradox of organic formalism where an emphasis on organic growth and fulfillment has to allow for the inseparable counterpart of organic death. Arnold, however, cannot conceive of the means of resolution, only the discomforting irony of unresolved juxtaposition: the scholar-gypsy and modern life must be kept separate, lest the second (the diseased real) will destroy the first (the pastoral ideal). Hence his apostrophe quickly transforms into admonition: "Fly hence, our contact fear!" (206).

Once, therefore, the poet-speaker reaches his moment of impasse (the insoluble contrast between the scholar's "perennial youth" [229] and the speaker's "mental strife" [222]), he has nowhere to go in order to achieve formal unity. The pastoral imagery upon which the poem is initially founded disallows resolution with the images of disease and infection that characterize "modern life." Certainly, Arnold does not provide organic metaphors that might produce such a settlement. Instead, the poem closes with what is formally an epic simile: an extended image describing the manner in which the scholar-gypsy should flee, like "some grave Tyrian trader" (232) escaping the intruding "Grecian coaster" (237). Yet, as is often the case with epic similes, the vehicle of the comparison (the trader) becomes so elaborate that it becomes a separate aesthetic object, losing touch with the source of the comparison (the scholar). Consequently, critics have expended considerable energy in attempting to integrate the metaphor of the trader with the imagery of the earlier sections of the poem. Some commentators read this metaphor as an allegory for sustaining an alternative lifestyle; others relate it to the power of imagination.[14] But in whatever way this epic simile is read, its imagery and formal devices neither provide a unified closure for the poem nor present a solution for the poet-speaker. He is left corrupted by disease, celebrating an unrealizable dream-vision: the empty form of an outmoded literary convention. Thus Arnold's mid-century experiment with pastoral, his attempt to repeat Romantic formalism, transforms itself into the ironic experience of a divided sensibility.[15]

This sense of division or ambivalence has become a focus for discussions of Victorian poetic form. In an important essay on the idealist legacy in Victorian poetry, W. David Shaw refers to the way that "Victorian poets experiment with genres in which the true subject of the poem is bracketed."[16] The result, he claims, is "generic indeterminacy."[17] By this term, Shaw identifies two tendencies. First, he means forms where the main subject of the poem remains elusive: Is "The Scholar-Gipsy" a narrative about the gypsy, a disrupted dream-vision, a lyrical expression of loss and regret, a satirical critique of social ennui, or a dramatization of a cultural impasse? Second, he distinguishes a "radical failure" to satisfy expectations: "The Scholar-Gipsy" begins as a pastoral idyll but does not end as one. In a similar vein, George Bornstein focuses on a distinction between the Greater Romantic Lyric and the Greater Victorian Lyric. Where the Romantic Lyric rests upon a shifting relationship between speaker and nature, the Victorian Lyric emphasizes linguistic self-consciousness and textual defensiveness. Both forms, however, manifest a tension between visionary and ordinary experience. This tension, Bornstein claims, provokes a potential for self-division, one that "the Romantics tend to mitigate and the Victorians to exacerbate."[18]

An obvious example of this exacerbation is always provided by Tennyson's "The Two Voices" (1842). But the ultimate Victorian experiment with self-division is arguably Clough's *Dipsychus* (1865). This poem, arranged into various scenes and couched in various verse forms, is written as a dialogue between a pragmatic tempter and a naive idealist. The dialectical interplay in this contest offers a subtle exploration of the multiplying divisions of consciousness and of its inconstant relationships with external phenomena and cultural ideologies – phenomena and ideologies that may or may not be the consequence of the speaking subject's self-projections.

Exacerbation of the potential for division sustains Isobel Armstrong's remarkable analysis of what she calls the Victorian double poem: a poem in which the Victorian poet dramatizes and objectifies the simultaneous existence of unified selfhood and fracturing self-awareness. Her crucial point is that this doubleness is structural, built into the basic processes of the poem. In this respect, it formalizes the link between poetry and culture, both testing the systematic ambiguities of language and drawing attention to "the nature of words as a medium of representation."[19] The result is consistent with Shaw's theory of "generic indeterminacy," where lyrics, for instance, become reclassified as drama. In other words, a poem that presents itself as lyric expression turns that expression around so that the utterance itself, as well as representing the speaker's outpouring of personal feeling, becomes the object of analysis and critique. Bearing this point in mind, Armstrong gives the example of Tennyson's "Mariana," where the speaker's account of her tortured isolation is "the utterance of a subjective psychological condition." At the same time, the poem incorporates the narrative overtones of a ballad into its lyrical expressiveness so that the act of narration restructures the utterance into a "symptomatic" cultural form, turning it into an "object of analysis." Victorian poets thus wrote texts that present utterance as both subject and object. Hence they were able to experiment with forms that simultaneously represent psychological processes (the self as internalized subjectivity) and the phenomenology of a culture (the self as an externalized manifestation of social practice). It follows that for Armstrong the Victorian double poem functions as a skeptical form: "It draws attention to the epistemology which governs the construction of the self and its relationships and to the cultural conditions in which those relationships are made."[20] To suggest that epistemological and hermeneutic problems characterize Victorian poetic forms is again to allude to "generic indeterminacy" and the consequential problems for critical interpretation. This approach also focuses a growing awareness in recent decades about the manner in which Victorian double poems – especially the dramatic monologue – challenge the epistemological assumptions that are so strongly embedded in post-Cartesian idealist traditions.[21] Indeed, the way that many Victorian poems portray expressive desire in relation to cultural conditions locates ironic displacement within the very processes of experience, where expressive form and cultural construction are part of the same utterance.

One of the more obviously innovative poetic forms of the period, Clough's *Amours de Voyage*, explores this displacement with subtlety and finesse. In this work, Clough combines an epistolary method (written in hexameters) with lyrics and cantos. The letters are written by Claude, an English visitor to Rome during the French intervention in the Risorgimento of 1849, to his friend Eustace. The descriptive and expository nature of these letters, therefore, grounds the poem in specific historical circumstances. At the same time, as Claude recounts his experiences in Rome, including a potential love affair with another English tourist, Mary Trevellyn, his correspondence becomes a record of a personalized and intricate introspection. Claude repeats Hamlet's problem, where the doubts of a skeptical intelligence induce psychological paralysis; he resists acting upon perceptions and descriptions that seem endlessly problematic, particularly in the way he articulates them in his letters to Eustace. Hence in the very act of reporting what he sees of events in Rome, Claude ties empirical reality to subjectivity and discourse: "there are signs of stragglers returning; and voices / Talk" and "on the walls you read the first bulletin of the morning" (*AHC* II. 141–43). Signs, readings and bulletins, an already textualized world, were all he "saw" and knew of "the battle" (II. 144). Another level of discursive action is added to the poem, however, by one of its complex structural elements: the separate lyrics, or elegiacs, that open and close each canto. These lyrics disperse the authority of Claude's central consciousness, since they refer both outwardly to the indeterminate continuities of lyric convention and internally to the content of the poem. For example, the apostrophe at the end of Canto I to Alba, the hills outside Rome, transforms the hills into a realm of cultural and lyrical abstraction while at the same time making a direct reference to the immediate Roman context: "Beautiful can I not call thee, and yet thou has power to o'ermaster, / Power of mere beauty" (I. 281–82). That is to say, the structural arrangement of the intervening lyrics reverses the usual referential pattern for poetic formalism. In these elegiacs, intrinsic reference, which is conventionally self-enclosed, points instead to the historically contextualizing narrative of Claude's letters. By contrast, extrinsic reference, which is normally historical, points to the formalist conventions of lyricism: namely, the detached timelessness experienced by unspecified poetic voices. In *Amours de Voyage*, then, the combination of elegiacs and letters produces a double level of indeterminacy and lack of closure. At the narrative level of the letters, Claude experiences no closure of resolution or decision, only a moving on to Egypt. For him the epistolary act is one of differentiation: the production of a divided self-consciousness and a subject-in-process, a self that is never complete or fixed. At the lyrical level of the elegiacs, the poem is released into the instabilities of textual production: acknowledged artifice (*"Go, little book!"* [V. 218], which echoes Geoffrey Chaucer's directive in *Troilus and Criseyde* [1385]); historical reference (*"writ in a Roman chamber"* [V. 223]); and ambiguous readings (*"flitting about many years from brain unto brain"* [V. 221]). By combining an array of formal methods in this manner, the poem displays a complex interrelationship of cultural and subjective practices.

Moreover, the kind of dialectical intertwining of social action and subjective process that is evident in *Amours de Voyage* emerges in hybrid forms that combine lyric and narrative. One lyric may embody a frozen moment of emotional intensity but a series of lyrics may produce a shifting temporalized narrative. As a consequence, we find a growing experimentation among Victorian poets with relationships between smaller discrete units – such as couplets, sonnets, or stanzas – and extended, often loosely constructed, narrative sequences. Tennyson's *In Memoriam* and *Maud* (1855); Barrett Browning's *Sonnets from the Portuguese* (1850); Arnold's "Empedocles on Etna" (1852); Clough's *Amours de Voyage* and *Dipsychus*; George Meredith's *Modern Love* (1862); Dante Gabriel Rossetti's *The House of Life* (1881); and Christina Rossetti's "Monna Innominata" (1881): all of these poems provide diversified forms constructed from component parts – separate lyrics or sonnets, differing stanzas and various sections, scenes, cantos, letters, and interspersed lyrics. The obvious nine-teenth-century paradigm for such structures, particularly those that employ lyrics of varying stanzas and length, is the monodrama. This genre developed in the eighteenth and early nineteenth century as a flexibly structured work that represented sequential phases of varying feelings – usually those of a distracted female character who is torn by conflicting passions and who shifts rapidly between moods.[22] For most monodramas the sequence is determined by formal considerations, as in music, whereas the narrative dimensions of these more sophisticated Victorian forms develop ethical, political, and psychological significances that extend beyond those required by pure form or merely oscillating moods. It is the narrative implications of these lyric sequences that develop modes of cultural experimentation, even more than the dramatic analogies that applications of monodrama tend to emphasize – such as when Tennyson famously remarked that in *Maud* he substituted "different phases of passion in one person" for "different characters."[23]

Narrative adds a political dimension to lyrical formalism. Lyricism tends to reflect back on itself, on the expressive quality of the moment – the feeling states and verbal display of the lyrical voice. The result is frequently the portrayal of an experience that is formally aestheticized or ideologically homogenized. By contrast, narrative modes, insofar as they are often associated with realist fiction, tend to encourage a relationship with referential contexts, whether explicit (as in *Amours de Voyage*) or implicit (as in *Modern Love*). As a result, the addition of narrative to lyric forms reinforces a move toward social connections and ideological contextualiza-tion. It locates otherwise solitary speakers within cultural and therefore political circumstances. In doing so, the addition of narrative creates two effects in Victorian poems. First, narrative induces a sense in which the speech acts of separate speakers are commensurate with the historical contexts of other social discourses. In these terms, the hybrid tendencies of Victorian poetry anticipate principles of dialogism that have been argued by the twentieth-century Soviet theorists, V.N. Voloshinov and Mikhail Bakhtin. In their influential work, individual speech is always simulta-neously social; any single utterance is always contaminated by the already preceding cultural use of the terms and phrases.[24] Second, narrative elements invoke a concern with cause and effect relationships. Such relationships provide the ideological grounding on which most narrative proceeds: they promote the difference between events that are merely sequential and events that are integrated with one another, or the difference between random action and motivated behavior. Both of these effects allow possibilities for cultural critique, whether to expose cultural ideologies or indicate the material grounding of lyrical idealism.

Tennyson's *Maud* illustrates both features. This poem was virtually written backward: Tennyson started from an already written lyric, "O that 'twere possible," and added both preceding and ensuing contexts. The result provides a series of lyrics, all of which differ in stanzaic structure and size, that represent the shifting and oscillating moods of the protagonist-speaker, much in the manner of a monodrama (a subtitle Tennyson added in 1875). True to the format of monodrama, the speaker remains embroiled in his (or her) own highly wrought sensitivities; he is obsessed with Maud, his childhood sweetheart, and he rails periodically at the increasingly bourgeois culture ruined by *laissez-faire* economics that he feels has dispossessed him of his birthright as a man from the landed classes. In attempting to indict his society, he remains aloof. But the poem extends beyond the tenets of monodrama precisely to the extent that it exploits the irony of a maniacal personality whose mania may reflect the very social ills of which he complains. In the climactic moment at the end of Part II, the speaker enacts what has become known as the madhouse cell scene. He believes that he killed Maud's brother in a duel and he has consequently fled England. Now isolated from Maud's influence and from his own landed society, he becomes further enclosed within his own introspective processes. His introspection culminates in a fantasy of burial: "my heart is a handful of dust, / And the wheels go over my head" (*AT* II. 241–42). Yet the quietness of the grave is contaminated by the unceasing utterance of other people. These figures represent social icons – lord, physician, statesman – and all participate in an "idiot gabble" (II. 279) that for him begins to characterize all human speech, whether inside or outside the madhouse. Personal and social discourses thus become coextensive; private utterance is social speech: "For I never whispered a private affair / . . . / But I heard it shouted at once from the top of the house" (II. 285–88). Following this episode, in Part III the speaker leaves his "cells of madness" (III. 2) and proposes to rejoin his "kind" (III. 58), to fight in the Crimean War with his countrymen. If, however, the noticeable brevity of Part III and its shift into the public rhetoric of war hardly provides an acceptable resolution for the poem, then echoes of earlier images and an identification between protagonist and society through the battle-cry of a nation nevertheless imply a closure of the gap between self and culture which has been a source of irony throughout. It can, therefore, be argued that several elements of the poem combine at this point: poetic structure (form), psychological need (content), and cultural belief (theme). All coalesce in the concluding embodiment of public and private rhetoric, in the private commitment to public and cosmic fate: "I embrace the purpose of God, and the doom assigned" (III. 59). Formalist closure in *Maud* draws attention to the dialogical link between subjective and public constitution, asking implicit questions about the connections between public and private sanity and morality.

Maud also exploits the impetus toward referential reality in narrative method for another purpose: to disrupt any cultural assumption of a simple cause and effect relationship between social reality and subjective perception. The poem frequently encourages the sense of a literal context within which the speaker's story takes place, and yet referents are notoriously vague. Is the "dreadful hollow" (I. 1), where the speaker's father died, literal or figurative? It appears to be literal and yet it functions figuratively. Did the betrothal to Maud when she and the protagonist were children actually happen? We might observe that expression in the poem, the speaker's utterance, continually responds to the demands of experience. But in *Maud* these are demands that require experience to be always already a fusion of event and interpretation. Experience – active observation or participation – is not therefore simply a literal event: it is always an articulated (and in the poem lyrically formalized) embodiment of the speaker's thinking and expression. In other words, experience is constituted as much by figuration as by literalness. A classic example occurs in Part I (lines 190–284), where the speaker posits a range of explanations for Maud's smile. In this lyric, his experience comprises *both* smile and speculation. Consequently, the section reads as a lyrical endeavor whose explanatory excesses refuse any easy separation of event (smile) from effect (speculation). What the reader receives is therefore predominantly effect: cause is continually an inference. As Herbert F. Tucker observes, *Maud* is "a poem not only written backward but inevitably read backward as well, from moment to moment, despite the forward thrust of its plot." "This monodramatic retrospection," he adds, "kinks up the chain of cause and effect by compelling us to gather the story by extrapolation from what the hero tells us."[25] The thematic result, however, of this inverted reading process is that cause becomes diffused through an array of effects (since it is left to the reader to extrapolate events). Thus the usual narrative structure of a plot based on cause and effect connections is broken apart, challenging conventional narrative expectations and their inherited cultural assumptions about causality and continuity. With this point in mind, Tucker suggests that the poem exposes how the question of causal linkage in any narrative remains potentially "arbitrary and inferential." Yet given that each section of the poem habitually presents a response to events that have already occurred (Maud's arrival, Maud's kiss, Maud's smile, Maud's song), the extent to which the speaker's expression is reactive means that external causes (social conditions, social events) cannot be ignored either. Rather, in *Maud* cultural determination, subjective responsibility, and cosmic purpose all become intermingled within imagistic and rhetorical connections.

Finally, Barrett Browning's *Aurora Leigh* and Browning's *The Ring and the Book* (1868–69), poems by the wife and husband poets, offer what remain arguably the most ambitious literary experiments in the period. *Aurora Leigh* – the result of Barrett Browning's desire to write a new form with which I began – is a verse novel that features the autobiography of a woman poet. Its combination of genres (autobiography, dialogue, narrative, prophecy, satire, treatise) comprises an attempt to write a modern epic where the protagonist's mythic quest becomes regendered and historicized as the desire of a woman poet to achieve both artistic and personal fulfillment within contemporary Victorian society. As the poem theorizes its own production (Aurora's famous reflection on poetry in Book V), the dominating aesthetic question is how to combine conflicting domains of experience: the external boisterous age which "brawls, cheats, maddens, calculates, aspires" (*EBBAL* V. 204) and the internal stage of "the soul itself, / Its shifting fancies and celestial lights" (V. 340–41). Aurora's answer to that question ("What form is best for poems?" [V. 223]) might be taken from Coleridgean poetics: "Trust the spirit, / As sovran nature does, to make the form / . . . Inward evermore / To outward" (V. 224–8). In the Fifth Book, Barrett Browning appears to follow this dictate by shifting from retrospective (inward) narration, where Aurora is in control of her narrative, to the unfolding of (outward) events as they happen. From this book onward, Aurora's narration resembles journal entries that have been recorded daily where we see once again the ambiguous narrative formalism of a poem like "Childe Roland" with its past-tense account told from a present-tense perspective.

The aesthetic trick, however, is to combine the poem's formalist method with the protagonist's personal dilemma, since Aurora realizes in Book V that her personal success as a poet has left her socially isolated. While her reading public appropriates her work, using her poems to represent their own feelings of love and joy, she remains solitary and loveless (see V. 439–77). The alteration in mode from retrospective narrative to journal writing thus registers Aurora's own transformation from the controlled and known world of her autobiographically constructed childhood and youth to the less secure exigencies of fate and social action. The later books consequently focus more and more on dialogue, as a dialectic of internal and external discourses shapes Aurora's experiences. This dialectic has already begun with her childhood move from the masculine world of her father's books ("Which taught her all the ignorance of men" [I. 190]) to the feminine world of her aunt's passive renunciation ("she had lived / A sort of cage-bird life" [I. 304–05]). But it continues through several crucial interactions with the disturbing social events relating to the working-class character Marian Erle (such as rape [VI. 1219–34] and single parenting [VI. 566–81]). The resulting interplay of constitutive discourse (the affective power of figurative language) with referential discourse (narrative or historical description) becomes particularly arresting in its presentation of female images and their relationship to patriarchal convention. Ultimately, *Aurora Leigh* remains consistent with other Victorian narrative poems – like *Amours de Voyage*, *Maud*, and *Modern Love* – because it makes the protagonist's self-consciousness the focus of dramatic action. Yet Barrett Browning's grand experiment produces a more distinct embodiment of the intermingling constructions of private and public processes. It extends social reference into a greater variety of class and political contexts – such as "drawing-rooms" (V. 206) and "Fleet Street" (V. 213). And it achieves a more intensive mixing of discursive elements. Gothic ("Ghost, fiend" [I. 154]), classical ("A loving Psyche" [I. 156]) and Christian ("Our Lady of the Passion" [I. 160]) images mingle with what Aurora calls "the woman's figures" (VIII. 1131): "Her. . . forehead braided tight" (I. 273); "behold the paps we all have sucked!" (V. 219); "puckerings in the silk / By clever stitches" (VIII. 1129–30).

A decade later, Browning's *The Ring and the Book* takes the dramatic monologue's potential to direct an ironic and discursive gaze on that same mutual construction of self and world to an altogether new extreme. Browning selects a Renaissance historical event concerning a middle-aged husband's murder of his fourteen-year-old spouse, and turns it into a series of monologues representing various perspectives: the three protagonists (husband, wife, and the priest who tried to rescue her), members of the public, the lawyers from the trial, and the Pope who acted as an ecclesiastical court of appeal. These ten monologues are framed by two from the poet, thus constructing a twelve-book form of epic status. If the formalist methods of *Aurora Leigh* ask questions about gender, then the epic structure of *The Ring and the Book* raises urgent questions about epistemology – on the production of knowledge, the search for the truth, and the evidence that supports them. Does the addition of each monologue add a further perspective that eventually completes a circular whole, a ring of truth? Or does the addition of each account simply obfuscate events, dissipating the truth? If we expect a conventional narrative conclusion or a teleological climactic moment, then the "generic indeterminacy" of this poem is bound to disappoint us. "Here were the end," says the poet in Book XII, invoking the irresolution of the subjunctive, "had anything an end" (*RBRB* XII. 1). Rather than providing a terminal explanation for his poem, Browning instead suggests a structural supplementarity: each speaker enacts a pattern of retrospective narration which claims a truthful account but each monologue is also succeeded by another that extends the context and alters the meaning of the previous one. Through the monologue form, Browning draws attention to the ironic limits of each speaker, to the contingent circumstances of any claim to total or transcendent truth. Yet, by means of serial juxtaposition and recurring images, and through the contestation of institutional languages (of church, law, and literature), he also displays the structuring processes of social practices. The result is a subtle critique of the complex interrelationships among private and public discourses. Meaning, perception, and understanding are all rendered fundamentally textual in this story of citations, citations within citations, eyewitness accounts, hearsay, and letters, with one textual version suc-ceeding another.

The Ring and the Book provides a climax for the formalist claim that underpins this whole discussion: that poetry, through its intensive linguistic formalizing, foregrounds the inseparability of experience and discourse. *The Ring and the Book* overtly asks the question that implicitly lurks in other Victorian poetic experiments: In a culture where signs and texts continually proliferate, "how else know we save by worth of word?" (I. 837). If there is no other means of knowing, then all knowledge is mediated. We are, therefore, thrust back onto the epistemological dilemma of a relationship between self and world that is always already constituted through representation, through the discursive descriptions and expression that characterize all our versions of experience. An awareness of this formalist dilemma, and the way it characterizes acts of human perception as well as acts of poetic creation, is the legacy of Victorian revisionary formalism. Through adapting and restructuring previous conventions, poems such as *Amours de Voyage, Aurora Leigh, Maud,* and *The Ring and the Book* explore possibilities for combining poetic expression with cultural critique. They contest, extend, and transform perceptual conditions and ideological assumptions. In this sense, they manifest cultural experiments, textual testing grounds where various discourses – epistemological, litur-gical, poetic, political, psychological – meet, mingle, and question one another.

NOTES

1 Elizabeth Barrett Browning, "To Mary Russell Mitford," 30 December 1844, in *The Brownings' Correspondence*, ed. Philip Kelley et al., 14 vols. to date (Winfield, KS: Wedgestone Press, 1984–), IX, 304.

2 See, for example, Donald S. Hair, *Browning's Experiments with Genre* (Toronto: University of Toronto Press, 1972); and F.E.L. Priestley, *Language and Structure in Tennyson's Poetry* (London: Andre Deutsch, 1973).

3 Robert Con Davis and Ronald Schleifer, *Criticism and Culture: The Role of Critique in Modern Literary Theory* (Harlow: Longman, 1991), 23–25. For further discussion, see E. Warwick Slinn, "Poetry and Culture: Performativity and Critique," *New Literary History* 30 (1999), 57–74.

4 This connection was pointed out to me by Herbert F. Tucker somewhere in the Buller Gorge, New Zealand, on 27 January 1998. See also *The Shorter Oxford English Dictionary*.

5 Quotations from Arthur Hugh Clough's poetry are taken from Clough, *Amours de Voyage*, ed. Patrick Scott (Brisbane: University of Queensland Press, 1974); line references appear in parentheses.

6 See William Clyde DeVane, *A Browning Handbook*, second edition (New York: Appleton-Century-Crofts, 1955), 229.

7 Samuel Taylor Coleridge, *Biographia Literaria; or Biographical Sketches of My Life and Opinions*, ed. James Engell and Walter Jackson Bate, 2 vols. Bollingen Series (Princeton, NJ: Princeton University Press, 1983), II, 13.

8 Coleridge, *Coleridge's Writings on Shakespeare*, ed. Terence Hawkes (New York: Capricorn, 1959), 68.

9 On the interpenetration of space and time in Victorian poetry, see Herbert F. Tucker, "Of Monuments and Moments: Spacetime in Nineteenth-Century Poetry," *Modern Language Quarterly* 58 (1997), 269–97.

10 Coleridge, *Coleridge's Writings on Shakespeare*, 67.

11 See, for example, Cleanth Brooks, *The Well Wrought Urn: Studies in the Structure of Poetry* (New York: Harcourt Brace, 1947).

12 Matthew Arnold, "The Study of Poetry," in Arnold, *English Literature and Irish Politics*, ed. R.H. Super, *The Complete Prose Works of Matthew Arnold*, 11 vols. (Ann Arbor, MI: University of Michigan Press, 1960–77), IX, 161.

13 Joseph Glanvill, *The Vanity of Dogmatizing; or, Confidence in Opinions. Manifested in a Discourse on the Shortness and Uncertainty of Our Knowledge, and Its Causes; with Some Reflexions on Peripateticism; and an Apology for Philosophy* (London: H. Eversden, 1661), 196.

14 See, for example, A. Dwight Culler, *Imaginative Reason: The Poetry of Matthew Arnold* (New Haven, CT: Yale University Press, 1966), 189–93, and George Bornstein, *Poetic Remaking: The Art of Browning, Yeats, and Pound* (University Park, PA: Pennsylvania State University Press, 1988), 44–45. David G. Riede recognizes that the poem provides no resolution, noting that adverse judgments about its aesthetic failure are based on expectations about organic unity, and concluding instead that the poem's "inability to resolve a dialectic is a proper and inevitable reflection of a godless society in which no goal can be posited and no quest is possible": *Matthew Arnold and the Betrayal of Language* (Charlottesville, VA: University Press of Virginia, 1988), 147.

15 Such an effect should be distinguished from the work of the "Spasmodic" poets (Philip Bailey, Alexander Smith, Sydney Dobell), also writing in mid-century, who sustained an elaborate expressionism seeking the truths of personal subjectivity. Their unquestioning absorption of Romantic aesthetics is illustrated by a remark about creativity in Smith's "A Life Drama" (1854): "it was his nature / To blossom into song, as 'tis a tree's / To leaf itself in April" (Smith, *Poems* [Boston, MA: Ticknor, Reed, and Fields, 1854], 18). For further information on the "Spasmodics," see Mark A. Weinstein, *William Edmondstoune Aytoun and the Spasmodic Controversy* (New Haven, CT: Yale University Press, 1968).

16 W. David Shaw, "Philosophy and Genre in Victorian Poetics: The Idealist Legacy," *ELH* 52 (1985), 472.

17 Shaw, "Philosophy and Genre in Victorian Poetics," 473.

18 Bornstein, *Poetic Remaking*, 39.

19 Isobel Armstrong, *Victorian Poetry: Poetry, Poetics and Politics* (London: Routledge, 1993), 12.

20 Armstrong, *Victorian Poetry* 13.

21 See, for example, Loy D. Martin, *Browning's Dramatic Monologues and the Post-Romantic Subject* (Baltimore, MD: Johns Hopkins University Press, 1985), and E. Warwick Slinn, *The Discourse of Self in Victorian Poetry* (Charlottesville, VA: University Press of Virginia, 1991).

22 See A. Dwight Culler, "Monodrama and the Dramatic Monologue," *PMLA* 90 (1975), 366–85.

23 Tennyson, *The Works of Alfred, Lord Tennyson*, ed. Hallam Tennyson, Eversley edition, 6 vols. (London: Macmillan, 1908), IV, 271.

24 There has been debate about whether or not Voloshinov and Bakhtin are the same person. For a dialogical view of utterance, see V.N. Voloshinov, *Marxism and the Philosophy of Language*, trans. Ladislav Matejka and I.R. Titunik (New York: Seminar Press, 1973); this work was first published in Russian in 1929.

25 Herbert F. Tucker, *Tennyson and the Doom of Romanticism* (Cambridge, MA: Harvard University Press, 1988), 413.

4

CORNELIA D.J. PEARSALL

The dramatic monologue

Early in Augusta Webster's dramatic monologue, "An Inventor" (1870), the speaker expresses his frustration over a contraption that he has not yet perfected. "It *must*," he insists, "perform my thought, it *must* awake / this soulless whirring thing of springs and wheels, / and be a power among us" (119).[1] These desperate imperatives ("it must") are followed by a question that might betray a sense of futility were it not also the question of any innovator: "Aye but how?" The speaker seeks public exhibition or display of his thought; only then can the object be "a power among us," and so enjoy a social and cultural import beyond even its maker. But the phrase also suggests a more pragmatic, less theatrical, and less hierarchical imperative for the object: it must execute his thought, it must accomplish or fulfill some action or deed, and it must be effectual.[2]

The notion of creating a vehicle for the performance of thoughts may remind us of another nineteenth-century invention: the dramatic monologue itself. This chapter explores the element of performance in the dramatic monologue, the ways these poems enact or express aspects of their speakers, and the ways in which these varied monologues are "dramatic." It will also, however, pursue what we might term the performative element of the dramatic monologue, the methods by which these discursive forays, these words, accomplish various goals – some apparent, others subtle and less readily perceptible.[3] Given this genre's interest in the exploration of character, it may not be surprising that "the first book on the dramatic monologue," according to A. Dwight Culler, was by an elocution instructor, Samuel Silas Curry.[4] Himself president of Boston's School of Expression, Curry, in his 1908 *Browning and the Dramatic Monologue*, stresses the form's overtly theatrical elements, the modes in which they might be literally performed. He also suggests in passing that the poems themselves are performative and seek some effect: "There is some purpose at stake; the speaker must . . . cause decisions on some point of issue."[5] In contrast, Robert Langbaum, among the leading theorists of the dramatic monologue, claims in *The Poetry of Experience* (1957) that these mono-logues are superfluous and unnecessary; he hears in these works "a super-abundance of expression, more words, ingenuity and argument than seem necessary for the purpose." He adds that the "impression of gratuitousness is heightened by the fact that the speakers never accomplish anything by their utterance, and seem to know from the start that they will not."[6] Critics have long joined him in this claim, the primary corollary of which is that dramatic monologists invariably reveal far more than they intend. Referring specifically to the paradigmatic monologues of Robert Browning, Herbert F. Tucker argues, "What . . . speakers say gains ascendancy over what they set out to mean."[7] A monologist such as the Duke in Browning's "My Last Duchess" (1842) "simply gets carried away," according to Clyde de L. Ryals, speaking "simply because . . . one utterance . . . engenders another."[8]

Countering Langbaum's perspective on the dramatic monologue, my discussion will suggest that a major feature of this poetic genre is its assumption of rhetorical efficacy. Speakers desire to achieve some purpose, looking toward goals that they not only describe in the course of their monologues but also labor steadily to achieve through the medium of their monologues. In reading dramatic monologues, I propose, we must ask what each poem seeks to perform, what processes it seeks to set in motion or ends it seeks to attain.[9]

The transformation of the monologue

In large measure a Victorian invention, the dramatic monologue is a central genre in a period rich with an extraordinary array of generic experimenta-tion. We identify a genre by its differentiation from other kinds, and part of the way this genre distinguishes itself is its discursive, even conversational, nature. Classical epic and lyric forms (themselves profoundly altered by Victorian practitioners) have their origins in song, while the dramatic monologue emphatically represents speech (even if presented as an interior monologue or written letter), sometimes though not always addressed to an auditor.[10] This discursiveness is part of what allies these poems so assiduously with drama. But the contexts and modes of these discourses are so radically varied that the question of generic uniformity has from the start attended this type of poetry. The significant body of criticism occasioned by the dramatic monologue has often attempted to establish this poetic form's defining characteristics, the signs by which the genre announces itself. Some critics have debated classifications and intricately argued distinctions among such terms as "dramatic lyrics," "lyrical dramas," "mask lyric," and "monodrama."[11] And yet, as Tucker wisely remarks, "'Dramatic monologue' is a generic term whose practical usefulness does not seem to have been impaired by the failure of literary historians and taxonomists to achieve consensus in its definition."[12] Indeed, these distinctions have their clear uses. As Alastair Fowler reminds us, "to decide the genre of a work, then, our aim is to discover its meaning."[13] What, then, might be the use of a generic term, and specifically, how does the umbrella term "dramatic monologue" contribute to our reading of these poems?

Among the finest descriptions of the form remains Arthur Henry Hallam's 1831 pronouncement, which actually predates the prototypical examples of the Victorian dramatic monologue produced by Tennyson and Browning soon thereafter. In a review of Alfred Tennyson's early work, the friend who would become the subject of Tennyson's great elegy *In Memoriam* (1850) wrote, "we contend that it is a new species of poetry, a graft of the lyric on the dramatic, and Mr. Tennyson deserves the laurel of an inventor."[14] While the dramatic monologue was seen even in its time as a new literary form, however, it was not without multiple precedents. Culler suggests that its origins lie in the classical rhetorical form of *prosopopoeia*, or impersonation, while Benjamin Fuson recalls us to Ovid's *Heroides* (a series of verse letters from mythical heroines to their lovers), as well as the long line of precursors within the English literary tradition, from Geoffrey Chaucer to Felicia Hemans, the early-nineteenth-century poet. (Hemans is herself often credited with inaugurating the century's use of this form, in her 1828 collection *Records of Woman*.[15]) But it nevertheless appears that the dramatic monologue *as we now know it* derives prominently if not exclusively from the work of Tennyson and Browning, and is one of the few literary genres whose first instances we can date. In early November 1833, Tennyson read "St. Simeon Stylites," the first of its kind, to a group of friends, while Browning was first in print, publishing "Porphyria's Lover" and "Johannes Agricola in Meditation" in the *Monthly Repository* in January 1836. At the time the poets did not know each other, and cannot have known of their concurrent experimentation with what was to become a new genre.

It is instructive to remember, however, that the term "dramatic monologue" did not attain currency until late in the nineteenth century; Browning, the foremost practitioner of the genre, appears never himself to have employed the phrase.[16] Intermediary terms used by poets, often as titles for collections, such as "Dramatic Lyrics," "Dramatic Romances," "Dramatic Idylls," "Dramatic Studies," "Dramatis Personae," as well as "Monodrama," indicate their own attempts to place and even to formalize literary production that was for some time unnamable. Significantly, the best-known title of a collection made up chiefly of dramatic monologues, Browning's *Men and Women* (1855), names not the generic form but the subject matter, identifying social interaction, and especially gender relations, as constitutive of the form. In the aggregate, these titles seem to indicate significant shifts in the conception of the precise nature of this poetic mode. Can it finally be said that at the moment of composition there was for the majority of Victorian poets the assumption of a fixed and discernible genre, with clearly established rules? Hovering as it does among other generic kinds that it resembles but forcefully deviates from, such as lyric or drama, the dramatic monologue eluded classification even by its makers.

In their desire to define at least some unifying principle, critics most often seem to waver between definitions so restrictive as to discount many dramatic monologues, and definitions so expansive as to include any number of poems. For example, in summarizing a reigning critical assumption Elisabeth A. Howe observes, "Only one feature is common [to dramatic monologues] . . . namely, their identification of the speaker as someone other than the poet, whether a mythical figure . . . a historical one . . . or a fictional [one]."[17] This viewpoint would appear to be supported by no less an authority than Browning, who in his prefatory Advertisement to *Dramatic Lyrics* (1842) provides one of his few formal statements regarding the genre, calling the poems, "though for the most part Lyric in expression, always Dramatic in principle, and so many utterances of so many imaginary persons, not mine."[18] And yet even so focused and credible a distinction as Howe's is open to challenge. Langbaum warns that if our definition of this genre involves "every lyric in which the speaker seems to be someone other than the poet," then the category can include innumerable epistles, laments, love songs, orations, soliloquies, and "first person narratives," including such works as Geoffrey Chaucer's *Canterbury Tales*.[19] Alan Sinfield defends precisely this line of "historical continuity," positing that such forms as the complaint and the epistle are in fact early examples of the dramatic monologue, as are "all first-person poems where the speaker is indicated not to be the poet."[20] Nevertheless, Langbaum's resistance to any definitions grounded in "mechanical resemblance" remains instructive. He urges that instead we "look inside the dramatic monologue . . . [to] consider its effect, its *way* of meaning"; by doing so, we shall see that "the dramatic monologue is unprecedented in its effect, that its effect distinguishes it, in spite of mechanical resemblance, from the monologues of traditional poetry" (76–77). Through focusing on its "effect," Langbaum insists, we may more fully distinguish the dramatic monologue from other genres, and more fully follow its own internal workings, "what the form is essentially doing" (78).

Distinguishing what he considers to be "an effect peculiarly the genius of the dramatic monologue," Langbaum argues for the necessary presence in the poems of "the tension between sympathy and moral judgment" (85). Encountering Browning's paradigmatic "My Last Duchess," for example, a reader is divided, understanding and even identifying with the speaker's position, and yet drawn to render moral judgment about what the speaker appears to reveal. Langbaum's focus, therefore, is chiefly on reception, and he is surely right to recognize the centrality of the effects of these words on auditors or readers. I shall argue here, however, that these effects of reception are broader and still more complex than the dichotomy that he suggests. These effects, moreover, are everywhere bound to the equally compelling issue of anticipated production, which we might define as the alteration the monologue is laboring to perform or cause. Dramatic monologues, especially the most vital examples of the genre, are distinguished by their transformative effects. The genre might ultimately be defined less by its technical elements than by the processes it initiates and unfolds. My larger claim regarding the dramatic monologue is that a speaker seeks a host of transformations – of his or her circumstances, of his or her auditor, of his or her self, and possibly all these together – in the course of the monologue, and ultimately attains these, if they can be attained, by way of the monologue.

One of the most expressive examples of this genre's performance of thoughts is Browning's "The Bishop Orders His Tomb at St. Praxed's Church" (1845), which Fuson calls an example of the form at "its highest technical virtuosity."[21] Even the title indicates the monologue's intention to be efficacious. When first published, the poem was titled simply "The Tomb at St. Praxed's"; the revised specification of the speaker and his particular verbal activity points to the speaker's intention to attain this object, his own monument, by way of his speech. Certainly, he also "orders" his tomb in the sense of designing and imaginatively arranging all its components, from the building materials to the decorations at its base to its crowning effigy of himself. There has always been debate over whether the sons whom he addresses will actually undertake his commission; the Bishop himself suspects they will not. But I would argue that the question is to some extent irrelevant, since the tomb takes definitive shape in the course of the monologue, by way of the monologue. As I have argued elsewhere, the terms that he uses to conjure the image of the mistresses with which he would reward his sons, objects possessed of "great smooth marbly limbs"

(*RB* 75), pertain to the alterations that his own body undergoes as the monologue progresses.[22]

In the course of his speaking, the Bishop's body begins to experience its own form of transubstantiation, as he stretches his feet "forth straight as stone can point" (88) and his vestments and bedclothes petrify "Into great laps and folds of sculptor's-work" (90). He alludes to "marble's language" (98), referring specifically to the Latin epitaph that he deems appropriate. But the monologue itself is composed of this surprisingly fluid lapidary tongue, and it is this discursive substance that constructs a tomb that takes shape before our eyes. The dramatic monologue turns toward the ongoing marriage between his body and stone, imagined now in terms of the possible dissolution of both: "Gritstone, a-crumble!" (116), inadequately housing "the corpse . . . oozing through" (117). While repeatedly stressing his body's inertia and incapacity (he reiterates, "As I lie here," "As here I lie" [10, 86]), the monologue nevertheless keeps his body in motion, commanding its own myriad transformations.

In multiple ways, then, the Bishop orders his tomb; the monologue is fully aware that even monumental construction is a discursive art. And indeed most speakers of dramatic monologues hold overt ambitions for some definite if occasionally indefinable result from their speaking. The speaker of Tennyson's "Ulysses" (1842) seeks escape from his island, the speaker of Tennyson's "Tithonus" (1860) seeks escape from his painful immortality, the speaker of Browning's "Soliloquy of the Spanish Cloister" (1842) seeks damnation of a colleague, while the speaker of Browning's "'Childe Roland to the Dark Tower Came'" (1855) seeks, of course, the tower. This list can continue, and include virtually every dramatic monologue by Tennyson or Browning, though in some cases the goals that help precipitate or sustain speech are less readily identifiable. This pattern in itself should prompt us to probe more deeply into the ways that dramatic monologists are all engaged in ordering, in arranging or dictating various aspects of their experience. Each speaker brings a complex of ambitions to his or her discursive moment. A dramatic monologue works actively to accomplish something for its speakers, perhaps the something they are overtly seeking – Ulysses's next voyage, the Duke's next duchess – but also something infinitely more subtle, some other kind of dramatic transformation of a situation or a self.

Monologic conversations

In November 1833, when Tennyson read "St. Simeon Stylites" (considered the first Victorian dramatic monologue) to friends, one member of his audience described it appreciatively but noted: "It is to be feared however that the men of this generation will hold it to be somewhat too unwholesome."[23] When Browning published the first dramatic monologues in January 1836 ("Porphyria's Lover" and "Johannes Agricola in Meditation"), he placed them under the combined heading "Madhouse Cells." In its earliest incarnations, then, the form featured monologists whose deviance was in some sense their subject, and Browning's heading marks his attempt to educate his reader concerning the centrality to this genre of what Ekbert Faas terms "abnormal mental states."[24] A theme of transgression, or unwholesomeness, seems to have been characteristic of the genre from its inception, itself constituting part of the ingenuity and becoming part of the tradition of the form. It should be noted that this transgressive bent is not *necessarily* integral to the monologic form, only that this strain of identifiable peculiarity, transgressiveness or even subversiveness was present from the start, and became almost immediately conventional. It is important, though, to bear in mind that other kinds of poem besides the dramatic monologue feature characters who might be termed demented. There are as well a number of dramatic monologues whose speakers voice opinions that their authors endorse wholeheartedly and rationally. Yet frequently the newfound flexible poetic conventions of this genre provided a forum for speakers who strain against the restrictions of societies that their monologues go far in representing. Thus in these poems the form's distance from convention is expressed on a thematic level as well as a generic one.

The majority of dramatic monologists are not criminals or charlatans, only searchers after some transformation, whether spiritual, professional, or personal. And yet these speakers display a marked tendency toward adopting extreme positions, including those not represented in any way as disturbing or insane. This tendency helps to explain why the genre is so suited to representing complex moral dilemmas, spanning a notably broad range of religious beliefs and personal opinions, while cutting a wide historical and social swathe. From their inception, dramatic monologues roam through much of the world and myriad historical periods, themselves at once responding to and propelling the larger Victorian appetite for exploration and appropriation of other cultures, however distant geographically or chronologically. How, then, might one claim generic kinship among such varied poets and poetic styles as the Victorian period offers us? And how can we yoke together such disparate and frequently desperate speakers? Their interrelation may partly have its basis in their unfitness for any community other than the generic one that they join in forming. Attending to echoes and affiliations among speakers can help us track what criticism of this genre has only begun to explore: namely, the range of conversations that engage these highly individual, even alienated monologists.

The Victorian workings of this genre present to us an apparent contradiction: namely, that these criminals, iconoclasts, individualists, misfits, and rebels themselves form what we might term a community. For all their removal from any norm, they collectively present adherence to certain patterns, constituting a conformation of nonconformists. Individual speakers, moreover, can gather into still more focused groupings. One such community is a loose coalition of "fallen women," populated by female figures whose sexual history is a governing concern, who either are spoken of or speak themselves. Prostitution was a predominant social issue of mid-Victorian Britain, the subject of numerous debates, sermons, periodical articles, and parliamentary bills. Elizabeth Barrett Browning's epic *Aurora Leigh* (1856) gave the subject significant literary expression but the topic seems to have been especially suited to the medium of the monologue. A work such as Dante Gabriel Rossetti's "Jenny" (1870), in which a man considers a silent, sleeping prostitute, unconscious of the implications of her life as she is of his commentary, is countered by a number of monologues spoken by "fallen women" themselves, including poems by Dora Greenwell, Augusta Webster, and Amy Levy, in which speakers assert thoroughgoing understanding of their situations.

Rossetti's "Jenny" – originally drafted in 1848, then revised and published after he retrieved the manuscript some years later from his wife Elizabeth Siddall's exhumed grave – is punctuated by the monologist's sense of the prostitute's relative states of consciousness. His words are posited on the assumption that Jenny is his subject and not his auditor; the poem is an especially notable example of an "interior monologue," defined by Daniel A. Harris as "unsounded self-questioning" or "silent thought."[25] Jenny is so far from functioning as an interlocutor or respondent that she is portrayed initially as a "thoughtless queen / Of kisses" (*DGR* 36) and later as a "cipher" (41). Her comprehensive incomprehension is dramatized by the fact of her unshakable drowsiness. The speaker repeatedly attempts to rouse her, urging "handsome Jenny mine, sit up: / I've filled our glasses, let us sup" (37). Failing to stir her, he concedes, "What, still so tired? Well, well then, keep / Your head there, so [long as] you do not sleep" (37). She does sleep, as he comes to exclaim ("Why Jenny, you're asleep at last!" [39]), resisting his final attempt at arousal: "Jenny, wake up . . . Why, there's the dawn!" (41). Reflecting on the world outside her window, he finally grants, "Let her sleep" (42).

Jenny's wavering unconsciousness prevents various modes of interaction,

but it functions nevertheless to provide a climate for the potent performance of her patron's thoughts. Her discursive absence, amid his silent
prolixity, leads to the attainment for the monologist of a pointed goal. He
refers, as he prepares to leave, to "Jenny's flattering sleep" (42). He has
noted throughout how appealing she is in repose, and it is this visual
pleasure that helped prompt the monologue. But this term also refers, in
some sense, to how "flattering" her sleep has been to him. While slumbering
in the company of a client hardly appears complimentary, in doing so she
has enabled him to formulate an opinion of himself as different from her
other customers, and in the end, as radically altered by this encounter.
Early in the monologue he admits that rooms like hers were more familiar
to him "Not long ago" (36), but now he needs to see this night as different
from all the others. He needs, moreover, to have a sense that, for all her
other patrons (and her other "double-pillowed" mornings [42]), this night
with him will be memorable for her also: "Why, Jenny, waking here alone /
May help you to remember [me]" (42).

For all the speaker's assessment of Jenny, which comprises the body of
the monologue, it is her voiceless judgment of him that preoccupies his own
unspoken words, in their titillating conjunction of illicit sexuality and
covert discursivity. He speculates, "I wonder what you're thinking of" (37),
and he is especially curious about her estimation of him: "If of myself you
think at all, / What is the thought?" (37). Ultimately, his concern is less
with his "reading" of her ("You know not what a book you seem," he tells
her [37]), than hers of him: "What if to her all this were said?" (39). He
imagines that when she wakes she will remember him not only because he
left in so timely a manner, but because all he has indulged in is a
monologue, one she was not even obliged to hear. And this is of course
what he pays her for so handsomely: he has acquired through her the
opportunity to develop this voiceless monologue, with its overt claims of
having both marked and caused some transformation in himself, and
perhaps in her.

Jenny's lack of alertness or comprehension might have been seen as
enviable by the speaker of Dora Greenwell's "Christina" (composed 1851,
published 1867), a dramatic monologue of which Dante Gabriel Rossetti
may have been aware, since his sister Christina Rossetti was a friend of the
author's and interested in her work.[26] The speaker, a fallen woman,
describes seeking imaginative refuge in the life of her childhood friend
Christina, in order "to lose / The bitter consciousness of self, to be / Ought
other e'en in thought than that what I was" (109–11).[27] So powerful is this
desire for annihilation that she admits, "I sought not death, for that were
but a change / Of being" (175–76) but rather "to cease utterly to be" (178).

The genre of the dramatic monologue, however, is eminently one that requires and therefore affirms a speaking self, working always toward creation rather than destruction of identity, imagining always further changes "Of being." The speaker's salvation, deriving in religious terms from the aptly named Christina and subsequent spiritual retreat, might be seen to draw also from the very medium of her speaking.

In Webster's "A Castaway" (1870), the speaker Eulalie's wide-ranging review of her own past is prompted by her having dipped into a previous exercise in recording the details of her life, her "Poor little diary" (35) which we might consider a precursor to her present monologue.[28] The diary's pathos for her is largely in its record of her naive efforts and plans, her "good resolves" (35). But she also calls these by a sharper name, "ambition": "(was there ever life / that could forego that?) to improve my mind / And know French better and sing harder songs" (36). Ambition has not been entirely forsaken; the speaker muses throughout her monologue on the potential financial advantages her profession has presented her. And yet the diary's girlish ambition for self-improvement, pitied and mocked here, is seen as a kind of lost ideal, one that, because lost, contributed to the chain of circumstances that has led to her current position as a high-level prostitute. The speaker in "Jenny" refers to his own "cherished work" (36) among his "serried ranks" of books (36), while the Castaway presents a life in which the possibilities of such work are early blighted. After "teaching myself out of my borrowed books" (56), a strained and inadequate tutelage, Eulalie loses a post as governess because, she regretfully recalls, "I . . . must blurt out / my great discovery of my ignorance!" (50). Set on her present course because of withheld or castaway education, her monologue is itself an exercise in prismatic autodidacticism, in "teaching myself."

Rossetti's speaker imagines Jenny "waking alone," and thinking of him, but the speaker in "A Castaway" provides a different, and perhaps surprising, sense of the line of thought that Jenny might pursue in solitude. Indeed, Eulalie suggests such a woman might not be entirely grateful for being left to her own devices; she herself finds solitude abhorrent. An earlier attempt to leave her profession fails because of the enforced seclusion at a refuge: "as if a woman / could bear to sit alone, quiet all day" (45). Her wide-ranging autobiographical review is peppered with exasperated variations on the question "Will no one come?" (43), while the poem ends with the arrival of friend she calls a "cackling goose" who is nevertheless received warmly in the poem's final line: "Most welcome, dear: one gets so moped alone" (62). Part of what her monologue accomplishes is that it engages her in conversation with a range of other monologues by fallen women, thus acknowledging her solitude while breaking her silence.

Eulalie has not, however, been entirely alone in the course of the monologue, but rather flanked by past and future selves. Angela Leighton writes of this speaker: "For all her clarity of perception, the Castaway cannot see *herself*."[29] It may be, though, that this speaker observes too many selves, each of which is potentially self-destructive. Like many of Webster's dramatic monologists, the speaker of "A Castaway" is well aware of her own self-division; referring to the author of the diary, her younger avatar, she declares: "it seems a jest to talk of me / as if I could be one with her" (36). In thinking of her future self as "Old," she concludes, "that's to be nothing," only to modify this nihilistic prediction: "or to be at best / a blurred memorial that in better days / there was a woman once with such a name" (43). The Castaway derisively mimics prevalent social theory that argued that there are, as she puts it, "too many women in the world" (48).[30] And yet while she is bitterly mocking in her attribution of the cause of her own situation to "woman's superfluity" (48), the medium of the monologue itself allows her at once to resist and entertain the theory of a superfluous self.

The Castaway's adopted moniker refers not only to a woman flung aside but also to one who is herself adept at abandoning other people, including what she represents as her various past and potential selves. With her monologue, she can cast away and yet rescue an identity straining against itself. Her searching self-examination may help to show that the prostitute whom the speaker of "Jenny" was addressing was far beyond his discursive reach. Before he leaves, Rossetti's monologist arranges gold coins in Jenny's hair, for visual and presumably psychological effect. What might Jenny say when she does finally awaken, amid a shower of coins? We learn from Greenwell's and Webster's speakers that this community of "fallen women" shares an impulse toward self-annihilation, one that the medium of the dramatic monologue at once indulges and forestalls. But these speakers also express an instinct and indeed hunger for self-possession, one that undercuts the most basic premise of their profession. When Jenny the "fallen" woman rises she might anticipate the statement that the ruined and dying speaker of Amy Levy's "Magdalen" (1884) imagines making to her seducer: "I am free; / [And] you, through all eternity, / Have neither part nor lot in me" (*AL* 83–85).

Monologic ends

The final section of this chapter examines the relation of the form of the dramatic monologue to emotional and sometimes actual destruction, whether of another person or of the speaking self; these are among the most extreme examples of the performance of thoughts that this genre presents to us. The prevalence of so much seemingly random devastation would appear to run counter to the work of construction, innovation, or revision in which, in one way or another, we see so many dramatic monologists engaged. And yet destruction, even to the point of self-annihilation, can be a creative act, providing the means to advance ambitions or effect desired alterations in persons or situations. In tracking this phenomenon in examples from a few well-known dramatic monologues and in two lesser known works, Webster's "Circe" (1870) and Levy's "A Minor Poet" (1884), we can witness this inventive genre's complex commitment to varieties of spoliation and ruin.

If the speaker of "Jenny" is finally preoccupied less with his apprehension of Jenny than hers of him, then he intersects with another community of dramatic speakers with a similar fascination. The dramatic monologue from the start, in such foundational works as Browning's "Porphyria's Lover" and "My Last Duchess" concerned itself with female subjectivity, including and perhaps especially the modes of consciousness of women whom we do not hear speak. The speaker of "Porphyria's Lover" not only draws his name from his intimate relationship to her but also claims that the actions he describes, including that of murdering her, are based on his apprehension of her desires, her "one wish" (*RB* 57). He surmises, "Porphyria worshipped me" (33); it is this insight that leads him to find "a thing to do" (38), to render his houseguest a permanent fixture. He represents both her "struggling passion" (23), which prompts her to come to him, and the corresponding lack of struggle or feeling with which she acceded, or so he believes, to his inspiration to strangle her: "No pain felt she; / I am quite sure she felt no pain" (41–42).

Porphyria's lover finds his most immediate confrère later in the century, in Swinburne's "The Leper" (1866), featuring another monologist who still more ecstatically eroticizes a corpse, in this case that of his leprous love-object: a highborn woman whose trysts with lovers he had watched surreptitiously. Now diseased and rejected, she is taken in by the speaker, who exalts in an obsessive lovemaking that only intensifies with her death. While he reviews his increasing ardor we gain glimpses of her appalled exhaustion and dismay (even he recognizes her "sad wonder" [*ACS* I, 123]), reactions all the more distressing for their confinement within his impassioned account. These monologues serve to elucidate their speakers' actions, but still more to prolong them, to detain these men and their lovers forever in the present tense. Although Browning's original heading "Madhouse Cells" indicates the solitary incarceration of the Lover, the murderer's monologue insists in closing, "we sit together now" (58), while the now diseased speaker of "The Leper" claims that in spite of his beloved's death, and his own impending demise, "I sit still and hold / In two cold palms her two cold feet" (I, 122).

The monologue of Porphyria's lover makes faint suggestion that it is only with him, at "*That* moment" that she was "Perfectly pure and good" (36–37; emphasis mine). Her "soiled gloves," (12) "vainer ties" (24), and attendance at "to-night's gay feast" (27) may point, he hints, to other lovers of Porphyria. Such conjecture attends the Duchess in "My Last Duchess," who may be the victim either of excess fidelity or imprudent infidelity. That the Duchess "liked whate'er / She looked on, and her looks went everywhere" (*RB* 23–24), and that she "thanked men" (31) rather too profligately, may indicate that she was either charming or promiscuous; in either case, the speaker claims that *her* passions led to her removal, not his. The Duke's monologue begins with the question that he knows any viewer of her portrait will have, regarding "How such a glance came there"; he assures the envoy, "not the first / Are you to turn and ask thus" (12–13). In a sense, the monologue is an attempt to answer that question, to explain the glance, the "spot / Of joy" (14–15) on her cheek, the "faint / Half-flush" now perpetually dying "along her throat" (18–19). One might argue, indeed, that the enigmatic and potentially wayward nature of her subjectivity as well as her expression is part of what prompted the Duke to fix a single image of her. In these and other dramatic monologues, female desire (linked, as it is, to complex and perhaps indefinable sexualities) is viewed as causative, as tending toward some effect. In pursuing a woman even unto death, each speaker is himself altered by an elusive female consciousness, although he often avers that it is her thought that he is performing.

I have been arguing that the dramatic monologue seeks to dramatize, as well as to cause, performative effects. This tendency makes the genre especially useful in cases where both the speaker and the poet are attempting to create reactions and larger social transformations in the world outside the poem. We noted that one of the Castaway's explanations for her current position stressed that had her education been stronger her profession might have been different. While this is only one of the critiques that the speaker brings to society's failings and her own, we know that Webster was a passionate advocate of women's education, and that the monologue obliquely but firmly reflects the poet's external social commitments. Perhaps no Victorian poet used the genre of the dramatic monologue to more· powerful polemical effect than Elizabeth Barrett Browning, whose poem "The Runaway Slave at Pilgrim's Point" first appeared in an American anti-slavery publication in 1848. The runaway slave, the speaker of the dramatic monologue, presents an appalling indictment of the system of slavery, one in part attempting to account for her murder of her own child, offspring of her rape by her master. Other dramatic monologues, such as Webster's "Medea in Athens" (1870) and Levy's "Medea" (1884), probe the dynamics of maternal destructiveness. The spectacle these works contemplate is that of a creator destroying what she has herself generated and produced, of destruction constituting an act of responsive innovation. These poems present as speakers mothers whose profoundest act is laying waste to their children, a devastation figured as a form of radical protest. Barrett Browning's "Runaway Slave" exhibits the extended enactment of a child's murder at the center of the poem (possibly an influence for and certainly a precursor to Toni Morrison's acclaimed novel *Beloved* [1987]). She uses the genre's tendency to feature speakers in extremity to powerful dramatic effect, seeking for a multiplicity of transformations to take place not only in the course of the poem but also in the world beyond it. In such works we may trace the creative transformation of violence, as destructive acts mutate into inventive ones through the very medium of the monologue.

As in these other monologues featuring speakers who seek transformations of selves and situations through emotional depredation, Webster's "Circe" especially interests itself in the ruinous effects that one sex can wreak upon the other. Circe, the woman who holds Ulysses in an enervating thrall when we first see him in Homer's *Odyssey*, is in both writers' works an overseer of masculine transfigurations. Hard-laboring mariners shipwrecked on the speaker's island are seduced by their sudden luxurious leisure into drinking from her charmed cup, and as a result are transformed into animals. Webster finds Circe mistress of a menagerie of former men, the only human speaker among a community of grunting animals "who wallow in their styes, . . . / . . . or munch in pens and byres, / or snarl and filch behind their wattled coops" (18).[31] Like other dramatic monologists who are catalysts for distressing alterations in other people, however, Circe claims that the modifications she causes could not occur were the seeds of change not already dormant in her victims. She insists that drinking from her cup only "revealed them to themselves / and to each other" (21). Indeed, she denies, in spite of the howling and barking of her companions, that any alteration occurred: "Change? there was no change; / only disguise gone from them unawares" (21).

For Circe, the problem with her domain is that in fact change of any sort is so unaccustomed; the dilemma that she confronts is wholesale stagnation. At the start of her monologue, she calls for a powerful storm to wrack her island: "let it come and bring me change, / breaking the sickly sweet monotony" (15). This still air is suffocating to her; at the end of the monologue, she complains, even as she views distant lightning, "the air / Clings faint and motionless around me here" (22). Leighton, in one of the rare extended discussions of this poem presently available, notes the resemblance of this island's voluptuous stillness to the ultimately untenable stasis sought by the speakers of Tennyson's "The Lotos-Eaters" (1832, revised 1842), themselves mariners seeking respite from the rigors of Ulysses's journey in Homer's *Odyssey*.[32] And yet Circe herself undergoes a daily experience of multiple transformations, wrought, in an autoerotic fashion, by herself upon herself. Looking at her image she exclaims, "oh, lips that tempt / my very self to kisses" (19). Like Narcissus, she addresses the reflection of her own "perfect lovely face" (19) in a still pool, and asks, "should I be so your lover as I am, / drinking an exquisite joy to watch you thus / In all a hundred changes through the day?" (19). Her most intense pleasure is in her own diurnal transformations; in this respect she most resembles Aurora, the goddess of the dawn in Tennyson's dramatic monologue "Tithonus," who daily experiences "mystic change" (*AT* 55) only gaining in beauty with every new morning.

This intense experience of self-satisfaction leads paradoxically to the sort of self-division we remarked in Webster's "A Castaway"; addressing her own reflection, Circe declares: "I love you for him till he comes" (19). At a number of points in her monologue Circe refers to the man whom she knows is destined to wash ashore, one who might drink from her cup and stand "unchanged" (19–20). The arrival of this man (whom we know to be Ulysses, not only through Homer but also through Tennyson's "Ulysses," a dramatic monologue with which this poem is in implicit dialogue) may well occur this very night. As she speaks, a storm is rising and she sees a ship, now a "shuddering hulk" (19) in the distance, struggling vainly against it; her monologue ends, "It were well / I bade make ready for our guests to-night" (22). These final lines suggest further transmutations of her guests into zoological specimens. But in pointing to the future arrival of Ulysses, her closing remarks suggest also a kind of violent alteration to be wreaked upon herself. Leighton writes that Circe "wants the thrill of change and experience [of the sort enjoyed by Ulysses] for herself."[33] We might extend this insight still further, however, in surveying the modes of change to which Circe desires to submit herself.

In the course of her monologue, Webster's Circe articulates a longing, I would argue, to pursue experience less like that of Ulysses than like that of the nameless men whom she transforms into creatures only more truly themselves. A creature of self-division, Circe idealizes the revelation of a coherent, if abased, identity. Certainly, she defines herself in the context of being mastered by another person. In response to her central monological question, "why am I who I am?" (18), her answer is, "for the sake of him whom fate will send / one day to be my master utterly" (18). While she imagines this fateful man standing "unchanged" in her presence, she wants for him to "[look] me in the eyes, / abashing me before him" (22). She proves and values this man by his adamant ability to withstand change, to be a self less mutable than any other. Yet even as she disdains radical transmutation in other individuals, she seeks it for herself. In harboring this desire she comes in the course of the monologue, by way of the monologue, to resemble all too closely her feral men wracked by storm. We can now see that this ambition was announced at the opening of the monologue, in which she calls for a violent storm, "though it rend my bowers" (14), precisely because it will shatter every aspect of her existence. Their sensuous delight in her hospitality changes her guests into (or rather, as she claims, reveals them as) beasts. For her, too, self-pleasuring transmutes into self-abasement and submission. A dramatic monologue like "Circe" demonstrates the complexity of the genre's figurations of "men and women" (as the title of Browning's well-known collection has it). In a dazzling display of the possibilities and dangers of gendered transfiguration, the speaker desires to become "mastered," like the storm-riven subjugated men whom she oversees. More than any narcissistic pool, the men whom she derides as inhuman (calling them "these bestial things" [18]), provide the image that she chooses to see herself as reflecting.

We have noted some of the ways that this genre, while founded on the primacy of the speaking subject, is drawn to the representation of various forms of self-annihilation. With these examples in mind, it is useful to close with a poem in which such self-destruction is still more direct, and indeed stands as the premise of the monologue. Levy's "A Minor Poet" intersects with aspects of the dramatic speakers of the two major poets of this genre. Readers have long heard in the speakers of Tennyson's "Ulysses" and "Tithonus" an urge toward release from existence, a yearning toward death. This is a desire sought as intensely by Levy's male speaker. He is also linked to a line of Browning monologists convinced of and yet resistant to the notion of their own failure, including the speakers of "Pictor Ignotus" (1845), "Andrea del Sarto" (1855), and "Childe Roland to the Dark Tower Came." What Levy's speaker is determined not to fail in, despite a lifetime of shortcomings and frustrations, is his own suicide.[34] The poem begins with the speaker locking himself into his rooms; later he notes of his earlier botched attempts, "I wrought before in heat ... / ... scarcely understanding; now I know / What thing I do" (AL 158–60). The monologue maintains, then, a clear sense of deliberation; equally decisive is his sense of self-definition: "I am myself, as each man is himself" (21). It appears, however, that it is precisely his keen self-awareness that is now to culminate in his self-annihilation.

This dramatic monologue has an Epilogue, in a sense a companion or pendant monologue, spoken by the Minor Poet's friend Tom Leigh. Leigh describes to an unnamed auditor his having "burst in" to the poet's room, "And found him as you know" (172–73). Leigh enumerates reasons that others have suggested for the poet's suicide – his unrequited love for a woman, his poverty, his despair over "carping critics" (202) – but he himself reserves judgment: "I, Tom Leigh, his friend / I have no word at all to say of this" (202–03). And yet it seems to me that Leigh has already supplied the chief reason when he observes, "There was no written word to say farewell, / Or make clear the deed" (176–77). This inexpressiveness is precisely what the Minor Poet struggles with in the course of his mono-logue. As he prepares to swallow his phial of poison, he looks to his books, telling them, "you've stood my friends / . . . yet now I'll turn / My back on you, even as the world / Turns it on me" (78–81). He seems to turn from their serried ranks because the public reception of his works has painfully disappointed him. But his next comment indicates that he is still more hounded by the frustrations inherent in his own conditions of production. He compares himself to another poet who experiences "no silent writhing in the dark, / No muttering of mute lips, no straining out / Of a weak throat a-choke with pent-up sound, / A-throb with pent-up passion" (95–98). His description of what this other poet did not suffer depicts in vivid detail his own writhing, straining, choking, and throbbing attempts at speech. Even in this moment of a distress so radical as to require suicide, he feels himself unable to articulate his emotions; he says of this other poet: "At least, he has a voice to cry out his pain" (94).

While the Minor Poet stresses how "silent" and "mute" he has been, he nevertheless figures his own failed eloquence in musical terms. He claims early in the monologue that "From very birth" he has been out of place, "A blot, a blur" (50). But in continuing this self-canceling line of description, he calls himself something that at least points to a potential lyricism: "a note / All out of tune in this world's instrument" (50–51). Later he complains, "My life was jarring discord from the first," but concedes, "Tho' here and there brief hints of melody, / Of melody unutterable, clove the air" (165–67). Yet even this attempt to salvage some attainment points to the inescapability of his failure. With the oxymoronic "melody unutter-able," he conveys that even this hint of music was fleeting and inchoate. While Tom Leigh finds "no written word" to "make clear the deed" (179–80), he does find scrawled marginalia in the poet's books, as well as "sketches on the wall / Done rough in charcoal" and "Large schemes of undone work. Poems half-writ / Wild drafts of symphonies; big plans of fugues" (183–84). These abortive works themselves constitute a lucid account of his motivation for suicide; the speaker believes that his thoughts can find no performance, can neither be voiced by him nor heard by any public. On the one hand, the monologue is itself the completed work, the pain and the poem fully voiced, the "big plan" accomplished. On the other hand, he now remains forever mute, since his monologue's only auditor is a self engaged in its own overthrow. In the course of destroying himself, he has produced another oxymoronic discursive situation, one akin to the "melody unutterable" that he only faintly discerned; he has performed an unspeakable monologue.

The absolute annihilation of Levy's monologist is unusual – though this is a genre that is often interested in the concurrence of creativity and destruction, the simultaneous representation and termination of a speaking self. Unlike the Minor Poet, however, the speaker of Webster's "An Inventor" – the dramatic monologue with which this essay began – resolves, "I'll not die with my work unfulfilled" (13). He notes, as do so many dramatic speakers, that for some people the path to accomplishment is easy, for others hard: "each of his kind; / but can you change your kind?" (65–66). None of the speakers we have considered – however dire, disturbing, frustrating, or comical their situations are – would change their kinds. The Bishop perpetually ordering his tomb, the prostitutes and their clients, the lovers and their doomed beloveds, the poets and the inventors: many of these speakers might desire to change their situations but never, finally, the selves they may even consider extinguishing. So aware is he of the complexity of identifying, let alone changing, one's kind that the Inventor goes on to ask: "who would pray (say such a prayer could serve) / 'Let me be some other, not myself'?" (72–73). Prayer is of course also a kind of discourse through which an individual may seek transformative effects, clearly a more sanctified mode of address but one perhaps allied to aspects of the dramatic monologue. The form of the dramatic monologue itself represents speech seeking to be efficacious, to cause a variety of transformations. The act of the dramatic monologue, its performance of thoughts, simultaneously creates a self and alters that self, and may perhaps ultimately destroy the self it held so dear.

The works of Tennyson, Browning, Barrett Browning, Dante Gabriel Rossetti, Swinburne, Webster, Levy, and other Victorian poets demonstrate that the dramatic monologue has long wrestled with the intricacies of desire, sexual or otherwise. While Modernist poets such as T.S. Eliot and Ezra Pound put the form to rich use, it continues to provide a vital and relevant forum for a range of voices. The monologic speakers in Richard Howard's *Untitled Subjects* (1969) are the Victorians themselves, while W.D. Snodgrass's *The Führer Bunker* (1995) features monologues of Hitler and his circle. The panoply of speakers in Anna Deavere Smith's *Fires in the Mirror* (1993) and *Twilight: Los Angeles 1992* (1994) intensively explore recent events of racial violence and civic chaos. The Victorians' relentless but constantly shifting focus on the variables of human longing and frustration continues in such recent works as Eve Ensler's *The Vagina Monologues* (1998), a series of vocalizations concerning that female body part. Like Smith, Ensler draws her voices from numerous interviews, and she performs the monologues on stage. The linked monologues that make up each of these late-twentieth-century collections are all involved in conversation with one another, in some ways more direct than in Victorian examples we have considered, and in others still more oblique. The audience frequently gains a distinct sense of how little speakers are willing to listen to each other, and therefore how difficult any transformation, whether of a self or of a society, might be. These speakers appear strikingly different from their Victorian forebears, and yet they might be seen as engaging in conversation with these previous monologic performances, and therefore viewed less as deviating from than extending the tradition. The form of the dramatic monologue from the start dealt in transformations involving myriad sexualities, controversial contemporary and historical figures, and tangled affiliations and prejudices. Attending to so vast an array of speakers, we might hear these works finally build less to a conversation than an orchestration; they announce how much the dramatic monologue still has to say to us.

NOTES

1 Quotations from Augusta Webster's poetry are taken from Webster, *Portraits* (London: Macmillan, 1870); page references appear in parentheses.
2 According to the *Oxford English Dictionary*, the word "performance" derives from "parfournir," an Old French word signifying "to complete" or "to carry out thoroughly."
3 Dorothy Mermin has explored the genre's emphasis on communication, observing that a "dramatic monologue with or without an auditor is a performance: it requires an audience." But she does not read the performative element as also causative, seeking transformations. In her view, the "monologue lacks the resources to develop the temporal dimension, the notion of life as a continuing process of growth and change": *The Audience in the Poem: Five Victorian Poets* (New Brunswick, NJ: Rutgers University Press, 1983), 11, 10.
4 A. Dwight Culler, "Monodrama and the Dramatic Monologue," *PMLA* 90 (1975), 368.

5 Samuel Silas Curry, *Browning and the Dramatic Monologue: Nature and Interpretation of an Overlooked Form of Literature* (1908; reprinted New York: Haskell House, 1965), 13.

6 Robert Langbaum, *The Poetry of Experience: The Dramatic Monologue in Modern Literary Tradition* (New York: Random House, 1957), 182–83; further page references appear in parentheses.

7 Herbert F. Tucker, Jr., "From Monomania to Monologue: 'St. Simeon Stylites' and the Rise of the Victorian Dramatic Monologue," *Victorian Poetry* 22 (1984), 121–37.

8 Clyde de L. Ryals, *Becoming Browning: The Poems and Plays of Robert Browning, 1833–1846* (Columbus, OH: Ohio State University Press, 1983), 150–51.

9 While he does not emphasize the notion that dramatic monologues may labor toward particular *teloi* or endpoints, E. Warwick Slinn explores aspects of the genre's interest in change and transformation. He reads these poems chiefly in the context of the Hegelian dialectical process, focusing on longer works such as Tennyson's *Maud* (1855), Arthur Hugh Clough's *Amours de Voyage* (1855), and Browning's *The Ring and the Book* (1868–69); see *The Discourse of the Self in Victorian Poetry* (Charlottesville, VA: University of Virginia Press, 1991).

10 For discussions regarding the representation of speech in perhaps the most representative author of dramatic monologues, see Daniel Karlin on Browning's "vocal" style in John Woolford and Daniel Karlin, *Robert Browning*, Studies in Eighteenth- and Nineteenth-Century Literature (Harlow: Longman, 1996), 55–64, and E.A.W. St. George, *Browning and Conversation* (Basingstoke: Macmillan, 1993).

11 Among the most comprehensive examples of this approach are Ralph W. Rader, "The Dramatic Monologue and Related Lyric Forms," *Critical Inquiry* 3 (1976), 131–51, in which he draws distinctions between "expressive lyric," "dramatic lyric," "dramatic monologue," and "mask lyric"; and Culler, "Monodrama and the Dramatic Monologue."

12 Tucker, "From Monomania to Monologue," 121–22.

13 Alastair Fowler, *Kinds of Literature: An Introduction to the Theory of Genres and Modes* (Cambridge, MA: Harvard University Press, 1982), 38.

14 Arthur Henry Hallam, *The Writings of Arthur Hallam*, ed. T.H. Vail Motter (New York: MLA, 1943), 197.

15 Benjamin Willis Fuson, *Browning and His English Predecessors in the Dramatic Monolog*, State University of Iowa Humanistic Studies, VIII (Iowa City, IA: State University of Iowa, 1948). Isobel Armstrong also suggests Letitia Elizabeth Landon's *The Improvisatrice* (1824) as an originary instance of the form, and argues that "it was the women poets who 'invented' the dramatic monologue": *Victorian Poetry: Poetry, Poetics and Politics* (London: Routledge, 1993), 326.

16 Karlin makes this point, and notes that the term was first applied to Browning in 1864; see Woolford and Karlin *Robert Browning*, 38, n. 3. Culler dates the first use to 1857, as a title to a collection of poems by George W. Thornbury: "Monodrama and Dramatic Monologue," 356.

17 Elisabeth A. Howe, *The Dramatic Monologue*, Studies in Literary Themes and Genres (New York: Twayne, 1996), 3.

18 Robert Browning, *The Poems*, ed. John Pettigrew and Thomas J. Collins, 2 vols. (Harmondsworth: Penguin Books 1981), I, 347. For a discussion of the relation of the dramatic monologue to what Browning calls "Lyric . . . expression," see Tucker, "Dramatic Monologue and the Overhearing of Lyric," in *Lyric Poetry: Beyond New Criticism*, eds. Chaviva Hošek and Patricia Parker (Ithaca, NY: Cornell University Press, 1985), 226–43.

19 Langbaum, *Poetry of Experience*, 75.

20 Alan Sinfield, *Dramatic Monologue* (London: Methuen, 1977), 42. Sinfield argues that, while this poetic form "had an unprecedented importance for the Victorians . . . there is no single aspect of it that was not anticipated" (53).

21 Fuson, *Browning and His English Predecessors*, 22.

22 For a more detailed examination of the processes the Bishop undergoes by way of his monologue, see Cornelia D.J. Pearsall, "Browning and the Poetics of the Sepulchral Body," *Victorian Poetry* 30 (1992), 43–61.

23 The diary entry is by W.H. Thompson and dated 11 November 1833, cited in Peter Allen, *The Cambridge Apostles: The Early Years* (Cambridge: Cambridge University Press, 1978), 163.

24 Ekbert Faas, *Retreat into the Mind: Victorian Poetry and the Rise of Psychiatry* (Princeton, NJ: Princeton University Press, 1988), 51.

25 Daniel A. Harris, "D.G. Rossetti's 'Jenny': Sex, Money, and the Interior Monologue," *Victorian Poetry* 22 (1984), 197. Harris suggests various reasons for the speaker's silence, including his internalizing of "a powerful public censorship" (201) on the subject of prostitution, his fear of "an explosive and hostile reply" (202), and his ultimate "revulsion with deceptive male speech" (209).

26 Christina Rossetti herself performed extensive volunteer work for a number of years at St. Mary Magdalene Penitentiary, Highgate, an Anglican refuge for prostitutes founded in 1855. Her own "fallen women" poems include the dramatic monologue "The Convent Threshold" (1862); for a discussion of Christina Rossetti's works in this context see Leighton, "'Because Men Made the Laws': The Fallen Woman and the Woman Poet," *Victorian Poetry* 27 (1989), 109–27.

27 Quotations from Dora Greenwell, "Christina" are taken from *Victorian Women Poets: An Anthology*, eds. Angela Leighton and Margaret Reynolds (Oxford: Blackwell, 1995); line references appear in parentheses. The poem is also reprinted in *Nineteenth-Century Women Poets: An Oxford Anthology*, eds. Isobel Armstrong and Joseph Bristow with Cath Sharrock (Oxford: Clarendon Press, 1996), 439–48.

28 Webster's "A Castaway" is reprinted in *Victorian Women Poets: An Anthology*, eds. Leighton and Reynolds, 433–48, and in *Nineteenth-Century Women Poets*, eds. Armstrong and Bristow with Sharrock, 602–17.

29 Angela Leighton, *Victorian Women Poets: Writing Against the Heart* (Charlottesville, VA: University Press of Virginia, 1992), 200.

30 A chief proponent of this theory was W. R. Greg, in "Why are Women Redundant?" *National Review* 14 (1862), 434–60. Webster takes up aspects of the redundant woman question in her essay "The Dearth of Husbands," in *A Housewife's Opinions*, 239–45. See also Greg's "Prostitution," *Westminster Review* 53 (1850), 238–68. Mary Poovey briefly discusses Greg's essays in

Uneven Developments: The Ideological Work of Gender in Mid-Victorian England (Chicago, IL: University of Chicago Press, 1988), 1–6.

31 Webster's "Circe" is reprinted in *Victorian Women Poets: An Anthology*, eds. Leighton and Reynolds, 428–33, and in *Nineteenth-Century Women Poets*, eds. Armstrong and Bristow with Sharrock, eds., 591–9.

32 Leighton, *Victorian Women Poets: Writing against the Heart*, 193–95.

33 Leighton, *Victorian Women Poets: Writing against the Heart*, 195.

34 While Levy herself committed suicide, one would want to avoid attaching the statements of this speaker too directly to the poet. The genre in which she chose to explore these sentiments, the dramatic monologue, demands that some distance be assumed between the poet and the poem's speaking subject.

5

YOPIE PRINS

Victorian meters

In Victorian poetry we see a proliferation of poetic forms, departing from eighteenth-century heroic couplets and neoclassical odes, and further developing the Romantic revival of ballads, sonnets, and blank verse into increasingly refined and rarefied metrical experiments. Alongside the English fashion in Italian sonnets, French stanzaic forms, Germanic accentual verse, and various kinds of dialect poetry – as well as a fascination with the literary recreation of songs, ballads, hymns, refrains, and other musical forms – there was a return to meters inspired by ancient Greek and Latin poetry. Victorian prosody – the study of meter – also became increasingly elaborate: in addition to counting the number of stresses or syllables per line, as in the tradition of English accentual-syllabic verse, prosodists tried to measure the length (or "quantity") of syllables in English according to the tradition of classical quantitative verse. The publication of historical surveys and theoretical treatises on meter rose dramatically throughout the Victorian period, ranging from Edwin Guest's *A History of English Rhythms* (1838, revised 1882) to George Saintsbury's *History of English Prosody* (1906–10), and peaking mid-century with the New Prosody of Coventry Patmore and his contemporaries, and again at the end of the century, with the circulation of numerous polemical pamphlets and scholarly debates about meter.[1] What are the implications of this preoccupation with form? In my own history of Victorian meters, I will begin telling the long and short of that story.

Nineteenth-century theories of meter are often considered antiquated by twentieth-century readers, as metrical analysis has been reformulated on a linguistic model and traditional foot-scansion called into question.[2] Rather than setting aside Victorian metrical theory as an obsolete science, however, let us take more seriously John Hollander's claim that "prosodical analysis is a form of literature in itself."[3] It is a literary genre that raises important historical and theoretical questions about the interpretation of poetry, beyond a merely technical, seemingly ahistorical approach to the scansion of a particular text. Hollander calls for a diachronic as well as synchronic approach to metrical analysis, demonstrating how meters operate contextually and intertextually: "To analyze the meter of a poem is not so much to scan it, as to show with what other poems its less significant (linguistically speaking) formal elements associate it" (162). The formal elements of a poem that appear to be "less significant (linguistically speaking)" but nevertheless have historical significance are its non-semantic properties: the phonemic arrangement of the poem and its graphic notation, or what Hollander calls "the poem in the ear" and "the poem in the eye." The relationship between these "material" forms of language – how a poem materializes in sound and how it materializes on the page – proves to be a central concern in Victorian metrical theory, as it develops an account of meter that is neither an imitation of voice nor a script for voice but a formal mediation that makes "voice" a function of writing.

The Victorians increasingly conceptualized meter as a formal grid or pattern of spacing, created by the alternation of quantifiable units. Their interest in quantification has the effect of detaching poetic voice from spoken utterance, and marks – literally, in the making of metrical marks – a graphic distinction between meter and rhythm. Thus, when Patmore writes in his "Essay on English Metrical Law" that "the sequence of vocal utterance shall be divided into equal or proportionate spaces," the very process of measuring such "proportionate spaces" turns "vocal utterance" into a temporal or spatial "sequence."[4] Voice is no longer understood in terms of "natural" speech rhythm but measured in predictable intervals. This abstraction of metrical law is enforced by the rules of scansion and recitation taught in schools, where schoolboys learn to distinguish "false" from "true" quantities, and to modulate their voices accordingly. A popular schoolbook such as *English Lessons for English People* (1871) describes the modulation of speech rhythms into a metrical pattern in order to make the voice "rise" from prose to poetry: "Now just as the voice rises from (a) conversational non-modulation to (b) rhetorical modulation, and from modulation to (c) singing, so the arrangement of words rises from (a') conversational non-arrangement to (b') rhetorical rhythm, and from rhythm to (c') *metre*."[5] The idealization or uplifting of the voice depends on turning speech into song and rhythm into *metre* but the analogy between singing and metrical form also raises a question about what befalls the spoken utterance. Does speech fall silent as "the voice rises"? Does meter follow the rhythms of a speaking voice, or does voice follow meter? The measurement of utterance by division and quantification turns voice into an abstract pattern: a series of intervals for enumeration rather than enunciation.

This metrical mediation of voice is already implicit in earlier nineteenth-century accounts of meter. In his 1802 "Preface" to *Lyrical Ballads*, William Wordsworth endorses metrical composition in so far as it serves to regulate an "unusual and irregular state of the mind" with "the co-presence of something regular," and thus creates "an intertexture of ordinary feeling."[6] Not only does the regularity of meter impart "ordinary" feeling through repetition and habituation but it also introduces an "intertexture" between voice and text: an intermediate voice, composed by the meter rather than spoken aloud. Wordsworth consciously enacts this kind of metrical manipulation in his own lyrical ballads. But in his 1815 "Preface" he also warns against meter when its rules and regulations begin to dictate how a poem should be voiced: "The law of long syllable and short must not be so inflexible, – the letter of metre must not be so impassive to the spirit of versification, – as to deprive the Reader of all voluntary power to modulate, in subordination to the sense, the music of the poem."[7] Here Wordsworth insists on the reader's "voluntary power" to breathe life into a poem and modulate its music according to the "spirit of versification," rather than reading mechanically according to "the letter of metre." There is, however, the possibility of becoming involuntarily overpowered by the meter, which – while seeming "impassive to the spirit" – animates the poem. Rather than reading the music of the poem "in subordination to the sense," we might find our reading subordinated to another kind of sense: the material properties of language that materialize, in part, through meter. Spiritual and material elements are therefore intertwined in a way that complicates the opposition between vocal utterance and the dictates of meter, the spoken and the written, the spirit and the letter, in order to create another "intertexture" between voice and text.

Victorian poets develop this Wordsworthian insight into a vision of voice – one that reflects "a doubled consciousness of metrical language itself," as Eric Griffiths suggests.[8] Emphasizing how Wordsworth points to a "break with the organic functions of metre, by virtue of rendering the passage from visible to audible rhythmic patterns less secure" (74), Griffiths argues that Victorian poetry arises out of that very break. If the circulation of poems in nineteenth-century print culture already troubles the relation of person to voice, then in Victorian metrics we see a further transformation of voice into a spectral form, simultaneously present and absent, and strangely detached from spoken utterance. In close readings of various Victorian poems, Griffiths seeks to demonstrate how "the printed page which retains the poetic voice ('retains' in the double sense of 'keeps back' and 'preserves') becomes the dramatic scene of [a] searched and searching utterance" (70). What Griffiths calls the "printed voice of Victorian poetry" can no longer be located in a single speaker. Instead, the reader discovers it in a mediation between the ear and the eye that produces the possibility of multiple voicings: "The intonational ambiguity of a written text may create a mute polyphony through which we see rather than hear alternatively possible voicings, and are led by such vision to reflect on the inter-resonance of such voicings" (16). Nevertheless an investment in an idea (or ideal) of voice remains central to his understanding of Victorian poetry. In this respect Griffiths is a very Victorian reader, his ear attuned to the resounding echoes and interruptions of sounds that cannot be heard, except by reflecting on their "inter-resonance." Other contemporary critics, such as Dennis Taylor and Matthew Campbell, have likewise turned to Victorian prosody in order "to re-create or listen again to the voice of nineteenth-century poetry," hoping to hear the rhythms inspired by a living, breathing voice through "understanding the breadth of nineteenth-century innovations and experiments in verse."[9]

While these critics read Victorian poems (still) as dramas of speaking, however, I wish to emphasize that the figure of voice also resists being reduced to utterance in Victorian poetry. One of the legacies of the New Criticism – by now not so new – is to understand poems as the representation of a personal utterance that may or may not be attributed to the "actual" author but nevertheless assumes the actualization of a speaking voice. On this theory we approach all poems as if they were dramatic monologues, by inferring a "speaker" whose utterance is "overheard" by the reader. But if New Criticism seems to derive its theory of reading from the Victorian dramatic monologue in particular, then this poetic genre already points to the difficulty of locating voice. Indeed, the historical emergence of the dramatic monologue revolves around the problem of reading a poem as a spoken utterance, rather than resolving that problem. Although twentieth-century readers would like to discover the spiritualization of voice in Victorian poetry, I will argue that nineteenth-century theories of meter also uncover a form of linguistic materialism that complicates the claim to vocal presence. Instead of hearing voice as breath or spirit, we see it materialize through the counting of metrical marks. It is important, then, to read the poetry in conjunction with the prosody of the period, in order to develop a critical understanding of Victorian meters.

The English ear

Ranging "from the twelfth century to the present day," Saintsbury's three-volume *History of English Prosody* chronicles an historical progression culminating in the latter half of the nineteenth century. Volume 3 ("From

Blake to Mr. Swinburne") of this rather idiosyncratic narrative summarizes prior developments in the history of English versification – "the progressive constitution of rhythm up to Chaucer; its emphasizing and regimenting by him; the break-up under his successors, and the restoration by Spenser and his contemporaries; the rise of blank verse, its decay in drama, and its reorganisation as a non-dramatic form by Milton; the battle of the couplets and the victory of the enclosed form; its tyranny, and the gathering evasions of it and opposition to it" – in order to conclude quite confidently in the present tense: "These stages are past: each of the progressive and constructive ones has left its gain, and each of the retrograde and destructive intervals its warning, for good and all. Now, things are different" (III, 170). With the "abolition of the strict syllabic theory" and "the admission of Substitution and Equivalence," Saintsbury claims that nineteenth-century verse has entered a new era of freedom (III, 171), and by the middle of the century Victorian poetry has gained "full entrance on the heritage which had been gained in the past: the exercise, deliberate and unrestrained, of the franchise of English prosody" (III, 296).

Presenting prosody in a series of "stages," Saintsbury seems to open English literary history itself to a form of metrical analysis: he marks out "intervals" that are alternately "progressive" or "retrograde," and measures these alternations as part of a larger historical pattern that can only be discerned in retrospect. From a very late- (or even post-) Victorian perspective, Saintsbury surveys the entire history of English poetry as conveyed by Victorian poets in particular, whose poetry exercises "the franchise of English prosody" with new variety and freedom (III, 296). "Tennyson is at once the earliest exponent, and to no small extent the definite master, of this new ordered liberty" (III, 296), and its latest exponent is Algernon Charles Swinburne, whose "unsurpassed versatility and virtuosity" reflects "the growth and development of seven centuries of English language and English literature" (III, 351). Saintsbury's reconstruction of the past newly enfranchises Victorian poetry through a genealogy of English poets including Chaucer, Spenser, and Milton (with Shakespeare standing in the wings), whose prosodies are historically embedded in the English language, and now inherited by poets such as Tennyson and Swinburne. English prosody becomes a national heritage, with a political as well as a poetical purpose in resisting "tyranny" and establishing a "new ordered liberty" for the English nation. It has its own law and order, and even while appropriating other traditions of versification, it will not be ruled by any tradition except its own.

In keeping with this nostalgic and nationalist strain in his reading of lyric history, Saintsbury often emphasizes the difference between an English ear and foreigners who are deaf to English prosody. He criticizes a "loose *sloppiness* in the German or Germanised ear, which cannot understand elasticity combined with form" (III, 336), and asks with patriotic fervor, "What law can a French ear give to an English tongue?" (III, 468). Neither the German ear nor the French ear is attuned to the harmonization of order and liberty in English prosody, according to Saintsbury: the Germans are "prone to exaggerate the accentual and 'irregular' element in English" while "the French try to introduce syllabic regularity" (III, 463). And finally, most emphatically in his conclusion to *History of English Prosody*, Saintsbury refuses all forms of prosodic analysis "foisted in from abroad, and developed by persons lacking English tongues or English ears, and mostly under the domination of an artificial and arbitrary system of phonetics" (III, 511). He patriotically rallies to the defense of an early Tennysonian lyric, criticized by some for its apparent metrical irregularity: "One reads it, wondering how any human ear could be 'tortured' by it, but wondering still more how any *English* ear could be in the least puzzled by its meter" (188). Likewise he quotes two lines in the context of his discussion of Swinburne as self-evident examples of poetry that "should appeal to every one: 'To doubt its music were to want an ear, / To doubt its passion were to want a heart'" (III, 390). Although Tennyson and Swinburne inspired very different political sentiments in late-Victorian England,[10] what they have in common is an appeal to the human heart that seems inseparable from their appeal to the English ear – as indeed, the very word "ear" is already contained within the "heart" of the English language.

And yet Saintsbury's *History of English Prosody* is haunted by an unspoken question: How can meter be heard by ear? In the concluding remarks to his third volume, Saintsbury celebrates "the great multiplication of metres" in the nineteenth century, and praises Victorian poetry in particular for "the strenuous and constant endeavour to increase the range of appeal to the reader's faculties of mental sight and hearing" (III, 508). But in doing so he also points to the abstraction of Victorian meters: they are recognized, by the faculties of "mental sight and hearing," as a function of reading. The notion of an inner ear suggests why Saintsbury is skeptical of phonological, acoustical, and musical approaches to prosody, all of which are emerging in nineteenth-century England alongside comparative philology and scholarly inquiry into the history of the English language. The study of Old English pronunciation, for example, seems as obscure to Saintsbury as attempts to reconstruct the sound of ancient Greek. He finds phonetics of limited use even in analyzing the sound of English: "Phonetics may possibly tell us something about a certain sound when heard; and it may tell us, for ought I know infallibly, by what physical movements that sound is produced. But how can it tell us what a sound *was*?" (III, 432). The question resonates not only in our reading of dead languages but also in the way that we "hear" English poetry, where hearing proves to be a figure for reading a text that cannot really ever "tell us what a sound *was*." Saintsbury complains of "the phoneticians who are frequently deaf, though unfortunately not dumb, guides" to English prosody (III, 467) because they have too much to say about the sound of spoken English, and not enough about its appeal to an inner ear.

In Tennyson's poetry, however, Saintsbury discovers the perfection of an English ear attuned to the mediation of voice by meter. Saintsbury presents the poet's early lyric, "The Dying Swan" (1830), as "a diploma piece from the prosodic point of view" (III, 192). He reads it in detail not only to display Tennyson's precocious metrical skill but also to insist on the interplay between meter and voice, or "body" and "soul": the material and spiritual dimensions of poetry. In Saintsbury's reading of the poem, the spiritualization of voice cannot be separated from the way it is embodied or materialized in the meter: one must apprehend "the soul-substance" without "stripping it of its essential and inseparable body of poetry" (III, 193). The poem introduces the dying swan as a solitary figure in a melancholy landscape, where the river runs "with an inner voice" (*AT* 5) and the wind seems to "sigh" (15) through the reed-tops and weeping willows. But by stanza 3, these barely audible murmurs and whispers are amplified into resounding echoes of the swan's lament:

> The wild swan's death-hymn took the soul
> Of that waste place with joy
> Hidden in sorrow: at first to the ear
> The warble was low, and full and clear;
> And floating about the under-sky,
> Prevailing in weakness, the coronach stole
> Sometimes afar, and sometimes anear;
> But anon her awful jubilant voice,
> With a music strange and manifold,
> Flowed forth on a carol free and bold;
> As when a mighty people rejoice
> With shawms, and with cymbals, and harps of gold,
> And the tumult of their acclaim is rolled
> Through the open gates of the city afar,
> To the shepherd who watcheth the evening star.
> And the creeping mosses and clambering weeds,
> And the willow-branches hoar and dank,
> And the wavy swell of the soughing reeds,
> And the wave-worn horns of the echoing bank,

And the silvery marish-flowers that throng
The desolate creeds and pools among,
Were flooded over with eddying song.   (21–42)

While "we have merely had the *fact* of the swan's lament noted" in the first two stanzas, Saintsbury emphasizes that the final stanza simultaneously describes and enacts "the death-song itself" through metrical manipulation: "the metre lengthens, unrolls, is transformed by more and more infusion of the trisyllabic foot, till the actual equivalent of the 'eddying song,' the 'awful jubilant voice,' the 'music strange and manifold,' is attained" (III, 192–93).

With this remark, Saintsbury marks the meter as a necessary condition for hearing the sound of the poem. He notices how the poem gathers momentum from stanza to stanza in tetrameter, with an increasing number of anapestic feet. We can extend this reading of the poem into our own metrical notation. (I will use the following metrical notation: / = stressed syllable, x = unstressed syllable, [ ] = foot boundaries, and || = caesura.) For example, the seemingly despondent spondees in

[x   /] [/   /] [/   /] [x   /]
The wild swan's death - hymn took the soul

give way to trisyllabic rhythms as follows:

[/   x   x] [/   x] [x /   ] [x x   /   ]
Hidden in sorrow: at first to the ear

[x /] [x x   /   ]
The warble was low.

Here dactyls and anapests emerge from the iambic meter to reanimate the lament, rapidly accelerating in the description of the swan's voice:

[x x   /] [x   /] [x /] [x x   /]
But anon her awful jubilant voice,

[x   x /] [x   /   ] [x   /] [x /]
With a music strange and manifold.

The strange music of the second line makes the meter itself seem manifold, as two iambs shade into a dactyl in the word "manifold." This orchestration of manifold meters is conveyed in the description of music that follows,

[x   /   ] [x   x /] [x   x   /   ] [x /]
With shawms, and with cymbals, and harps of gold

and further echoed by nature in a gradual amplification of anapests:

[x   x   /] [x   /] [x x   /   ] [x /   ]
And the wavy swell of the soughing reeds,

[x   x   /] [/   /   ] [x x   /] [x x   /]
And the wave-worn horns of the echoing bank

This musical crescendo has its climax in the final line:

[x   /] [x /] [x   x   /] [x x   /]
Were flooded over with eddying song.

It is through this kind of metrical reading that Saintsbury asks us to find "various forms of 'suiting sound to sense'" hidden in Tennyson's poem (III, 192), just as in Tennyson himself he would find a poet with true "command of sound" (III, 193). Much as the "inner voice" of the river is heard when the "echoing bank" resounds with the song of the dying swan, so also the inner ear is meant to hear the resonance of this strange music in the manifold meters of the poem.

Yet the swan, doomed to die at the very moment of singing her "death-hymn," also serves as allegorical figure for a voice that is no longer heard; the resurrection of song is predicated on its death. Indeed, when Saintsbury introduces "The Dying Swan," he does so in order to resurrect Tennyson himself as "a fresh Phoenix-birth of an English 'poet of the century'" (III, 192) – a poet who rises from the ashes with a new kind of song, giving life to its dying cadences through metrical manipulation. The survival of his poetry depends on the death of a living breathing voice, so it may materialize in written form: an appeal to the inner ear that is mediated by an appeal to the eye. Of course from Saintsbury's late-Victorian perspective, the afterlife of Tennyson as "poet of the century" necessarily presupposes such a death. But even when Tennyson was still alive his poetry was read as a dying cadence.

Arthur Henry Hallam's early review of the 1830 *Poems*, for example, famously praises "the variety of his lyrical measures and exquisite modulation of harmonious words and cadences to the swell and fall of the feelings expressed."[11] The expression of feelings is so exquisitely modulated in Tennyson's poetry that "the understanding takes no definite note of them" but "they leave signatures in language" (194) when the "tone becomes the sign of the feeling" (195). Although the reader takes "no definite note," the modulation of lyrical measures produces "the tone" of which the signature is a metrical *notation*, the reinscription of *notes* as *tones*. Like Saintsbury's later reading of Tennysonian meter, Hallam maintains that "the proportion of melodious cadences" in Tennyson's poetry "could not be diminished without materially affecting the rich lyrical expression" (195); the expression can only materialize through its metrical reinscription, the measuring of the cadence. "A stretch of lyrical power is here exhibited which we did not think the English language had possessed," Hallam proclaims, and his review demonstrates this lyrical range by taking note of the continual rise and fall of tones in Tennyson's poetry, "the soft and melancholy lapse, as the sounds die" (196).

The "stretch of lyrical power" through Tennysonian tones can be understood within the context of nineteenth-century theories of language. As Donald S. Hair points out, Victorian philology associated "tone" (derived from the Greek verb *teino* and the Sanskrit *tan*, to tense or stretch out) with the extension of voice, and the etymology of "cadence" was also common knowledge: "The word is derived from the Latin verb *cadere*, to fall, and refers, strictly speaking, only to the dropping of the voice, but in practice the word refers to the whole rhythmical unit, with its swelling and falling, tensing and relaxing."[12] But if Tennyson's poetry seems to stretch the voice, it does so by extending vocal utterance into rhythm, and rhythm into meter. The cadence of speech falls into measured units before it can be sublimated or uplifted into "voice." Even in reading his own poems aloud Tennyson performed a peculiar kind of voicing, more like a low drone or monotonous chant, according to various auditors. Edward FitzGerald heard the poet reading in "his voice, very deep and deep-chested, but rather murmuring than mouthing," and Aubrey de Vere also describes hearing the poems in "the voice which rather intoned than recited them." While Hair interprets such "ear-witness accounts" as "evidence of the voice's expressive power" (64–65), they also leave the impression of a voice haunted by writing. In his low-voiced "murmuring," Tennyson "intoned" a metrical pattern inscribed in the poem rather than "mouthing" words to be recited in a speaking voice. His recitation was a meticulous reinscription of the meter, which Tennyson considered inadequately voiced in any reading except his own.

Tennyson's "natural" ear for meter was created by extensive metrical training. Like most well-educated boys in Victorian England, he learned to scan Greek and Latin meters by marking the long and short syllables, and later in *A Memoir* he claimed to know the quantity of every word in the English language except "scissors."[13] This double-edged comment ironically holds open and closes down the possibility of writing English poetry based on quantities: How can words be divided and measured when even "scissors" – an instrument for cutting and dividing – is a word that can not be quantified with any measure of certainty? Only a poet with an educated ear should be able to tell the difference between false and true quantities. But in order to transform this seemingly mechanical process of quantification into voice, his ear must also be naturally attuned to the innate music of the English language. Another anecdote in *A Memoir*, recollected by the poet himself at the age of 80, serves as a primal scene for this revelation of voice: "Before I could read, I was in the habit on a stormy day of spreading my arms to the wind and crying out, 'I hear a voice that's speaking in the wind'" (I, 11). The voice is seemingly without origin, as it is heard simultaneously in the sound of the wind and the resounding cry of the child: a moment of inspiration when hearing and speaking seem to converge. The perfect ear coincides with the perfect voice, whose utterance is written in iambic pentameter:

[x /] [x /] [x   /   ] [x /] [x   /   ]
I hear a voice that's speaking in the wind

This reinscription of metrical convention turns the act of "spreading my arms to the wind" into a scene of reading where voice is mediated by meter.[14] Thus Tennyson's anecdote records a voice that proves to be a prior inscription, even if it is remembered as pure inspiration

The memory is included in *A Memoir* because it supposedly inspired Tennyson's earliest poem, a quatrain written around age eight and inserted in the second stanza of a later poem entitled "Whispers."[15] Here again Tennyson recalls "a voice that's speaking in the wind" as whispers that seem to rise and fall without clear articulation:

> Whate'er I see, where'er I move,
> These whispers rise, and fall away,
> Something of pain – of bliss – of Love,
> But what, were hard to say.
> I could not tell it: if I could
> Yet every form of mind is made
> To vary in some light or shade
> So were my tale misunderstood.   (*AT* 9–16)

In lines 9 to 12 (Tennyson's poem from boyhood) a whispering is heard all around. But exactly what these whispers are heard to say proves "hard to say"; they are heard but not understood. The second four lines further suggest that any attempt to "tell" their tale will also be "misunderstood"; neither the wind nor the "I" has a voice to speak.

And yet the poem does "tell" something without saying it, not only in the interplay of rising aspirated rhythms ("Whate'er I see, where'er I move / These whispers rise") and low susurrations ("and fall away, / Something of pain – of bliss – of Love") but also in its careful counting out of the meter. Tennyson's anecdote is reframed in iambic tetrameter, fading into trimeter and echoing in diminished form the iambic pentameter of his earlier outcry. It is as if "I hear" were left out of that pentameter line, leaving only "a voice that's speaking in the wind." This metrical reinscription is both a misunderstanding of the prior utterance and a way of understanding it after all; indeed, since "every form of mind is made / To vary in some light or shade," it is only by varying the form that the poem can retell its tale, not as something heard but as something written. The variation from tetrameter to trimeter in the fourth line is telling because we see the missing foot *without* hearing it; what is missing is difficult to tell, unless we count the space between "but what" and "were hard to say." We seem to find an answer to the question that haunts Saintsbury – how can any poem "tell us what a sound *was?*" – in the telling example of Tennyson's poem: "I could not tell," but "if I could," it would be told by measuring the meter. Thus we come to understand Tennyson's meter not as the transcription of voice but as a form of inscription, where "telling" turns out to be the counting and recounting of metrical marks.

The hexameter mania

The viability of writing verse in classical meters was an ongoing debate, if not an obsession, among poets and prosodists throughout the Victorian period. Not since the sixteenth century had there been as much interest in classical meters in English poetry, with an appeal to educated readers in particular. The quantitative movement in Elizabethan England was influenced by Latin prosody taught in grammar schools, where schoolboys scanned poetry on the model of classical verse: after marking the long and short syllables of a Latin text and dividing lines into feet, they would read it aloud according to the rule that they had memorized. Such techniques of scansion emphasized the intellectual apprehension of durational patterns through the written rather than the spoken word, as Derek Attridge has argued in further detail: Elizabethan verse in classical meters tried to move "away from any conception of metre as a rhythmic succession of sounds, akin to the beat of the ballad-monger or the thumping of a drum" toward an abstract mathematized order "where words [were] anatomised and charted with a precision and a certainty unknown in the crude vernacular."[16] This transformation of the vernacular proved unpopular (by definition) until the nineteenth century, when poets returned with new enthusiasm to the transformation of classical meters into a popular form.

If sixteenth-century experiments attempted to classicize English verse by removing it from the vernacular, then Victorian experiments had the reverse effect of popularizing classical meter by drawing it closer to the vernacular. While Elizabethan verse in classical meters was primarily modeled on Latin prosody, Victorian prosody increasingly turned to Greek models, especially Homeric hexameter (a six-beat line written mostly in dactyls). With the proliferation of nineteenth-century translations of Homer's *Iliad* and *Odyssey*, the idea of reviving dactylic hexameter became a popular ideal – so popular that Saintsbury devotes an entire chapter to "The Later English Hexameter and The Discussions On It." He does not take a favorable view, however, of "the battle of the hexameter" that dominated early Victorian metrical theory (III, 173), and subsequently developed into "the hexameter mania in the middle of the century" (III, 207). His chapter is a long tirade against "English Quantity-Mongers" (III, 411) and "classicalisers" (III, 422), who introduce quantities that are difficult to measure or hear in English. "With the self-styled quantitative hexameter you must either have a new pronunciation, or a mere ruinous and *arrhythmic* heap of words," writes Saintsbury (III, 400). His own unspoken ambivalence about the problem of pronouncing meter is intensified by the question of quantitative verse, and he therefore dismisses the recreation of Homeric hexameters in English as an experiment "reinforcing lack of ear" and "foredoomed to failure" (III, 415).

Even Tennyson seems doomed to fail in writing a hexameter couplet, as quoted by Saintsbury: "These lame hexameters the strong-winged music of Homer? / No, but a most burlesque, barbarous experiment." The syllables must be forced into improper pronunciation to make the quantities audible, according to Saintsbury: "you have to pronounce, in a quite unnatural way, 'experime*nnnnnnt*,' 'hexamete*rrrrr*'" (III, 421). Of course the poetic success of Tennyson's hexameter couplet is measured precisely by that apparent failure of pronunciation. But Saintsbury takes Tennyson at his word. Quantitative versification is a "barbarous experiment" that reduces syllables to meaningless sounds, rebarbarizing the English tongue by forcing it into an "unnatural" composition, derived from a dead language that is taught in schools but no longer spoken. To emphasize that scanning ancient Greek is not the same as reading English verse, Saintsbury scans the phrase "dons, undergraduates" and ironically points to the difficulty of pronouncing "unde*rrr*graduate" according to antiquated rules of quantity – an instructive academic exercise for dons and undergraduates, perhaps, but too artificial for those of us ready to graduate from metrical instruction and begin reading English verse on its own terms. "Our business is with English;" Saintsbury insists, "And I repeat that, *in English*, there are practically no metrical fictions, and that metre follows, though it may sometimes slightly force, pronunciation" (III, 434–35).[17]

But if, as Saintsbury concedes, pronunciation may (and even must) be forced by the meter "sometimes," the widespread reinvention of dactylic hexameter in the nineteenth century shows to what degree this metrical fiction can be naturalized in English, and was already circulating as a popular idiom. Indeed, the popularity of English hexameters makes it increasingly difficult to distinguish between reading meter as a sign of advanced literacy or as a sign for common literacy. Early in the century Robert Southey caused controversy with his defense of dactylic hexameters in *The Vision of Judgment* (1821), and by the 1840s the conversion of quantitative into accentual hexameter – in which quantity is made to coincide with a pattern of accents, or is replaced by stressed syllables – became increasingly common, as in Henry Wadsworth Longfellow's *Evangeline* (1847) and Clough's *The Bothie* (1848). Saintsbury is suspicious of both these efforts in hexameter, albeit for different reasons. He first acknowledges "the distinct popular success" of *Evangeline*, if only as an appeal to "popular taste" that is "cheap enough" (III, 404), and then remarks how "its marked singsong is a quality which undoubtedly appeals more to untrained ears" (III, 406). By contrast, he considers Clough's attempt to retrain the ear of the reader to be lacking in melody. While the American popular prosody of Longfellow seems too smooth, the manipulation of meter by Clough is too rough, and too much like prose (III, 408–09).

An assessment of Clough's hexameters as rough, irregular, and prosaic is not unusual among his critics. Even the headnote to *The Bothie* encourages such a reading: "The reader is warned to expect every kind of irregularity in these modern hexameters: spondaic lines, so called, are almost the rule; and a word will often require to be transposed by the voice from the end of one line to the beginning of the next."[18] Combining the conventions of classical epic with more conversational rhythms of speech in *The Bothie*, Clough asks the reader to mediate between what is written and what is spoken. Words must be "transposed by the voice" to make the meter of his poem audible. Yet this assumption of "voice" also depends on scanning the lines visually. His "modern hexameters" move beyond an imitation of classical meter, however, by breaking the rules of scansion that educated readers have been taught to expect. Instead, the reader must expect the unexpected. In a detailed analysis of Clough's "radical metre" in *The Bothie*, Joseph Patrick Phelan traces the early outlines of a radically innovative theory of musical prosody: "a new and essentially musical understanding of the hexameter as a series of 'isochronous intervals' between accents, intervals which can be filled with words or pauses and which can span written line-endings."[19] Placing Clough within the context of scholarly debates about classical prosody in the 1840s and 1850s, Phelan demonstrates how traditional modes of reading Greek and Latin prevent Clough's critics from understanding his English hexameters. Further, he argues that the metrical innovations of *The Bothie* should be understood in the broader social context of nineteenth-century university reform. Written just after Clough left Oxford, his poem is a critique (in its metrical form as well as its narrative content) of Oxford's narrowly traditional approach to the Classics.

Thus, although Clough can certainly be counted among those "dons, undergraduates" trained to scan classical meters, *The Bothie* reflects quite self-consciously on the remaking of its own metrical form. The poem narrates "A Long-Vacation Pastoral" of a group of Oxford students, led by their Tutor on a pastoral retreat to Scotland, and begins with a reflection on the formal appearance of each character, dressed for dinner like epic warriors armed for battle. The introduction of the Tutor in particular suggests how self-consciously tutored the writing of this poem will be:

> Still more plain the Tutor, the grave man, nicknamed Adam,
> White-tied, clerical, silent, with antique square-cut waistcoat
> Formal, unchanged, of black cloth, but with sense and feeling beneath it;
> Skilful in Ethics and Logic, in Pindar and Poets unrivalled;
> *Shady* in Latin, said Lindsay, but *topping* in Plays and Aldrich.
>
> (*AHC* I. 20–24)

The Tutor's style of dress suits the style of the poem, measured out in "antique, square-cut" hexameter that may appear "formal, unchanged" to the eye at first but "with sense and feeling beneath it." The appearance of the Tutor, like the seemingly traditional use of meter in *The Bothie*, is animated by "skilful" exercise of intellect: "Skilful in Ethics and Logic, in Pindar and Poets unrivalled" – a perfect line in dactylic hexameter to emphasize the performance of poetic skill. But if the Tutor has mastered the meters of Pindar in Greek (quite a feat), he remains not so well-versed in Latin, as we learn in the next line, where the elevated formal diction falls into a colloquialism, "*Shady* in Latin." The ideal model for Clough's hexameters is ancient Greek, it would seem, but the combination of formal and informal language in the poem, along with its "irregular" deployment of metrical rules, produce a more hybrid and heterogeneous form, illuminated by Greek but also shadowed by Latin.

To convey the range of Clough's modern hexameters, different characters embody different ways of speaking in hexameter. Indeed, in presenting these various "voices" mediated by the meter, the poem often seems to allegorize its own metrical effects. The metrical mediation of voice is most fully developed in the central character of "Hewson, the chartist, the poet, the eloquent speaker" (II. 19), otherwise known as "Philip who speaks like a book" (II. 158). In contrast to other students in his cohort, his speech is smoothly modulated in perfect dactylic hexameters, as he effortlessly enumerates the ancient Greek authors who have taught him to speak in this way:

```
[ /    x  x] [ /   x   x] [ /    x    x] [ / x x ] [ /    x   x ] [ / / ]
```
Aeschylus, Sophocles, Homer, Herodotus, Pindar, and Plato.

(II. 289)

But he is eager to take a vacation from books and proclaims himself ready to pursue new paths, untrodden by familiar feet: "Weary of reading am I, and weary of walks prescribed us" (II. 304). In the winding course of the narrative, as Philip ventures into the Highlands where he will discover his bride, the hexameters seemingly "prescribed" by classical convention also change their course. Here the poem begins to project another kind of metrical allegory into the landscape, self-consciously naturalizing the formal mechanism of its verse.

In Book III of *The Bothie*, for example, we encounter the detailed description of a stream that flows through the Highlands and leads the students to a swimming hole:

> Springing far off from a loch unexplored in the folds of great mountains,
> Falling two miles through rowan and stunted alder, enveloped
> Then for four more in a forest of pine, where broad and ample
> Spreads, to convey it, the glen with heathery slopes on both sides:
> Broad and fair the stream, with occasional falls and narrows;
> But, where the lateral glen approaches the vale of the river,
> Met and blocked by a huge interposing mass of granite,
> Scarce by a channel deep-cut, raging up, and raging onward,
> Forces its flood through a passage, so narrow, a lady would step it.

(III. 21–29)

The stream running down from distant mountains corresponds to the movement of the verse, as it streams along in one continuous sentence, "springing far off" in the first line, "falling two miles" in the second line and "four more" in the next four lines, moving laterally across each line and ever downward, until it is forced along a channel "deep-cut." Here we see a caesura, a mid-line pause in the comma after "cut" that literally cuts the line in two and redirects the flow of language:

```
[ /    x  x] [ /   x   x  ] [ /   | |
```
Scarce by a channel deep-cut

This strong masculine caesura (so designated because it comes after the accented syllable of the third foot) is followed by a double feminine caesura (a weaker pause, placed after unaccented syllables) in the next line:

[/ x x] [/   x   x] [/ x || x] [/ x ||x][/ x x   ][/ x]
Forces its flood through a passage, so narrow, a lady would step it

This formal play with caesuras recreates a narrow passage across the water, a lady's foot-crossing over the final trochee ("step it") where the turbulent dactyls subside briefly enough for us to cross to the next line.

The meter gathers momentum by running along in such variable feet, "with occasional falls and narrows," and even when "met and blocked" by interposing caesuras, it continues "raging up, and raging onward" with greater rapidity. The words that flow so rapidly through the hexameter lines of the poem are thus rediscovered in the natural landscape, and assimilated into the larger flow of the poem itself. This cascading verse leads to a waterfall where the water "frees itself" for a moment, as it falls into a self-mirroring pool that is measured yet again in feet:

> But in the interval here the boiling, pent-up water
> Frees itself by a final descent, attaining a basin
> Ten feet wide and eighteen long, with whiteness and fury
> Occupied partly, but mostly pellucid, pure, a mirror.   (III. 34–37)

The poem artfully reflects on its own naturalization of meter, "in the interval here," where the water and the meter seem a reflection of each other. It also reflects further on some of the metrical effects Clough learned from Longfellow, whose hexameters he admired: "Mr. Longfellow has gained, and has charmed, has instructed in some degree, and attuned the ears of his countrymen and countrywomen . . . upon both sides of the Atlantic, to the flow and cadence of this hitherto unacceptable measure."[20] Longfellow's flowing cadences are recreated by Clough in the stream of his own verse, and it is possible to read the stream flowing "in a forest of pine" in *The Bothie* as a reflection on the famous opening line in *Evangeline* – "This is the forest primeval. The murmuring pines and the hemlocks."[21] Like Longfellow, Clough manipulates the caesura within each line, and enjambment between lines, to create a sense of continual flow through measured interruption.

But although Clough claims to have imitated Longfellow in *The Bothie* – "it was a reading of his Evangeline aloud . . . which, coming after a reperusal of the Iliad, occasioned this outbreak of hexameters"[22] – he also breaks out of Longfellow's influence through the "irregularity" of his own modern hexameters. Just as Clough's stream emerges from the pine forest into a space "where broad and ample / Spreads, to convey it, the glen," Clough's hexameters are conveyed with a broader and more ample sense of boundaries. Like the course of his stream with "slopes on both sides: / broad and fair," his line endings can be transposed by the voice to the next line and read metrically on "both sides" of the hexameter. Here Clough extends Longfellow's hexameters in a new direction. Indeed, as Phelan argues, his most radical metrical innovation is a musical understanding of hexameter as an eight-foot line, in which the caesura and the line-end pause are counted as suppressed feet. These silent intervals are measured as "empty time" that is "theoretically and temporally equivalent to the 'full times' of the line itself, and could, therefore on occasion simply be 'filled in' without destroying the essential rhythm of the line" (180). This is the effect conveyed in the cadence of Clough's stream, "enveloped" in a meter associated with Longfellow but further amplified and broadened by Clough.

Simultaneously describing and enacting the hexameters in which the story is told, *The Bothie* therefore tells multiple allegories of its own metrical making. Subtitled "A Long-Vacation Pastoral," the poem recounts a time away from formal instruction in classical meters, yet during this interval it is continually marking forms of measurement, duration, calculation, and enumeration: times of day, days of the week, months of the calendar, numbers of people, catalogues of places, lists of names, length and width of objects, dimensions of space, all formalized into abstract quantities. The evolution of English hexameters beyond Longfellow and Clough increasingly revolves around this imperative to quantification, a search for mechanisms to measure intervals of space and time as interchangeable, vacated forms. In this respect the highly specialized hexameter debates among nineteenth-century poets and prosodists are part of a larger cultural pattern in Victorian England, a turn toward abstraction that subordinates other definitions of value to quantification and increasingly formalizes the trope of counting.

Fancy prosody

The formalization of metrical theory coincides with a general nineteenth-century tendency toward the codification of numerical modes of analysis and the production of abstract space, which Mary Poovey has discussed in detail.[23] It also corresponds more specifically to the convergence of economic and literary formalisms later in the century, as described by Regenia Gagnier. Gagnier traces a revolution in economic theory in the 1870s that leads to the abstraction of value on a quasi-mathematical model, and she further argues that this transformation of economics into a quantifying science runs parallel to a shift in aesthetics, where the quality of aesthetic experience is quantified through increasingly subtle discriminations of taste. In Gagnier's argument, Walter Pater exemplifies the convergence of "economic" and "aesthetic" man. He begins his "Preface" to *Studies in the History of the Renaissance* (1873) with a demand for quantification – "discriminating between what is more or less" – and concludes his book with another impulse to quantify, in his famous dictum to "get as many pulsations as possible into the given time."[24] I would add that this should also be understood as a metrical impulse. Although Pater measures out his own cadences in prose, he appears to be rearticulating ideas about meter that he learned at Oxford during the 1860s: the years of his classical training and no doubt his initiation into heated debates about the New Prosody. That decade was a significant turning point for Victorian metrical theory, when meter was being theorized as a principle of spacing that is mentally perceived or internally "felt" as an abstract form, rather than heard.

An early and influential example of this abstraction of meter is Patmore's "Essay on English Metrical Law." First published in 1857, it circulated in different versions for several decades and contributed to the emergence of the New Prosody in Victorian England, both in theory and in practice.[25] Patmore defines English meter as "the function of marking, *by whatever means*, certain isochronous intervals." He adds that "*the fact of that division shall be made manifest* by an 'ictus' or 'beat,' actual or mental, which, like a post in a chain railing, shall mark the end of one space and the commencement of another" (15). The conflation of temporal and spatial measurement allows Patmore to understand meter as the demarcation of space *between* dividing marks, which can be either "actual" or "mental," and he stresses that this division into equal spaces can be marked "*by whatever means*." But he goes on to emphasize that meter is best understood as an imaginary mark: "*it has no material and external existence at all*, but has its place in the mind, which craves measure in everything, and, wherever the idea of measure is uncontradicted, delights in marking it with an imaginary 'beat.'" (15). The perception of such mental spaces is independent of actual pronunciation; it is an "idea of measure" that can be abstractly schematized and quantified, because "the mind . . . craves measure in everything."

The New Prosody combines this philosophical idea of meter with a desire for ever more complex measures, a "craving" that coincides with the insatiable desires produced by fin-de-siècle formal aesthetics. Thus Saintsbury comments on "the *polymetric* character of the century" (III, 317), as he surveys the ongoing multiplication of meters in several generations of poets who follow Patmore in developing their own, increasingly intricate, variations on prosody. Patmore's essay was avidly read and discussed among the Pre-Raphaelites, and critics have noted his later influence on the metrical experiments of Gerard Manley Hopkins, Thomas Hardy, and Yeats.[26] Even the tour-de-force of meters in Swinburne's *Poems and Ballads* (1866) can be read as a virtuosic elaboration of Patmore's principles. Although Patmore maintains that "the language should always seem to *feel*, though not to *suffer* from the bonds of verse" (8), Swinburne's poems are made to both feel *and* suffer those bonds as the articulation of an exquisitely painful desire. The rhythmic beating of the body in "Anactoria" and the pangs of pain in "Dolores" – to name just two poems from this notorious volume – anticipate the economizing aestheticism of Pater by getting in as many pulsations as possible in the given time. Indeed, throughout *Poems and Ballads* Swinburne seems to take pleasure in inventing infinitely varied ways to perform his subjection to English metrical law. "The variety and the individuality of the construction of these measures becomes almost bewildering, though every one of them responds, with utmost accuracy, to the laws," Saintsbury writes in awe of Swinburne (III, 342).

In Saintsbury's survey of the New Prosody, Christina Rossetti emerges as another important figure. "Pages would not suffice for a full analysis of her infinite variety," Saintsbury concludes, in a treatment of her poetry that follows immediately after his discussion of Swinburne. He ranks her alongside Swinburne in metrical virtuosity: "On the whole, late nineteenth-century prosody has hardly, on the formal side, a more characteristic and more gifted exponent than Christina Rossetti" (III, 358–59). If Swinburne's metrical virtuosity anticipates the convergence of economic and aesthetic man, then Rossetti's manipulation of meter marks the convergence of economic and aesthetic woman as well. Her wide metrical range is evident in "Goblin Market" (1862) – "the more the metre is studied, the more audacious may the composition seem," Saintsbury notes (III, 354) – as it produces various discriminations of value that correspond thematically to the logic of the marketplace. In this way her poem meditates on the production of insatiable desires, not only in its content but also through its very form. The wide range of lyrics in Christina Rossetti's *Goblin Market and Other Poems* can thus be understood – like Swinburne's *Poems and Ballads*, published not long after Patmore's essay first began to circulate – as a poet's response to current ideas about prosody. From this decade onward we see the emergence of "fancy prosodies," invoked by Saintsbury to describe the metrical complications of poems in which "*various* scansions of the same line and piece present themselves" (III, 475).

In "Winter: My Secret," for example, Rossetti playfully responds to new ways of telling meter by refusing to "tell" a secret:

> I tell my secret? No indeed, not I:
> Perhaps some day, who knows?
> But not today: it froze, and blows, and snows,
> And you're too curious: fie!
> You want to hear it? well:
> Only, my secret's mine, and I won't tell.   (CR 1–6)

Throughout the poem, the existence of the secret remains ambiguous and its content uncertain. Indeed, in the manuscript version of the poem, an empty space serves as a placeholder for the very word "secret": "Only my < > mine . . ." Even while the poem holds forth on the secret, it therefore withholds it as well:

> Or, after all, perhaps there's none:
> Suppose there is no secret after all,
> But only just my fun.   (7–9)

Here again a word is missing from the manuscript: "Or after all perhaps < > none." Perhaps there is no "there" there. Perhaps Rossetti is playing with the idea of an empty space, asking us to fill in the blank by imaginary measures, by measuring the mental spaces of an abstract metrical form which (as Patmore asserts) *"has no material and external existence at all, but has its place in the mind."*

Perhaps, then, the puzzle of Rossetti's poem can be solved metrically by counting the number of accents per line. At first the poem seems to lack a clear pattern, since the accents vary in lines that expand from four to five accents, or contract from four to three, as in the following enumeration of months:

> Spring's an expansive time: yet I don't trust
> March with its peck of dust,
> Nor April with its rainbow-crowned brief showers,
> Nor even May, whose flowers
> One frost may wither thro' the sunless hours.   (23–27)

The variable number of accents is reminiscent of *The Shepherd's Calendar* of Edmund Spenser, who also measures out each month in different meters. In fact, the metrical pattern that emerges in Rossetti's poem is associated with the month of February, written by Spenser in an ambiguous meter that prompted debates among nineteenth-century prosodists: a loosely constructed four-beat line, sometimes verging on iambic pentameter. Guest, for example, singles out the February eclogue of Spenser as an example of "tumbling verses" which "generally have four accents . . . but they sometimes take three or five accents, and the rhythm shifts, accordingly, to the triple or to the common measure" (535). Rossetti replays this ambiguity throughout her own poem, where two metrical norms are juxtaposed from one line to the next, and even superimposed within lines that can be scanned simultaneously as pentameter or tetrameter. "Nor April with its rainbow-crowned brief showers" allows for various scansions (depending on how briefly we scan "brief"). It thus exemplifies what Saintsbury calls "fancy prosody." If this metrical tale sounds too fanciful to be true, then it is nevertheless prompted by the final lines of the poem, where the reader is invited to speculate: "Perhaps my secret I may say, / Or you may guess." The secret, it would seem, is that the month of February has been speaking all along. What "I may say" and "you may guess" may not be spoken, but can be told in the meter. In other words, what speaks here is neither a person nor a voice but a temporal unit, an "I" measured by the calendar and spatialized in a series of metrical marks.

The examples I have chosen reverse Matthew Campbell's argument about rhythm and will in Victorian poetry, in so far as these forms of metrical writing run contrary to "the performance of speech in verse" and "the dramatic representation of human agency in verse" that prove central to Campbell's readings of Victorian poetry (63). A different selection of Victorian poets (or a selection of different poems by the same poets) can serve to illustrate how the formulation of meter also has the effect of suspending the "rhythm of will," especially if this is figured as the purpose, intention, determination, or agency of a speaker. Following my brief account of Victorian meters, we can read Victorian poetry not only as the dramatic representation of voice in verse, but also as its reversal: the writing of voice, inverse. Reading poems by Tennyson, Clough, and Christina Rossetti alongside Victorian theories of meter, I have argued that the poetry and prosody of the period are mutually implicated in an ongoing effort to mediate between enunciation and enumeration, between two different ways of "telling" meter. If lyric poetry as a genre is marked by the counting and recounting of utterance, then what distinguishes Victorian poetry is both the self-conscious reinscription of the marking function and a heightened consciousness about the metrical mediation of voice. The claim to voice may seem a contradictory impulse in Victorian metrical theory, where meter is understood to be a formal mechanism as well as an organic form, simultaneously "artificial" and "natural" in graphing the rhythms of English as it is (no longer) spoken. Nevertheless this proves a productive contradiction for nineteenth-century discourses on meter, as these proliferate with increasing variety and complexity in articulating – in theory and in practice – the materiality of language.

Rather than assuming a transhistorical definition of meter, or presuming an ahistorical grammar for metrical analysis, I have placed Victorian debates about meter within their own historical context in order to emphasize the cultural significance of formalist reading. Herbert F. Tucker has recently called for such an approach to Victorian poetry, concluding that "the theory of such a cultural neoformalism has yet to be written."[27] I would conclude that its history has already been written in Victorian metrical theory, and is yet to be read. By reading Victorian meters, we can develop a theoretical perspective on lyric voice, and a historical perspective on the analysis of form; we can understand the relevance of metrical debates to the formation of national identity and histories of the nation; we can interrogate the formal instruction of the English ear, the reconstruction of classical traditions, and the construction of a vernacular idiom in nineteenth-century England; we can trace the quantification of value, the abstraction of form, and the engendering of aesthetics; and so, in short or at length, can go on enumerating why, and how much, Victorian meters count.

NOTES

1 Edwin Guest, *A History of English Rhythms: A New Edition, Edited by Walter W. Skeat* (London: George Bell, 1882); further page references appear in parentheses. George Saintsbury, *A History of English Prosody, from the Twelfth Century to the Present Day*, second edition, 3 vols. (London: Macmillan, 1923); volume and page references appear in parentheses. For twentieth-century surveys of Victorian metrical theory, see T.S. Omond, *English Metrists* (Oxford: Oxford University Press, 1921) and the section on nineteenth-century prosody in T.V.F. Brogan, *English Versification, 1570–1980* (Baltimore, MD: Johns Hopkins University Press, 1981).

2 Thus, for example, W.K. Wimsatt introduces *Versification: Major Language Types* (New York: New York University Press, 1972) with the assertion that traditional prosody has been "pre-empted by modern linguistics" (xix). For a lucid survey of metrical analysis ranging from traditional approaches ("classical" and "temporal") to linguistic approaches ("phonemic" and "generative"), see Derek Attridge, *The Rhythms of English Poetry* (Harlow: Longman, 1982). For a guide to foot scansion and glossary of terms, see Timothy Steele, *All the Fun's in How You Say a Thing: An Explanation of Meter and Versification* (Athens, OH: Ohio University Press, 1999).

3 John Hollander, *Vision and Resonance: Two Senses of Poetic Form*, second edition (New Haven, CT: Yale University Press, 1985), 19; further page reference appears in parentheses.

4 Coventry Patmore, *Essay on English Metrical Law: A Critical Edition with a Commentary*, ed. Sister Mary Roth (Washington, DC: Catholic University of America Press, 1961), 15; further page references appear in parentheses.

5 Edwin A. Abbott and J.R. Seeley, "Meter," in *English Lessons for English People* (London: Selley, Jackson, and Halliday, 1871), 144.

6 William Wordsworth, 1802 '"Preface" to *Lyrical Ballads*, in *The Prose Works of William Wordsworth*, ed. W.J.B. Owen and Jane Worthington Smyser, 3 vols. (Oxford: Clarendon Press, 1974), I, 146.

7 Wordsworth, "Preface of 1815," in *The Prose Works of William Wordsworth*, III, 29–30.

8 Eric Griffths, *The Printed Voice of Victorian Poetry* (Oxford: Oxford University Press, 1989), 73; further page references appear in parentheses.

9 Matthew Campbell, *Rhythm and Will in Victorian Poetry* (Cambridge: Cambridge University Press, 1999), 48, further page reference appears in parentheses; Dennis Taylor, *Hardy's Metres and Victorian Prosody* (Oxford: Clarendon Press, 1988).

10 On this topic, see John Lucas, "Voices of Authority, Voices of Subversion: Poetry in the Late Nineteenth Century," in this volume, 280–301.

11 [Arthur Henry Hallam,] "On Some Characteristics of Modern Poetry," *Englishman's Magazine* 1 (1831), 616–28, reprinted in *The Writings of Arthur Hallam*, ed. T.H. Vail Motter (New York: MLA, 1943), 192; further page references appear in parentheses.

12 Donald S. Hair, *Tennyson's Language* (Toronto: University of Toronto Press, 1991), 61–62; further page reference appears in parentheses.

13 Hallam Tennyson, *Alfred Lord Tennyson: A Memoir by His Son*, 2 vols. (London: Macmillan, 1897), II, 231; further volume and page reference appears in parentheses.

14 Herbert F. Tucker notes the iambic pentameter in *Tennyson and the Doom of Romanticism* (Cambridge, MA: Harvard University Press, 1988), 40. Matthew Rowlinson meditates further on the metricality of the child's cry, as it encodes a rhythm and records a voice whose origins remain uncertain, in *Tennyson's Fixations: Psychoanalysis and the Topics of the Early Poetry* (Charlottesville, VA: University Press of Virginia, 1994), 13.

15 "Whispers" is dated 1833, and published only partially in *A Memoir*; the entire poem is reassembled from manuscript by Ricks in *The Poems of Tennyson*, I, 609.

16 Derek Attridge, *Well-Weigh'd Syllables: Elizabethan Verse in Classical Metres* (Cambridge: Cambridge University Press, 1974), 77–78.

17 Saintsbury excerpts the phrase "dons, undergraduates" from the verse introduction to C.B. Cayley's 1877 translation of Homer: "Dons, undergraduates, essayists, and public, I ask you, / Are these hexameters true-timed, or Klopstockish uproar?" Saintsbury's response to this rhetorical question is a staunch refusal of quantitative scansion, for to do so "is to speak a language that is not English" (III, 411–12).

18 Arthur Hugh Clough, *The Bothie*, ed. Patrick Scott (St. Lucia: University of Queensland Press, 1976), 4. Quotations are taken from the original 1848 text printed in this edition, published under the title *The Bothie of Toper-na-Fuosich: A Long-Vacation Pastoral*; line references appear in parentheses. The title of Clough's poem was subsequently changed to *The Bothie of Tober-na-Vuolich*, and portions of the text were revised for an edition of Clough's collected poetry in 1859.

19 Joseph Patrick Phelan, "Radical Metre: The English Hexameter in Clough's *Bothie of Toper-na-Fuosich*," *Review of English Studies* 50 (1999), 167. Phelan also focuses on the 1848 version of the poem in order to emphasize the radical metrical innovations made by Clough, before he revised his hexameters into a less irregular, more "orthodox," form.

20 Clough, "Two Letters of Parepidemus," in *The Poems and Prose Remains of*

Arthur Hugh Clough, ed. Blanche Clough, 2 vols. (London: Macmillan, 1869), I, 397; this article first appeared in *Putnam's Magazine* 2 (1853), 72–74 and 138–40.

21 Longfellow, "Evangeline: A Tale of Acadie," in *The Works of Henry Wadsworth Longfellow*, ed. Samuel Longfellow, 14 vols. (Boston, MA: Houghton Mifflin, 1886), II, 19.

22 Clough, "To R.W. Emerson," February 10, 1849, in *The Correspondence of Arthur Hugh Clough*, ed. Frederick L. Mulhauser, 2 vols. (Oxford: Clarendon Press, 1957), I, 240–41.

23 On this topic, see especially chapter 2 in Mary Poovey, *Making a Social Body: British Cultural Formation, 1830–1864* (Chicago, IL: University of Chicago Press, 1995), 25–54.

24 Regenia Gagnier, "Is Market Society the *Fin* of History?" in *Cultural Politics at the Fin de Siècle*, ed. Sally Ledger and Scott McCracken (Cambridge: Cambridge University Press, 1995), 298–99. Regenia Gagnier elaborates in more detail the example of Pater in "On the Insatiability of Human Wants: Economic and Aesthetic Man," *Victorian Studies* 36 (1993), 145–46.

25 In Omond's survey of *English Metrists*, the New Prosody is inaugurated by Patmore (171). Patmore's essay first appeared as a review of "English Metrical Critics," *North British Review* 27 (1857), 127–61, and was subsequently revised as "Prefatory Study on English Metrical Law," in *Poems*, 4 vols. (London: George Bell, 1870), I, 3–85; it was revised again as "English Metrical Law" in *Poems*, second collective edition, 2 vols. (London: George Bell, 1886), II, 217–67, and widely read in subsequent editions.

26 Dennis Taylor offers an excellent overview of Patmore's influence on the New Prosody in *Hardy's Metres and Victorian Prosody* 8–42; see also Margaret Stobie, "Patmore's Theory and Hopkins' Practice," *University of Toronto Quarterly* 19 (1949), 64–80; Matthew Campbell, *Rhythm and Will in Victorian Poetry*, 226–27.

27 Herbert F. Tucker, "Introduction," in *Critical Essays on Alfred Lord Tennyson*, ed. Tucker (New York: G.K. Hall, 1993), 8. Tucker further elaborates the claims of formalist reading in "The Fix on Form: An Open Letter," *Victorian Literature and Culture* 27 (1999), 531–35.

6

HILARY FRASER

Victorian poetry and historicism

I

"A poet in our times is a semi-barbarian in a civilized community," announced Thomas Love Peacock in his satirically anti-Romantic essay "The Four Ages of Poetry" (1820),[1] an essay whose vocabulary anticipates Matthew Arnold in the 1860s but which in fact takes a position quite antithetical to that of the later apostle of Culture and Hellenism. "He lives in the days that are past," writes Peacock. "The march of his intellect is like that of a crab, backward" (21–22). Mischievously appropriating the standard historicist idea of the four ages that originally derives from the Greek poet Hesiod (8th century BC) who charts the decline of a golden age in *Works and Days*. Peacock derisively consigns modern poetry to the age of brass. He claims that the poets of his own time "wallow . . . in the rubbish of departed ignorance," parasitically weaving "disjointed relics of tradition and fragments of second hand observation" into "a modern-antique compound of frippery and barbarism, in which the puling sentimentality of the present time is grafted on the misrepresented rugged-ness of the past into a heterogeneous congeries of unamalgamating manners" (19–20). Peacock exhorts the modern reader to eschew such "artificial reconstructions of a few morbid ascetics in unpoetical times" (18) in favor of the genuine item, and thus "that egregious confraternity of rhymesters, known by the name of the Lake Poets" (18) is peremptorily dismissed.

Peacock's early-nineteenth-century view of the brassy attempts of modern poetry to emulate the golden age of literature underlines the obvious point that the Victorians were by no means the first to turn to the past for a kind of poetic authenticity felt to be lacking in the present time. Yet, as the nineteenth century wore on, that precious commodity poetry was to become more tarnished still by its persistent traffic in history. The use of the past was to grow both more self-consciously theorized and more diverse in ways that were distinct from earlier forms of historicism – including that so wickedly satirized by Peacock. This chapter explores the range and eclecticism of Victorian historicism, the cultural and ideological uses to which history was put, and the representational forms that it assumed in the poetry and poetics of the period. My discussion concentrates on the most popular touchstones for the nineteenth century: Ancient Greece, the Middle Ages, and the Renaissance. Yet I do not wish to suggest too fixed and over-schematized a picture of Victorian attitudes to – as well as reconstructions of – the past. Tastes and enthusiasms were constantly undergoing revaluation. We need to recognize that historicism itself was subject to the movement of history. The literary production of Hellenism, medievalism, and the idea of the Renaissance in Victorian England was based on dynamic and contested, and in some respects competing, cultural concepts.

History was ubiquitous in Victorian cultural and intellectual life. It did not confine itself to the museum or the chronicle but found expression in the art, architecture, and literature of the period, just as it did in the political treatise and the religious tract. As A. Dwight Culler has demonstrated: "the great Victorian debate about science, religion, art, and culture always had a historical dimension, always was concerned with the relation of the present to the past."[2] While the study of history became increasingly professionalized during the Victorian era,[3] instilling a new respect for the integrity – indeed, the difference – of the past, there was nevertheless a strong sense of the connections between antiquity and modernity. Victorian intellectuals viewed history as a continuum. They researched the suggestive significance of past events and past cultures to understand the most pressing intellectual and personal concerns of the present. In 1831 John Stuart Mill observed in the "Spirit of the Age" that the Victorians' desire to locate themselves in history was a novel phenomenon: "The idea of comparing one's own age with former ages, or with our notion of those which are to come, had occurred to philosophers; but it never before was itself the dominant idea of any age."[4] Similarly, in 1843 the influential historian and cultural critic Thomas Carlyle claimed that the purpose and value of writing about the past was to "illustrate the Present and the Future."[5] Comparisons between past and present could reflect well on a modern world seen, according to the Whig view of history, to have progressed toward a more advanced state of civilization. But the Victorians by no means always felt that their contemporary age was superior to that of previous generations.

Certainly, the imagined pre-industrial past evident in some Victorian writing provides escape from the ugliness of modern life. Take, for example, how William Morris begins the prologue to *The Earthly Paradise*

(1868–70), a poem consisting of twenty-four tales on classical and medieval – especially Norse – subjects:

> Forget six counties overhung with smoke,
> Forget the snorting steam and piston stroke,
> Forget the spreading of the hideous town;
> Think rather of the pack-horse on the down,
> And dream of London, small, and white, and clean,
> The clear Thames bordered by its gardens green. (WM III, 3)

Yet, in a style notable at once for its directness and indirection, Morris's historicist poetry performs a complex balancing-act between aesthetic displacement and transformational socialist engagement. Where his epic poems such as *The Earthly Paradise* retreat into the past, his later prose romances *The Dream of John Ball* (1888) and *News from Nowhere* (1890) project into a utopian future – as part of a larger political vision.

It was not, then, generally mere nostalgia for a pre-industrial golden age that impelled the Victorians' historicist turn. The strategic uses of history in the nineteenth century were manifold. For a newly empowered yet still insecure middle class seeking cultural and ideological as well as economic and political definition, history could serve as a means of legitimacy, conferring respectability by offering a lineage that connected the modern bourgeoisie to such persons as Italian Renaissance merchant princes and patrons. For a nation conscious of its role on the world stage, history provided moral lessons and political guidance in the form of parallels and precedents. And for an age that was self-consciously modern, it offered insights into the very meaning of modernity. Articulated in the full range of artistic forms, the past was always and inevitably imbricated in the very textures of Victorian ideology. Further, Victorian representations of the past, as of everything else, are notable for their ideological instability. On the one hand, John Ruskin's Gothic cathedral epitomized the pre-capitalist order at the same time as it promoted the decidedly bourgeois ideals of personal freedom and individuality. On the other hand, Morris's neo-medieval furnishings were conceived in homage to the creativity of the pre-industrial craft worker yet their production paradoxically involved laborious, repetitive, and highly regulated techniques, and they were soon to become synonymous with the very elitist aesthetic that Morris ostensibly despised.

Victorian critics and readers themselves were hardly naive interpreters of historical poetry, novels and paintings, any more than they were of historical treatises. Victorian commentators were acutely aware of the varieties of classicism and medievalism displayed among contemporary poets, just as they were alert to the mediating role of the poet, together with the stylistic and cultural differences between the modern historicist poem and its putative model from the past. By contrast, late-twentieth-century readers have placed greater emphasis on the ideological work of history, as well as on the importance of identifying what and whose history is under construction. With the advantage of hindsight, modern diagnoses of nineteenth-century historicism have contextualized the Victorians' evident fixation on the past and its reproduction by explaining it in terms of the radical destabilization of traditional understandings of humanity's place in history. Such destabilization occurred as people began to examine the implications of both evolutionary science, as it unfolded from Charles Lyell to Charles Darwin, and the new historicist biblical scholarship emanating from Germany, which exposed the unreliability of the gospel narratives. It has often been suggested that Victorian theories of organic and teleological historical development were erected to counteract a disabling sense of cultural dislocation consequential upon such intellectual developments. That is why the Victorian historicist project might be read, in Marjorie Levinson's words, as an attempt "to restore to the dead their own, living language, that they might bespeak themselves."[6] In *The Order of Things* – a groundbreaking analysis of the foundations and archaeology of the human sciences first published in 1966 – Michel Foucault demonstrates the critical role of history (albeit a history radically reconfigured) in the Victorians' self-conceptualization, at the very cultural moment when "man" was "dehistoricized":

> [T]he imaginative values then assumed by the past, the whole lyrical halo that surrounded the consciousness of history at that period, the lively curiosity shown for documents or for traces left behind by time – all this is a surface expression of the simple fact that man found himself emptied of history, but that he was already beginning to recover in the depths of his own being, and among all the things that were capable of reflecting his image . . . a historicity linked essentially to man himself.[7]

By such accounts, nineteenth-century historicism was fraught with internal tensions and ambiguities. The "lyrical halo" that surrounded historical consciousness can be reinterpreted in terms of its hollow center. According to such a view, Victorian writers attempted to resuscitate the past in their poetry in order to regain access to their own threatened historicity.

II

This viewpoint has interesting implications for our understanding of how and why poets such as Matthew Arnold and Algernon Charles Swinburne subjected the past to new kinds of scrutiny through their engagement with the cultural ideal of Hellenism. For a start, Arnold's poetry articulates in a particularly poignant register the kind of historical disinheritance that Foucault discusses. In this respect, his best-known poem "Dover Beach" (1867) may be said to offer a more compelling example of Arnold's historicist poetics than his Hellenic drama *Merope* (1857): the long poem that prompted Swinburne to ask: "the clothes are well enough but where has the body gone?"[8] "Dover Beach" is set firmly in what Arnold in 1849 called the deeply *"unpoetical . . . age"*[9] of mid-nineteenth-century Britain – a "darkling plain . . . / Where ignorant armies clash by night" (*MA* 35–37). Yet at the same time "Dover Beach" refers to "Sophocles long ago" (15), the classical philosopher who heard the same "eternal note of sadness" (14) in the sounds of the sea. In addition, the temporal backdrop to the poem conforms to an evolutionary time-scale and an historical perspective more vertiginous than the cliffs of Dover themselves. The very *mise en scène* is suggestive of the accumulations and encrustations of geological time, in contrast to the spiritual bankruptcy of the all-too-human poetic subject. As such, it eloquently exemplifies Foucault's theory of humanity's historical dispossession in the face of the newly acknowledged historicity of the natural sciences. In "Dover Beach," we witness a reformulated world where, as Foucault says, "nature no longer speaks to [humanity] of the creation or the end of the world, of his dependency or his approaching judgement; it no longer speaks of anything but a natural time."[10]

Arnold's historicist poetry is driven by a profound sense of loss, and also by a keen awareness of historical processes. His Hellenism forms part of a broader cultural project to reassert human historicity in the face of the dispossession that Foucault identifies. But this project is marked by ideological contradiction. Chapter 4 of *Culture and Anarchy* (1869) offers what is perhaps the most famous statement of Victorian humanistic Hellenism: a philosophical position founded upon a belief in the transhistorical uniformity of human nature.[11] And yet modern historicist ideas that radically undercut such a formulation run throughout Arnold's best poetry. Although Arnold often appears as the proponent of a unitary concept of Greek civilization characterized by a rational and calm "sweetness and light,"[12] in some of his early poetry – such as "Empedocles on Etna" (which first appeared in 1852) – he depicts an ancient Greek culture as conflicted as his own. Indeed, in the famous "Preface" to his *Poems* (1853), where he expresses his unease with "Empedocles" and explains why he has refused to reprint it in the volume, Arnold portrays late-fifth-century Greece as a time when "the dialogue of the mind with itself has commenced."[13] This is an era, he says, when "modern problems have presented themselves." "[W]e hear already the doubts," Arnold adds, when "we witness the discouragement, of Hamlet and of Faust." His Empedocles is based on the Greek poet-philosopher who lived in Sicily circa 440 BC but his profound sense of spiritual exile and his alienated self-consciousness owe much to the Romantic poet George Gordon Byron. Empedocles's dystopic world is one where "Heaven is with earth at strife" (*MA* I. 122), and in which "we feel, day and night, / The burden of ourselves" (I. 127–28). Uncannily prescient of the alienating cultural dislocations of the nineteenth century, this poet-philosopher announces: "we are strangers here; the world is from of old" (181). "To tunes we did not call," he declares, "our being must keep chime" (I. 196). As Peter Allan Dale points out, "Empedocles on Etna" "is at least as much a poem about history and historical process as it is about the dialogue of a mind with itself."[14] Like his spiritual heirs, Empedocles looks in vain to the past for redemption:

> And we shall fly for refuge to past times,
> Their soul of unworn youth, their breath of greatness;
> And the reality will pluck us back,
> Knead us in its hot hand, and change our nature.   (II. 383–86)

Arnold himself was plucked back from these "past times" by the critical essays that came to dominate his career as a writer from the 1860s onward. Following his resolution to emulate instead the *"grand style"* and "the calm, the cheerfulness, the disinterested objectivity" of "the great monuments of early Greek genius" ("Preface," I, 5, 1), his muse deserted him, and he thereafter endorsed the Hellenic cultural ideal chiefly in prose.

"Empedocles on Etna" was not reprinted until *New Poems* (1867). In his review of the volume, the younger poet Swinburne praised the poem, saying of the songs that the harpist Callicles plays to soothe Empedocles: "No poet has ever come so near the perfect Greek; he has strung with a fresh chord the old Sophoclean lyre."[15] In the same essay, however, Swinburne (who had recently gained notoriety as a controversial critic and poet) has a fictitious French writer complain of the English "ils ont la manie de vouloir réconcilier les choses irréconciliables" ('they always want to reconcile things irreconcilable' [57, 59]). Swinburne clearly has little time for Arnold's endeavors in other poems to reconcile the irreconcilable – rationalism and religion, art and morality – within a moralized form of Hellenism:

Elsewhere . . . Mr. Arnold also has now and then given signs of an inclination for that sad task of sweeping up dead leaves fallen from the dying tree of belief; but has not wasted much time or strength on such sterile and stupid work. Here, at all events, he has wasted none; here is no melodious whine of retrospective and regretful scepticism; here are no cobwebs of plea and counterplea, no jungles of argument and brakes of analysis. (62)

Of his own *Atalanta in Calydon* (1865) – a magnificent verse-drama styled after Aeschylus – Swinburne wrote: "I think it is pure Greek"[16] (on the grounds, presumably, that it is unaccompanied by the aforesaid "melodious whine"). But Swinburne's own reviewers, although generally enthusiastic about the poetic drama, begged to differ. Richard Holt Hutton, for example, observed:

> Nothing can be more striking than the contrast between the workmanship of Mr. Swinburne and the workmanship of his great models. The attempt to imitate the Greek tragedians in English verse has once before been made in our time by Mr. Matthew Arnold in *Merope*. That poem was a great failure as a poem, for it was unluckily quite devoid of life and interest. Merope sighed out her melancholy like a languid Oxford gentleman rather than like Antigone or Electra. There was nothing of the keen and solemn irony of the Greek sadness in her. Still the drama had its merits, not as a poem, but as a lesson in the singleness of conception which belongs to the Greek school of imagination. Mr. Arnold succeeds in imitating the fine thin fibre of thought or feeling which winds through a Greek tragedy. *Merope* was dull, but it was in some respects classical. Mr. Swinburne is curiously unclassical in his workmanship. His fancies and illustrations throng upon us with the short, quick panting breath of [Percy Bysshe] Shelley rather than with the single, measured chaunt of the Greek imagination.[17]

Hutton makes it clear that historicism in poetry embraces not only the choice of historical subject matter, language, and form but also the poet's ability to evoke the "thought or feeling" and period style of an earlier culture. Even Richard Monckton Milnes, who vigorously sponsored Swinburne's early poetic career, condemned the verse-drama's moral tone and its "bitter, angry anti-theism, which has its place among the aberrations of human nature, but not in Greek culture."[18] Swinburne was captivated by the Marquis de Sade's anti-theism as well as by his flagellant enthusiasms, and both influences find their way into his erotic and decadent invocation of classical paganism. The Chorus in *Atalanta* first accuses the gods of having "circled pain about with pleasure, / And girdled pleasure about with pain" (*ACS* IV, 285) before proceeding to denounce "the supreme evil, God." (IV, 287). Such sentiments certainly strike a different note from Arnold's poetic renditions of the ancient Greek world. Swinburne explains their differences in terms of their respective classical allegiances, with Arnold emerging as "a pupil of Sophocles" while he himself stands as "a disciple of Aeschylus."[19] But it was not simply a matter of following one or another classical model. Swinburne was the protégé of the Oxford classicist Benjamin Jowett. The young poet probably assisted Jowett in his popular English translation of Plato. The author of *Atalanta* belonged to a new generation of Oxford-educated Hellenists: scholars who were to carve out for themselves alternative versions of Ancient Greece for modern times from the humanistic Hellenism endorsed by Victorian liberal intellectuals such as Arnold, Jowett, and Mill.

Swinburne himself developed a form of Hellenism that generally celebrated the paganism of ancient Greece. In his "Hymn to Proserpine" (1866), the speaker – a fourth-century Roman follower of the ancient pagan faith – foresees the passing of the old religion after the proclamation of Christianity in Rome. By contrast with Arnold's lament for the retreat of the Christian "sea of faith" in "Dover Beach," Swinburne's poem offers a view of the tides of history in which regret for the ebb of pagan faith with the establishment of Christianity is framed by an acceptance of Heraclitean flux. (Heraclitus [*c.*535–*c.*475 BC] stated the idea that all things remain in a state of flux, differentiated from fire – the first element, and single mobile principle – only through incessant strife.)

> All delicate days and pleasant, all spirits and sorrows are cast
> Far out with the foam of the present that sweeps to the surf of the past:
> Where beyond the extreme sea-wall, and between the remote sea-gates,
> Waste water washes, and tall ships founder, and deep death waits:
> Where, mighty with deepening sides, clad about with the seas as with wings,
> And impelled of invisible tides, and fulfilled of unspeakable things,
> White-eyed and poisonous-finned, shark-toothed and serpentine-curled,
> Rolls, under the whitening wind of the future, the wave of the world.
>
> (*ACS* I, 69–70)

Against the "grey" religion of Christ (the "pale Galilean"), Swinburne opposes a classicism whose colorful energy is dynamically realized in the elevated rhetoric and rhythmical vigor of his metrical experimentation with ancient prosodic models.

Swinburne's affinity with the Oxford don Walter Pater's relativist historicism, and with his particular construction of ancient Greece, is readily apparent. Pater's famous study titled "Winckelmann" first appeared in the *Westminster Review* in 1867, and it caused as much of a stir as most of the poems (including "Hymn to Proserpine") that appeared in Swinburne's *Poems and Ballads* the previous year. In this essay, Pater represents the eighteenth-century German art historian as a student of Plato, in a manner that signals a radical modification of the cultural meanings of Hellenism. He argues that the Greek philosopher to whom Winckelmann is drawn is not the Plato of "[t]he modern student" – the one who "most often meets

Plato on that side which seems to pass beyond Plato into a world no longer pagan, and based upon the conception of a spiritual life" – but the Plato who is "wholly Greek, and alien from the Christian world, represented by that group of brilliant youths in the *Lysis* . . . finding the end of all endeavor in the aspects of the human form, the continual stir and motion of a comely human life."[20] Pater, a classics tutor at Brasenose College, was intimately associated with the transformation of Oxford Hellenism that took place in the latter half of Victoria's reign as an unforeseen consequence of the successful attempt by Jowett and other university reformers to establish in the study of ancient Greek culture the basis for an alternative social and ethical value-system to that grounded in Christian theology. As Linda Dowling has consummately demonstrated, the liberal reformers' representation of Plato as a source of transcendental authority created a cultural context in which male love – the "spiritual procreancy" celebrated in Plato's *Symposium* and generally associated with ancient Greece – might be experienced and justified in ideal terms.[21]

Timothy d'Arch Smith has coined the term "Uranian" to describe nine-teenth-century poetry that celebrates the spiritual love between males discussed in Plato's *Symposium*.[22] This type of writing began to appear in the 1850s and it was well established by the time Oscar Wilde went up to Oxford in 1874. Wilde's poetry, like Swinburne's, presents a Hellenism in conflict with Christianity. "Humanitad" (1881), for example, echoes the idiom of both Swinburne and Pater. Here Wilde laments the passing of ancient Greece, a time "When soul and body seemed to blend in mystic symphonies." Such an era is superseded by the advent of "the new Calvary" (*OW* 410), to which "[we] pass / With weary feet" (409–10). By compar-ison, the final lines of his "Sonnet Written in Holy Week at Genoa" (1877) sigh: "Ah, God! Ah, God! those dear Hellenic hours / Had drowned all memory of Thy bitter pain, / The Cross, the Crown, the Soldiers, and the Spear" (12–13). Although the speaker's pagan adventures are here checked by his penitential Christian feelings of pity for Christ's suffering, aroused by the song of a "young boy-priest" (9), Hellenism emerges as a temptation to which he has understandably surrendered and will, it is implied, return. Such poetry indicates that by the 1880s the culture of ancient Greece offered a coded language for the emerging discourse of homosexuality.

Dowling throws considerable light on both the evolution of Oxford Hellenism and the cultural moment of Wilde's trial in 1895 when he made his legendary defense of love between men as a love "such as Plato made the very basis of his philosophy."[23] She shows how closely enmeshed Victorian historicist methodologies and discourses are with the histories of sexuality and with the construction of gendered poetics. But the gendered aspects of Victorian Hellenism extended well beyond the largely male world of Oxford. If, as Dowling and other post-Foucauldian critics such as Herbert Sussman have contended,[24] the emergence of a diversity of masculinities and masculine poetics can be traced through the various uses of historicism in Victorian writing, then what can historicist poetry tell us about understandings of femininity in the period? In other words, how did the distinctive gendering of historicism affect women writers at this time?

III

Christina Crosby proposes that "in the nineteenth century 'history' is produced as man's truth," enabling "'man' [to] . . . know himself in history, find his origin there and project his end."[25] By contrast, she argues, women stand outside history, remaining "intrinsically unhistorical." Moreover, women who wished to write historical poetry were doubly disadvantaged, for it can be said that of all literary forms poetry depends most on rules and conventions mediated through tradition. Not only did women often receive little or no formal education in the classical authors who defined those rules and conventions but they also lacked their own aesthetic models. Even Elizabeth Barrett Browning, who was probably as deeply read in classical literature as any other poet of the time, memorably complained: "I look everywhere for Grandmothers and see none."[26] Further, women poets were frequently obliged to develop strategies to negotiate or subvert the masculine literary history that was their only inheritance in order to intervene as speaking subjects in a literary tradition that had them typecast as silent objects of desire and inspirational muses. Thus Christina Rossetti wrote a sonnet sequence entitled "Monna Innominata" (1881) in which the anonymous lady of a Renaissance sonneteer speaks "for herself."[27] Each of the fourteen sonnets has epigraphs from both Dante and Petrarch, and each provides the unknown woman's perspective on a love affair known in literary history only from the man's point of view. Sonnet 5, for example, is prefaced by the lines "Amor che a nulla amato amar perdona" ("Love, who exempts no loved one from loving"), from Dante, and "Amor m'addusse in sì gioiosa spene" ("Love led me into such joyous hope"), from Petrarch. It begins with reference to the traditional elevation of the man to a state of perfection through his noble love of a woman, then shifts perspective in the sestet:

> So much for you; but what for me, dear friend?
> To love you without stint and all I can

> Today, tomorrow, world without an end;
>> To love you much and yet to love you more,
>> As Jordan at his flood sweeps either shore;
> Since woman is the helpmeet made for man.   (CR 9–14)

The whole sonnet sequence, through its ironic engagement with the fathers of an immensely influential literary and cultural tradition, cumulatively critiques the gender ideology of that tradition.

There was, though, one notable female poet in the ancient tradition upon whom Victorian women could model themselves. Sappho – the great classical poet of Lesbos – became an iconic figure that enabled many women poets to articulate their own poetic identity. As Joan DeJean shows, Sappho has been the subject of critical debate, editorial intervention, fabrication, speculation, and translation over the past four centuries.[28] In the nineteenth century, the sexual politics of Sappho's reception focuses questions of authorship, gender, history, and sexuality. A significant tradition of poems about Sappho by early-nineteenth-century women writers such as Felicia Hemans, L.E.L. (Letitia Elizabeth Landon), Caroline Norton, and Christina Rossetti – just to give the prominent examples – celebrates and develops the prevailing idealized heterosexual myth of her life, portraying a drama of love and betrayal, a story of heroic female creativity, even in the face of loss. Norton, for example, writes in "The Picture of Sappho" (1840):

> FAME, to thy breaking heart
>> No comfort could impart,
> In vain thy brow the laurel wreath was wearing;
>> One grief and one alone
>> Could bow thy bright head down –
> Thou wert a WOMAN, and wert left despairing![29]

But only the bare contours of Sappho's life could be inferred from the fragments that remained of her work, and Norton explicitly acknowledges the Lesbian poet's ambiguity, questioning the narrative that has been constructed from the piecemeal evidence:

> Yet, was it History's truth,
>> That tale of wasted youth,
> Of endless grief, and Love forsaken pining?
>> What wert thou, thou whose woe
>> The old traditions show
> With Fame's cold light around thee vainly shining?[30]

As Yopie Prins points out: "These two questions present Sappho as an increasingly impossible personification."[31]

Assuredly, determining "History's truth" in relation to Sappho was no easy matter. With the publication of Henry Thornton Wharton's 1885 edition of her poetry, a radically alternative Sappho was proposed from either the paragon of chastity or the supreme expression of heterosexual female desire of earlier modern tradition. The volume opened with John Addington Symonds's anonymous homoerotic prose translation of Sappho's "Ode to Aphrodite" where for the first time in the English language readers saw that the Lesbian poet's object of desire was female.[32] Wharton's controversial edition exerted considerable influence in shaping the coded articulation of female same-sex desire. It is in the poetry of Katherine Bradley and her niece Edith Cooper, who published collaboratively under the name Michael Field, that the pagan emphasis of the new Hellenism is given a Sapphic inflection.

In this regard, Michael Field's most significant publication is the volume *Long Ago* (1889), where the author's preface acknowledges the inspiration of Wharton's edition:

> When, more than a year ago, I wrote to a literary friend of my attempt to express in English verse the passionate pleasure Dr. Wharton's book had brought to me, he replied: "That is a delightfully audacious thought – the extension of Sappho's fragments into lyrics. I can scarcely conceive anything more audacious" . . .
>
> Devoutly as the fiery-bosomed Greek turned in her anguish to Aphrodite, praying her to accomplish her heart's desires, I have turned to the one woman who has dared to speak unfalteringly of the fearful mastery of love.   (iii)[33]

Audacious in more ways than one, Michael Field's poems are translations and extensions of the Sapphic fragments, some of which are explicitly homoerotic. "Come Gorgo, put the rug in place, / And passionate recline" is the seductive opening of Poem xxxv: an elaboration of fragment 35, which translates as "But do not put on airs for the sake of a ring" (56). By comparison, Poem xxxiii declares:

> Maids, not to you my mind doth change;
> Men I defy, allure, estrange,
> Prostrate, make bond or free:
> Soft as the stream beneath the plane
> To you I sing my love's refrain;
> Between us is no thought of pain,
>   Peril, satiety.   (52)

At the head of each poem in *Long Ago*, there are epigraphs taken from Sappho's Greek fragments, recalling Rossetti's use of Dante and Petrarch in "Monna Innominata." But rather than signifying a masculinist tradition from which the woman poet is excluded, Michael Field's epigraphy legitimizes female creativity and female sexuality through its invocation of an unimpeachable feminine cultural authority. As Prins observes: "Literally and figuratively, their Sapphic lyrics are located in the spaces between the Sapphic fragments – the lacunae in Wharton's text – in order to open a textual field that Bradley and Cooper may enter together as 'Michael Field.'"[34]

As fragments from which full poems are pieced together, Michael Field's epigraphs emblematize – in a particularly telling way – the Victorian historicist project of reconstituting the dismembered fragmentariness of the historical record. Sappho serves as a figure of the past of which what remains are only fractured shards, incoherent effects. The realization of that "delightfully audacious thought" – the extension of Sappho's fragments into lyrics – articulates a broader historiographical desire to recover in antiquity an imagined originary wholeness that would confer integrity upon the constituting subject.[35] Even more suggestively, the authorial name Michael Field, which designates the constructed unitary male voice speaking for two transgressive women, may be read as both exemplifying and deconstructing the idea of the modern historicizing and constituting subject as an agent of integrity and coherence.

IV

This interest in exposing the fabricated identity of both the historical past and the historicist poet is a feature that may be seen in many other Victorian poems, if in rather different forms and modes. In particular, Robert Browning is noted for his poetic exploration of the implications of historicism's embrace of ambiguity, perspectivism, and plurality. Indeed, Browning is celebrated for his recognition that, although our access to the past can only be partial, accidental, and interested, it is nevertheless valuable to find imaginative ways of entering history as a means of coming to terms with modernity. In one respect, his poetry enacts the Victorians' historiographical longing to reintegrate the broken and incomplete remains of history. His astonishingly metonymic imagination seizes on the fragments of past cultures – an antiquarian book, a bust, a painting, a statue, a tomb – to conjure up an entire age. In Book I of *The Ring and the Book* (1868–69), the poet-speaker declares:

> "I can detach from me, commission forth
> Half of my soul; which in its pilgrimage
> O'er old unwandered waste ways of the world,
> May chance upon some fragment of a whole,

> Rag of flesh, scrap of bone in dim disuse,
> Smoking flax that fed fire once: prompt therein
> I enter, spark-like, put old powers to play." (*RBRB* I. 749–55)

Here the poet compares himself to a magus. But the imagery also suggests that the poet, like Aeneas, has the power to descend into the underworld, just as he is a Promethean figure who can bring the past "spark-like" to life and rescue what might otherwise be lost to oblivion.

But in other respects, like Michael Field, Browning critiques the dream of wholeness that so many of his contemporaries found so seductive. Elsewhere he offers instead an ironic acknowledgment of the contingency, fictiveness, and indeed partiality of any attempt to reconstruct the past in such a way as to undermine the truth claims of history. In the much earlier *Sordello* (1840) – a long poem of epic dimensions featuring the life of a thirteenth-century troubadour during the Guelf–Ghibelline wars – the poet is figured as a grave-snatching impresario: "poets know the dragnet's trick, / Catching the dead" (*RB* I. 35–36):

> . . . Here they are: now view
> The host I muster! Many a lighted face
> Foul with no vestige of the grave's disgrace;
> What else should tempt them back to taste our air
> Except to see how their successors fare?
> My audience! (I. 44–49)

The past is made before our very eyes, the scene is set, exploding into view, conjured like a genie from a lamp:

> Lo, the past is hurled
> In twain: up-thrust, out-staggering on the world,
> Subsiding into shape, a darkness rears
> Its outline, kindles at the core, appears
> Verona. (I. 73–77)

Browning's historicist convictions are inscribed even more tellingly in the formal constitution of his poetry, which does not aspire to coherence, and deliberately demands of the reader an active engagement in the process of producing the past. As Joseph Bristow has shown, the unusual structure of *Sordello*, which veers alarmingly between the writer's present and the historical setting, and which "chops up its narrative sequence – so that the story . . . has to be pieced together, bit by bit," should be read as the poet's deliberate attempt "to put an avant-garde method of historiography into poetic practice."[36]

It is in the dramatic monologue that Browning's interrogation of both history and the historical subject is most dynamically realized. J. Hillis

Miller describes this form as "par excellence the literary genre of historicism" in that "[i]t presupposes a double awareness on the part of its author, an awareness which is the very essence of historicism."[37] If the epic proportions of both *Sordello* and *The Ring and the Book* may be said to contest history's conventionally singular and linear narrative, then Browning's dramatic monologues, in their exploration of human duplicity, complicate our understanding of the past in other ways. This distinctive type of poetry reveals that the human subject is constituted by language, a feature that not only problematizes earlier Romantic assumptions about the integrated and authentic poetic subject but also ironizes the authorized version of the past by showing history in the making. Thus we can see Browning as the inhabitant of an age self-consciously in a state of transition: a period in which, according to John Stuart Mill, "[m]ankind have outgrown old institutions and old doctrines, and have not yet acquired new ones."[38] Browning was fascinated by the idea of history as a series of transitional moments. To be sure, he and his own contemporaries were articulate about their sense of suspension between past and future at a moment of change. Arnold's speaker in "Stanzas from the Grande Chartreuse" (1855), for example, declares himself to be "Wandering between two worlds, one dead, / The other powerless to be born, / With nowhere yet to rest my head" (*MA* 85–87). But Browning's monologists generally have little sense of their pivotal place in history. Take, for instance, Fra Lippo Lippi, the maverick artist of the Italian Renaissance whose name titles one of the most admired dramatic monologues in Browning's *Men and Women* (1855). Lippi presents his apologia for the ingenious dramatic realism of his pictorial work, just as he remains conscious of generational differences in taste and skill – of "the old grave eyes / . . . peeping o'er my shoulder as I work" (*RB* 231–32) and the opportunities to be enjoyed by future painters: "Oh, oh," he exclaims, "It makes me mad to see what men shall do / And we in our graves!' (312–13). But as dawn breaks over Lippi's quattrocento Florence ("There's the grey beginning. Zooks!" he cries [392]), the reader knows, as the painter does not, that this moment heralds a significant new phase in Renaissance art.

Such poems brilliantly demonstrate an ability to make history live. Herbert F. Tucker argues that "they enact the reciprocation of historicist desire, whereby the reader's backward yearning to know the past feelingly meets the historical agent's projective will to survive into the future."[39] This is nowhere more dazzlingly the case than in "The Bishop Orders His Tomb at St Praxed's Church" (1845), spoken by an outrageously corrupt sixteenth-century Bishop of Rome. Focused as he is on his rivalry with his predecessor "Old Gandolf" (17), and imagining the figure he will cut in effigy for future generations, the Bishop remains blithely unaware of all that his funerary monument will signify about the High Renaissance for future generations. Ruskin counted among the noted Victorian critics who appreciated the economy with which this poem portrayed "the Renaissance spirit, – its worldliness, inconsistency, pride, hypocrisy, ignorance of itself, love of art, of luxury, and of good Latin." "It is," Ruskin added, "nearly all that I said of the central Renaissance in thirty pages of *The Stones of Venice* [1851–53] put into as many lines."[40] Browning depicts the Bishop trying to bribe and cajole his illegitimate sons into building him a splendid tabernacle in which he imagines himself reclining, with a huge lump of lapis lazuli between his knees, surrounded by nine columns of "Peach-blossom" marble (29), and with antique-black basalt for his slab. "How else," declares the Bishop, "Shall ye contrast my frieze to come beneath?" (54–55). As his imagination runs wild, he imagines this "frieze" featuring "some tripod, thyrsus, with a vase or so" (58), a picture of Jesus Christ preaching "his sermon on the mount" (59), and "one Pan, / Ready to twitch the Nymph's last garment off" (60–61). The tasteless jumble of materials in this riotous display of conspicuous consumption signifies for Ruskin the aesthetic, moral, and spiritual disorder of the High Renaissance. Above all, it is through such material objects as the Bishop's tomb that "the Renaissance spirit" can be accessed.

V

By contrast with such a monstrous spectacle of cultural incoherence as the Bishop's tomb, the Middle Ages represented for Ruskin what Alice Chandler has aptly termed "a dream of order."[41] Ruskin's medievalism draws on a view of the Middle Ages that developed during the eighteenth century, a view that emphasized its naturalism, its social stability under feudalism, its faith, and most of all its organic cultural unity. But the Victorians' approach to the Middle Ages was neither more singular nor more unified than their perception of Ancient Greece or Renaissance Italy. If for some writers the Middle Ages connoted Roman Catholicism (and, depending on a writer's viewpoint, this connection with Rome could be a good or a bad thing), then for others it signified a characteristic Englishness. Where Tories associated medievalism with the old feudal values, socialists believed it represented the pre-capitalist laboring classes and the Guilds. While some poets discovered the Middle Ages through Thomas Malory's *Le Morte Darthur* (1485), others found them in the works of Geoffrey Chaucer, in the early Italian paintings by artists such as Giotto and Cimabue, and in the gargoyles and arches of a Gothic cathedral.

Quite often, indeed, single writers embraced different aspects of medievalism in their work. Morris, who was captivated in his youth by Malory and the romance of chivalry, wrote beautiful poems in archaic language on medieval subjects that powerfully suggested both the decorative loveliness and the danger of a Middle Ages that owed much to Keatsian Romanticism. But Morris was a student of Karl Marx as well as of Keats and Malory, and it was through Marx's dialectical materialism that Morris came to view the fourteenth century as another transitional period: a time of relative prosperity for the laboring poor between feudalism and capitalism. Even in Morris's own day, his poetry was thought to represent a medievalism shaped by his own culture and temperament. Pater observed that Morris's poetry draws on a past age "but must not be confounded with it."[42]

Isobel Armstrong has demonstrated that Morris's first volume of poetry *The Defence of Guenevere and Other Poems* (1858) presents a Middle Ages mediated specifically by Ruskin's memorable formulation of the "Grotesque" in *The Stones of Venice*. Ruskin defines this mode as a "tendency to delight in fantastic and ludicrous, as well as in sublime, images" that is a product of the "Disturbed Imagination" of the Gothic builder.[43] According to Armstrong, Ruskin's reading of "The Nature of Gothic" (1853) – which Morris was to describe in his "Preface" to the Kelmscott Press edition of 1892 as "one of the very few necessary and inevitable utterances of this century"[44] – provided a framework for Morris's own poetic exploration of "the modern Grotesque."[45] In particular, this "modern Grotesque" characterized "the ways in which modern poetic form and consciousness are materially shaped by the form and nature of work in nineteenth-century society." In Armstrong's view, the medieval subject matter and forms deployed by Morris are thus neither "a simple proxy" nor a "disguise for contemporary conditions." Rather, the poems "are an attempt to *be* the form in which modern consciousness shaped by work and labour sees, experiences and desires, to be what it imagines and the myths it needs to imagine with."[46] Such a reading enables us to trace the "fantastic" effects to be found in the dramatic monologue that titles the volume back to the "Disturbed Imagination" induced by oppression and disempowerment under industrial capitalism. "The Defence of Guenevere" is full of extraordinary images of distortion, especially ones of bodily estrangement, dislocation, and even dismemberment. "See through my long throat," says Guenevere, "how the words go up / In ripples to my mouth; how in my hand / The shadow lies like wine within a cup / Of marvellously colour'd gold" (*WM* I, 8). An equally weird sense of physical exhaustion emerges from her description of her first kiss with

Lancelot: "When both our mouths went wandering in one way, / And aching sorely, met among the leaves; / Our hands being left behind strained far away" (I, 5). Such images are profoundly expressive of an industrial economy built on the division of labor and the alienated modern consciousness that, by a Marxist reading, is its inevitable product.

The refraction of the past through modern consciousness, then, took many forms in the nineteenth century. Such imaginative appropriations are invariably double-focused. Thus Tennyson's quarrying of Arthurian legend, both early and late in his career, is mediated by a framing device that underwrites the allegorical reverberations of the myth of the rise and fall of a society for modern times. His early poem "Morte d'Arthur," probably composed in 1837–38, is later framed by "The Epic" (1842): an introduction and conclusion to the poem whose title alludes to the poet's plans, eventually abandoned, to write his own modern epic based on the Arthurian legends. Instead, he was to produce a series of fragments in the Romantic tradition, realizing that if he "meant to make his mark at all, it must be by shortness."[47] Where Malory compiled his great work from a range of heterogeneous sources, Tennyson dismantles the medieval corpus that is his inspiration to provide a series of "idylls" – framed pictures representing incidents from the narrative of Arthur's life, written over a period of fifty-five years – that were eventually put together as *Idylls of the King* (1859–85). The nationalistic legends of Arthur and his Round Table were traditionally read as an allegory of the historic authority and virtue of the British monarchy. This association with the Crown becomes clear in Tennyson's sequence by the "Dedication" to Prince Albert and the closing address "To the Queen." Although the poem explores important Victorian preoccupations such as the dualism of the body and the soul, the symbolic use of the Middle Ages – in particular the implied parallel between Arthur and Albert ("He seems to me / Scarce other than my king's ideal knight" [*AT* "Dedication," 5–6]) – is not altogether successful. In 1879 Gerard Manley Hopkins commented privately: "'He shd. have called them *Charades from the Middle Ages* (dedicated by permission to H.R.H. etc)."[48]

But Tennyson also wrote poetry that resonates like no other with a profoundly moving sense of what historicism implies for an understanding of the human predicament. His greatest work is haunted by another Arthur – his beloved friend Arthur Hallam, whom he lost at a young age and mourned thereafter as a poignant signifier of mortality. In the dramatic monologue "Ulysses" (1842), begun in 1833 just a few days after Hallam's untimely death, Tennyson draws on Homer's and Dante's accounts of Ulysses's decision to undertake a final sea voyage as a way of articulating what Tennyson saw as "the need of going forward, and braving the struggle of life."[49] The poem culminates in Ulysses's exhortation:

> Come, my friends.
> 'Tis not too late to seek a newer world.
> Push off, and sitting well in order smite
> The sounding furrows; for my purpose holds
> To sail beyond the sunset, and the baths
> Of all the western stars, until I die.
> It may be that the gulfs will wash us down:
> It may be we shall touch the Happy Isles,
> And see the great Achilles, whom we knew.
> Though much is taken, much abides; and though
> We are not now that strength which in old days
> Moved earth and heaven; that which we are, we are, –
>
> (AT 56–67)

Here the ironic double focus afforded by the dramatic monologue places Ulysses's resolution against our knowledge of the fatal outcome of his final voyage. The power of the poem, like so many of Tennyson's lyrics, lies in his choice of a critical historical moment, his suspension of a story at its penultimate point. This feature reveals the human subject of the poem as subject to the inexorable movement of time.

"What first comes to light in the nineteenth century," observes Foucault in *The Order of Things*, "is a simple form of human historicity – the fact that man as such is exposed to the event."[50] As we look back from the vantage-point of the twenty-first century at the multiform attempts by Victorian poets to come to terms with their fundamental exposure to the fact of their own historicity, we are reminded that, just as each period of history has its past, so it has its future. This is a point made particularly clear when the medievalist poet and Roman Catholic convert the Rev. Frederick William Faber sanctimoniously observes:

> The Future is the open trench, the ground
> Whereon our deeds are built, wherein we cast,
> As though we did a reverend temple found,
> The corner-stones to build another Past.[51]

Faber is conscious of his own and his contemporaries' responsibilities to posterity. Published in 1845 when he followed his spiritual leader, John Henry Newman, to Roman Catholicism – after the Tractarians' long and ill-fated struggle to rebuild a revitalized Anglican Church for the nineteenth century on the historical cornerstone of the Early Church – these lines suggest the almost religious seriousness with which the Victorian poet contemplated his place in literary history.

But what are *our* responsibilities to the text of the past? Gillian Beer points out: "Engaging with the *difference* of the past in our present makes us aware of the trajectory of our arrival and of the insouciance of the past – their neglectfulness of our prized positions and our assumptions."[52] Attending respectfully to that difference, looking at the Victorians' own strategies for positioning themselves in history, can perhaps enable us to confront our own historicity under post-modernity with greater wisdom and equanimity, mindful of Tennyson's Ulysses who perceives that "all experience is an arch wherethrough / Gleams that untravelled world, whose margin fades / For ever and for ever" (19–21).

NOTES

1 Thomas Love Peacock, "The Four Ages of Poetry," in Peacock, *Essays, Memoirs, Letters, and Unfinished Novels, The Works of Thomas Love Peacock*, 10 vols. (London: Constable, 1924), VIII, 20; further page references appear in parentheses. Arnold develops his ideas about the cultural role of the poet and intellectual in an uncivilized society ruled by "Barbarians" (the aristocracy) and "Philistines" (the middle classes) in *Culture and Anarchy: An Essay in Political and Social Criticism* (1869): see *Culture and Anarchy with Friendship's Garland and Some Literary Essays*, ed. R.H. Super, *The Complete Prose Works of Matthew Arnold*, 11 vols. (Ann Arbor, MI: University of Michigan Press, 1960–77), V, 85–256.

2 A. Dwight Culler, *The Victorian Mirror of History* (New Haven, CT: Yale University Press, 1986), viii.

3 On the professionalization of history, see J.P. Kenyon, *The History Men: The Historical Profession in England since the Renaissance* (London: Weidenfeld and Nicolson, 1983).

4 John Stuart Mill, *The Spirit of the Age* (Chicago, IL: University of Chicago Press, 1942), 1. Mill's essay originally appeared in parts in the *Examiner* between 23 January 1831 and 29 May 1831.

5 Thomas Carlyle, *Past and Present, The Works of Thomas Carlyle*, centenary edition, 30 vols. (London: Chapman and Hall, 1896–99), V, 38.

6 Marjorie Levinson, "The New Historicism: Back to the Future," in *Rethinking Historicism: Critical Readings in Romantic History*, Levinson, Marilyn Butler, Jerome McGann, and Paul Hamilton, (Oxford: Basil Blackwell, 1989), 52.

7 Michel Foucault, *The Order of Things: An Archaeology of the Human Sciences*, trans. Alan Sheridan (London: Tavistock Publications, 1970), 369.

8 Algernon Charles Swinburne, "To Pauline Trevelyan," 15 March 1865, *The Swinburne Letters*, ed. Cecil Y. Lang, 6 vols. (New Haven, CT: Yale University Press, 1960), I, 115.

9 Arnold described his own age as "[not] unprofound, not ungrand, not unmoving: – but *unpoetical*": "To Arthur Hugh Clough," February 1849, in *The Letters of Matthew Arnold*, ed. Cecil Y. Lang, 2 vols. to date (Charlottesville, VA: University Press of Virginia, 1996–), I, 131.

10 Foucault, *The Order of Things*, 368.

11 On Arnold's Hellenism, see Frank Turner, *The Greek Heritage in Victorian Britain* (New Haven, CT: Yale University Press, 1981), 15–36; and David J. DeLaura, *Hebrew and Hellene in Victorian England: Newman, Arnold, and Pater* (Austin, TX: University of Texas Press, 1969), 181–91.

12 Matthew Arnold, *Culture and Anarchy*, 90.

13 Matthew Arnold, "Preface to the First Edition of *Poems* (1853)," in Arnold, *On the Classical Tradition*, ed. R.H. Super, *The Complete Prose Works of Matthew Arnold*, 11 vols. (Ann Arbor, MI: University of Michigan Press, 1960–77), I, 1; further page references appear in parentheses.

14 Peter Allan Dale, *The Victorian Critic and the Idea of History: Carlyle, Arnold, Pater* (Cambridge, MA: Harvard University Press), 77.

15 Algernon Charles Swinburne, "Matthew Arnold's New Poems," in *Swinburne as Critic*, ed. Clyde K. Hyder (London: Routledge and Kegan Paul, 1972), 68; further page references appear in parentheses. This essay first appeared in the *Fortnightly Review* n.s. 2 (1867), 414–45. Swinburne added the first long passage assigned to the French critic when the essay was revised for *Essays and Studies* (London: Chatto and Windus, 1875).

16 Swinburne, "To Pauline Trevelyan," 15 March 1865, *The Swinburne Letters*, I, 115.

17 Richard Holt Hutton, *A Victorian Spectator: Uncollected Writings of R.H. Hutton*, ed. Robert Tener and Malcolm Woodfield (Bristol: The Bristol Press, 1989), 88; this essay was first published in *Pall Mall Gazette*, 18 April 1865, 11.

18 [Richard Monckton Milnes,] Review of *Atalanta in Calydon*, *Edinburgh Review* 122 (1865), 202–16.

19 Swinburne, "To William Michael Rossetti," 21 August 1875, *The Swinburne Letters*, III, 55.

20 Walter Pater, *The Renaissance: Studies in Art and Poetry, The 1893 Text*, ed. Donald L. Hill (Berkeley, CA: University of California Press, 1980), 145. Pater's "Winckelmann" first appeared in the *Westminster Review* 87 (1867), 80–110.

21 Dowling, *Hellenism and Homosexuality in Victorian Oxford* (Ithaca, NY: Cornell University Press, 1994), xiii.

22 Timothy d'Arch Smith, *Love in Earnest: Some Notes on the Lives and Writings of English 'Uranian' Poets from 1889–1930* (London: Routledge and Kegan Paul, 1970).

23 H. Montgomery Hyde, *The Trials of Oscar Wilde* (London: William Hodge, 1948), 236.

24 See Herbert Sussman, *Victorian Masculinities: Manhood and Masculine Poetics in Early Victorian Literature and Art* (Cambridge: Cambridge University Press, 1995).

25 Christina Crosby, *The Ends of History: Victorians and "The Woman Question"* (London: Routledge, 1991), 1.

26 Elizabeth Barrett Browning, "To Henry Fothergill Chorley," 7 January 1845, *The Brownings' Correspondence*, ed. Phillip Kelley et al., 14 vols. to date (Winfield, KS: Wedgestone Press, 1984–), X, 14.

27 Christina Rossetti, *The Complete Poems of Christina Rossetti: A Variorum Edition*, ed. R.W. Crump, 3 vols. (Baton Rouge, LA: Louisiana State University Press, 1979–90), III, 86.

28 Joan DeJean, *Fictions of Sappho 1546–1937* (Chicago, IL: University of Chicago Press, 1989).

29 Caroline Norton, *The Dream and Other Poems* (London: Henry Colburn, 1840), 205.

30 Norton, *The Dream and Other Poems*, 202.

31 Yopie Prins, "Personifying the Poetess: Caroline Norton, 'The Picture of Sappho,'" in *Women's Poetry, Late Romantic to Late Victorian: Gender and Genre, 1830–1900*, eds. Isobel Armstrong and Virginia Blain (Basingstoke: Macmillan, 1999), 58.

32 Henry Thornton Wharton, *Sappho, Memoir, Text, Selected Renderings, and a Literal Translation* (London: David Stott, 1885), 46.

33 Quotations from Michael Field's poetry are taken from Michael Field, *Long Ago* (London: George Bell and Sons, 1889); page references appear in parentheses.

34 Yopie Prins, "A Metaphorical Field: Katherine Bradley and Edith Cooper," *Victorian Poetry* 33 (1995), 137.

35 My argument here draws on and adapts Page DuBois's stimulating discussion of Sappho, using a Lacanian model of historicism, in "Sappho's Body in Pieces," in *Textual Bodies: Changing Boundaries of Literary Representation*, ed. Lori Hope Lefkovitz (Albany, NY: State University of New York Press, 1997), 19–33.

36 Joseph Bristow, *Robert Browning* (New York: St. Martin's Press, 1991), 76–77.

37 J. Hillis Miller, *The Disappearance of God: Five Nineteenth-Century Writers* (Cambridge, MA: The Belknap Press of Harvard University Press, 1963), 108.

38 Mill, *The Spirit of the Age*, 6.

39 Herbert F. Tucker, "Wanted Dead or Alive: Browning's Historicism," *Victorian Studies* 38 (1994), 31.

40 John Ruskin, *Modern Painters*, IV, in *The Works of John Ruskin*, eds. E.T. Cook and Alexander Wedderburn, 39 vols. (London: George Allen, 1903–12), VI, 449.

41 Alice Chandler, *A Dream of Order: The Medieval Ideal in Nineteenth-Century English Literature* (London: Routledge and Kegan Paul, 1971).

42 [Walter Pater,] "Poems by William Morris," *Westminster Review* n.s. 34 (1868), 300.

43 Ruskin, "The Nature of Gothic," *The Stones of Venice, The Works of John Ruskin*, X, 239, 184.

44 J.W. Mackail, *The Life of William Morris*, 2 vols. (New York: Longmans Green, 1922), II, 289.

45 Isobel Armstrong, *Victorian Poetry: Poetry, Poetics and Politics* (London: Routledge, 1993), 235–36.

46 Armstrong, *Victorian Poetry*, 236.

47 Hallam Tennyson, *Alfred Lord Tennyson: A Memoir*, 2 vols. (London: Macmillan, 1897), I, 166.

48 Gerard Manley Hopkins, "To Richard Watson Dixon," 27 February 1879, in *The Correspondence of Gerard Manley Hopkins and Richard Watson Dixon*, second edition, ed. Claude Colleer Abbott (London: Oxford University Press, 1955), 24.

49 Hallam Tennyson, *Alfred Lord Tennyson: A Memoir*, I, 196.

50 Foucault, *The Order of Things*, 370.
51 Frederick William Faber, "The Present, 1," in "Thoughts while Reading History," *Poems*, third edition (London: Thomas Richardson, 1857), 517.
52 Gillian Beer, *Arguing with the Past: Essays in Narrative from Woolf to Sidney* (London: Routledge, 1989), 1.

7

DANIEL BROWN

Victorian poetry and science

I

In the 1802 "Preface" to *Lyrical Ballads*, William Wordsworth states that "Poetry is the breath and finer spirit of all knowledge; it is the impassioned expression which is in the countenance of all Science."[1] In other words, he presents poetry as an informing principle: a "breath" or "spirit" that gives contingent physical attributes, the discrete facts of science, an identifiable face. Although many Continental scientists of the time – notably the German *Naturphilosophen* – shared this Romantic metaphysic, the strong tradition of British empiricism was far less receptive to it. The economic and technological successes of the Industrial Revolution vindicated the type of empiricist research based upon sensory experience and practical experiment that Francis Bacon had theorized in the early seventeenth century. Doctrines of positivism, which maintain that the information which science extracts from sense-perception is the only nonanalytic knowledge possible, exercised a powerful influence over British intellectual life from the middle of the nineteenth century onward. They led science to break its traditional ties to philosophy and religion and to emerge as the paradigmatic form of knowledge. Poetry enters the Victorian era endowed by Romanticism with a metaphysical and cultural authority that it struggles to preserve in the face of such scientism. The present chapter explores the ways in which a range of poems reify, reinflect, or reject both this familiar narrative of combat and contrasting fortunes, and its ideological underpinning: namely, the hierarchical distinction between poetry and science that Wordsworth asserts in his "Preface."

An episode from the early 1860s helps to focus what was at stake in the conflict between poetry and science during the Victorian period. Here is the physicist John Tyndall's account of a Spiritualist séance that he attended:

> The spirits were requested to spell the name by which I am known in the heavenly world. Our host commenced repeating the alphabet, and when he

reached the letter "P" a knock was heard. He began again, and the spirits knocked at the letter "O." I was puzzled, but waited for the end. The next letter knocked down was "E." I laughed, and remarked that the spirits were going to make a poet of me. Admonished for my levity, I was informed that the frame of mind proper for the occasion ought to have been superinduced by a perusal of the Bible immediately before the *séance*. The spelling, however, went on, and sure enough I came out a poet. But matters did not end there. Our host continued his repetition of the alphabet, and the next letter of the name proved to be "O" . . . The knocks came from under the table, but no person present evinced the slightest desire to look under it. I asked whether I might go underneath; the permission was granted; so I crept under the table . . . I continued under that table for at least a quarter of an hour, after which, with a feeling of despair as regards the prospects of humanity never before experienced, I regained my chair. Once there, the spirits resumed their loquacity, and dubbed me "Poet of Science."[2]

Spiritualist phenomena, such as the table-rappings that Tyndall investigates here, manifest physical effects that the laws of science cannot explain. An import from the United States, the Spiritualist movement became immediately and immensely popular in mid-Victorian England. For a generation whose Christian beliefs were under threat from the positivist science of Darwin and his peers, Spiritualism offered a credible alternative to materialistic atheism or reactionary religious conservativism because it apparently fulfilled the positivist criterion for knowledge by offering observable evidence of an immaterial human spirit and its life after death.

The spirit world is justifiably nervous of Tyndall, the fierce public advocate for the autonomy of science who insisted upon testing such phenomena as prayer[3] and Spiritualism according to positivist experimental principles. The "spirits" try to placate him by invoking the Romantic identification of science with poetry. But for Tyndall, the two fields of cultural activity are quite distinct, and he is accordingly amused at the prospect of being called a "Poet." He writes that the spirits "dubbed" him "Poet of Science," as if they were conferring upon him an aristocratic title. The honorific use of the word "Poet" relegates "science" to a merely contingent and subject dominion, in a manner similar to Wordsworth's 1802 "Preface." Principles that are directly opposed to Victorian scientism and belong to Spiritualism, such as divine inspiration, faith, prophecy, and transcendentalism, are canonized in Romantic poetry. Here the ghostly figure of the Romantic poet functions as the real medium between the spirits and the scientist. But Tyndall of course accepts no such mediation. Far from looking heavenward for truth, he gets down on all fours and crawls under the table, relying exclusively on his senses in his positivist quest to find a material basis for Spiritualist phenomena.

Poetry furnishes an interesting alternative to Spiritualism in Alfred Tennyson's *In Memoriam* (1850), a long series of elegiac lyrics in which the poet communes with his dead friend Arthur Henry Hallam. Tennyson developed a close friendship with Hallam at the University of Cambridge, where they were both elected to the "Apostles," an elite undergraduate society whose twelve members debated pressing intellectual matters of the day. It is to these more abstract issues that Tennyson returns in *In Memoriam*, which he began after Hallam's early death in 1833 and continued writing at intervals until the year before the poem went on sale. The "Prologue," which dates from 1849, brings the principle of religious faith into relief against the poem's implicit acceptance of the current scientistic criterion for knowledge: "We have but faith: we cannot know; / For knowledge is of things we see" (*AT* 21–22). These lines mark a rupture with natural theology, the influential doctrine that allied empiricism with Christianity by claiming that the existence and nature of God could be inferred from natural phenomena. Tennyson knew of this system of thought from at least two documents: first, William Paley's frequently reprinted *Natural Theology; or Evidences of the Existence and Attributes of the Deity, Collected from the Appearances of Nature* (1802); and second, the Bridgewater Treatises (1833–37), a series originating with a bequest left by the eighth Earl of Bridgewater to which such prominent natural philosophers as William Whewell, Tennyson's lecturer at Cambridge, contributed "On the Power, Wisdom, and Good of God as Manifested in the Creation."[4] On several occasions in the poem, Tennyson states that natural theology cannot serve as the basis for his belief in God: "I found Him not in world or sun, / Or eagle's wing, or insect's eye" (CXXIV, 5–6).

Throughout the Victorian era, Tennyson was widely regarded as the principal heir of Romanticism. He was also, according to his friend the Darwinian naturalist T.H. Huxley, "the first poet since Lucretius who has understood the drift of science."[5] For Tennyson and his peers, the most momentous secular application of empirical science prior to Darwin was Charles Lyell's *Principles of Geology* (1830–33), a book that Tennyson – according to his son – was "deeply immersed in" during 1837.[6] Lyell developed James Hutton's theory of uniformitarianism, which claims that what are seemingly the most stable group of natural phenomena, those of the earth beneath our feet, have changed gradually but momentously over history through the actions of such currently observable terrestrial forces as volcanic activity, strata-building, and wind and water erosion. Uniformitarianism demonstrates that the earth is very much older than the biblical account suggests, and that its geological formations can be explained without recourse to such divine interventions as the Great Flood.

Tennyson describes astronomy and geology in his late poem "Parnassus" (1889) as "terrible Muses" (*AT* 16). Both sciences had been formidable sources of inspiration from an early point in his career. His wide reading acquainted him with P.S. Laplace's nebular hypothesis that had by 1800 eliminated the need to invoke God to explain the origin and regular movements of the planets. Laplace argued that the planets orbited in the same plane and the same direction because they had been formed together, in accordance with the laws of physics and chemistry, as the condensation of the sun's revolving gaseous atmosphere. Tennyson alludes to the theory in section CXVIII of *In Memoriam*: "The solid earth wheron we tread / In tracts of fluent heat began" (8–9). Laplace's nebular hypothesis was complemented by the speculations of G.L.L. Buffon and Jean-Baptiste Lamarck on the mutability of species. Lyell's *Principles* was probably the main source for Tennyson's early familiarity with Lamarck's doctrines of evolution, in which an animal's continuous use of specific attributes ensures that certain physical features become more prominent. Lamarck believed that such changes were heritable, so that in his famous example of the giraffe, the neck and front legs of the creature enlarged over time as each generation strove for edible leaves that lay beyond their reach.

The nebular hypothesis, the evidence of the fossil record, and Lamarckian models of species development: all are synthesized in the speculative evolutionary cosmology that Robert Chambers presented anonymously in his popular *Vestiges of the Natural History of Creation* (1844). Tennyson read a review of the book in November 1844 that prompted him to remark: "it seems to contain many speculations with which I have been familiar for years."[7] Section CXVIII presents a progressive evolutionary history that echoes the broad sweep of Chambers's cosmology. Beginning with Laplacian and Lyellian principles of "fluent heat" and "cyclic storms" (11), the stanzas advance to the appearance of humanity and its possible future evolution. At this point, Tennyson appeals to a Lamarckian principle in which human beings strive to purge themselves of their animal inheritance, so that they can "Move upward, working out the beast" (27). But it is noticeable that Tennyson opens the long sentence that features these ideas with the conditional phrase "They say" (7). The skeptical inflection of this phrase emerges more clearly in section CXX, where the poet feels able to dismiss materialist science, even if it should finally establish that human beings are nothing more than "cunning casts in clay": "Let Science prove we are, and then / What matters Science unto men, / At least to me?" (5–8). This is the strongest of Tennyson's challenges to the validity of the scientific project, which he sees as driven inexorably toward materialist conclusions.

But it is not just the status of scientific knowledge that *In Memoriam* brings into question. Early in the poem, Tennyson formulates a dictum about language and nature, and the extent to which they present us with their truths: "For words, like Nature, half reveal / And half conceal the Soul within" (V, 3–4). Although Tennyson retains the Christian-idealist metaphor of spirit that Wordsworth and other Romantics identified with poetry, he suggests that this principle of truth may be undermined by the duplicitous nature of the words that comprise it. If Nature and words are evenly poised between revelation and concealment, between Romantic expressivism and materialist skepticism, how can we know whether their representations in poetry or science actually convey "the Soul within"? This profound uncertainty creates a decisive break not only with the epistemological surety of natural theology but also the optimistic Romantic metaphysic expounded in Wordsworth's "Preface."

In Memoriam proposes that science and poetry "feel" Nature in different ways; they have different "dreams" of Nature. Indeed, the image of the dream that recurs throughout much of the poem[8] provides a series of curious shifting and skeptical commentaries on both positivistic science and Romantic metaphysics. The dream – a state of consciousness in which products of the imagination are experienced with the conviction that they are in fact actual sense-impressions – critiques the positivist faith in sense-data. But in Tennyson's work it soon becomes clear that the dream represents only an unsteady version of idealism. In modern times the ideal – the principle of rational form – has largely been banished from the physical world in which Aristotle entrenched it. As a consequence the ideal has been exiled to individual consciousness. That is why Romantic poets such as Samuel Taylor Coleridge, like Tennyson, are apt to figure it as shadowy and dream-like. In Coleridge's "Constancy to an Ideal Object" (1828), for example, thought "haunt'st" the persona. He compares it to the ghostly effect of the Brocken-specter, an Alpine trick of light and mist in which the spectator perceives the shape of a giant figure unaware that it is he who "makes the shadow, he pursues."[9] According to this modern perspective, there is no guarantee that subjective perception corresponds to an external reality unaffected by individual states of mind. In Tennyson's poem the feeling of sorrow, for example, makes nature succumb to the pathetic fallacy. He perceives "the phantom, Nature" solipsistically: "all the music in her tone" is a "A hollow echo of my own" (III, 9–11).

The Coleridgean epistemological metaphors of dreams, ghosts, and mists are given greater point in Tennyson's poem by contemporary scientific discoveries, ones that question the principle of the "type" (LV, 7; LVI, 1), of a core, soul-like, essence that fixes identity in the face of historical change. As Tennyson mourns his dead friend, his most urgent concern is with the human soul and its immortality: "that of the living whole / . . . / No life may fail beyond the grave" (LV, 1, 4). Here he appears to base his faith in the Aristotelian doctrine of *nous*: "The likest God within the soul." Aristotle claims that this individual soul distinguishes human beings from all other creatures, which have only a reproducible species soul.[10] Consequently, the casual brutality of organic nature – "so careful of the type she seems, / So careless of the single life" (LV, 7–8) – does not threaten Tennyson's hopes for human immortality. As long as nature respects the principle of "type," of species identity, then there is reason to believe with Aristotle that humanity is distinguished from all other species by the divine element of *nous*.

Once the fossil evidence of extinct creatures is introduced, however, this argument by analogy with species-souls yields alarming conclusions about the meaning of human life:

> "So careful of the type?" but no.
> From scarpèd cliff and quarried stone
> She cries "A thousand types are gone:
> I care for nothing, all shall go.
>
> "Thou makest thine appeal to me:
> I bring to life, I bring to death:
> The spirit does but mean the breath:
> I know no more."   (LVI, 1–8)

Here nature articulates the voice of materialism, for which the "spirit" means nothing more than its etymological origins in the Latin *spiritus* as "breath" or "air." Such facets of nature, which were brought to the fore by contemporary geology, generate another dream of nature and its creation that Tennyson experiences as a nightmare. This is what Mother Nature yields as a consequence of the approaches of "Science" in section XXI: "Science reaches forth her arms / To feel from world to world, and charms / Her secret from the latest moon" (18–20). Although it is gendered feminine, Science is attributed with a conventionally masculine boldness that roams over the curvaceous forms of nature's worlds with active exploratory hands and charms cold and remote moons into revealing their secrets. Viewed in the wider perspective of the poem, "To feel" in such a lascivious manner means to interpellate Mother Nature as both primitive and amoral. She thus becomes a chthonic principle alienated from God and the other male protagonists of the poem: "God and Nature [are] then at strife, / That Nature lends such evil dreams" (LV, 5–6). If "love reflects the thing beloved" (LII, 2), then conversely the profane love of positivist science summons "evil dreams" from an abject Mother Nature that is "red in tooth and claw" (LVI, 15). An affront to God, such science "shriek'd against his [i.e. humanity's] creed" (LVI, 16) and found its originary myth for humankind not in Genesis but in the prehistoric world of the dinosaurs that was disclosed by fossil remains:

> Man, her last work, who seemed so fair,
> Such splendid purpose in his eyes,
> Who rolled the psalm to wintry skies,
> Who built him fanes of fruitless prayer,
>
> . . .
>
> No more? A monster then, a dream,
> A discord. Dragons of the prime,
> That tare each other in their slime,
> Were mellow music matched with him. (LVI, 9–12, 21–24)

Toward the close of the poem, the poet feels free to state his acceptance of a Lyellian view of the earth: "They melt like mist, the solid lands, / Like clouds they shape themselves and go" (CXXIII, 7–8). The original idealists Parmenides and Plato confidently equated such flux with unreality. Parmenides (c. 515–after 450 BC) uses strict logic to establish that Being is one, unchanging and consistent with itself, so that conversely the principles of multiplicity and change must be illusory. Plato (428–347 BC) develops this logic in his doctrine of the Forms, which posits the necessary existence of pure, unchanging ideas that are understood only through reason and exist separately from the fluctuant world of sensible things. Tennyson struggles to work within this idealist tradition: "What hope of answer, or redress? / Behind the veil, behind the veil" (LVI, 27–28). By bringing classical idealist criteria to bear upon the thin "veil" of appearances privileged by positivism, he diminishes this view of the world and strengthens his conviction in a private vision: "But in my spirit will I dwell, / And dream my dream, and hold it true" (CXXIII, 9–10). Truth is dreamed here. It is a seemingly arbitrary matter of self-will and personal conviction: a private refuge from a world increasingly colonized by positivistic science.

II

Many English Romantics sought to escape from the effects of British practical science – the factories, crowded cities, and railways of the industrial revolution – by entering into a self-affirming dialogue with nature. Wordsworth's "Lines Composed a Few Miles above Tintern Abbey" (composed 1798, published 1807) dramatizes this flight from modern life, taking solace in the optimistic belief that "Nature never did betray / The heart that loved her."[11] Half a century later *In Memoriam* marks the trauma of this Romantic sensibility as nature, reconceptualized by the new theoretical science of Laplace and Lyell, withdraws from this dialogue. This forced retreat from a Wordsworthian communion with nature is clearly evident in Matthew Arnold's poem "Dover Beach," which was probably composed in 1851 (although not published until 1867). Like *In Memoriam*, "Dover Beach" is often seen as one of the representative poems of its age because it registers a deep sense of spiritual alienation that many educated mid-Victorians felt with the decline of Romanticism and natural theology. But its intellectual preoccupations resonate with a later – arguably more momentous – development in Victorian science: Charles Darwin's theory of evolution.

"Dover Beach" is a monologue addressed to the persona's "love" (*MA* 29). It begins with the speaker meditating upon a scene of serene natural beauty:

> The sea is calm to-night
> The tide is full, the moon lies fair
> Upon the Straits; – on the French coast, the light
> Gleams, and is gone; the cliffs of England stand
> Glimmering and vast, out in the tranquil bay.
> Come to the window, sweet is the night air! (1–6)

Such an opening invites a generic response from its readers, one drawn from their reading of such canonical Romantic poems as "Tintern Abbey," where nature prompts a poet's reveries and presents a stable restorative beauty. Fixed visual imagery renders the sense of stasis in this reverie. Hence the tableau of the sea framed by the window, which is cast in lines that proceed slowly with a basically iambic rhythm weighed down by full vowel sounds. But this sea is not always calm, it only happens to be so "to-night," and is maintained in this state artificially, as a picture, through the perpetual present tense of these lines. The quiet moonlit night is the calm before the storm that gathers as the poem proceeds. Once we are exhorted to focus upon the auditory effects, the reverie is broken, a transition that the poem dramatizes with a series of onomatopoeic techniques and metrical variations upon the established iambic pattern: "Listen! you hear the grating roar / Of pebbles which the waves suck back and fling" (9–10). The reversed rhythm of the trochee enhances the imperative "Listen!" Similarly, the pyrrhic and spondaic substitutions of the second line – which contribute to a sequence of three unstressed and three stressed syllables – mimic the hurried movement of waves sweeping outward and then drawing back slowly and powerfully before the quickened momentum of the final iambic foot. We are thrust into a world familiar to us from Tennyson, a world of fluctuating, treacherous, and violent natural process.

Bereft of the old grounds of faith, the persona of "Dover Beach" scales down the demands that he makes upon the external world:

> Ah, love, let us be true
> To one another! for the world, which seems
> To lie before us like a land of dreams,
> So various, so beautiful, so new,
> Hath really neither joy, nor love, nor light,
> Nor certitude, nor peace, nor help for pain;
> And we are here as on a darkling plain
> Swept with confused alarms of struggle and flight,
> Where ignorant armies clash by night.   (29–37)

Here truth no longer exists in a direct correspondence between the subject and the object world of nature (conceived of either as a Romantic pantheist principle or as the Creation of natural theology). Instead, truth inhabits the relation between the subject and another person who can be trusted to share a private vision and reflect one's selfhood. While the reciprocating subjectivities of the lovers can "be true / To one another," the external "world . . . seems," in an interesting pun, "To lie before us." Arnold's speaker presents the Romantic perception of a benign and beautiful world as mere solipsism. Its existence is conditional upon its viewer; it only "seems" and is "like" an imaginary vision, "a land of dreams" that may be more accurately described as a "lie." Tennyson's idealist metaphor of the phenomenal world as a "veil" – a "veil" behind which "answer, or redress," may be found to affirm his vision (LVI, 28, 27) – has been reversed. Transformed by their vision, the world that "lie[s]" before the lovers is ultimately a veil that obscures the truth of a disturbing, if not vicious, reality.

Placed prominently at the beginning of the second volume of Lyell's *Principles of Geology* is a fold-out map that illustrates the dramatic change over geological time of "the space occupied by Europe, from the conditions of an ocean interspersed with islands to that of a large continent."[12] Arnold uses the phenomenon figuratively to describe a gradual waning of religious belief: "The sea of faith / Was once, too, at the full, and round earth's shore / Lay like the folds of a bright girdle furl'd" (21–23). The chalk cliffs of Dover certainly provide spectacular evidence of the Lyellian process of erosion. But the poem describes another instance of this process in "the grating roar / Of pebbles which the waves suck back, and fling." Indeed, this "roar" can be identified as a treacherous Lyellian undertow to "The sea of faith": "Its melancholy, long, withdrawing roar" (21, 25). Caught in the ceaseless mechanistic cycle of the waves, the pebbles on the beach are, as M.W. Rowe observes, a way of imaging the atomist hypothesis, which sees the ultimate reality of all matter to consist "of nothing but undifferentiated micro-particles clashing ceaselessly in a vacuum."[13] In an age when materialist science is eclipsing traditional Christian belief, the ocean eventually represents not "The sea of faith" but a vast indifferent mechanistic universe of matter in motion.

In its final stanza, "Dover Beach" comes to a precarious rest on dry land. The retreat of "The sea of faith" at the close of the penultimate stanza exposes the shoreline, "the vast edges drear," and introduces the terrestrial world as an atomistic substrate, the "naked shingles of the world." These descriptions are of the beach, the stretch of land shaped and defined by the reach of the tide as it both deposits the pebbles and sand it forms, along with shells and other marine detritus, and partially sweeps away such deposits and erodes exposed coastal rock. As a consequence of these tidal actions, beaches are formed smooth and flat. They retain this nature as geological upheavals push them upward as terraces or plateaus above a new beach. It is as such a raised beach, entirely removed from "The sea of faith" and composed of the atomistic pebbles or sand produced by the tides, that Arnold's "darkling plain" should be understood.

The atomistic "roar" of pebbles finds a further echo in the "clash by night" that closes the poem. The "darkling plain" is no longer "Swept" with the tides that originally formed it but "with confused alarms of struggle and flight": the similarly involuntary but organic dynamism of creatures as they act out of the imperative for survival. To a readership acquainted with Darwin's researches – as indeed most of its readership is likely to have been following the publication of "Dover Beach" since its first publication eight years after *The Origin of Species by Means of Natural Selection* (1859) – the "confused alarms of struggle and flight" may suggest a phrase that Darwin introduces in the subtitle of his book: *The Preservation of Favoured Races in the Struggle for Life*. These "confused alarms" suggests a desperate cacophony as animals prey upon one another in an ongoing "struggle," responding instinctively with "fight or flight" reflexes. In this reading Arnold's "ignorant armies" are identified with contending species: the "type[s]" that Tennyson's Mother Nature, many years before Darwin's *Origin*, values over and above the individuals that comprise it. "Dover Beach" figures this "struggle for life" in the military world where the welfare of the individual is subordinated to that of the group. Similarly, individuals within species are "ignorant" in their actions, behaving with reflexive obedience to the dictates of instinct, much as armies do to the commands of their officers.

Whereas in Lamarck's schemes the engine of biological evolution is the will of the organism, for Darwin the evolutionary process occurs as organisms act involuntarily because of the imperative of species survival. Darwin explains the phenomena of evolution through his principle of natural selection. This theory maintains that heritable variations within species, coupled with keen competition for material sustenance, will ensure that those individuals with advantageous variations will survive and breed, and so come to prevail over those members of their species (and of other species) that are less well adapted to their environment. Darwin's principle makes atoms of individual organisms, which clash with one another to form and maintain the tentative dynamic equilibrium that constitutes the survival of a species within its habitat. The doctrine is consistent with that of physiological reductionism, which was available to Arnold and his peers from the 1840s. The poem's "confused alarms" can be understood in reductionist terms as neurological vibrations that sweep through organisms to issue in the audible actions of "struggle and flight": an energy like that of the tides which sets bodily matter in motion. A raised beach occupied by clashing mechanistic organisms, Arnold's "darkling plain" is both literally and figuratively a higher plane of atomism.

As evolution shifted from being a speculative hypothesis to a scientific doctrine, the natural world became for many Victorian poets a correspondingly more disturbing place. Thomas Hardy consolidates and expands upon Arnold's vision of the "darkling plain." His poem "In a Wood" (composed 1887, published 1896) begins with its Wordsworthian persona, "Heart-halt and spirit-lame, / City-opprest" (TH 9–10) hoping to find in "Nature a soft release / From men's unrest" (15–16). What he discovers in practice, however, is a reality similar to the one that concludes "Dover Beach": the Darwinian "war of nature"[14] mentioned at the end of *Origin of Species* where a belligerence once identified only with humanity now characterizes all vegetable life:

> Great growths and small
> Show them to men akin –
> Combatants all!
> Sycamore shoulders oak,
> Bines the slim sapling yoke,
> Ivy-spun halters choke
> Elms stout and tall.   (18–24)

Hardy's poem exploits the pared-down syntax of newspaper headlines to represent the Darwinian characterization of nature. Here Darwinism is news. It is a new paradigm that strips nature of romantic lushness and reduces it to a mechanistic determinism: a conception that is reinforced by the poem's jolting idiom and hammering rhythm.

Small wonder, then, that in other poems – such as "To Outer Nature" (1898) – Hardy remains deeply nostalgic for a pre-Darwinian and humanized nature: "Show thee as I thought thee / When I early sought thee" (*TH* 1–2). The identical rhymes suggest that in his earlier experiences of nature there was little to distinguish his knowledge from his will, that his understanding of nature was solipsistic. Such Romantic "thought" has been revealed by the progressive force of "Time" to be an idealist encumbrance upon reality, an embellishment that obfuscates the facts of nature: "such readorning," Hardy writes, "Time forbids with scorning" (16–17). The frustrated Will to Truth featured in "To Outer Nature" emerges in the 1866 poem "Hap" as theological. There he argues that even the hypothesis of a cruelly "vengeful god" (*TH* 1) would ensure that the universe was informed with some purpose. In "Hap," the lack of cosmic intent disclosed by modern (principally Darwinian) science means that "joy lies slain" (9). An atomistic "Crass Casualty obstructs the sun and rain" (11), disallowing him from finding in them an intrinsic principle of meaning. Hardy's poem nominates "Hap" as the name for nature's First Principle, a three-letter word to supersede "God."

III

In Memoriam, "Dover Beach," and the poems by Hardy all charge science with draining the natural world of spiritual and metaphysical meaning. George Meredith provides an interesting contrast to such defensive stances in his mischievous sonnet "Lucifer in Starlight" (1883), which contemplates a purely naturalistic universe not with anxiety but amusement. Lucifer rises from Hell "On a starred night" (*GM* 1) to survey the earth:

> Soaring through wider zones that pricked his scars
> With memory of the old revolt from Awe,
> He reached a middle height, and at the stars,
> Which are the brain of heaven, he looked, and sank.
> Around the ancient track marched, rank on rank,
> The army of unalterable law. (9–14)

"The army of unalterable law" – the elaborately lawful universe that modern science discloses – proceeds in supreme indifference to Lucifer. In stark contrast to his old sparring partner God, this "army" offers no prospect of even acknowledging his existence let alone of entering into a contest with him. The Dark Ages cosmology of Lucifer's "dark dominion" is simply incommensurable with the rationalist post-Enlightenment cosmology of modern science: the superstition and myth of this Christian cosmology is banished by the rule of "unalterable law." "Lucifer in Starlight" is an approving allegory that upholds science's disenchantment of the natural world.

Meredith's poem carefully extricates the scientific understanding of the starry heavens from the conclusions drawn by natural theology. The sublime prospect of the stars at night provided Paley and his followers with their most enduring ground. As late as 1888, the *Encyclopaedia Britannica* asserted: "'God's glory in the heavens' . . . is in some degree visible to the naked eye and uninstructed intellect, but it becomes more perceptible and more impressive with every discovery of astronomy."[15] While developments in the biological sciences had radically undermined a large part of natural theology's territory, astronomy could still be called upon to sustain it. But in Meredith's poem the regularities of the heavenly world represent not the mind of God, as they did in Pythagorean and Newtonian traditions, but "the brain of heaven."

The advent from mid-century of the reductionist science of neurophysiology effectively attacked the metaphysical and theological principles of mind and soul by locating the seat of human rationality and individual identity in the physical organ of the brain. Throughout *Principles of Psychology* (1855), Herbert Spencer argued that this material basis for thought was the product of evolution: a hypothesis that gained credibility during the following decades through the work of Darwin and Huxley, among others. Meredith expounds a version of this evolutionary understanding in some of the companion poems to "Lucifer in Starlight," such as "The Woods of the Westermain" (1883): "Each of each in sequent birth, / Blood and brain and spirit" (*GM* 169–70). By describing the stars as "the brain of heaven," Meredith does not simply import a principle of materialist science into what had been traditionally regarded as the metaphysical, theological and poetic realm of the heavens. He also implies an understanding of the universe according to the nebular hypothesis and other developmentalist theories.

Lucifer's acquiescence to the universe of "unalterable law" marks his demythologization. The conceit by which "he looked, and sank" plays on the meaning of the devil's title of Lucifer, which derives from Isaiah 14: 12: "How you are fallen from heaven, / O Day Star, son of Dawn!'" Lucifer is a name for the morning (or day) star, the planet Venus, which appears daily just before sunrise like a bright star and once every eight years in its transit across the face of the sun as a dark circle, "the black planet" (8). Rather like Bunbury in Wilde's *The Importance of Being Earnest* (1895), whom

"The doctors found out . . . could not live . . . – so Bunbury died,"[16] Lucifer is discovered by science to be a myth and forced to revert to being the natural phenomenon that gave rise to it. He resumes his humble part within "The army of unalterable law." Like the "Red Sails in the Sunset" of the old song, "Lucifer in Starlight" becomes barely perceptible, submerged in the indirect light that it reflects and shares with other celestial bodies.

Meredith's witty poem can be read as an unobjectionable instance of biblical criticism. Just as the science of Lyell and his peers broke from the guiding principles of natural theology to explain natural phenomena exclusively by terrestrial laws, so biblical criticism similarly approached the Bible rationally and naturalistically, as Robert Browning put it in "Christmas-Eve" (1850), "To sift the truth of it from fable" (RB 931). Each refuses to credit the supernaturalism that traditionally provided the premise for studies of the twin books of Nature and Revelation. Although biblical criticism has its roots in the Enlightenment, its most momentous statement comes in 1835 and 1836, with the publication in Germany of David Friedrich Strauss's two-volume *Life of Jesus*. Strauss uses the category of myth to explain Biblical accounts of miracles and other phenomena that he judges to be inconsistent with the universals governing experience, such as the laws of cause and effect. Thus miracles are regarded as the culturally specific ways in which religious ideas are imaginatively expressed. They are stories that belong to the folklore of their time and place. Biblical criticism came to public attention in Britain with the publication of George Eliot's translation of Strauss's *Life* in 1846. Meredith's treatment of the Lucifer myth is a whimsical afterthought to the devastating impact of biblical criticism in England during the middle years of the century.

Browning's "Christmas-Eve" features a representative "Critic" of the Bible lecturing on the Straussian theme of the "Myth of Christ" (RB 859). The persona of the poem marks Christmas Eve by attending several church services. He begins in the chapel of some Dissenters. In the nineteenth century, the Dissenters were largely synonymous with the Evangelical movement, which by insisting upon very literal readings of the Bible as the basis of faith and the guide to conduct are dramatically opposed to the liberalism of the biblical critics. Similarly, the simplicity of the Dissenters' practices of worship contrasts starkly with the elaborate rituals of Roman Catholicism, the other type of Christianity represented in Browning's poem. After leaving the Dissenters' service, Browning's persona proceeds, with God as his silent guide (and mode of transport), to St Peter's in Rome, before reaching the door of the German lecture theatre where the biblical critic delivers his address. Browning's speaker then takes stock of all that he has seen that night, drawing upon science for a metaphor to facilitate his comparison of biblical criticism with Roman Catholicism and Dissent:

> This time he would not bid me enter
> The exhausted air-bell of the Critic.
> Truth's atmosphere may grow mephitic
> When Papist struggles with Dissenter,
> Impregnating its pristine clarity,
> – One, by his daily fare's vulgarity,
>   Its gust of broken meat and garlic;
> – One, by his soul's too-much presuming
> To turn the frankincense's fuming
>   And vapours of the candle starlike
> Into the cloud her wings she buoys on.
>   Each, that thus sets the pure air seething,
>   May poison it for healthy breathing –
> But the Critic leaves no air to poison;
> Pumps out with ruthless ingenuity
> Atom by atom, and leaves you – vacuity.   (897–913)

The "air-bell" is a glass bell-shaped apparatus that was used in experiments on the processes of combustion and respiration, most momentously by Joseph Priestley and Antoine Lavoisier in the second half of the eighteenth century. By placing a living organism (or burning matter) in the bell, the gaseous transactions between it and the enclosed air can be contained and observed. The poem figures both the "Dissenter" and the "Papist" as distinctive organisms that, in asserting their complementary modes of Christianity, pollute the eternal realm of "Truth's atmosphere." The former exhale the honest and abject reek of ordinary mortal life, a "gust of broken meat and garlic," while the latter respire the cleansing fumes of incense and candles, which offer to transcend such intimations of mortality. Browning's metaphor builds on the ancient analogy of the breath with the spirit, which can be traced back both to the pre-Socratic philosopher Anaximenes (c.587–c.527 BC), who claimed "our soul . . . being air holds us together and controls us,[17] and to the Bible, which maintains that God breathed the soul into the original human body (Wisdom 15: 11). The Dissenters and the Roman Catholics inflect the divine spirit, the ground of their respective modes of Christianity, with their physical – and thus finite – nature. In the late eighteenth century, experiments with the "air-bell" established that all such forms of combustion (including animal respiration, as Laplace and Lavoisier proved) exchange oxygen in the air for irrespirable carbon dioxide: the distinctive "poison" that "sets the pure air seething" in the poem. "When Papist struggles with Dissenter," the heated expulsion of their breath makes the air "mephitic," filling it with the waste gas carbon dioxide (which Priestley observes was often termed mephitic air or acid).[18]

Browning's analogy presents the poisonous "struggles" between the Dissenting churches and Roman Catholicism as a natural excrescence of these human institutions. Moreover, the Dissenters' chapel and St. Peter's "miraculous Dome of God" (529) are open both to the purifying, uplifting, divine spirit and the sinful, self-poisoning, human spirit. They are, then, open air-bells, analogous to the respiration apparatus that Henri Victor Regnault and Jules Reiset presented to the world in 1849; Regnault and Reiset were the first scientists to both feed oxygen to the bell chamber and remove the carbon dioxide produced by the captive animal.[19] The mixture of eternal spirit and mortal breath in the open air-bells of the Catholics and Dissenters is sanctioned by the peculiar nature of Christ as God Incarnate: "He himself with his human air" (432).

While the Catholics and the Dissenters make the air "mephitic" with their exhalations, "the Critic leaves no air to poison." The poem presents the "laboratory of the Professor" (1243): the "air-bell" of his lecture theatre that is not only hermetically sealed but also equipped with an air-pump that draws out all air, leaving only a vacuum. This mechanism appears in Joseph Wright's painting *An Experiment on a Bird in the Air Pump* (1767–68). Wright depicts the dramatic moment when a scientific demonstrator, having pumped out the air from a glass chamber holding an almost asphyxiated bird, is about to restore it to the vacuum, though probably too late to save the animal. The biblical critic in Browning's poem is, like the demonstrator in Wright's painting, charged with a crime of vivisection, a spiritual asphyxiation. The lecturer, with "his cough, like a drouthy piston" (893), is the mechanism that extracts all air, all breath and spirit from the "air-bell," thus suffocating and desiccating all about him. The parallel that Browning's analogy draws of the biblical critic to the vivisecting scientist highlights the broadly scientistic approach that they share.

IV

The scientific knowledge of air advanced greatly in the decades that separate Browning's "Christmas-Eve" from Gerard Manley Hopkins's poem "The Blessed Virgin Compared to the Air We Breathe," which was composed in 1883. Hopkins's "world-mothering air" (*GMH* 1, 124) is not only the medium supporting both physical and spiritual life but also the medium through which sunlight passes. By analogy, the Virgin Mary figures as the medium through which "God's infinity" (18) assumes the finite human form of Christ: God's "light / Sifted to suit our sight"

(112–13). The poem describes the air as a "fine flood": a physical medium like water. The sky, the body of air which surrounds the earth, shares Mary's color: it is a "bath of blue" able to "slake / His fire" (95–96). Gillian Beer has traced the scientific explanation that informs Hopkins's understanding of "How air is azurèd" (74), thereby softening the harshness of the sun's rays, to Tyndall.[20] In 1870, Tyndall established that minute particles in the atmosphere cause the refraction of solar rays, especially of those that have a small wavelength, which our eyesight registers as the color blue. That the air of the sky is not, as was previously supposed, stained blue is clear from the fact that

> this blue heaven
> The seven or seven times seven
> Hued sunbeam will transmit
> Perfect, not alter it.   (86–89)

In these lines, the sunbeam splits not only into the seven hues of the Newtonian spectrum but also into the much finer gradations disclosed by the new science of spectroscopy. During the 1850s Robert Bunsen and Gustave Kirchhoff proved that each chemical element, when added to a clean gas flame, produced a definitive wavelength of light. When such light is passed through a prism, it discloses a "bright line" of color at a particular point of the spectrum. As an undergraduate at Oxford during the 1860s, Hopkins was aware of "the spectral analysis by wh[ich] the chemical composition of non-terrestrial masses is made out."[21] His "seven times seven / Hued sunbeam" is an aptly approximate reference to the growing but often contested tallies of solar chemical elements that scientists were making in the latter part of the century. The astronomer Norman Lockyer, for example, writing in 1878, counted "more than thirty" of the fifty-one known terrestrial metals from solar light.[22]

Spectroscopy provides Hopkins with an apt analogy to describe his ontology, which values individual difference as an expression of God's nature. It is for Hopkins the very specificity – the tightly focused distinctiveness – of the "bright line" that makes an instance of being integral to the ultimate Being of God. The inclusive yet transcendent white light of the Sun is, scientifically speaking, the source of all energy and life in the universe. Each creature is necessary as the means to disclose, by absorption and reflection, aspects of the vast spectrum of Being that, as pure transparent white light, would otherwise be imperceptible. This is a feature evident in the untitled poem, dating from 1877, that begins:

> As kingfishers catch fire, dragonflies draw flame;
>   As tumbled over rim in roundy wells

> Stones ring; like each tucked string tells, each hung bell's
> Bow swung finds tongue to fling out broad its name   (*GMH* 1–4)

Here the optical spectrum has come to parallel the musical scale. Just as the distinctive being of the creatures is caught in the manner of spectroscopy in a definitive flash of light, so too the respective natures of the stones, string and bell issue as specific sounds.[23] The common principle is a physical dynamism: the regular pattern of agitation in the respective media of the luminiferous ether (posited by the wave-theory of light), together with the air through which sound is also propagated in the form of waves. Indeed, the formal analogy of the wave is neatly presented by Hopkins's punning image of "stones" that "ring" both visibly through the surface of the water and audibly through the air. Such semantic richness marks an instance of the saturated participation in being, in activity, that Hopkins's poetry insists upon. These lines require that the reader "find . . . tongue" and exercise it by moving through the obstacle course of their prosody: a sequence of alliteration, internal rhymes, and crisp consonants wrapped around closely packed contrasting vowel sounds often marked by strong stresses. He emphasizes that he wrote his poetry to be read aloud. In a fragment written in 1865, he understood speech as a physical activity and sound as vibration: "Where is the tongue that drives the stony air to utterance?" ("O what a silence in this wilderness!" [*GMH* 14–15]). Most of his mature poetry implicitly poses this question, demanding that the latent energy of print be actualized by speech.

The analogy that Hopkins draws between sound and light is based upon an understanding of each as a dynamic formal principle, a particular pattern of movement in a material medium. Such understandings presuppose thermodynamics, the science that emerged in the 1820s from the study of the steam engine. By the 1860s, this area of scientific research conceived of not only heat and work but also electricity, magnetism, light, and sound as translatable modes of an abstract quantitative principle that was becoming known as energy. The principle of the conservation of energy maintains that whatever transformations such principles undergo there is always, as Henri Poincaré puts it, "*a something which remains constant.*"[24] Hence energy is described either as potential or as actual. The movement from the latent to the actual state appears in Hopkins's poem "Tom's Garland: On the Unemployed" (composed 1887) where the friction of the working man Tom's boots on paving stones generates a spark: it "rips out rockfire" (*GMH* 3). For Hopkins, the source of all such energy is God: "As kingfishers catch fire" they manifest this energy as a distinctive pitch of light. Hopkins conceives of God's presence as a huge charge of energy that can be actualized at any moment, as we see in the opening of "God's Grandeur" (written in 1877): "The world is charged with the grandeur of God. / It will flame out, like shining from shook foil" (*GMH* 1–2).

The equation of God's power with energy that we find in "God's Grandeur" is elaborated systematically in the doctrine of "stress," "instress," and "inscape" that Hopkins develops in his 1868 reading of the pre-Socratic monist Parmenides.[25] Hopkins, like many of his peers in the 1860s, recognizes that the new ontology of energy physics effectively reinstates metaphysical monism, the theory that ultimate reality consists of one thing (such as Being, spirit, or thought). Indeed, the simultaneous discovery of the energy principle during the 1840s was probably the consequence of scientists working independently within the organicist traditions of Romantic science. Many of these scientists began with the Romantic presupposition of an overarching unity to nature, which they put on a scientific footing with the discovery and development of energy physics.[26] Not only was the energy principle of foundational importance to neurophysiology (where it fitted into a reductionist ontology that countered the Romantic hypothesis of vitalism), it also served to resuscitate the grand Romantic cosmology that Coleridge summed up in his poem "The Eolian Harp" (1795) as "the one Life within us and abroad."[27] It provided Hopkins with the means of developing his peculiarly dynamic version of natural theology during the Darwinian decades of the 1860s, 1870s, and 1880s.

In "Duns Scotus's Oxford" (composed 1879), the world is for Hopkins an energy plenum: "Cuckoo-échoing, bell-swármed, lark-chármèd, rook-rácked, river-róunded" (*GMH* 2). This line demonstrates the way in which Hopkins's well-known theory and practice of "Sprung Rhythm" registers the ontological status of what he calls, in his spiritual writings, "stress or energy."[28] "Sprung Rhythm" makes the stressed syllable the measure of each metrical foot. On this model, a strong stress can carry with it up to three other "slack" syllables.[29] This method means that, along with such other formal features as internal rhyme and alliteration, lines such as this one from "Duns Scotus's Oxford" reproduce in microcosm the barely contained dynamism of Hopkins's world.

"That Nature Is a Heraclitean Fire and of the Comfort of the Resurrection" (composed 1888) is a caudated sonnet – that is, a sonnet with "a tail" – that enlarges this dynamic vision to consider the earth's atmosphere:

> Cloud-puffball, torn tufts, tossed pillows I flaunt forth, then chevy on
>   an air-
> Built thoroughfare: heaven-roysterers, in gay-gangs I they throng; they
>   glitter in marches.

Down roughcast, down dazzling whitewash | wherever an elm arches,
Shivelights and shadowtackle ín long | lashes lace, lance, and pair.
Delightfully the bright wind boisterous | ropes, wrestles, beats earth
    bare
Of yestertempest's creases; in pool and rutpeel parches
Squandering ooze to squeezed | dough, crúst, dust; stánches, stárches
Squadroned masks and manmarks | treadmire toil there
Fóotfretted in it. Million-fuelèd | nature's bonfire burns on.   (*GMH* 1–9)

The meteorological phenomena of wind, clouds, and evaporation illustrate
"nature's bonfire." A closed system of heat and water vapor comparable to
that of the steam engine, the physics of this "bonfire" is understood to be
that of thermodynamics. The diurnal and seasonal variations in the
exposure of atmospheric air to the sun's heat, along with such factors as the
amount of moisture in the air (which holds such heat better than dry air),
cause differences in pressure among bodies of air. In 1868 a series of maps
was published that chart the distribution of the air pressure in the earth's
atmosphere and the pattern of the prevailing winds for each month of the
year. From these charts came the understanding that wind occurs as the
flow of high-pressure air to areas of lower pressure. Clouds are formed as
the temperature of bodies of air drop, thus causing the condensation of
their moisture. Particular cloud formations and their alterations in shape
and position make visible the changing patterns of heat, moisture, and
pressure distribution in the earth's atmosphere. Put more radically, all such
phenomena have their source in complicated thermodynamic relations
between bodies of air and water: "All things," Heraclitus declares, "are an
equal exchange for fire and fire for all things."[30] The swiftly moving
glittering and protean clouds, like the efficacious evaporative effects of the
wind on the "ooze" that are also described by the poem, make "nature's
bonfire" visible and identify it with the entire atmosphere of the earth.
Indeed, we are made to replicate the changes in air pressure that determine
the phenomena of clouds described at the beginning of the poem when we
read these lines aloud. In doing so we have to deploy breath with sufficient
pressure to mark each of the discrete and deliberate staccato stresses and
long vowel sounds of the opening phrases – "Cloud-puffball, torn tufts,
tossed pillows | flaunt forth" – before the more rapid even exhalation
required for the pyrrhic sequence in the phrase "then chevy on an air- /
Built thoroughfare," which describes the quick light movement of the
clouds that is facilitated by an expanse of warm rising air. Through such
techniques, Hopkins makes us enact gestures that reciprocate God's graces,
giving the breath of life and other graces back to God, their source. "Resign
them, sign them, seal them, send them, mótion them with breath," he

writes in "The Golden Echo and the Leaden Echo" (composed 1882; *GMH* 33). Here he literalizes – makes physical – the Christian-idealist analogy of spirit and breath that absorbs Wordsworth's, Tennyson's, and Browning's attention. He collapses the abstract and the concrete: the idealist and positivist understandings of "breath" that Wordsworth relies upon in making his influential "contradistinction . . . of Poetry and Matter of Fact, or Science."[31]

NOTES

1 William Wordsworth, "Preface" (1802) to *Lyrical Ballads*, in *Wordsworth's Literary Criticism*, ed. W.J.B. Owen (London: Routledge and Kegan Paul, 1974), 80–81.

2 John Tyndall, "Science and Spirits," *Fragments of Science for Unscientific People* (London: Longmans, Green, 1871), 433–34.

3 See Tyndall, *Fragments of Science for Unscientific People*, 29–37, 38–68, 445–49.

4 William Whewell, *Astronomy and General Physics, Considered with Reference to Natural Theology* (London: William Pickering, 1833).

5 T.H. Huxley, *Life and Letters of Thomas Henry Huxley*, ed. Leonard Huxley, 2 vols. (London: Macmillan, 1900), II, 338, cited in D.R. Oldroyd, *Darwinian Impacts: An Introduction to the Darwinian Revolution*, second edition (Kensington, NSW: New South Wales University Press, 1983), 312.

6 Hallam Tennyson, *Alfred Lord Tennyson: A Memoir by His Son*, 2 vols. (London: Macmillan, 1897), I, 162.

7 Tennyson, "To Edward Moxon," 15 November 1844, in *The Letters of Alfred Lord Tennyson*, ed. Cecil Y. Lang and Edgar F. Shannon Jr., 3 vols. (Cambridge, MA: Harvard University Press, 1981–90), I, 230.

8 See, for example, the following lines: X, 9; XIII, 15; XLII, 4; XLVII, 11; LV, 6; LXIV, 17; LXVI, 14; LXVIII, 4; LXIX, 1; LXXXIX, 36; CXXIII, 10.

9 Samuel Taylor Coleridge, *The Poems*, ed. Ernest Hartley Coleridge (London: Oxford University Press, 1912), 456.

10 See Aristotle, *De Anima*, II. 4. 415a23–415b15 on the reproducible species soul, and *Nicomachean Ethics* X. 7. 1177b26–78a8 on *nous*.

11 Wordsworth, "Lines Composed a Few Miles above Tintern Abbey, on Revisiting the Banks of the Wye during a Tour, 13th July 1798," in *Lyrical Ballads and Other Poems, 1797–1900*, ed. James Butler and Karen Green, The Cornell Wordsworth (Ithaca, NY: Cornell University Press, 1992), 119.

12 Charles Lyell, *Principles of Geology*, second edition, 3 vols. (London: John Murray, 1832–33), II, 308. The map faces the first page. See Lyell's commentary on the fold-out map (II, 304–10) and his discussion of chalk and the geology of south-east England in III, 285–323.

13 M.W. Rowe, "Arnold and the Metaphysics of Science: A Note on 'Dover Beach,'" *Victorian Poetry* 27 (1989), 216–17.

14 Charles Darwin, *The Origin of Species*, ed. Gillian Beer, World's Classics (Oxford: Oxford University Press, 1996), 396.

15 Robert Flint, "Theism," *Encyclopaedia Britannica*, ninth edition (Edinburgh: Adam and Charles Black, 1888), XXIII, 249.

16 Oscar Wilde, *The Importance of Being Earnest: A Trivial Comedy for Serious People*, ed. Russell Jackson (London: Ernest Benn, 1980), 87.

17 See G.S. Kirk, J.E. Raven and M. Schofield, *The PreSocratic Philosophers*, second edition (Cambridge: Cambridge University Press, 1983), 158.

18 Joseph Priestley, *Experiments and Observations on Different Kinds of Air*, 3 vols. (Birmingham: Thomas Pearson, 1790), I, 8.

19 V. Regnault and J. Reiset, "Recherches chimiques sur la respiration des animaux des diverse classes," *Annalles de chimies et de physiques*, 3me série, 26 (1849), 299–519.

20 Gillian Beer, "Helmholtz, Tyndall, Gerard Manley Hopkins: Leaps of the Prepared Imagination," in Beer, *Open Fields: Science in Cultural Encounter* (Oxford: Clarendon Press, 1996), 264–6.

21 Gerard Manley Hopkins, "The Tests of a Progressive Science" (MSS, Campion Hall, D. IX 2, folio 3), in Hopkins, *Journals and Papers*, ed. G. Castorina (Bari: Adriatica, 1974), 181.

22 Norman Lockyer, "What the Sun is Made of," *Nineteenth Century* 4 (1878), 79.

23 For a fuller discussion of this point see Daniel Brown, *Hopkins's Idealism: Philosophy, Physics, Poetry* (Oxford: Clarendon Press, 1997), 247–51.

24 Henri Poincairé, *Science and Hypothesis*, trans. W.J.G. (London: Walter Scott, 1905), 127.

25 Gerard Manley Hopkins, "Parmenides," in Hopkins, *The Journals and Papers*, ed. Humphry House and Graham Storey (London: Oxford University Press, 1959), 127–30.

26 See Thomas Kuhn, "Energy Conservation as Simultaneous Discovery," *Critical Problems in the History of Science*, ed. Marshall Clagett (Madison, WI: University of Wisconsin Press, 1959), 321–56.

27 Coleridge, *The Poems*, 101.

28 Gerard Manley Hopkins, *The Sermons and Devotional Writings*, ed. Christopher Devlin (London: Oxford University Press, 1959), 137.

29 For an account of Hopkins's unique prosodic terms, see his "Author's Preface on Rhythm," reprinted in *The Poetical Works*, 115–17.

30 Fragment 219, in Kirk, Raven and Schofield, *The PreSocratic Philosophers*, 198.

31 Wordsworth, "Preface" (1802) to *Lyrical Ballads*, 95.

8

CYNTHIA SCHEINBERG

Victorian poetry and religious diversity

I

Among the Romans a poet was called *vates*, which is as much a diviner, foreseer or prophet . . . so heavenly a title did that excellent people bestow upon this heart-ravishing knowledge . . . And may not I presume a little further, to show the reasonableness of this word *vates*, and say that the holy David's Psalms are a divine poem? . . . Neither let it be deemed too saucy a comparison to balance the highest point of man's wit with the efficacy of nature; but rather give right honour to the heavenly Maker of that maker.

– Sir Philip Sidney, *The Defence of Poetry* (1595)[1]

Vates means both Prophet and Poet; and indeed at all times, Prophet and Poet, well understood, have much kindred of meaning. Fundamentally indeed they are still the same; in this most important respect especially, that they have penetrated both of them into the sacred mystery of the Universe, what Goethe calls "the open secret!" . . . But now I say, whoever may forget this divine mystery, the Vates, whether Prophet or Poet, has penetrated into it; is a man sent hither to make it more impressively known to us.

– Thomas Carlyle, "The Hero as Poet" (1841)[2]

By placing Sir Philip Sidney's remarks on the poet as vates or prophet next to Thomas Carlyle's similar invocation of the Poet as Prophet, it becomes clear that by the Victorian age the concept of poetry has been linked to religious utterance for at least two hundred and fifty years. Both writers claim that the poet and the prophet have access to the divine. Yet if for both Sidney and Carlyle the poet is represented as a prophet and the prophet a kind of poet, the distinct differences that each writer offers in their understanding of the vates are important to note as well. On the one hand, Sidney's references to ancient Jewish and classical cultures give specific historical and religious contexts for this notion of the *vates*, while on the other, Carlyle suggests the connection between poetry and prophecy is fundamental, and therefore transcends cultural or historical boundaries. Situating the poet-prophet within the literary and religious realm of

Christianity – which claims that God is a Heavenly Maker who in turn makes the poet, and asserts that the holy Psalms were authored by King David – Sidney's notions of poetry are rooted in a particular set of religious preconceptions about biblical authorship, divine creation, and scriptural history that he readily assumes that his audience will share. By comparison, Carlyle uses altogether vaguer references to spirituality, referring to "the sacred mystery of the Universe, what Goethe calls 'the open secret!'" Calling on a distinguished German Romantic writer rather than specific scriptural or doctrinal allusions, Carlyle noticeably avoids defining a specific religious context for the divine knowledge that his *vates* receives. Indeed, Carlyle's open-ended descriptions of the very nature of the "divine secret" reflect significant shifts in literary and religious cultures since the time when Sidney's famous essay appeared.

In this chapter, I argue that one way to explain the decisively "open" language that characterizes Carlyle's naming of the prophetic nature of the vates is that in nineteenth-century England it had become increasingly difficult to designate any one theological position as a source of universal truth for the nation. Despite the fact that England still had a state religion (Anglicanism), Carlyle's society was differentiated from Sidney's by an increased presence of diverse religious communities that were gaining economic, political, and social status. Victorian religious poetry became an important site for presenting divergent religious perspectives, providing a dynamic forum where writers frequently explored the fraught experience of living as a religious "other" in England.

It is perhaps easiest to understand the increasing diversity that marked Victorian poetic and religious identity by examining some of the salient historical changes that occurred in English culture between the sixteenth and nineteenth centuries. In Sidney's England, poetry was for the most part a courtly endeavor, one that had distinct ramifications for the relationships that poetry maintained with religious authority, religious discourse, and religious doctrine. In 1534 Henry VIII had broken from the Roman Catholic Church and established the Anglican Church, placing himself at its head. After the death of Henry VIII's heir Edward VI in 1553, however, Queen Mary returned the monarchy to the Roman Catholic Church, and religious and national turbulence ruled in England during her five-year reign. It was Henry VIII's younger daughter Elizabeth who eventually gained the throne in 1558 and solidified the bonds between the English government, the Anglican Church, and the nobles of the court who supported the newly formed state religion. In Elizabethan England, poets and poetry were supported through royal and noble patronage, and so in essence poetry was also bonded to the Anglican institutions to which all of the Elizabethan court were subject. As Gary Waller writes: "The Court . . . appropriated poetry as one of the many practices by which it tried to exercise cultural dominance."[3]

There was, of course, a degree of religious diversity in sixteenth-century England despite the dominance of Anglican literary and religious culture. While there was no significant Jewish community in Renaissance England – since all Jews had been expelled from England in 1290, and were not to return until 1656 when Oliver Cromwell held power as Lord Protector – there were other religious groups who did not profess allegiance to the Church of England. In this respect, the most obvious group was the Roman Catholics who defied Henry VIII's Act of Supremacy. In addition, there were Dissenters (often termed Puritans) – including Baptists, Independents, and Presbyterians – who argued for a more thorough reform of the English Church. Whereas Henry VIII had changed certain aspects of authority and Church practice from Roman Catholicism, his reform nevertheless maintained many of the rituals and hierarchies of Church authority that Dissenters sought to transform even more radically.

If, however, there was a variety of Dissenters in Elizabethan England, their literary efforts remained largely outside the literary institutions linked to the court, and were therefore far less likely to have been preserved in later historical periods. In this respect, it is useful to observe that, although Sidney's *Defence of Poetry* is a canonized essay, the work that galvanized Sidney's critical discussion was the Dissenter Stephen Gosson's *School of Abuse* (1579), which declared that "the whole practice of Poets, either with fables to show their abuse, or with plain terms to unfold their mischief, discover their shame, discredit themselves, and disperse their poison through all the world."[4] Needless to say, Gosson's Puritan criticism has rarely been seen as a representative voice in English literary history. Instead, the literary canon has tended to focus, until quite recently, on men – such as the poets John Donne, George Herbert, Christopher Marlowe, and Edmund Spenser – who were, like Sidney, educated in Anglican institutions in preparation for holy orders (though not all chose to take that professional route). The literary opinions of the non-Anglican minorities were, when the threat of civil revolution loomed in the seventeenth century, increasingly dangerous to hold. The political and religious chaos that came with Mary's brief reign as a Roman Catholic monarch, and the later revolution by Cromwell and the various Puritan groups aligned with him indicate that religious diversity was often understood as a threat to the political stability of England.

When we turn our attention to the nineteenth century, significant contrasts immediately emerge in relation to both literary and religious history. The growing influence and state recognition of non-Anglican religious communities becomes most apparent in a series of Parliamentary acts throughout the middle decades of the century. Of central importance was the 1828 repeal of the Test and Corporation Acts that mandated that all public offices in England be held by members of the Church of England. Although these acts were primarily symbolic – since there were legal loopholes that allowed Dissenters to serve in public offices prior to this act – their abolition signaled, in Gerald Parsons's words, "the growing influence of Nonconformity and changing attitude towards religious establishments."[5] In 1829 the Catholic Relief Act granted Roman Catholics the same political rights held by Protestant Nonconformists. It would take until 1858 before Parliament voted to modify the Christian oath of office so that Jewish people could freely take up elected positions without having to swear "on the true faith of a Christian."

These significant political reforms reflected the increased influence of a number of different religious groups whose numbers and organizations had grown enormously in the late eighteenth and early nineteenth centuries. The Dissenters of the earlier centuries now tended to be referred to as Nonconformists. As Parsons has written: "the 1851 Religious Census" (the first of its kind in Britain) "made clear the diversity of Victorian Nonconformity . . . It revealed no less than thirty separate Non-conformist traditions"; he makes distinctions in these groups between "Old Dissent" (groups whose roots came out of the religious controversies of the seventeenth century) and "New Dissent" (which consisted of "Methodists, Calvinistic Methodists and a minority of Baptists . . . and was a product of the Evangelical Revival of the eighteenth century").[6] Along with a marked rise in the Nonconformist movements, the nineteenth century also witnessed considerable transformations in both Jewish and Roman Catholic communities. What linked these two quite different religious constituencies was the Anglican assumption that Roman Catholics might claim a primary allegiance to the Vatican and Jews might associate with a collective notion of "Israel" that saw itself to some degree independent from the English state. As a consequence, it was felt that both of these distinctive affiliations might limit Roman Catholic and Jewish loyalties to English national identity. The anxiety about Roman Catholic allegiance was surely augmented by the fact, as Parsons remarks, that "between 1800–1850 the number of Roman Catholics in England and Wales had increased dramatically from under 100,000 to approximately 750,000."[7] "Most of this increase," he adds, "was due to Irish immigration." Parsons notes that the rapid growth in this Roman Catholic minority was only one cause of the virulent anti-Catholicism evident in the mid-century. Other causes, he observes, were "anti-Irish immigrant prejudice, traditional doubts about the compatibility of loyalty and Catholicism, the vitality of converts and the unfamiliarity of their devotional life, and the internal disarray of English Protestantism."[8] Nevertheless, despite a prejudice against "Popery" in Anglican culture, Roman Catholicism "achieved the status of principal religious alternative to the established church."[9]

In the national debates about Jewish identity, the question that was repeatedly asked focused on whether Jews could be full citizens in an explicitly Christian nation. The Anglo-Jewish community had also grown significantly since readmission under Cromwell. In 1800, the Jewish population was estimated at 25,000, growing to 35,000 in 1850, and expanding to 60,000 by 1880 (the latter increase mostly coming from immigration from Eastern Europe). Indeed, these late-century immigrants had an important effect in changing certain aspects of Anglo-Jewry. The earliest generations of Jewish people to resettle in England in the seventeenth and eighteenth centuries had been Sephardic Jews who traced their roots to Portugal and Spain. It was primarily these earlier Sephardic families who also emerged in the nineteenth century as highly successful in English economic, political, and social life, as the history of families such as the Montefiores and the Disraelis demonstrated. Despite the fact that he was baptized in the Anglican Church as a child, Benjamin Disraeli was constantly referred to as the "Hebrew premier" and contributed greatly to the general population's awareness of Jewish identity in the nation. While the Sephardic community grew in cultural authority and economic prestige, later waves of immigrants in the latter part of the nineteenth century came from primarily from poorer Ashkenazi (Eastern European) backgrounds and were often associated, in the dominant English cultural consciousness, with poverty, crime, and disease. Israel Zangwill's novel *Children of the Ghetto: A Study of a Peculiar People* (1892) offers a unique glimpse into the distinctions between the lives of the Ashkenazic and Sephardic communities and cultures of late-nineteenth-century London.[10]

It was not only non-Anglican groups and institutions that underwent change in the nineteenth century. The Anglican Church itself was also deeply influenced by the broad spectrum of religious life in Victorian England. By the mid-century three different brands of Anglicanism – Broad (or Liberal); High (Anglo-Catholic); and Low (Evangelical) – had emerged as distinct groups within the Church of England. High Church Anglicanism, often termed Anglo-Catholicism, maintained the most complex rituals and adherence to Church hierarchy. Supported by the Oxford Movement – an influential group of clerics and scholars who from 1833 onward argued that the Anglican Church, rather than Roman Catholic

Church, was indeed the apostolic Church of Christianity – High Church Anglicans faced a crisis when one of their leaders, John Henry Newman, converted to Roman Catholicism in 1845.[11] At the opposite end stood the Low Church, often linked to the Evangelical revival of the eighteenth century, and where, as John Wolffe discusses, there was "a divergence between Evangelicals who remained loyal to the Church of England and those who ultimately moved into Methodism."[12] A third Anglican group in this period was the Broad Church, which Wolffe claims was "difficult to categorize or identify,"[13] since it was unified around a belief in the importance of the comprehensive national identity of the Church, drawing on a number of intellectual movements of the day. Occupying the middle ground between the High and Low Church, Broad Churchmen sought to maintain Anglicanism as an intellectual, liberal, and vital source of national unity.

Within these diverse Victorian movements, poetry was essentially linked to religion. This intrinsic connection between poetic and religious concerns comes into focus when we see how many influential Victorian clerics were also literary critics. John Keble, one of the central theologians of the Oxford Movement, was also Professor of Poetry at Oxford from 1832 to 1841. In lectures that combined both literary theory and theology, Keble argued that Christian belief has a "handmaid" in poetry: an essential theological tool to help bring Anglicans closer to God and the Church.[14] Significantly, Keble's own book of poetry, *The Christian Year* (1827), perhaps the single most popular book of verses of the age, is a series of poems organized around the daily Anglican liturgical cycle; it was clearly intended to encourage Anglican devotional practice.[15] Given the immense popularity of *The Christian Year* (379,000 copies were sold until the copyright expired in 1873),[16] it is perhaps ironic that Keble's poetry is rarely ever considered nowadays on syllabi devoted to Victorian literature. By contrast, the essays of Matthew Arnold are often seen as dominant in Victorian studies today, in part because of the powerful influence that his criticism exerted on the development of English studies, a discipline that, in its early stages, followed Arnold's lead in seeking to explain new kinds of relationship between religious and literary realms. Whereas Keble claimed that poetry might induce Christians to deeper acts of devotion, Arnold suggested – perhaps most clearly at the start of his essay "The Study of Poetry" (1888) – that the "strongest part of our religion to-day is its unconscious poetry,"[17] a statement indicating that poetry might become the best replacement for religion in an increasingly secular age. Representing a Broad Church position in widely debated works like *Culture and Anarchy* (1869), Arnold asserted that the cultivation of the intellect was a particularly Christian act, one in which "the idea of beauty and of a human nature perfect on all sides" formed "the dominant idea of poetry," a "true and invaluable idea" that in his view was "destined, adding to itself the religious idea of a devout energy, to transform and govern the other."[18]

Although Arnold tended to emphasize the importance of poetry in relation to the arts, classical literature, and the world of university life, other contexts for producing poetry also became visible in this period. If we return to our comparison with the sixteenth century, we find quite radical changes in education, literary culture, and publishing that transformed the ways in which poetry, including overtly religious poetry, was produced and received. As Richard D. Altick reminds us: "Victorian literature was a product of the first age of mass communication."[19] "By the end of the century," he adds, "English publishing had undergone a revolution. From a sleepy, unimportant trade whose practices differed little from those prevailing in Shakespeare's time it had grown into a bustling business, as inventive, competitive, and specialized as any other branch of Victorian commerce."[20] With perhaps the exception of the Poet Laureate, Victorian poets were for the most part no longer supported by the court or by upper-class patrons. Instead, poetry was a largely underpaid profession, and the professionalization of poetry meant that poets were now reliant on the rapidly growing and economically powerful publishing industry, rather than courtly patronage. Likewise, the Victorian audience for poetry had changed dramatically since the sixteenth century, specifically because of the changes in educational policy, as well as transformations in the class structure that offered the middle classes and even some members of the working class new opportunities for literacy. In fact, this shift in literacy rates was also linked to the Evangelical emphasis on the individual's ability to read Scripture for himself or herself, rather than relying on an educated clergy. Since literacy was no longer only available to an Anglican courtly society, poets and readers were more likely to come from a variety of religious perspectives and alliances, ones that authors and publishers sought to address.

While Anglican social and educational privileges in nineteenth-century England still ensured that a great number of publishing poets had an Anglican religious outlook, many of the non-Anglican religious institutions and communities published their own journals and thus supported their own writers. Religious periodicals started in this period included the following: the *Jewish Chronicle* (1841); the Unitarian *Christian Teacher* (1845), succeeded by the *National Review* (1855); the Quaker *Friend* (1843) and *Friends' Quarterly Examiner* (1867); the Roman Catholic *Dublin Review* (1836), *Month* (1864), and *Rambler* (1848; succeeded by the *Home and Foreign Review* in 1862); and the Wesleyan *Methodist Magazine* (1822).[21] Most of these journals included specific literary sections, and writers could start their careers in publishing by contributing to these forums. Early publication in these outlets could in turn launch a first volume of poetry, one that would be available to a more diverse readership. And while some poets sought to secure poems in periodicals aimed at likeminded readers, it is clear that other writers tried to place poetry wherever they could. For example, when the Jewish poet Grace Aguilar sent her work to the *Jewish Chronicle* and when that journal took too long to reply to her submission, she sent the same poem off to the *Christian Ladies Magazine*.[22]

Stepping back from this broad overview of the worlds of Victorian poetry and religion, I suggest that any Victorian poet, in contradistinction to a Renaissance writer such as Sidney, would have had a clear awareness of the heterogeneity of audiences for which he or she wrote. In what follows, I explore the work of three poets from disparate religious traditions, reading their poems with an eye to how they address, both implicitly and explicitly, the climate of religious diversity in Victorian England. My discussion focuses on the formal and intellectual strategies that individual poets use to represent their particular religious experiences to readers who might not share their beliefs and assumptions. In Grace Aguilar's "Song of the Spanish Jews" (1844), Christina Rossetti's "Consider the Lilies of the Field" (1862), and Gerard Manley Hopkins's "To Seem the Stranger" (probably composed in 1888), each speaker articulates a distinctive religious perspective that requires certain transformations of both English poetic conventions and the readerly assumptions embedded in those conventions.

II

Aguilar was undoubtedly one of the most widely read, and indeed respected, Jewish writers of the Victorian period. Novelist, poet, teacher, and theologian, as well as advocate for Jewish women's education, Aguilar thought that the creation of Jewish literature in English would provide both Jews and Christians with a better understanding of Jewish identity. Aguilar herself demonstrated enormous commitment to the production of an Anglo-Jewish literature in works published before her premature death at the age of thirty-one in 1847, as well as in volumes published posthumously by her mother. Much, though not all, of her work took up specifically Jewish issues and historical narratives, including numerous poems in American and British journals, a nonfiction work of theology (*The Spirit of*

Judaism [1842]), and the first history of the English Jews by an English Jew (in *Chambers' Miscellany* [1847]). She also published short stories on Jewish topics, such as *Records of Israel* (1844), and a very successful novel, *The Vale of Cedars; or, The Martyr* (1850). Aguilar came from a Sephardic background, she never married, and she often supported her family through her teaching and writing. Many critics have suggested that her life in the largely Christian environments of Hackney, rural Devon, and Brighton instilled in Aguilar a desire to create better understanding through Jewish-Christian literary relations. She had a broad knowledge of Christian literary writings, and she often called on those works as a way to engage readers and augment her own Jewish literary authority – an authority that was always suspect in Christian culture. Where poets affiliated with Christianity could appropriate the New Testament rhetoric of Christian universality into their poetic forms and voices (and thus claim their own poetic universality), Aguilar – a committed Jewish woman – chose to use many of the same formal conventions of English poetry to challenge specifically the idea that Jesus Christ (and, by extension, Christian theology) was universally accepted. Much of Aguilar's fiction and poetry seeks to recast Judaism as a deeply spiritual and loving religion in concerted response to the anti-Judaic rhetoric that argued that Judaism was a religion of the letter and the law rather than the spirit. Unable to claim a specifically Christian female poetic identity upon which so many of her Christian colleagues based their poetic eminence, Aguilar had to seek other grounds for claiming authority so that she could command the attention of both Christian and Jewish readers.

The full title of her poem is "Song of the Spanish Jews during their 'Golden Age,'" and it immediately locates Jewish identity in a particular historical context. The "Golden Age" appears in the epigraph attributed to the Victorian cleric Henry Hart Milman's popular account of Jewish history published in 1829: "It was in Spain that the golden age of the Jews shone with the brightest and most enduring splendour. In emulation of their Moslemite brethren, they began to cultivate their long disused and neglected poetry: the harp of Judah was heard to sound again, though with something of a foreign tone." This epigraph suggests Aguilar's awareness of the many Christian interpretations of Jewish history that were produced in the Victorian era. By absorbing Milman's highly regarded work into her poem, Aguilar bolsters her own literary authority in addressing the Christian members of her audience. Nevertheless, by choosing a collective "we" to represent the Spanish Jews of pre-Inquisition Spain, Aguilar offers a specific address contemporary Sephardic Jews in England who might make a special identification with this collective voice. Further, Aguilar's choice of the a first-person plural voice links her identity as an Anglo-Jewish Sephardic poet to the collective Jewish voices of the historical poets about whom she writes, suggesting that the very ability to create an Anglo-Jewish poem signals a "Golden Age" for Anglo-Jewry in her contemporary moment.

This self-reflexive aspect suggests that "Song of the Spanish Jews" not only is an historical recreation but also has specific meaning for Victorian England. Indeed, right from the start the poem challenges one of the major arguments used against the campaign for Jewish political enfranchisement in the first half of the nineteenth century. As David Feldman makes clear, this argument contended that "Jews could be members of a Christian society but not make laws for it; they were in the country but not of the nation."[23] In other words, there was a widespread belief that Jews could never have a complete national identification with England because of their commitments to Judaism and the theological imperative to return to Israel as the true locus of national identity. The opening stanza of Aguilar's poem reads:

> Oh, dark is the spirit who loves not the land
> Whose breezes his brow have in infancy fann'd,
> That feels not his bosom responsively thrill
> To the voice of her forest, the gush of her rill.[24]

In this and the next two quatrains, the collective "we" represents the idea that the Diaspora Jews do indeed have the capacity to "love" the "land" upon which they live. But the Spanish Jews go further by suggesting that without this intimate relationship of self to land, their spirit becomes "dark." Thus love of one's geographical home has distinct religious and spiritual implications as well as national ones. In fact, the third stanza concludes by referring to the "dark spirit" of one "Who treads not with awe where his ancestors lie / As their spirits around him are hovering nigh." These lines imply that the Spanish Jews of this "Golden Age" maintained a relationship to the "homeland" generally denied to Jews of the Diaspora, a relationship that was eventually denied to Spanish Jews in particular. Of course these lines carry with them a certain ironic distance in the nineteenth century, given that readers most likely knew about the Spanish Inquisition that in 1492 deemed that no Jews could remain in the land where their families were buried. For Jewish readers in particular, this deep sense of relationship to birth-land may have carried a special meaning, since so many of the Anglo-Jewish Sephardic families who eventually settled in England traced their lineage back to this Spanish soil, though they could not move directly to England during the fifteenth and sixteenth centuries since Jews were legally forbidden to enter England until 1656.

The fourth stanza moves from a more generic relationship to a natural landscape of birth to explore a patriotic connection to Spain. If love of the land that nurtures one's family proves necessary to the "spirit," then recognition of national and political identity for Aguilar is equally, if not more, necessary:

> Oh, cold is the spirit: and yet colder still,
> The heart that for Spain does not gratefully thrill,
> The land, which the foot of the weary has pressed,
> Where the exile and wand'rer found blessing and rest.

Here the collective voice imagines the deep national pride in Spain that characterized Jews before their era of expulsion, forced conversions, and martyrdom. In other words, the speakers address the very fears about the capacity for national pride that agitated English attitudes toward Jewish citizenship rights. Later, in one unified voice, the Spanish Jews argue that because "Spain has the exile and homeless received / . . . we feel not of country so darkly bereaved." The poem, therefore, emphasizes the Jewish capacity to pledge national affiliation with a government that protects and nurtures the Jewish community.

Yet the historical gap that Aguilar opens by setting this poem in the mouths of pre-Inquisition Jewry makes it impossible to read "Song of the Spanish Jews" without the awareness of the subsequent persecution of Jews in that same land, and it is this historical knowledge that renders their poetic utterance tragic and poignant, rather than the simple statement of national faith it appears to be. It suggests that the poem not only embraces the experience of the Sephardic community persecuted by the Inquisition but also contemplates fears for the Jews living in Victorian England. The fifth and sixth stanzas reinforce the irony of the Spanish Jews' sense of national identity that was ultimately not honored by their homeland:

> On the face of the earth our doom was to roam,
> To meet not a brother, to find not a home;
> But Spain has the exile and homeless received
> And we feel not of country so darkly bereaved
>
> Home of the exiles! Oh ne'er will we leave thee;
> As mother to orphan, fair land we now greet thee.
> Sweet peace and rejoicing may dwell in thy bowers,
> For even as Judah, fair land! thou art ours.

These lines remind both Christian and Jewish readers that while Jews are fully capable of forging deep national ties, the nations of the world have not always honored such Jewish national allegiance. When read from a Jewish perspective, the poem urges Jewish readers to consider the wisdom of total identification with nation-states that have, as history shows, frequently reversed their favorable national policies toward settled Jewish communities. "Song of the Spanish Jews," then, aims to convince Christian readers that Anglo-Jewry can be good English subjects, while reminding Anglo-Jews that their sense of safety and belonging in England may always be threatened.

III

Aguilar's double voice – which communicates different messages to Christian and Jewish readers – was a technique used not only by writers from seemingly marginal religious positions. To be sure, Christina Rossetti was deeply aligned with High Anglicanism in almost every facet of her life. But her poetry also engages a "double voice" to pose the question of religious diversity in relation to the specificity of women's Christian faith. In "Consider the Lilies of the Field," she takes on the challenge of proposing a distinctly female Anglicanism:[25] an issue that can be obscured when one bears in mind that Rossetti was reluctant to support both women's suffrage and a priesthood for women.

Both the title of Rossetti's poem and its subject matter refer to a well-known parable from Matthew 6: 27–30 and Luke 12: 27: New Testament passages where Jesus interrogates the role that intellect plays in developing true faith. In calling on the Bible directly, and then offering her own reworking and interpretation of chapter and verse, Rossetti claims an exegetical authority that is often denied to women. The passage from Matthew upon which the poem is based reads:

> Which of you by taking thought can add one cubit to his stature? And why take ye thought for raiment? Consider the lilies of the field, how they grow; they toil not, neither do they spin: And yet I say unto you, That even Solomon in all his glory was not arrayed like one of these. Wherefore, if God so clothe the grass of the field, which today is, and tomorrow is cast into the oven, shall he not much more clothe you, O ye of little faith?   (*King James Version*)

The parable explores the role that thought (the intellect) plays in religious faith. Employing the figure of raiment (clothing) for this intellectual work, Jesus's parable argues that the toiling and spinning that create thought have little significance in God's world. The lilies symbolize the most revered beauty that has no need of the raiment of thought but relies instead on God to clothe it. In "Consider the Lilies of the Field," Rossetti explores the relationship between Jesus's allusion to lilies and the common connection made between flowers and women that can be found in the Bible as well as throughout English literary history. By expanding on Jesus's use of the lily to represent idealized faith, Rossetti's poem extends the floral figure to represent a number of other female religious viewpoints.

Rossetti considers the biblical parable to examine the common Victorian assumption that women are creatures of faith rather than intellect. We need to read the poem in full to see how she connects this urgent theological issue to the ways in which women are often reified as silent objects of male visual pleasure, their words and ideas ignored.

> Flowers preach to us if we will hear: –
> The rose saith in the dewy morn:
> I am most fair;
> Yet all my loveliness is born
> Upon a thorn.
> The poppy saith amid the corn:
> Let but my scarlet head appear
> And I am held in scorn;
> Yet juice of subtle virtue lies
> Within my cup of curious dyes.
> The lilies say: Behold how we
> Preach without words of purity.
> The violets whisper from the shade
> Which their own leaves have made:
> Men scent our fragrance on the air,
> Yet take no heed
> Of humble lessons we would read.
>
> But not alone the fairest flowers:
> The merest grass
> Along the roadside where we pass,
> Lichen and moss and sturdy weed,
> Tell of His love who sends the dew,
> The rain and sunshine too,
> To nourish one small seed.   (CR 1–24)

At first glance, the poem would seem to follow the spirit of the biblical parable by exploring exactly how "Flowers preach to us": an idea generated by Jesus's argument that the lilies offer spiritual truths without being clothed in words or thoughts. In this respect, it is easy to see how this poem might be characterized as an example of simple orthodoxy. But Rossetti's expansions of the parable recast its central meaning in a number of intriguing ways. Her poem suggests that thought does indeed have a role in expressions of Christian faith. Taking up the familiar literary poetic trope of the catalogue of flowers – which Renaissance poets developed into standard figures for women and femaleness – Rossetti changes the idea that the lilies take no thought and no speech. In her revision of Matthew 6: 27–30, each of the flowers makes an intricate statement of religious faith. It is not that these flowers-cum-women reject the role of the intellect per se. Instead they use thought to create innovative links between the biblical text and their own feminine lives. Rossetti emphasizes that the perception of their intellectual passivity is the fault of an audience that fails to "hear" the preaching of the flowers. Indeed, the verb "preach" offers a subtle transformation of biblical authority. Whereas in the parable it is Jesus who "preach[es]" about the flowers, here Rossetti transfers agency to the flowers themselves, who repeatedly "say," "whisper," and "Tell." Linking their identity to Christian narrative, the "rose" and "poppy" call on images of the "thorn" or "scorn" and thus mirror Jesus's experiences on earth. If passive in action – neither "spinning" nor "toiling" – Rossetti's flowers are nevertheless remarkable for their obvious intellectual consideration of their own existence in light of Scripture. The larger point is that the flowers can be misread unless they offer their own readings of their spiritual significance.

Rossetti's most complex argument about the role of women's religious authority and women's intellect emerges in her reference to the "violets" at the end of the first stanza. Here the question of what the flowers actually make marks a clear divergence from the Bible. If the violets neither "toil" nor "spin," they nonetheless make "shade" and produce "fragrance," as well as give "humble lessons." These lines add to the biblical parable the idea not only that flowers do in fact make things but also that the things that they have made remain ignored by "men." "[M]en," the subject of the sentence, only "scent" the flowers, "tak[ing] no heed / Of humble lessons *we would read*" (emphasis mine). This last phrase, with its deceptive conditional tense, proves central to meaning of the whole poem, since it implies some hindrance to the violets' (and thus women's) ability to read for themselves. Indeed, the phrase suggests that the violets know the lessons that they would utter if they could. Moreover, it carries the idea that they "would read" Scripture for themselves if they had an audience of "men" who would authorize their "humble lessons." The manifest irony here is that the poem itself represents a woman poet's interpretation of Scripture. By displacing these meanings onto the flowers, Rossetti offers a subtle commentary on her own distinctly female poem – one in which "men" will most likely "take no heed."

Once Rossetti has made this contentious comment, however, the poem returns to safer ground by extending its message beyond the limits of gender difference. Her final references to the "grass" and "lichen and moss and sturdy weed" extricate her from the link between flowers and women.

This shift allows her to conclude her poem not as a direct polemic against men who "take no heed" but rather as an inclusive statement about the universality of divine Christian love. Rossetti's concern with speakers who might remain unheeded on earth certainly echoes a deeply significant concept in Christian theology: namely, that Christ was rejected by many people, only to be crucified. Taking Christ's example, therefore, the experience of communal rejection becomes a potential sign of divine authority. In this sense, Rossetti forges an implicit link between the status of existing as an unheeded woman in the Anglican world and the place of Jesus as a rejected prophet in his earthly suffering. (This is a connection that she makes repeatedly in one of her later prose works, *Seek and Find* [1879].) Finally, in her poetic appropriation of Jesus's words, Rossetti claims a canonized Christian text as her own. "Consider the Lilies of the Field" enables Rossetti to articulate her own particular theology as a Christian woman who "consider[s]" Christian gospel both intellectually and spiritually. That said, since this poem has rarely been interpreted for its female perspective on a biblical parable, it is clear that it proved remarkably unthreatening to a patriarchal religious and literary community that would sanction a woman's acts of religious poetry long before they would sanction her theological authority.

IV

Where Rossetti calls on an unheeded existence as a marker for Anglican women's poetic and religious endeavors, Gerard Manley Hopkins turns to this same figure of feeling "unheard" in his powerful sonnet "To Seem the Stranger": a poem that represents the stressful condition of his Roman Catholic identity in the Anglican culture that he chose to reject. Hopkins was raised in a well-to-do High Anglican family. He studied at Balliol College, Oxford, where he came under the influence of many religious controversies still raging in response to the legacy of the Oxford Movement. Eventually, Hopkins himself entertained doubts about the various Anglican schisms from Roman Catholicism, and in 1866 converted to Rome. Although Roman Catholic political disability had recently been removed in England, affiliation with Rome still carried minority status. For a prizewinning Oxford graduate like Hopkins, conversion meant that all university posts and positions in the clergy were closed to him. It also meant that even his family had certain suspicions about his contact with them. Writing to his father in October 1866, Hopkins mentions these concerns: "You are so kind as not to forbid me your house, to which I have no claim, on the condition, if I understand, that I promise not to try and convert my brothers and sisters."[26] In 1868, not long after finishing his degree at Oxford, Hopkins entered the order to Jesuits, and two years later he took the vows of the Society of Jesus, spending the rest of his life as a Jesuit priest.

Hopkins wrote poetry at many different times in his life as a Jesuit, often questioning whether poetry was a suitable pursuit, and often wary of publishing. His close friend Robert Bridges published most of Hopkins's poems in 1918, almost thirty years after the poet's death. This posthumous volume drew the attention of many Modernist writers and critics who highly esteemed Hopkins's works. Ever since, his prosodic and stylistic experimentalism has been thought to anticipate Modernist transformations of poetic technique. In this regard, Hopkins is perhaps best known for his metrical innovations with poetic stress. He developed an ingenious system of meter (known as sprung rhythm) that would produce what he sometimes called "inscape": a "pattern" or "design" that emerged, within his distinctive theological poetics, from a system of heavily stressed syllables that gave more vocal weight to a poetic line than either English grammar or traditional scansion would usually allow.

"To Seem the Stranger" arguably marks the culmination of a group of poems written in the mid-1880s – including "I Wake and Feel the Fell of Dark, Not Day" and "Carrion Comfort" – that are often referred to as the "Terrible Sonnets" or (less ambiguously) the "Sonnets of Desolation" because they explore the confounding complexities, intense difficulties, and profound terrors of faith. Daniel A. Harris sees this resonant poem as the summary of the crisis that this group of sonnets articulates; in his view, the marked emphasis throughout "To Seem the Stranger" on what it means to be "Heard" (*GMH* 14) or "unheard" (13) relates to many kinds of frustration, including the earthly failures of familial, ministerial, and national recognition, and the ultimate failure of being "heard" by God.[27] In this remarkable poem, Hopkins extends one tradition of the English sonnet with his own unique use of enjambment, diction, and rhythm, as the opening quatrain reveals:

> To seem the stranger lies my lot, my life
> Among strangers. Father and mother, dear,
> Brothers and sisters are in Christ not near
> And he my peace/my parting, sword and strife.　　　　(1–4)

Feeling like a "stranger... / Among strangers," Hopkins alludes here to his life in Ireland, a country with a majority Roman Catholic population, where he for the most part worked unhappily as a Professor of Greek and Latin Literature at University College, Dublin, from 1884 until his death in

1889. Yet his careful use of line breaks extends his English identity as a "stranger" in Ireland to his own Anglican family. Thus the line "Among strangers. Father and mother dear" reads not only as the start and end of two different sentences but also as a unit in itself, indicating that his "dear" parents are also "strangers" to him in some way. Likewise, the line "Brothers and sisters are in Christ not near" carries a double meaning. His siblings are at once literally not "near" him (geographically) and meta-phorically not "near" him (spiritually). This semantic and structural doubleness continues past the line break: "Christ not near / And he my peace/my parting." In short, his Roman Catholic alliance to Christ is simultaneously a cause for "peace" and "parting" – a source of both religious sustenance and social alienation. Despite their expression of religious estrangement from England, however, the first four lines show a commitment to aspects of English poetic convention. Hopkins establishes a clear pentameter in all four lines. But this adherence to traditional meter does not extend to rhythm as well as line length, for by the second line the iambs are clearly broken by the caesura after the significant phrase "Among strangers," a caesura that arises since "strangers" is a trochee. Here the common rhythms of English verse may not serve him, or at least come easily when living outside of England.

The complex negotiations of poetic, religious, and social identities become the focus of the next quatrain that focuses on marriage through a striking reference to "woo[ing]" England, figured as a wife. In addition, the metrical innovation also increases in this second half of the octave:

> England, whose honour O all my heart woos, wife
> To my creating thought, would neither hear
> Me, were I pleading, plead nor do I: I wear-
> Y of idle a being but by where wars are rife.   (5–8)

These lines institute a clear relationship between Hopkins's creative process and his religious affiliation. "England" fails to hear his wooing or pleading, two conventional activities of the traditional male sonneteer in pursuit of his lady. Hopkins makes it plain that while his religious commitments are to Roman Catholicism, his literary commitments have a national alle-giance. England stands as the "wife" or partner to his poetic production, and so the fact that England rejects him by not "hear[ing]" his Roman Catholic voice results in a block to his creative activity. To be heard, the poet suggests, is not a privilege that he would enjoy even if he did "plead" his case, and he notes that he does not "plead" because of his own internal "wars" that "wear- / Y" his being. Challenging the heterosexual desires that often motivate the traditional English sonnet, Hopkins offers a critical focus on the hegemonic assumption of sexual partnership, pointing to its difference from his religious and social identity as a celibate Jesuit priest.[28] In addition, this differentiation of his self from both familial and romantic relationships echoes the conditions of Christ's life, since Christ explicitly repudiated common ties to family and marriage because of his obedience to God the Father.

Once he recognizes that even "pleading" to be heard by "England" will do his religious and poetic case no good, Hopkins continues to dissolve his formal alliance with English literary tradition, abandoning any semblance of pentameter in the last line of the octave (which has thirteen syllables). This line similarly speaks of "wars" both within the speaker's battle to be heard as a religious other and within England's internal struggle to maintain Anglican hegemony. But by far the most daring aspect of this quatrain occurs in the startling line break in "wear- / Y," which suggests a failed attempt to maintain connections to common conventions of English grammar as well as poetry. Here, above all, is a representation of the strangeness of his poetic and religious voice in relation to English poetic tradition. The three repetitions of "I" in close proximity give way to the more truly strange version of "I" as "Y," suggesting that the identity of the speaker has likewise undergone drastic transformation in the "wars" that eventually determined his Roman Catholic identity.

The sestet opens with a return to seemingly clear language and a varied, if still expanding, pentameter:

> I am in Ireland now; now I am at a third
> Remove. Not but in all removes I can
> Kind love both give and get. Only what word
> Wisest my heart breeds baffling heaven's dark ban
>   dark heaven's baffling ban
> Bars or hell's spell thwarts. This to hoard unheard,
>   Thought unhoarded unheard
> Heard unhéeded, leaves me a lonely began.
>   [leave]   (9–14)

Here, too, the poem modulates between conformity and nonconformity to literary tradition. First of all, the metrical length varies. The opening line has twelve syllables, while the next two return to ten. At the same time, the grammatical simplicity of the opening clause yields to increasing complexity of meaning. Whereas the first two alienating "removes" named in the octave – his distance from his family, and his dissociation from a spousal love of England – were psychic "removes" that seemed to occur regardless of his physical location, the idea of existing at a "third /

Remove" reflects his literal removal to Ireland: the country where he could belong as a Roman Catholic but not belong as an Englishman. Yet none of these "removes" offers him the experience of "kind love" to be able to "both give and get." And, indeed, this re-emphasis on his disaffection galvanizes another loss of linguistic clarity, significantly marked by the phrase "only what word," as if he were questioning the very validity of speech itself because his utterance comes from a position outside of dominant conventions. In contemplating the value of his own speech, he returns to a desperate image of familial connection, this time through the verb "breeds." But the clause "Only what word / Wisest my heart breeds" depicts a figure of solitary creation, a man seeking to "create" without the benefit of familial, national, or spousal partnership. And this "word," produced out of a solitary heart, remains vulnerable to "dark heaven's baffling ban" and "hell's spell": two dark forces that "bar" and "thwart" his ability to create further. This memorable idea of existing as a "lonely began" – where the active movement of a verb strikingly transforms into an immobilizing noun – hearkens back to Christ's suffering on the cross, rejected and despised yet also, through his suffering, offering hope to those subsequent Christians who would claim his death as the sign of human salvation: a new beginning that has nonetheless emerged from terminal isolation.

V

Despite their very different religious perspectives and religious commitments – Aguilar to Judaism; Rossetti to High Anglicanism; and Hopkins to Roman Catholicism – all three poets take on the challenge of representing their own particular religious identities and commitments to an audience that might not otherwise comprehend their beliefs. In doing so, each poet undoes certain assumptions about national identity, poetic tradition, and the role of the *vates*. The echoes between Rossetti's figure of the Christian woman of whom men "take no heed" and Hopkins's image of the Roman Catholic struggle to be simultaneously "Heard" and "heeded" in Anglican society are certainly worthy of note. Correspondingly, while Aguilar suggests that a "Golden Age" of poetry can occur for specific groups when they live in relative cultural and political freedom, Hopkins links the creation of poetry – or in his sonnet, its seeming disintegration – to a contentious view of how Anglican intolerance makes him "seem a stranger." These poems endorse the idea that poetry, like prophecy, is always directed at an audience that has the power to confirm or discredit the poet's authority. In this sense, they implicitly call up the central paradox facing the religious prophet, who must either be believed or deemed mad. None of these poets could assume that their audience would only be made up of readers who shared their own viewpoints. If, as Carlyle put it, "the Vates . . . is a man sent hither to make it [the "open secret"] more impressively known to us," then Victorian poets sought to inform their readers of not only the content of that divine "secret" but also the diverse social and political dynamics involved in any act of prophetic poetry.

NOTES

I would like to offer special thanks to Joseph Bristow. His thoughtful responses and suggestions for revision have been almost universally incorporated.

1 Sir Philip Sidney, "The Defence of Poetry," in *Sir Philip Sidney*, ed. Katherine Duncan-Jones, The Oxford Authors (Oxford: Oxford University Press, 1989), 214–15, 217.

2 Thomas Carlyle, "The Hero as Poet," in Carlyle, *On Heroes, Hero-Worship and the Heroic in History*, The Works of Thomas Carlyle, centenary edition, 30 vols. (London: Chapman and Hall, 1896–99), V, 80–81.

3 Gary Waller, *English Poetry of the Sixteenth Century* (London: Longman, 1986), 17.

4 Stephen Gosson, *The Schoole of Abuse and a Short Apologie for the Schoole of Abuse*, ed. Edward Arber (London: Alex, Murray, and Son, 1868), 19. The Elizabethan spelling presented in this edition has been modernized here.

5 Gerald Parsons, "Reform, Revival and Realignment: The Experience of Victorian Anglicanism," in *Religion in Victorian Britain: Traditions*, ed. Parsons, 5 vols. (Manchester: Manchester University Press, 1988), I, 15.

6 Parsons, "From Dissenters to Free Churchmen: The Transition of Victorian Nonconformity," in *Religion in Victorian Britain*, ed. Parsons, I, 71.

7 Parsons, "Victorian Roman Catholicism: Emancipation, Expansion and Achievement," in *Religion in Victorian Britain*, I, 150. For more on Roman Catholicism see the aforementioned article and the excellent bibliography accompanying his article. See also Sheridan Gilley, "Roman Catholicism," in *Nineteenth Century English Religious Traditions: Retrospect and Prospect*, ed. D.G. Paz (Westport, CT: Greenwood Press, 1995), 33–56.

8 Parsons, "Victorian Roman Catholicism," *Religion in Victorian Britain*, I, 152.

9 Parsons, "Victorian Roman Catholicism," *Religion in Victorian Britain*, I, 181.

10 On Anglo-Jewish history and life in Victorian England, see, for example, David Englander, "Anglicized, not Anglican: Jews and Judaism in Victorian England," in *Religion in Victorian Britain*, I, 235–73.

11 For more on the influence of the Oxford Movement, see Geoffrey Faber, *Oxford Apostles: A Character Study of the Oxford Movement* (London: Faber and Faber, 1933), and G.B. Tennyson, *Victorian Devotional Poetry: The Tractarian Mode* (Cambridge, MA: Harvard University Press, 1981).

12 John Wolffe, "Anglicanism," in *Nineteenth-Century English Religious Traditions*, ed. Paz, 10.

13 Wolffe, "Anglicanism," *Nineteenth-Century English Religious Traditions*, 12.

14 John Keble, "Lecture XL," in Keble, *Lectures on Poetry 1832–34*, trans. Edward Kershaw Francis, 2 vols. (Oxford: Clarendon Press: 1912), II, 484.

15 For more on *The Christian Year* and its rather incredible publishing history, see Tennyson, *Victorian Devotional Poetry*, 72–113, 215–32.

16 This statistic is cited in Richard D. Altick, *The English Common Reader: A Social History of the Mass Reading Public, 1800–1900* (Chicago, IL: University of Chicago Press, 1957), 386.

17 Matthew Arnold, "The Study of Poetry," in Arnold, *English Literature and Irish Politics*, ed. R.H. Super, *The Complete Prose Works of Matthew Arnold*, 11 vols. (Ann Arbor, MI: University of Michigan Press, 1960–77), IX, 161.

18 Matthew Arnold, *Culture and Anarchy with Friendship's Garland and Some Literary Essays*, ed. Super, *The Complete Prose Works of Matthew Arnold*, V, 99–100.

19 Richard D. Altick, *Victorian People and Ideas* (New York: W.W. Norton, 1973), 64.

20 Altick, *Victorian People and Ideas*, 65.

21 See Alvin Sullivan, ed., *British Literary Magazines: The Victorian and Edwardian Age, 1837–1913* (Westport, CT: Greenwood Press, 1984). My list represents only a very small sampling of the religiously affiliated journals of the period; for more complete references, see Sullivan's "Appendix H: Nineteenth Century Religious Magazines with Literary Contents," 515–19.

22 On this point see Beth Zion Lask-Abrahams, "Grace Aguilar: A Centenary Tribute," *Jewish Historical Society of England Transactions* 16 (1945–51), 143.

23 David Feldman, *Englishmen and Jews: Social Relations and Political Culture, 1840–1914* (New Haven, CT: Yale University Press, 1994), 35.

24 Grace Aguilar, "Song the Spanish Jews in their 'Golden Age,'" *The Occident and American Jewish Advocate* 1 (1844), 289.

25 "Consider the Lilies of the Field" was published *Goblin Market and Other Verse* (1862). R.W. Crump identifies the date of composition as 1852; see *The Complete Poems of Christina Rossetti: A Variorum Edition*, ed. Crump, 3 vols. (Baton Rouge, LA: Louisiana State University Press, 1979–1900), I, 261.

26 Gerard Manley Hopkins, "To His Father," 16 October 1866, in Hopkins, *Further Letters of Gerard Manley Hopkins, Including His Correspondence with Coventry Patmore*, second edition, ed. Claude Colleer Abbott (London: Oxford University Press, 1956), 94.

27 Daniel A. Harris, *Inspirations Unbidden: The "Terrible Sonnets" of Gerard Manley Hopkins* (Berkeley, CA: University of California Press, 1982), 124.

28 Hopkins's play on the conventional form of heterosexuality points to the ways in which the Victorian anti-Anglo-Catholic and anti-Roman Catholic discourses often expressed antipathy toward homosexuality; on this issue, see David Hilliard, "UnEnglish and Unmanly: Anglo-Catholicism and Homosexuality," *Victorian Studies* 25 (1982), 181–210.

9

SUSAN BROWN

The Victorian poetess

I

> Thou hast given
> Thyself to Time and to the world. Thy strains
> In many a distant day, and many a clime,
> Shall be thy living voice – nay, not *that* voice;
> But the soul's voice, the breathing poetess.
>
> – [Anonymous,] "To a Poetess" (1856)[1]

This tribute "To a Poetess" may seem a perverse note on which to begin this chapter, not least because the poem was most probably written by a member of the Langham Place group: the first identifiably feminist organization to promote women's rights in England. Why would a feminist writer praise the figure of the poetess? After all, the very word poetess has for most of the twentieth century sounded unequivocally patronizing. As the feminized form of poet (a word that can sound gender-neutral), poetess suggests not the difference in degree implied by a modifier like "woman" but the absolute difference in kind implied by separate nouns. Despite the negative connotations that the term eventually acquired, it is worth remembering that it would be hard for Victorians to grasp the extent to which "poetess" sounds unnecessarily gendered to us. As Isobel Armstrong asserts: "It is probably no exaggeration to say that an account of women's writing as occupying a particular sphere of influence, and as working inside defined moral and religious conventions, helped to make women's poetry and the 'poetess' . . . respected in the nineteenth century as they never have been since."[2] In other words, the mark of gender was not necessarily uniformly oppressive for Victorian women. Poetess, although occasionally used interchangeably with "woman poet," was generally the preferred term, and as such it proved enabling as well as constraining for women writers in its insistence that masculinity and femininity mattered where poetry was concerned. It is misleading to suggest, as Stuart Curran does, that the category of the poetess was "a trap enforced by masculine disdain for cultural refinement" as the novel achieved dominance.[3] In much more complicated ways, the poetess designated a fiercely contested role in the literary market of a rapidly transforming society.

The term's instability emerges in "To a Poetess," a poem that typically for its time reveals considerable tensions in the figure of the female poet. In this metaphysical contemplation of her role, the poetess is pulled between a temporal world of imperial vastness and an eternal world of divine inspiration. Moreover, the relationship between the poetess and her voice remains perilously uncertain. The embodied utterance ("thy living voice") is curiously dissociated from the Poetry ("the soul's voice") that will live on. But at the same time the disembodied eternal voice of the soul itself is finally reidentified with the "breathing" poetess: the material presence from which it had just been severed. Ultimately, the living poetess, rather than her "living voice," is viewed as the true utterance of the poetess' soul. The poem is not alone in its confusion. Although its contradictions are more legible than in some other Victorian writings, throughout the nineteenth century the poetess represents a discursive site where certain cultural anxieties are particularly legible.

In this chapter, I explore how influential and often contradictory understandings of the Victorian poetess are informed by a commodified aestheticism that frequently conflates the woman poet's body with her literary corpus. This particular structure becomes clear in a pronouncement made in *Fraser's Magazine* in 1833: "Beauty is to woman what poetry is to a language, and their similarity accounts for their conjunction; for there never yet existed a female possessed of personal loveliness who was not only poetical in herself but the cause of poetry in others."[4] This idea circulated in various cultural forms, not only in literary writings but also in paintings, periodicals, and sculpture – all of which made the poetical body of a woman available for consumption. Similarly, this idea was advanced by authors of popular conduct books such as Sarah Stickney Ellis, who advised their readers that beauty and poetry were associated with a specifically female domain separate from the material concerns of the marketplace. In *The Daughters of England* (1837), Ellis argues that "to have the mind so embued with poetic feeling that it shall operate as a charm upon herself and others" may well be superior to "fill[ing] a book with poetry."[5] Poetry is for women a mode, not an occupation.

For women writers, the major problem in this formulation is that women *are* poetry. They live and inspire it but they do not write it, while other people – namely, men – have the privilege to do so. One of the balder articulations of this view suggests such exclusion may engender violence.

Edgar Allan Poe, having argued that "Beauty is the sole legitimate province of the poem," notoriously observed that "the death . . . of a beautiful woman is, unquestionably, the most poetical topic in the world."[6] But if Poe's remark threatens to make femicide (of a textual kind) an aesthetic criterion, the image of the dead or dying woman provided many women writers with a model for thinking about what it meant to exist as a poetess in the nineteenth century. In what follows, I consider how both women poets and male critics adopted differing perspectives on the mortified body of the poetess. Thereafter, I examine how this ideal resulted in part from the domestic ideology that solidified in the decade when Victoria ascended the throne, and consider how a number of women writers reconfigured the identity of the poetess in light of the kind of feminist campaigns that the Langham Place group was the first to mobilize.

II

Sappho is a figure whose death provides a source of inspiration and despair for women writers throughout the nineteenth century. Indeed, Yopie Prins finds that "Sappho emerges as the proper name for the Poetess" in Victorian England.[7] Both the putative life and the fragmentary works of this sixth-century BC Greek writer – the most prominent woman of the classical poets and the acknowledged head of the lyric tradition – powerfully inflect countless representations of the Victorian poetess as an abandoned woman.[8] Until the 1880s, women poets read Sappho in the biographical tradition promulgated largely by Ovid's *Heroides*, which emphasized her suicidal leap from the Leucadian cliff after her male lover Phaon abandoned her. (Only when Swinburne published "Anactoria" in 1866 did Sappho's lesbian desires become fully legible in English poetry.) Sappho's suicide became an allegory for women poets' dilemmas and an alibi for their voices: it focused their sense of the conflicts between art and love, vocation and gender, and the desire for literary fame and the demands of social convention. Sappho's last song is virtually a fixture in pre- and early Victorian women's writing.

Felicia Hemans – a Romantic poet who posthumously became the most popular woman poet of the Victorian period – explicitly connects Sappho's plight to her femininity. Hemans remarked of a statue depicting the poet newly deserted by her lover: "There is a sort of willowy drooping in the figure, which seems to express a weight of unutterable sadness, and one sinking arm holds the lyre so carelessly, that you almost fancy it will drop while you gaze. Altogether, it seems to speak piercingly and sorrowfully of the nothingness of Fame, at least to woman."[9] These remarks reveal how the poetess forms part of a structure of representation that both aestheti-cizes and commodifies her – in this particular case through a sculpture by John Gibson that was exhibited in Italy and England. Hemans observes how the statue embodies Sappho's paradoxical position as a woman who cannot find in her artistic vocation any compensation for the "unutterable sadness" that drags her down as a woman disappointed in love. Here Sappho literally droops and sinks, threatening (though not quite managing) to drop the instrument that represents her poetic calling, and indeed her fame.

Yet this Sapphic moment, which locates the futility of such vocation, ironically becomes for Hemans and many other women a prime vehicle for poetic utterance. Hemans's "The Last Song of Sappho" (1834) takes as its starting point a sketch by Richard Westmacott Jr. that depicts Sappho "penetrated with the feeling of utter abandonment." With this image in mind, Hemans articulates Sappho's own voice in the moment before the poet took her life. The "living strings" of her lyre are "quench'd," since "broken even as they, / The heart whose music made them sweet, / Hath pour'd on desert-sands its wealth away" (*FH* VII, 10–11). Yet Sappho's undoing occasions Hemans's poetic doing. In the final stanza, Hemans speaks through her famous precursor an ecstatic climax expressing a visionary poetic self that accords well not only with the Romanticism on which her work draws but also with a specifically female aesthetic:

> I, with this winged nature fraught,
> These visions wildly free,
> This boundless love, this fiery thought –
> – *Alone* I come – oh! give me peace, dark sea!   (VII, 11)

Here is an ostensibly lyric utterance that unexpectedly rejects the lyre, with a poet who is both "winged[ly]" transcendent and reliant on gravity to achieve her desired doom. Hemans is caught in a circular logic. She writes, as Marlon B. Ross observes, as if "fame, along with death, is the sole threat to the power of feminine affection – an irony, since the creative genius that makes [early-nineteenth-century] women famous resides in that power."[10] Sappho's death emphasizes the extent to which this feminine aesthetic is grounded in contradiction. In order to speak as a woman writer, Hemans offers up both the lyric voice and the sacrificial body of the paradigmatic poetess for consumption as an aestheticized object – what Poe called "the most poetical topic in the world."

Women poets were not alone in seeing correspondences between Sappho and themselves. Victorian critics constantly invoked Sappho as a precedent for the poetess. In 1841 Laman Blanchard, the biographer of Letitia

Elizabeth Landon (known as L.E.L.), claimed that she was "voted one" with Sappho when she published her second volume, *The Improvisatrice* (1824).[11] Blanchard's biocritical method formed part of a trend that plagued women writers throughout the century and beyond. Critics exploited the fact that more of Sappho's reputation than her actual poetry remained. The fragmented voice of the writer whom the ancients respected as the progenitor of lyric was largely obscured as commentators focused attention on her deeply unhappy biographical legend. In practice this meant that there was little basis for aesthetic judgment of poetesses' work but their lives were scrutinized for conformity to perceived womanly and poetic standards, however conflicting those might be. Sappho's putative biography conveniently enshrined the antagonism between respectable femininity and poetic aspiration. Biographers capitalized on memoirs of women whose lives seemed to rehearse the unhappy conjunction of the two, initiating – as Tricia Lootens shows – a pernicious form of hagiography.[12]

Although Sappho was by default the proper name for the poetess, it was not the sole one employed by women poets themselves, who speak in the voices of many others: Corinne, Eulalie, Arabella Stuart, Properzia Rossi, Caterina, Bertha, Beatrice, Laura, the Pythoness (based on the priestess at Delphi). The voice of the poetess for Hemans, L.E.L., and other poets after them took the form of a self-consciously feminine self-staging in verse that appropriated many bodies, lives, and identities. This voice represented a fertile space between the expression of self and the representation of others, between the spontaneous Romantic outpouring that becomes gendered as female gush and a distanced dramatic voice that developed over the course of the century into the dramatic monologue.

L.E.L. and Sappho might have been "voted one" on the publication of *The Improvisatrice* but even the *improvisatrice*, though sapphic, is not precisely Sappho. The contemporary urban performer of spontaneous verse to her own musical accompaniment derives from Germaine de Staël's *Corinne* (1807), one of the most influential novels for women writers in nineteenth-century Britain. De Staël's *improvisatrice* is also unhappy in love and finds no compensation in her fame, but she chooses a decorous demise over a pyrrhic leap. L.E.L.'s version of the narrative presents a complex layering of voices framed by that of her Florentine *improvisatrice*. Even though she has "poured [her] full and burning heart / In song" (*LEL* 1–2), she, like Hemans, provides lyric utterances that are responses to artistic objects rather than effusions of the heart. A series of descriptions of her paintings – *objets d'art* translated from one medium to the next – preface her songs, which are divided from her own utterances, and given their own titles. Hence a description of the speaker's painting precedes "Sappho's Song." It occupies more lines than the poem itself, offering no greater connection between herself and the one "Who proved what woman's hand might do, / When, true to the heart pulse, it woke / The harp" (3) than it had earlier between the *improvisatrice* and Petrarch, or than it does between the speaker's situation and the later "Hindoo Girl's Song" or "The Indian Bride." The prefatory verses become more personal as the poem progresses. But only when we read the final interpolated poem do we discover an explicit relationship between it and the initial framing verse, though the poem is still another's – her lover's – story retold. As if to undercut the growing sense of congruence between the frame and its pictures, the final verse paragraph steps beyond the frame to provide a posthumous denouement, spoken by an additional unidentified first-person voice. The asymmetrical framing jars, as if the layers of voices bearing a teasingly analogous but always artfully divorced relationship to one another might be extended indefinitely. Although early-nineteenth-century critics might have felt that *The Improvisatrice* was a transparent expression of a woman's identity, more recent readers are apt to find an ambiguous meditation on the relationship between the self, the other, and the lyric voice.

In this early volume by L.E.L., the paradox that attends the figure of artless performance or improvisation – a paradox that became strongly associated with women's poetry – emerges clearly in L.E.L.'s later "History of the Lyre" (1829). Here the Pythoness Eulalie, another incarnation of the *improvisatrice*, reveals that her poetic utterances proceed not from the experience and loss associated with Sappho or the *improvisatrice*, but from genius and imagination:

> "I have sung passionate songs of beating hearts;
> Perhaps it had been better they had drawn
> Their inspiration from an inward source.
> Had I known even an unhappy love,
> It would have flung an interest round life
> Mine never knew. This is an empty wish;
> Our feelings are not fires to light at will
> Our nature's fine and subtle mysteries;
> We may control them, but may not create,
> And Love less than its fellows. I have fed
> Perhaps too much upon the lotos fruits
> Imagination yields, – fruits which unfit
> The palate for the more substantial food
> Of our own land – reality."   (*LEL* 229)

There is no necessary relation here between Eulalie's "passionate song" and her topic of "beating hearts": the convergence of meter and emotion is not experientially authentic but rather artistically produced. Although the failure here is one of life – or rather love – and not the poetess's art, in the final lines of the poem the English male speaker attributes Eulalie's consumptive death to the artistic practices that make women into the material of their art: "Peace to the weary and the beating heart, / That fed upon itself!" (231). The critical circle closes as this coda on her life and art transforms the ethereal lotos-fruits of Eulalie's imagination into her heart. This is the very model of female artistic production – the emotions of woman as ground and vehicle of lyric expression – that Eulalie had explicitly disavowed. The disjunction between the *improvisatrice*'s poetic world and harsh "reality" gestures at the complex matrix of material and ideological factors that constructs the poetess in the 1830s. As Angela Leighton argues, "A History of the Lyre" responds to reviewers' claims that L.E.L. had done her talents a disservice in taking an easy route to poetic fame.[13] The poem astutely reflects the critical economy within which such facile self-construction was inescapable. The persona of L.E.L.'s poetess is a self-consuming artifact, self-consciously delivered as an aesthetic object to the reader. She enacts, as a number of critics have remarked, a profound cultural alienation. Her performance is the basis of her commodification of the female "self" in verse – but it remains empty: "A History of the Lyre" announces itself, almost like a pun, as a history of the liar by undercutting the naturalization of the feminine lyric. The poem exposes the commodification of both sentiment and the spectacle of the female body "undone," even as it rehearses that process for us as Eulalie again produces herself as aesthetic object. In the poem's final tableau she is indistinguishable from what is soon to be her epitaphic sculpture: " 'twas hard to say / Which was the actual marble" (231).

Only Hemans rivaled L.E.L. as the paramount poetess for early Victorian readers. But, as Virginia Blain argues, L.E.L. and Hemans represent two different strains of the poetess.[14] While both writers were ambitious, engaging extensively with male Romanticism while insisting on a distinctively feminine poetic sensibility, L.E.L. took more risks. She adapted Byronic poetics to her own purposes just as her life came to resemble the Byronic biography. L.E.L. was initially welcomed as a mysterious and titillating addition to the publishing scene while still in her teens. Edward Bulwer-Lytton's recollection of the response of Oxford undergraduates evokes this particular poetess as an eroticized commodity: "there was always, in the reading room of the Union, a rush every Saturday afternoon for the *Literary Gazette*, and an impatient anxiety to hasten at once to that

corner of the sheet which contained the three magical letters of 'L.E.L.'
And all of us praised the verse, and all of us guessed at the author. We soon
learned it was a female, and our admiration was doubled, and our
conjectures tripled. Was she young? Was she pretty?"[15] Bulwer-Lytton
notably attributes L.E.L.'s exponential popularity as much to the mystery
of her identity as to her poetry. His interest lies in female body that the
poetry simultaneously announces and veils.

The ensuing scandals surrounding L.E.L.'s professional life concentrated
more and more oppressive attention on her actual body than her extensive
body of writing. Speculation turned to the singular status of an unmarried
single woman living in a boarding house, in constant professional contact
with men. Take, for example, William Maginn's conclusion to a profile in
Fraser's in 1833: "But why is she Miss Landon? 'A fault like this should be
corrected.'"[16] Female publication already carried implications of self-
advertisement and immodest circulation in the market. Landon's circumstances, therefore, made her doubly vulnerable. Her life was eventually
soured by scandal to the point where she seems to have been driven into the
equivalent – for a woman without Byron's means – of Byronic exile: hasty
marriage took her out of England to West Africa, where she soon died in
circumstances that suggested suicide. The popularity that allowed her to
support herself independently, combined with ambiguous class origins that
made scandal difficult to face down, seemed literally to have proved fatal
when they led to the suggestion that not only her works but also her person
were circulating widely. Although Byron's sexual scandal drove him from
England, his exiled personae provided grist for his poetic mill for years
thereafter, and his reputation did not prevent his poetry from becoming the
most lucrative in England to date. In contrast, the sexual double standard
inflected rumors about L.E.L.'s sexual impropriety to the extent that her
death seemed to many a fitting if tragic denouement to a poetic future that
was already foreclosed. Blanchard's identification of L.E.L. with Sappho
thus aptly locates hers as the fate of a poetess rather than a poet.

III

Despite the scandalous potential of the poetess, there were also profound
continuities between cultural constructions of her role and that of the
respectable woman, and they strengthened during the early years of
Victoria's reign as public adherence to domestic ideology increased. There
is some truth in the widespread view that this period witnessed a consolida-
tion of the notion of separate spheres for middle-class men and women,
where men took responsibility for the public world of work and women

exercised moral authority in the domestic realm. In the minds of both critics and writers, poetry became rapidly feminized in a way that intensified the association between the poetess and altruism, domesticity, sentimentality, and indeed spirituality – qualities that were placed in opposition to harder, rougher, and more taxing demands of the masculine public sphere.

For poets such as Hemans the ideological associations accruing to poetry were largely welcome: in many respects she embraced her role as a British poetess.[17] Hemans located herself explicitly not only in the high poetic tradition of Sappho but also in relation to the idea of a transnational and transhistorical womanhood. Both *Records of Woman* (1828) and *Songs of the Affections* (1830) feature predominantly the situations of women from numerous cultures and historical periods. Notwithstanding separation from her husband and her avoidance of more mundane household management, Hemans managed to represent herself as a poet of the feminine domestic ideal. Critics quickly associated Hemans with Wordsworth, the male poet of domesticity and Byron's foil. In contrast to the London-based L.E.L., Hemans lived for most of her adult life in rural Wales. Further, her dedication to her mother and her children seemed to prove a more effective alibi in the absence of a husband than L.E.L.'s financial support of her mother and brothers while living separately from them in the metropolis.

The domestic ideology that Hemans's poetry often celebrates is as deeply invested in nationalism and imperialism as it is in gender. Grasping the appeal of a work such as her popular "Homes of England" requires holding onto the complementary senses of "domestic" as opposed to both the "public" and the "foreign." The poem, which opens with a rousing patriotic epigraph from Walter Scott's *Marmion* (1808) ("Where's the coward that would not dare / To fight for such a land?"),[18] moves systematically through the social ranks. It shifts from the deer, swans, and "tall ancestral trees" that connote the aristocracy of the "stately Homes of England" down to the "Cottage Homes of England," binding them conceptually into a single space within which "first the child's glad spirit loves / Its country and its God!" (*FH* V, 228–29). Hemans superimposes the roles of mother and poet in this lofty nationalist enterprise, which prospers where "woman's voice flows forth in song" (V, 228).

The treatment of women was assumed to be an index of the degree of civilization reached by a culture. Victorian poetesses, by such logic, were yoked to the nationalist project in the titles of two landmark anthologies, Alexander Dyce's *Specimens of British Poetesses* (1825) and Frederick Rowton's *Female Poets of Great Britain* (1848); Victorian anthologies, criticism, and biographies all assume that women poets reflect the elevated

British national character.[19] In 1847, for example, Gilfillan contended: "in proportion as civilisation advances, and as the darker and fiercer passions which constitute the *fera natura* subside, in the lull of that milder day, the voice of woman will become more audible, exert a wider magic, and be as the voice of the spring to the opening year."[20] In their persons, lives, and poetry, women poets were expected to represent the domesticity, refinement, and purity associated with specifically British or English women. Hemans's constructions of domesticity became so naturalized as descriptions of British identity that Maria Abdy wrote in tribute: "we half unconsciously repeat / Strains we have learned as household words to greet."[21]

Not surprisingly, many women followed Hemans's lead to extrapolate the poetess' role from the domestic ideal. They also drew on women's presumed maternal capacity, as when Sara Coleridge published her popular *Pretty Lessons in Verse, for Good Children* (1835). Sometimes, too, a poetess would characterize her work as an extension of the philanthropic activity prescribed for bourgeois women. During the 1850s and 1860s Mary Sewell wrote widely distributed didactic poetry. Her preface to *Homely Ballads for the Working Man's Fireside* (1858) argues that the working classes have "an instinctive love and appreciation of simple descriptive poetry," which is for them "an almost needful relaxation from the severe and irksome drudgery of their lot." Maintaining throughout the stance of a well-meaning gentlewoman visitor, she offers her poems as an expression of her "earnest sympathy and interest."[22]

IV

Thus it would appear that the Victorian discourse on women and poetry remains firmly grounded in the aestheticization of women, on the one hand, and the rhetoric of separate spheres and female influence, on the other. But this is only half the story. The language and precepts of domestic ideology have to some degree distracted historians from remarking the extent to which women's participation in public life broadened from the early decades of the nineteenth century on. Likewise, as several literary and social historians have shown, the belief that separate spheres were completely dominant can prevent us from understanding the interconnections between gender and other crucial categories such as class, nationality, race, reason, and sexuality.[23] The rhetoric of domestic ideology often sounded dogmatic because it served to consolidate bourgeois, imperial, and national interests at a time when women were making incursions into public and political affairs to an unprecedented degree. Indeed, Victorian women participated in the "public sphere" notwithstanding their exclusion from formal political representation and commercial and professional affairs. Even if she upheld domestic ideals, it is vital to note that a poetess was very much a public woman whose writings circulated in a variety of printed forms. Moreover, apparent celebrations of ideology by poets such as Hemans may reveal incisive critiques of colonialism, domesticity, and militarism.

The marked tension between domestic ideals and the professional work of the poetess becomes clear when we look closely at how this figure came into the public eye through an innovative and highly profitable mode of publication. During the 1820s and 1830s, the annuals or literary gift books became one of most popular outlets for poetry. The first annual in England was *The Forget-Me-Not*, which appeared in 1823 on the model of literary almanacs that enjoyed commercial success in Germany. Directed at the Christmas and New Year market in Britain and its colonies, these gift books were produced in the autumn with titles such as *The Keepsake, Friendship's Offering, The Amulet or Christian and Literary Remembrancer*, the *Literary Souvenir*, and the *Oriental Annual, or Scenes in India*. Beginning as quite plain little books with a small number of engraved illustrations and a large quantity of text, the annuals quickly became much more lavishly illustrated and were often beautifully bound in watered silk or embossed leather with gilt decoration. Their illustrations and bindings became major selling points. By 1832, sixty-three gift books were in production.[24] Their popularity waned by the middle of the 1850s, although some continued into the twentieth century.

Editors of annuals could make hundreds of pounds. L.E.L., for example, who had experience editing the popular *Fisher's Drawing Room Scrapbook* in 1832, was paid £300 for editing the *Book of Beauty* the following year. Marguerite, Countess of Blessington took over the *Book of Beauty* in 1834, and with her income from this, other annuals, and additional writings, she was believed to be earning the astonishing sum of between two and three thousand pounds per annum.[25] The competition among publishers for renowned literary or aristocratic editors and writers who could contribute to the quality or marketability of their firm's annual meant that extremely large sums were spent in editors' and authors' fees. Scott was rumored to have made £400 for a short story in *The Keepsake*; he certainly received £100 for "The Bonnets of Bonnie Dundee" (1828).[26] Even more modest remuneration compared very well to the amount that a woman would earn from employment as a governess, one of few "respectable" occupations available to middle-class women, for which she might earn between £25 and £100 per year. And, as has often been observed, writing had the economic and ideological advantage of allowing the author to pursue her career at home, without any obvious abdication of domestic responsibilities.

Quite apart from the important earning power that the annuals afforded to women poets, the fact that women edited as well as published in them fostered a network of women's writing that rippled down through the entire Victorian period. The sense of association with sister writers whose work appeared alongside their own, the opportunity to publish in a large-circulation market (popular annuals had editions of ten or fifteen thousand), and the correspondence between authors and editors all laid the foundation for a community of women writers that included such figures as Grace Aguilar, Eliza Cook, Mary Howitt, Anna Jameson, and Mary Russell Mitford. In addition, a sense of professional kinship undoubtedly nourished the ongoing conversation we feel when Victorian women poets allude or respond to each other's work. It served the editors well when they went on, as a number of them did, to edit periodicals. Unlike in periodicals (which were also sources of income for poets and critics) with their traditions of anonymity, pieces in the annuals were often signed with initials or full names. The annuals thus helped women authors to establish a reputation and a readership which could lead to single-author publications. Certainly, the annuals posed a challenge to anthologists and critics attempting to institute separate spheres in the literary domain, since female and male authors appeared in them side by side, and women most often took the role of editor.

The annuals also helped clear the path for challenges to separate spheres of ideology beyond literature. One thinks of the publication of *Victoria Regia* (1861), the showpiece of an explicitly feminist publishing venture, the Victoria Press. In fact, the Langham Place circle stood behind this all-women publishing and printing company, which aimed to train its employees in every stage of book production. *Victoria Regia* situated itself determinedly in the midst of a raging controversy over women's employment and proper sphere of activity. It upheld the principle of equal pay for work of equal value, regardless of sex. In response, male printers resorted to minor industrial sabotage including destroying machinery, inking women compositors' stools, and mixing up their boxes of type in an attempt to keep women out of their line of work.[27]

Advertised as a "Christmas book," *Victoria Regia* presents most of the lavish features of an annual – such as an embossed cloth cover decorated with gilt, and a size that approaches that of *Fisher's Drawing-Room Scrapbook*. This imposing publication contains a range of poetry and prose by a wide range of prominent authors from a range of political positions. Its contributors include Matthew Arnold, Anna Jameson, Geraldine Jewsbury, Harriet Martineau, F.D. Maurice, Caroline Norton, Coventry Patmore, Alfred Tennyson, and William Makepeace Thackeray, together with members of the Langham Place circle such as Bessie Rayner Parkes and Isa Craig. The editor of this landmark publication was Adelaide Anne Procter, who had established herself as a popular poet – indeed she was the Queen's favorite – through her contributions to Charles Dickens's *Household Words*. Procter was also a member of the Society for Promoting the Employment of Women, the organization that founded the Press. Her work demonstrates in microcosm the degree to which the notions of sexual difference mobilized in the construction of the poetess could both be assimilated to the values of a middle-class reading public *and* inform an active desire for feminist reform. It is fitting that *Victoria Regia* would be one of last of the gift books, for in a sense it crowns the achievement of the annuals in their function of fostering a female publishing community.

At the same time, the devaluation of the poetess had much to do with the annual as a mode of publication. The gift book was clearly part of a rapidly accelerating commodity market where a book was treasured as much for its features as a material object as for its literary content, which was often scorned as hack work. Moreover, since annuals served as gift books – with an elaborate engraved presentation page to be filled out by the donor – they accentuated the degree to which material goods increasingly mediated human relations. This was doubly uncomfortable, for both poetry and women were traditionally supposed to compensate for the cash nexus. Mary Ann Stodart echoed the views of many in arguing at the close of a discussion of poetesses, that poetry was sadly required "to prevent our sinking into materialism."[28]

Annuals were thus associated with the commercialization and professionalization of literature, and its commensurate debasement within a culture based on economic exchange. Despite contributions by prominent male poets such as Coleridge, John Clare, Thomas Moore, Shelley, and Wordsworth while the annual was relatively young, it became a particularly feminized and derided form of poetic publication. Hartley Coleridge uses the phrase "*annual* value" to disparage weak poetry by women.[29] Charlotte Brontë praised her sister Emily's poetry with a sweeping condemnation of such verse: "I know – no woman that ever lived – ever wrote such poetry before – Condensed energy, clearness, finish – strange, strong pathos are their characteristics – utterly different from the weak diffusiveness – the laboured yet most feeble wordiness which dilute the writings of even very popular poetesses."[30]

V

One particularly well-known Victorian poem sought to redefine the ways in which the poetess imagined herself as a self-consuming aesthetic artifact, became further commodified in demeaning memoirs, and made her reputation in a market that also yoked her to a debased exchange value. As Linda H. Peterson claims, in its early books Elizabeth Barrett Browning's epic *Aurora Leigh* (1856) responds to L.E.L.'s "A History of the Lyre," creating a shift "from a male viewer to the female poet, from art produced to satisfy masculine desire to art for the sake of the female poet, from a literary tradition of biographical memoirs *about* women poets to a new tradition of autobiography *by* women writers."[31] There are certainly compelling reasons for reading Barrett Browning's bildungs-roman-in-verse as a highly successful intervention in the construction of the poetess. Early in her career, Barrett Browning recognized what masculine poetic tradition did to women. An "Essay on Woman" (probably written in 1822 when she was in her teens) berates "Imperious Man" – represented by the famed satirist of woman, Alexander Pope – who would "teach her a lovely, object thing, to be!"[32] Over thirty years later, *Aurora Leigh* works in innumerable ways to make the woman and the woman poet – she pointedly eschews the term "poetess" – the subject rather than the object of her poem. Instead of presenting an aestheticized female object for consumption, this remarkable poem from the outset asserts the self-sufficiency of its project:

> Of writing many books there is no end;
> And I who have written much in prose and verse
> For others' uses, will write now for mine,
> Will write my story for my better self   (*EBBAL* I. 1–4)

To be sure, like Hemans and L.E.L. before her, Barrett Browning takes the woman poet, her body and her life, for her subject matter. But here we find a new aesthetic economy where self-consumption allows the woman poet to thrive rather than expire.

Barrett Browning's engagement with her female poetic precursors is oblique but pervasive, despite – or perhaps because of – her famous claim that she "look[ed] everywhere for Grandmothers and [could] see none."[33] Her work simultaneously affirms and repudiates the aesthetics of both Hemans and L.E.L. Significantly, she weaves that uneasy legacy together with other threads in earlier women's poetry – based in what Anne K. Mellor has called the tradition of the "woman poet" who draws on scriptural authority – to forge a poetic voice and vision.[34] *Aurora Leigh* explodes the generic and thematic scope of the Victorian poetess, fusing lyric with novelistic, dramatic, satiric, and "sage" discourse to create a new kind of epic.[35]

In her relationship with her philanthropic cousin Romney, Aurora – the woman poet whose autobiography the poem records – works both conceptually and practically through the cultural contradictions in the construction of the poetess. Ostensibly a socialist, Romney emerges as a sexual conservative who, like many Victorian critics, grounds his dismissal of Aurora's poetic ambitions in her gender – "You write as well . . . and ill . . . upon the whole, / As other women" (II. 146–47). Moreover, he dismisses the social efficacy of poetry for its feminized insulation from the world: "this same world, / Uncomprehended by you, must remain / Uninfluenced by you. – Women as you are, / Mere women, personal and passionate" (II. 220–21). Echoing the terms of Coventry Patmore's paean to wedlock (*The Angel in the House* [1854–61]), he urges Aurora to become his domestic angel and pursue both poetry and domesticity on the model of diffuse feminine influence: "let me feel your perfume in my home / To make my sabbath after working-days" (II. 832–33). Indubitably, these are Ellis's terms: woman as living poetry, not dedicated poet.

Aurora rejects Romney's domestic ideology and moves determinedly with her poetry into the public sphere. First, she settles in London to live an idealized and sanitized version of the professional woman writer's life, but doing the kind of work associated with the annuals, writing for the sake of money, grappling with the reviewers and their patronage of women. Her success, while not predicated on a Sapphic self-consumption for the sake of love, is explicitly based on sexual self-repression, since domestic womanhood proves incompatible with her vocation. As she instructs a friend:

> "[M]y dear Lord Howe, you shall not speak
> To a printing woman who has lost her place
> (The sweet safe corner of the household fire
> Behind the heads of children), compliments,
> As if she were a woman."   (V. 805–9)

Here the professional writer supplants the *improvisatrice* (whose mode is spontaneous oral performance). But the conflict between art and love reasserts itself in a different way. Aurora desexualizes herself to avoid being trapped by the aestheticization of female abandonment. Yet this maneuver threatens to become another species of self-consumption. Aurora's most despairing experience, when her desire for Romney threatens to turn her life into the one that Ellis promoted where women can "save men by love"

(VII. 185), is accompanied by a sense of self-dissolution like "some passive broken lump of salt" (VII. 1308). This image builds on an earlier metaphor of consumption as womanly fulfillment:

> where we yearn to lose ourselves
> And melt like white pearls in another's wine,
> He seeks to double himself by what he loves,
> And make his drink more costly by our pearls.   (V. 1078–81)

The threat of consumption from hankering after bourgeois femininity is finally resolved in large part through a violent reconfiguration of Romney's masculinity that makes possible a reversal, and perhaps a reconceptualization, of the gendered terms of Victorian culture. *Aurora Leigh* returns us to the poem from the Langham Place circle with which we began: the eponymous speaker's "living voice," which is also in its vatic capacity the "soul's voice," reveals the poetess politicized. Published the same year as Barrett Browning's monument to the Victorian woman poet, "To a Poetess" anticipates Aurora's claim to the entire domain of human activity in a poem that puts various social causes – women's oppression, class conflict, urban poverty – in dialogue with lofty aesthetic aims and incisive social satire. *Aurora Leigh* appeared when Barrett Browning, the most prominent English woman poet of her day, had shown practical solidarity with what was known as "The Woman's Cause" by collecting signatures for the Langham Place group's petition for married women's property reform.

Following her death in 1861, Barrett Browning became revered as the "Great Poetess of our own day."[36] These words come from the preface to "Monna Innominata" (1881), Christina Rossetti's response to both Barrett Browning's *Sonnets from the Portuguese* (1850) and the tradition of woman as silent object of love poetry.[37] The sheer scope of Barrett Browning's oeuvre and her critical status set the bar for women's poetry for the rest of the century. Even as late as 1888 Oscar Wilde, in an essay on the poetess, upholds her as "an imperishable glory of our literature," proclaiming her the greatest female poet since Sappho.[38] For those working through the cultural contradictions surrounding women as poetic producers, her poems regularly draw on sexual difference as the basis of poetic power. The salt that threatened to dissolve Aurora in self-pity over the conflict between gender and poetic vocation gives the sting to the powerful political poetry of Barrett Browning's final years: "A curse from the depths of womanhood / Is very salt, and bitter, and good" ("A Curse for a Nation" [1860]; *EBB* 47–48).

VI

Interest in Sappho did not simply disappear. But the sense that Sappho was, as Margaret Reynolds puts it, a "fixed icon rigidly posed at the moment of self-display and self-destruction" certainly did.[39] After the mid-century, she is frequently transformed into a more politicized, more overtly mediated figure. Mary Catherine Hume folds a critique of woman as aesthetic object into a feminist analysis of prostitution in "Sappho" (1861), and Catherine Amy Dawson – in a long poem of the same name (1889) – rewrites Sappho in the image of a Victorian feminist educator and reformer.[40] In women's poetry, negotiations of the fraught relationship between the female body, aesthetic and sexual consumption, and poetic production seem more free, perhaps most remarkably in Rossetti's "Goblin Market" (1862). Here the contradictory relations among gender, aesthetics, and economics that we have been tracing are resolved in a closed-circuit of homoeroticism when one sister saves the other from a fatally consuming desire for participation in the market, exclaiming: "Eat me, drink me, love me; / Laura, make much of me" (*CR* 471–72). The poem posits a form of sisterly consumption that brings increase, not decrease. Enabling ironies of production, however, persisted: Rossetti's publisher Macmillan envisioned the publication of *Goblin Market and Other Poems* in terms of "an exceedingly pretty little volume" for Christmas, marketing it in the tradition of the annuals.[41]

Augusta Webster, an associate of the Pre-Raphaelite circle in which Rossetti moved, depicts in a dramatic monologue, "A Castaway" (1870), another woman who manages to profit from the consumption of her own body. As a fashionable prostitute named Eulalie, she is the literalization of the poetess in "A History of the Lyre." But whereas L.E.L.'s Eulalie's heart consumed itself with unsatisfied desire, Webster's speaker takes a more materialist line that puns on the fact that her face is her fortune: "Aye let me feed upon my beauty thus, / . . . triumph in it, / the dearest thing I have."[42] Though by no means resolved, the cultural contradictions of the earlier part of the century have taken a different complexion. Webster was a learned classicist. Yet she is not compelled to take up Sappho. Instead, her powerful series of monologues turns to Medea: the classical archetype of the unwomanly woman who negates her assigned cultural role in response to male oppression.

From the 1870s onward, the explicit invocation of the poetess is more critical than poetic, even though the project of keeping poets and poetesses in separate literary spheres is breaking down. This point becomes clear when we look at Emma Caroline Wood's anthology called *Leaves from the Poets' Laurels* (1869) that appears in Moxon's Miniature Poets series. It leads off with Procter's poem "A Woman's Question" (1858), and proceeds to intersperse works by male and female writers, although the former considerably outweigh the latter. Wood's preface makes no issue of gender; there is one passing reference to "poets of my own sex."[43] Increasingly, critics were treating male and female poets side by side or categorizing them together in critical discussions, as in H. Buxton Forman's *Our Living Poets* (1871). There were of course those who defended the old terrain, most notably Eric S. Robertson's *English Poetesses: A Series of Critical Biographies with Illustrative Extracts* (1883). He asserts that "women have always been inferior to men as writers of poetry; and they always will be," since "children are the best poems Providence meant women to produce."[44] But Robertson seems to protest too much. He was influential for later critics who found in him an ally for excluding women writers from the canon. Read in the context of other anthologies and women's poetry of the time, however, his polemic seems outmoded. Elizabeth Sharp's *Women Poets of the Victorian Era* (1890) reflects the mood of the previous two decades of women's poetry more accurately. Sharp dedicates her volume to the New Woman novelist Mona Caird, "the most loyal and devoted advocate of the cause of woman," and her preface broaches her material with a sense of confidence: "The scope of the volume covers . . . practically new ground. I do not think that the poetry enshrined herein requires any apology from me or from any one: it speaks for itself." In language that links her project with Caird's, she asserts that the collection

> arose primarily from the conviction that our women-poets had never been collectively represented with anything like adequate justice; that the works of many are not so widely known as they deserved to be; and that at least some fine fugitive poetry could be rescued from oblivion. Women have had many serious hindrances to contend against – defective education, lack of broad experience of life, absence of freedom in which to make full use of natural abilities, and the force of public and private opinion, both of which have always been prone to prejudice their work unfavourably, or at best apologetically.[45]

Sharp's analysis stands up well today, and her selection of poets mirrors almost uncannily that of anthologies which have more recently engaged in the project of rescuing the still fugitive poetry by Victorian women from oblivion.

This new poetess, rather like her fictional counterpart the New Woman, ushered in experimentation in both content and form. The old one lingered, and her imprint can be found in critical and poetic discourse into the next century. But now the cultural dilemmas posed by female cultural production seemed less pressing, to women poets at least. The feminist movement continued to gather steam. It drove home its analysis of the implication of gender politics in exchange and commodification through its critiques of marriage, the regulation of prostitution, and the nation's legal, educational, and political structures, even as it demonstrated the ability of women to thrive beyond the home in the public sphere. The remarkable shifts in tone and the startling variety of theme, form, and technique in the texts of late-Victorian women poets such as Mathilde Blind, Mary Coleridge, Amy Levy, Constance Naden, and A. Mary F. Robinson may be due to a sense that women no longer need define themselves against the figure of the poetess. In this respect, these accomplished poets had considerably out-stripped critics such as Robertson. To be sure, gender often remained an issue for women poets, but understandings of masculinity and femininity had transformed considerably since the dawn of the Victorian era.

Immense changes in the publishing industry likewise had an impact on how and where women published, so that the precious limited editions of Michael Field are a result of changing material practices as well as a shift in aesthetics. In underwriting the cost of literary productions, the aunt and niece who wrote jointly as Michael Field retained a large measure of editorial control over their material. Such control was possibly a necessity, given that even the sympathetic Robert Browning appears from the manuscript of *Long Ago*, their frankly "audacious" completion of Sappho's fragments,[46] to have counseled the excision of more explicit lesbian love poetry. Yet the gorgeous production values of their books, which present themselves as aesthetic objects, hearken back to the annuals. Their sense of elitism, exclusivity, and sheer decorativeness recalls women's role in conservative gender ideology as the "perfume" – to invoke Barrett Browning's words – in men's homes. It uncomfortably suggests a parallel between the commodified form in which women represent themselves and the commodification of women themselves. To have behind them a century of successful female poets gave women new confidence as cultural producers, but the structures of aesthetic commodification remained heavily gendered.

Such structures fostered the continuing devaluation of the Victorian poetess. Only in the 1990s have many feminist critics begun to consider women poets other than Rossetti, Barrett Browning, and Emily Brontë. Their research has questioned the standards of value and literary inquiry that placed Hemans – the most popular woman poet of the nineteenth century – beyond the critical pale for almost a hundred years.

Few scholars would now dispute the historical and sociological interest of the poetess as a significant phenomenon in the early nineteenth century. But critics remain divided on questions of literary value. Some find a real complexity in their works. Glennis Stephenson discovers in L.E.L.'s large canon an almost post-modern performance of identity that explores female eroticism; Stephenson pronounces L.E.L.'s writing for annuals "subversive with . . . impunity."[47] Mellor argues that "[w]orking from *within* an essentialist construction of the female as the beautiful and the loving, Landon's poetry uncovers the emptiness, the self-defeating consequences, of such a construction." Similarly, she contends that Hemans's work "exhausts – both in the sense of thoroughly investigating, finding the limits of, and in the sense of using up, emptying out – the very domestic ideology it espouses."[48] Not everyone is receptive to such views, however. Blain remains unconvinced that Victorian readers "were in a position to share such a sophisticated vision" of these poems.[49]

Such debate suggests two points. First, individual figures must be reassessed in relation to the conditions under which they wrote and were read. Second, the traditional standards by which we evaluate poetry – many of them the legacy of Modernism and its critical progeny the New Criticism – appear woefully inadequate for the study of nineteenth-century women writers.[50] Despite the energetic scholarly activity of late, our grasp of their poetry is yet at an early stage. Armstrong and Joseph Bristow must still resort to "a vocabulary of [their] own making to describe the two principal poetic genres [used by women poets] of the early and mid-century."[51]

The Victorian poetess demands further attention. Her work has already helped us to reconsider our critical priorities and conceptual frameworks. In the latter part of the twentieth century, Victorianists have repeatedly debated canonicity and literary value, precisely because women poets occupy a vast, uneven, and culturally vexed terrain in which materiality and ideality, and aesthetics and commodification continually intersect in the construction of both identity and community. Virginia Jackson and Prins argue compellingly that, as "the embodiment of sentimental exchange" whose texts "proclaimed their status *as* cultural currency," poetesses problematize the foundational assumption that lyrics are "personal subjective utterance[s] of historical subjects."[52] The Victorian poetess encourages us to untangle threads that have remained entwined for more than two centuries. These investigations prove urgent since our culture continues, often violently, to aestheticize women's bodies. Despite economic gains, women inhabit a society of spectacle and commodification where the female body remains caught between the positions of subject and object within the forces of production and consumption. Gendered divisions, such as that between private and public, still structure our quotidian world. Further, the literary and critical domains appear marginalized and feminized to an unprecedented degree in an increasingly technologized global "information" culture. The Victorian poetess is a deeply contested marker of the vexed relationship between highly naturalized constructions of femininity, new modes of production, and changing patterns of cultural consumption. In this distant day, we can now see more clearly the local strategies that nineteenth-century women employed to negotiate – and on occasion shift – the discursive and material practices that would otherwise make a mortified body of a "breathing poetess."

NOTES

I would like to thank Christine Bold, Linda Mahood, Donna Pennee, and Ann Wilson, for reading an early draft of this essay, and Joseph Bristow for editorial midwifery beyond the call of duty.

1 [Anonymous,] "To a Poetess" (Privately Printed, 1856), 7.
2 Isobel Armstrong, *Victorian Poetry: Poetry, Poetics and Politics* (London: Routledge, 1993), 321.
3 Stuart Curran, "Women Readers, Women Writers," in *The Cambridge Companion to Romanticism*, ed. Curran (Cambridge: Cambridge University Press, 1993), 193.
4 [Anonymous,] "The Female Character," *Fraser's Magazine* 7 (1833), 601.
5 Sarah Stickney Ellis, *The Daughters of England: Their Position in Society, Character, and Responsibilities* ([1837] New York: D. Appleton, 1842), 98.
6 Edgar Allan Poe, "The Philosophy of Composition," in *Selections from the Critical Writings of Edgar Allan Poe*, ed. F.C. Prescott (New York: Gordian Press, 1981), 156, 158.
7 Yopie Prins, *Victorian Sappho* (Princeton, NJ: Princeton University Press, 1999), 14.
8 Lawrence Lipking, *Abandoned Women and Poetic Tradition* (Chicago, IL: University of Chicago Press, 1988).
9 Felicia Hemans, Undated Letter, Correspondent Unknown, cited in [Harriett Hughes,] "Memoir of the Life and Writings of Mrs. Hemans by Her Sister," in *The Works of Mrs. Hemans*, 7 vols. (Edinburgh: William Blackwood and Sons, 1839), I, 226.
10 Marlon B. Ross, *The Contours of Masculine Desire: Romanticism and the Rise of Women's Poetry* (New York: Oxford University Press, 1989), 298.
11 Laman Blanchard, *Life and Literary Remains of L.E.L.*, 2 vols. (London: H. Colburn, 1841), I, 38.
12 Tricia Lootens, *Lost Saints: Silence, Gender, and Victorian Literary Canonization* (Charlottesville, VA: University Press of Virginia, 1996), 49–50.
13 Angela Leighton, *Victorian Women Poets: Writing Against the Heart* (Charlottesville, VA: University Press of Virginia, 1992), 67.
14 Virginia Blain, "Letitia Elizabeth Landon, Eliza Mary Hamilton, and the Genealogy of the Victorian Poetess," *Victorian Poetry* 33 (1995), 31–51.
15 [Edward Bulwer-Lytton,] Review of L.E.L., *Romance and Reality*, *New Monthly Magazine* 32 (1831), 546.
16 William Maginn, "Gallery of Literary Characters XLI: Miss Landon," *Fraser's Magazine* 8 (1833), 433.

17 Deborah Kennedy, "Hemans, Wordsworth, and the 'Literary Lady,'" *Victorian Poetry* 35 (1997), 267–85.

18 Walter Scott, *Marmion*, in *The Poetical Works of Sir Walter Scott*, ed. J. Logie Robertson (London: Oxford University Press, 1964), 135.

19 Alexander Dyce, *Specimens of British Poetesses: Selected and Chronologically Arranged* (London: T. Rodd, 1825); Frederic Rowton, *The Female Poets of Great Britain: Chronologically Arranged with Copious Selections and Critical Remarks* ([1848] Philadelphia, PA: Baird, 1853).

20 George Gilfillan, "Female Authors – No. II: Mrs. Elizabeth Barrett Browning," *Tait's Edinburgh Magazine* 18 (1847), 620.

21 Maria Abdy, "Lines Written on the Death of Mrs Hemans," *Metropolitan Magazine* 13 (1835), 257.

22 Mary Sewell, *Homely Ballads for the Working Man's Fireside* (London: Jarrold and Sons, 1858), iii, iv.

23 See, for example, Linda Colley, *Britons: Forging the Nation, 1707–1837* (New Haven, CT: Yale University Press, 1992), 237–81; Mary Poovey, *Uneven Developments: The Ideological Work of Gender in Mid-Victorian England* (Chicago, IL: University of Chicago Press, 1989); Cathy N. Davidson, "Preface: No More Separate Spheres!" *American Literature* 3 (1998), 443–63.

24 Frederick W. Faxon, *Literary Annuals and Gift Books: A Bibliography 1823–1903* (1912), reprinted with supplementary essays by Eleanore Jamieson and Iain Bain (Pinner: Private Libraries Association, 1973), xi-xii.

25 Alison Adburgham, *Women in Print: Writing Women and Women's Magazines* (London: George Allen and Unwin, 1972), 249–50.

26 Mrs. Newton Crosland, *Landmarks of a Literary Life* (New York: Charles Scribner's Sons, 1893), 95; Andrew Boyle, "Preface," *Index to the Annuals* (Worcester: A. Boyle, 1967), not paginated.

27 James Stuart Stone, *Emily Faithfull: Victorian Champion of Women's Rights* (Toronto: P.D. Meany, 1994), 52–53, 55.

28 M.A. Stodart, *Female Writers: Thoughts on Their Proper Sphere, and on Their Powers of Usefulness* (London: R.B. Seeley and W. Burnside, 1842), 102.

29 [Hartley Coleridge,] "Modern English Poetesses," *Quarterly Review* 46 (1840), 381.

30 T.J. Wise and J.A. Symington, *The Brontës: Their Lives, Friendships, and Correspondence*, in *The Shakespeare Head Brontë*, ed. Wise and Symington, 19 vols. (Oxford: Basil Blackwell, 1931–38), XV, 256.

31 Linda H. Peterson, "Rewriting the History of the Lyre," in *Women's Poetry: Late Romantic to Late Victorian*, ed. Isobel Armstrong and Virginia Blain (Basingstoke: Macmillan, 1999), 116.

32 Eleanor Hoag, "Note on 'Fragment of an "Essay on Woman,"'" *Studies in Browning and His Circle* 12 (Spring–Fall 1984), 7; Elizabeth Barrett, "Fragment of an 'Essay on Woman,'" *Studies in Browning and His Circle* 12 (Spring–Fall 1984), 12.

33 Elizabeth Barrett, "To Henry Fothergill Chorley," 7 January 1845, in *The Browning Correspondence*, ed. Philip Kelley and Scott Lewis, 14 vols. to date (Winfield, KS: Wedgestone Press, 1984–), X, 14.

34 Anne K. Mellor, "The Female Poet and the Poetess: Two Traditions of British Women's Poetry, 1780–1830," in *Women's Poetry in the Enlightenment: The*

Making of a Canon, 1730–1820, ed. Isobel Armstrong and Virginia Blain (New York: St. Martin's Press, 1999), 84, 85.

35 See Marjorie Stone, *Elizabeth Barrett Browning* (New York: St. Martin's Press, 1995), 137–59.

36 Christina Rossetti, "Monna Innominata: A Sonnet of Sonnets," in *The Complete Poems of Christina Rossetti*, ed. R.W. Crump, 3 vols. (Baton Rouge, LA: Louisiana State University, 1979–90), II, 86.

37 See Susan Conley, "'Poet's Right': Christina Rossetti as Anti-Muse and the Legacy of the 'Poetess.'" *Victorian Poetry* 32 (1994), 365–86.

38 Oscar Wilde, "English Poetesses," in *The Artist as Critic: Critical Writings of Oscar Wilde*, ed. Richard Ellmann (New York: Random House, 1969), 102. This essay originally appeared in *Queen*, 8 December 1888.

39 Margaret Reynolds, "'I lived for art, I lived for love': The Woman Poet Sings Sappho's Last Song," in *Victorian Women Poets: A Critical Reader*, ed. Angela Leighton (Oxford: Blackwell, 1996), 299.

40 Mary Catherine Hume, "Sappho," *Intellectual Repository*, 1 May 1862, 222–26; Catherine Amy Dawson, *Sappho* (London: Kegan Paul, Trench, 1889).

41 Alexander Macmillan, "To Dante Gabriel Rossetti," 28 October 1861, in *The Rossetti–Macmillan Letters*, ed. Lona Mosk Packer (Berkeley, CA: University of California Press, 1963), 6.

42 Augusta Webster, *Portraits* (London: Macmillan, 1870), 37. This poem is reprinted in *Nineteenth-Century Women Poets*, eds. Isobel Armstrong and Joseph Bristow with Cath Sharrock (Oxford: Clarendon Press, 1996), 602–30; and in *Victorian Women Poets: An Anthology*, eds. Angela Leighton and Margaret Reynolds (Oxford Basil Blackwell, 1995), 433–48

43 Emma, Lady Wood, *Leaves from the Poets' Laurels*, Moxon's Miniature Poets (London: E. Moxon, Son, 1869), xi.

44 Eris S. Robertson *English Poetesses: A Series of Critical Biographies, with Illustrative Extracts* (London: Cassell, 1883), xv, xiv.

45 Elizabeth Amelia Sharp, ed., *Women Poets of the Victorian Era* (London: Walter Scott, 1890), xxix, xxx. Alfred H. Miles also gave women substantial attention in his monumental *Poets and Poetry of the Century*, 10 vols. (London: Hutchinson, 1892–97).

46 "Preface," *Long Ago* (London: George Bell, 1889), iii.

47 Glennis Stephenson, *Letitia Landon: The Woman Behind L.E.L.* (Manchester: Manchester University Press, 1995), 172.

48 Anne K. Mellor, *Romanticism and Gender* (New York: Routledge, 1993), 120, 142.

49 Virginia Blain, "'Thou with Earth's Music Answerest to the Sky': Felicia Hemans, Mary Ann Browne, and the Myth of Poetic Sisterhood," *Women's Writing* 2 (1995), 259; and "Letitia Elizabeth Landon, Eliza Mary Hamilton, and the Genealogy of the Victorian Poetess," *Victorian Poetry* 33 (1995), 46.

50 See Curran, "The I Altered," in *Romanticism and Feminism*, ed. Anne K. Mellor (Bloomington, IN: Indiana University Press, 1988), 185–207.

51 Isobel Armstrong and Joseph Bristow, "Introduction," in *Nineteenth-Century Women Poets*, xxxvi.

52 Virginia Jackson and Yopie Prins, "Lyrical Studies," *Victorian Literature and Culture* 27 (1999), 527, 528, 531.

10

THAÏS E. MORGAN

The poetry of Victorian masculinities

Representations of masculinity – what men should think and feel, how they should look, and what sorts of work they should do – shifted several times in Victorian England. During the first half of the nineteenth century, as Herbert Sussman demonstrates in *Victorian Masculinities: Manhood and Masculine Poetics in Early Victorian England* (1995), a discourse about manliness was constructed in response to industrialization and changes in the socioeconomic class system. The traditional distinction between upper-class landowning aristocracy versus lower-class unpropertied laborers was complicated by the rise of a middle class of industrialists, bankers, merchants, and a variety of professionals. Historians Leonore Davidoff and Catherine Hall point to the "delineation of gender difference" as one of the main features of the Victorian middle class.[1] In particular, the balance between brawn and brains in the paradigm of masculinity was transformed. Manhood now involved work that might be more mental than physical. Rigorous moral as well as economic self-discipline became the hallmark of masculinity and the basis of claims to cultural authority, according to James Eli Adams in *Dandies and Desert Saints: Styles of Victorian Masculinity* (1995). For example, the early Victorian sage Thomas Carlyle defined manliness in terms of strenuous effort, both in the workplace and in the soul. His *On Heroes, Hero-Worship, and the Heroic in History* (1840) became a guidebook for several generations of Victorian men seeking a firm gender identity.

The other major force in the construction of the Victorian ideal of manliness was the increasing presence of women as moral guides and popular writers in English culture since the latter part of the eighteenth century. Nancy Armstrong's study of novels and conduct books reveals that "writing for and about the female introduced a whole new vocabulary for social relations."[2] An ideology of separate spheres for men and women took hold during the beginning of the nineteenth century. The definition of womanliness complemented that of manliness: the true woman was devoted to care of the family and maintenance of the home, while the true man dedicated himself to pursuit of economic success and his role as paterfamilias. This domestic ideology meshed with the larger political goals of the middle class: manly aggressiveness ensured the prosperity not only of the family but also the nation, while womanly spirituality provided support for both men and their heirs.

We find several Victorian masculinities represented by Alfred Tennyson, Matthew Arnold, and Algernon Charles Swinburne not only when their poetry is compared but within each poet's work. To clarify these differing models of manhood, this essay adopts Raymond Williams's model for analyzing the competing discourses that constitute culture. The first section, "Domestic Masculinities," looks at how the male poet positions himself in relation to domestic ideology: the "dominant" ideological formation that, to draw on Raymond Williams's terminology, comprises the "central system of practices, meanings and values" which "constitute[d] a sense of reality for most people" in Victorian England.[3] The second section, "Heroic Masculinities," considers the importance of both medievalism and classicism to constructing the ideal of manliness. These "residual" ideologies provide a means of representing "experiences, meanings and values, which cannot be . . . expressed in terms of the dominant culture" but were "nevertheless lived and practiced on the basis of" the past (40). The third section, "Emergent Masculinities," explores the "new meanings and values, new practices, new significances and experiences" which were "continually being created" in response to both dominant and residual ideologies (41).

Dominant domestic ideology operates as a "hegemony," establishing a hierarchized sexual difference between men and women.[4] Hegemonic masculinity sets a norm of patriarchal organization in both private and public life. Manliness entails homosociality or close relationships among men that exclude women, but homoeroticism or male–male desire remains taboo. Hegemonic masculinity must be "continually . . . renewed, recreated, and defended" in response to "alternative" as well as "oppositional" viewpoints (38). Tennyson, Arnold, and Swinburne put into play a range of ideological effects at the contested site of Victorian masculinities.

Domestic masculinities

Victorian male poets inhabited an ambiguous cultural space: as poets, they were expected to express deep feelings and explore private states of consciousness, yet this was identified in domestic ideology as the preserve of the feminine. Tennyson's early poetry exemplifies the tension between the masculinity of the poet and the femininity of his genre: Victorian critics found the texts about women and their emotions in domestic settings in *Poems, Chiefly Lyrical* (1830) unacceptably effeminate.[5] Consider the poem "Mariana" (1830) which describes the heightened senses of a woman waiting for her lover in a "lonely moated grange" (*AT* 8). Staring at the "rusted nails" (3) on the "gable-wall" (4) imprisoning her, Mariana sees not a rescuer but a "gnarlèd" (42) tree on the "level waste" (44). The refrain emphasizes her extreme despair: "I am aweary, aweary, / I would that I were dead!"; she is like the Victorian woman who, denied access to the world of action, depends on a man and marriage to realize herself. Mariana goes mad from waiting: "the mouse / Behind the mouldering wainscot shrieked, / . . . Old voices called her from without" (63–64, 68). Framing Mariana's experience in the descriptive narrative, the male poet ventriloquizes her voice in the refrain; he adopts a feminine persona. Imagining the domestic situation of women enables Tennyson to represent feelings different from those of Victorian men engaged in public life. But the fact that Mariana wishes to die suggests that the male poet's appropriation of the feminine preserves rather than changes the dominant ideology of separate spheres.

Matthew Arnold struggles with the relation between poetry and the feminine under domestic ideology throughout his career. His work often represents men and women interacting but always from a male point of view. "The Forsaken Merman" (1849) raises questions about the Victorian doctrine of separate spheres within a distanced setting of fairy tale. The merman calls to his children to come back home to the undersea world: "let us away; / Down and away below!" (*MA* 1–2). The paterfamilias has been "forsaken" by his wife who has betrayed her womanliness in preferring "the white-walled town" (25) to his "Sand-strewn caverns, cool and deep" (35). As the merman realizes that Margaret will not return, the poem turns elegiac; he laments days past of domestic bliss when "Once she sate with you and me, / . . . And the youngest sate on her knee" (50, 52). Familiar gender roles are reversed: the mother ventures out into the social world while the father takes refuge with the children in the "kind sea-caves" (61): "She said, 'I must go, for my kinsfolk pray / In the little grey church on the shore to-day'" (56–57). Arnold speaks the feminine through the voice of the merman: "She sits at her wheel in the humming town / Singing . . . / . . . 'O joy, O joy'" (87–89). A wounded but defiant masculinity characterizes "The Forsaken Merman." Margaret's refusal of her maternal and spousal roles has led to her "sorrow-clouded eye, / And a heart sorrow-laden" (103–04). A figure for the male poet, the merman remains bitterly nostalgic for a lost ideal harmony between man and woman, symbolized by the gap between the realms of land and sea: "Here came a mortal, / But faithless was she! / And alone dwell for ever / The kings of the sea" (120–23).

Algernon Charles Swinburne approaches the equivalence between the lyric and the feminine ensuing from the doctrine of two spheres oppositionally. In the long dramatic monologue "Anactoria" (1866), he ventriloquizes Sappho in order to attack both Victorian sexual morality and Christianity. His perverse rendition of Sapphic "song" is calculated to shock the middle class that hypocritically refuses to acknowledge the sensuality in literature. The ideological effects of Swinburne's ventriloquism of the feminine differ from those in Tennyson and Arnold. Swinburne focuses on female eroticism as realized in a gynosocial or all-female world that radicalizes the very notion of a separate woman's sphere. Swinburne undercuts the Victorian idealization of woman's nature as spiritual and chaste. Sappho and Anactoria engage in sadomasochistic lovemaking: "I would my love could kill thee; . . . / I would find grievous ways to have thee slain, / . . . Vex thee with amorous agonies" (*ACS* I, 58). The conventional description of woman as a flower for her beauty and delicacy is reencoded through ironic evocation of the color symbolism associated with the Virgin Mary. After Sappho's violent pleasures, the young Anactoria has

> eyes the bluer for all those hidden hours
> That pleasure fills with tears and feeds from flowers,
> Fierce at the heart with fire that half comes through,
> But all the flowerlike white stained round with blue[.]   (I, 58)

Swinburne focuses our eye on the female body: Anactoria's "fervent underlid" and her "amorous girdle, full of thee and fair / And leavings of the lilies in" her "hair" (I, 58). Victorian critics were outraged at this portrait of woman: "Is purity to be expunged from the catalogue of desirable qualities?" one demanded.[6]

Unquestionably, Swinburne radicalizes the issue of the femininity of poetry. In allowing Sappho to speak a long monologue without an omniscient narrator's interruption, Swinburne pays homage to her. Nevertheless, as in Tennyson's early poems, the identification of sensuality and femininity ultimately aligns him with mainstream Victorian gender ideology: woman's sphere includes the body and passion. As a poet, Sappho triumphs over the classical gods, the Christian God, and even death: she will immortalize the mortal "flower" Anactoria in the "high Pierian flower" of "song" (I, 63). Sappho's poems will be eternal and pervasive in their power: "Men shall not see bright fire nor hear the sea, / . . . But in the light and laughter, in the moan / And music, and in grasp of lip and hand / . . . Memories shall mix and metaphors of me" (I, 63–64).

Yet as a woman, Sappho dies. Although ever defiant of the dominant order ("But, having made me, me he [God] shall not slay" [I, 65]), and although asserting her right to desire ("neither moon nor snow nor dew / Nor all cold things can purge me wholly through" [I, 66]), Sappho finally takes her life by plunging into "Thick darkness and the insuperable sea" (I, 66). To what purpose does the male poet appropriate the feminine here? Arguably, the woman herself is expelled (Sappho's death) while the poet himself (Swinburne speaking as Sappho) remains.

Near mid-century, Tennyson represents the disturbances and adjustments in Victorian men's and women's gender identities in a long mock-heroic narrative poem, *The Princess: A Medley* (1847). Tennyson's strategy is to accommodate the gathering Victorian women's movement while reassuring his readers that the Chartist revolts of the 1840s do not signal a revolution in England like the French one of 1789. Both the masculinized Princess Ida ("Grand, epic, homicidal" like a formidable warrior ["Prologue," 218]) and the feminized Prince ("With lengths of yellow ringlet, like a girl" [I. 3]) are unconventionally gender-crossed. But the medievalizing setting of the story places them under the sign of courtly love, thereby carrying forward a residual ideology of gender and power relations into Victorian times. The Princess has left home and refused marriage in order to found a college for women who have historically been denied an education and equality with men. The Prince and two friends breach this chaste gynotopia by disguising themselves in "female gear" (I. 196) and speaking in falsetto. When in the presence of Ida herself, though, the Prince several times undergoes "weird seizures" (I. 14), as if he is overcome by the power of the feminine. The paradigm of courtly love allows for male submission to the female within the sphere of feelings but promotes a heroic ideal of manliness in the realm of action: the Prince rescues the Princess from a fall and he is wounded while jousting to save the Princess's cause.

Hegemonic masculinity is modified but not overthrown in *The Princess*. Although she finds them out early on, Lady Psyche does not expose the cross-dressed men to punishment because they appeal to a shared domestic ideal. Princess Ida traduces femininity by insisting on "theories . . . / Maintaining . . . / The woman were an equal to the man" (I. 128–30), instead of accepting her natural role of engaging in "Sweet household talk, and phrases of the hearth" (II. 294). The Prince seems more liberal in his sexual politics. Infused with a feminine "gentleness" (V. 160), he repudiates his father's aggressive style of manliness – "Man is the hunter; the woman is his game" (V. 147) – and absolutist patriarchalism: "Man for the field and woman for the hearth: / Man for the sword and for the needle she; / Man to command and woman to obey" (V. 437–40). But look closely at the plot and narrative frame of *The Princess*: action and its resolution depend on marriages sanctioned by the patriarchal order; the tale is told by young men who ventriloquize both the feminine (Ida and her followers) and the effeminate (the cross-dressed Prince and his friends). As Eve Kosofsky Sedgwick has shown in *Between Men: English Literature and Male Homosocial Desire* (1985), Tennyson's *The Princess* sets up a structure of exchange triangles in which a woman is the object of desire through which men bond with each other and against her. In Part VII and the "Conclusion," the Prince reasserts the masculine prerogative in a series of ambiguous equivalences even as he seems to accommodate Ida's feminism. "The woman's cause is man's" (VII. 243), he declares, as long as she embodies "All that harms not distinctive womanhood. / For woman is not undevelopt man, / But diverse . . . / Not like to like, but like in difference" (VII. 258–62).

Sidestepping the issue of gender equality, the Prince confirms the rightness of sexual difference. Princess Ida and her followers are transfigured by images of flowers and light when they realize true womanhood by turning the college into a hospital in Part VI to care for the men after the fighting in Part V. A salient theme throughout the poem, the maternal feminine provides a cornerstone of its resolution of gender conflict – from the masculine point of view. By way of encouraging the Princess to become a wife and mother, the Prince adduces his own mother as the paragon of womanhood: "all dipt / In Angel instincts, breathing Paradise" (VII. 301–02). He himself has been infantilized by fainting after the jousts and by relying on Ida's sympathetic nursing care. A charming child, Lady Psyche's Aglaea, circulates among the women as if to remind them and us of woman's truest destiny. Typifying mid-Victorian liberalism, Tennyson maintains a hierarchized opposition between male and female in which the former is always already superior to the latter.

Tennyson's *Princess* makes a strategic cultural intervention: the poem exceeds the bounds of hegemonic masculinity without destroying it. Victorian feminism is at least partially accommodated; aspects of femininity are appropriated (the androgyny, "weird seizures," and cross-dressing of the Prince); masculine hegemony (the chivalrous ideal of manliness, the homosociality of the frame and the plot, the overall superiority of men to women) is left standing. Nonetheless, gender trouble leaves its trace in the mixed genre of *The Princess*, a "strange experiment," a "medley" which at times turns into a melee between the sexes ("Prologue," 228, 230). As a *male* poet, Tennyson must mediate between the requirements of membership in patriarchy and the desire as well as the demands represented by the feminine. The issue of the female poet threads anxiously throughout the poem. One of the ladies in the frame wishes that she were a "mighty poetess" ("Prologue," 132); the "strange Poet-princess" (III. 255) has written "awful odes" (I. 137) which her father wryly admits are "masterpieces": "They mastered *me*" (II. 144–45), he quips. Ida mocks the Prince's attempt at poetry ("O Swallow . . . / Fly to her . . . / And tell her . . . what I tell to thee" [IV. 75–77]). In the end, womanly "Tenderness" (VII. 99) for the Prince overcomes her discursive ferocity and the Princess becomes a reader rather than a writer of poetry ("'Come down, O maid, from yonder mountain height" [VII. 175–207]). By adding in 1850 the "songs" to the 1847 text, Tennyson stages the battle between the sexes as a contest between lyric (feminine, maternal) and narrative (masculine, martial) modes, with himself as the voice of both. His bigendered poetic persona "move[s] as in a strange diagonal, / And maybe neither pleased myself nor them" ("Conclusion," 27–28) – the audience both inside and outside of the text.

Arnold often laments the passing of an ideal convergence between men and women. The speakers in the group of lyrics called "Switzerland" (1849) express alienation and loneliness that stem from a loss of the moorings of Victorian masculinity. The male lover in "Isolation: To Marguerite" had "faith" (*MA* 10) in the conventional domestic paradigm – "I bade my heart . . . / . . . grow a home for only thee" (2, 4) – but, finding his love unrequited, reluctantly resigns himself to "isolation without end" (40). Apostrophizing not the beloved but his "lonely heart" (13), he renounces "passions" (17) and tries to embrace "solitude" (18). Arnold allegorizes the ineluctable separation between man and woman in terms of a seascape in "To Marguerite – Continued": "Yes! in the sea of life enisled, / With echoing straits between us thrown" (1–2), he declares, "We mortal millions live *alone*" (4).

Arnold's representation of masculinity as a lost, unattainable, or even repressive identity informs much of his poetry. He uses the dramatic monologue to allow a male persona to express the full range of his emotions to an implied female listener, thereby framing an unconventional feminized masculinity within conventionally binary terms. "Fate" is taken to task for dictating strict gender roles in "The Buried Life" (1852): the speaker pleads for recognition of "The unregarded river of our life" (*MA* 39), specifically the "nameless feelings" (62) which men experience but dare not express lest they be thought effeminate. The internal seascape of "To Marguerite – Continued" becomes a "buried stream" (*MA* 42) of emotions that "course on for ever unexpress'd" (63). Both men and women possess a "hidden self" (65) but the male speaker focuses on his own need for "a beloved hand" (78), a sympathetic exchange of glances, and "the tones of a loved voice" (83) to realize the "pulse of feeling" otherwise "lost" (85) to his awareness. The poem raises an unanswerable question: Is the feminine presence that completes masculinity outside Arnold's speakers, inside them, or both/and?

Swinburne in the first series of *Poems and Ballads* (1866) takes aim at the Christian moralism and patriarchalism dear to the Victorian middle class. Besides critiquing Victorian notions of love and God, "Faustine" hyperbolizes the enshrinement of the feminine in Victorian domestic ideology to a deliberately outrageous extreme. "Faustine" portrays Woman as a gorgeous desiring machine that vampirically metamorphoses over time, destroying men with pleasure. By the same token, the ascetic norm of manhood is undermined: the male speaker in "Faustine" remains prostrate with desire. Swinburne exposes the discourse of courtly love as oppressive to both men and women in "Les Noyades," set during the French Revolution, where desire triumphs over the class system and the sacrament of marriage is trumped by lust and death: "Shall she not know me [carnally, in the Biblical sense] . . . / Me, on whose heart as a worm she trod? / You [the executioners] have given me . . . / What man yet never was given of God" (*ACS* I, 50). Whereas Tennyson deploys the residual ideology of courtly love to support the Victorian ideology of separate spheres in *The Princess*, Swinburne turns courtly love against ideals of manliness and womanliness throughout *Poems and Ballads*. "He is either the vindictive and scornful apostle of a crushing iron-shod despair, or else he is the libidinous laureate of a pack of satyrs," commented a disgusted contemporary.[7]

Heroic masculinities

Cultural sages and literary critics called upon the Victorian male poet to represent paradigms of heroism. Responding to the medieval revival in Victorian culture, Tennyson, Arnold, and Swinburne each draw on Thomas Malory's *Le Morte Darthur* (1485) to represent heroic masculinity but with divergent ideological effects.[8] A residual formation in which sexual difference is strongly marked, courtly love supports domestic ideology: the chivalric knight ventures forth in the world of action in order to serve and protect the lady who adorns his castle home with her beauty, both physical and spiritual. This kind of heroism in many ways extends, if only to complicate, the domestic manliness that these poets would elsewhere explore.

Arnold reorients the external glories of combative masculinity into the internal sufferings of male melancholy in "Tristram and Iseult" (1852). In

Part I, Tristram, once a "peerless hunter, harper, knight" (*MA* I. 22), lies on his deathbed; he appears "weak with fever and pain" (I. 85) helpless and in "deep distress" (I. 209) – the very anti-type of the "brilliant youthful knight / In the glory of his prime" (I. 109–10). Pain, both physical and psychological, feminizes the hero. Tristram recalls a battle during which his prowess failed him because he was consumed by passion for Iseult of Ireland. Arnold, after giving voice to Tristram, uses third-person narration to emphasize Tristram's falling away from his knightly duty under the pressure of emotion: while his comrades-in-arms revel in "the ringing blows" (I. 259) as "the trumpets blow" (I. 264), Tristram suffers from "Sick pining" (I. 261) for a woman: "Ah! what boots it . . . / If oneself cannot get free / From the clog of misery?" (I. 267–68).

In Part II of "Tristram and Iseult," Arnold invents a meeting between the doomed lovers at Tristram's deathbed. Whereas Part I alternates dialogue between the characters with narration, Part II focuses on a dialogical exchange of feelings of regret, loss, and love. Gentleness, a feminine quality introduced into masculinity in several other poems by Arnold, tempers the harshly heroic in the dying Tristram. Illicit passion has been spiritualized by mutual suffering – "Both have pass'd a youth consumed and sad" (II. 54) – which unites the lovers eternally. Iseult of Ireland, once a "cruel" lady, returns to true womanliness ("I am now thy nurse" [II. 70]), enabling Tristram to indulge in a melancholy manliness that replaces the pugnacious virility conventionalized for medieval heroes. Part III of "Tristram and Iseult" doubles this reinscription of the domestic feminine. The narrator presents Iseult of Brittany caring for her "laughing children" (III. 77), unhappy in her love for the now dead Tristram but content with her "home" (III. 76), "her broidery-frame" (III. 82) and "her prie-dieu" (III. 92). The narrator observes that suffering may make passion transcendent but that passion remains dangerous in "subdu[ing] our souls to it, / Till for its sake alone we live and move" (III. 128–29).

The narrator further urges that men's "fool passion" (III. 134) for women creates an imbalance of power between them and that this "unnatural" (III. 136) situation – "Being, in truth, but a diseased unrest" (III. 135) – destroys the men: "They straightaway are burnt up with fume and care" (III. 139). "Tristram and Iseult" ends with the story of the once mighty magician Merlin and Vivian, that "lovely" (III. 164) but "false fay" (III. 161) who seduced him and left him to waste away in "a sleep . . . / . . . more like death, so deep" (III. 213–14). Desire for a woman undoes both Tristram and Merlin, two heroes of Arthurian legend. Is "Tristram and Iseult" an oppositional poem because Arnold represents a feminized, gentled masculinity in the hero Tristram? Or is it a misogynistic text because Arnold represents women as temptresses who destroy men? The answer is both. Told by that "Sweet flower" (III. 325) of domestic femininity, Iseult of Brittany, the tale of Merlin's downfall at the hands of a seductress resonates with that of Tristram and Iseult of Ireland, becoming a moral exemplum of "How this fool passion gulls men potently" (III. 134). At the same time, Tristram represents a new kind of male heroism: he dies not for king and country but for love and longing.

In the first group of *Idylls of the King* (1859), Tennyson focuses on four female figures – "Enid," "Elaine," "Vivien," and "Guinevere" – by way of problematizing the representation of heroic masculinity in relation to the feminine. In "Enid" (divided into two parts in 1873, then retitled "The Marriage of Geraint" and "Geraint and Enid" in 1886), Geraint embodies a physical ideal of manhood: we admire his splendid body through Enid's eyes: "The massive square of his heroic breast, / And arms on which the standing muscle sloped" ("The Marriage of Geraint," *AT* 75–76). Nevertheless, his "mere uxoriousness" (60) puts into question his masculinity, leading him to take Enid on a brutal test-quest in order to prove that he has not descended into "mere effeminacy" through domestic bliss (107). Heroic masculinity is also destabilized in "Elaine" (renamed "Lancelot and Elaine" in 1870). Sir Lancelot is nearly unmanned by "melancholy" (323) and displays a deheroicized male body when ill: "His battle-writhen arms and mighty hands" (807) seem as useless as his legendary "name / Of greatest knight" because he has failed to live up to the moral ideal of manhood (1402–03). Compare this problematic representation of masculinity with Tennyson's earlier idealizing treatment of Lancelot in "The Lady of Shalott" (1832).

In "Vivien" (retitled "Vivien and Merlin" in 1870), an emasculating combination of desire and melancholy overcomes the "gentle wizard" Merlin (*AT* 906). "[O]vertalk'd and overworn," he "Yield[s]" (963–64) his secret knowledge, hence his power, to the wily enchantress, Vivien. Expressing a traditional misogyny ("Too much I trusted when I told you that, / And stirr'd this vice in you which ruined man / Thro' woman the first hour" [359–61]), Merlin nonetheless gives in to a fascination with Vivien's "lissome limbs" (221) and the "ease of heart" (891) which her blandishments lend to his patriarchal notions. A central topic of their debate is masculinity in general and King Arthur's in particular. Vivien questions the very basis of the Round Table's manhood: the "utter purity" (26) championed by Arthur, "blameless king and stainless man" (777), has put him in the effeminized position of a cuckold: "Man! is he man at all, who knows and winks?" (779). Through Vivien, Tennyson casts doubt on the efficacy of male courtliness: perhaps if men were more manly in asserting their masculine prerogatives, then women would be more womanly in accepting their subordination to men.

Masculinity proves inextricable from femininity in Tennyson's *Idylls of the King*. Arthur emphasizes that gender complementarity is the cornerstone of the world of Camelot in "Guinevere." Like the Prince in *The Princess*, the King relies on the woman's performance of femininity as the guarantee that legitimizes his own performance of masculinity. Authorized not by patrilineal culture but by a principle of the feminine in nature (the Lady of the Lake bestows the magic sword, signifier of phallic power, upon him), Arthur initially defines heroic masculinity in terms of a quest for a perfect feminine counterpart: "But were I join'd with her / Then might we live together as one life / And reigning with one will in everything / Have power on this dark land to lighten it" ("The Coming of Arthur" *AT* 89–92). He attempts to forge a new mode of masculinity based on moral *ascesis* or self-discipline rather than brute force: "I knew / Of no more subtle master under heaven / Than is the maiden passion for a maid, / Not only to keep down the base in man, / But teach . . . / . . . all that makes a man" ("Guinevere," *AT* 474–78, 480).

Arthur's project, however, involves a slippage from heroic to domestic masculinity that risks a slide from virility into effeminacy. Throughout the *Idylls*, Arthur tries to navigate between a martial male subjectivity – evidenced by his quests, battles, and rulership – and a spiritualized "gentleness" marked as feminine. In order to maintain the masculine position as dominant, this appropriation of the feminine must be partial (moral qualities only) and must remain clearly distinguishable from the other attributes of woman (physical weakness, maternity). Refusing to perform the patriarchally sanctioned feminine (the roles of wife and mother), Queen Guinevere's barren infidelity deconstructs the hierarchized opposition of sexual difference that underpins King Arthur's experiment in domesticating heroic masculinity: "thou has spoilt the purpose of my life," he tells her (450). Put on the defensive in the battle of the sexes, Arthur falls back on traditional misogyny in his denunciation of Guinevere as a threat to the entire social order; she is "like a new disease" (515). He remasculinizes himself by invoking his manly duty to reassert patriarchal priority on a domestic level: "I hold that man the worst of public foes / Who . . . / . . . lets his wife / Whom he knows false abide and rule the house" (509–12).

The conflict between heroic and domestic masculinities brings about the downfall of the Knights of the Round Table. In "Balin and Balan" (1885), the effeminizing ineffectuality of King Arthur's "gentleness" drives two brothers to an extreme of homosocial violence (*AT* 180). Christian salvation is marked as inaccessibly feminine in "The Holy Grail" (1869); only the androgynous Sir Galahad can see the Grail that repulses the virile warriors. The Red Knight in "The Last Tournament" (1871) mocks Arthur: "art thou not that eunuch-hearted King / . . . The woman-worshipper?" (444, 446). Tennyson's exploration of contradictory masculinities in *Idylls* has ambiguous implications for the political order of Queen Victoria's Britain: Can a "female king" serve as the national icon of manhood?[9]

The effeminacy of King Arthur is one of Swinburne's targets in *Under the Microscope* (1871) where he refers to *Idylls of the King* as "the Morte d'Albert": "by the very exaltation of his hero as something more than man he has left him in the end something less."[10] Swinburne finds that Tennyson has "lowered and degraded" the "moral tone" of the Arthurian legend by portraying the main characters of its central love triangle too closely in relation to the death of Victoria's beloved consort. "The story is rather a case for the divorce-court than for poetry," a sordid and effeminizing piece of gossip rather than a noble and manly narrative, Swinburne charges (57). King Arthur is "a wittol" (57), emasculated by cuckoldry and his failure to take action against it; although Vivien is a "base and repulsive . . . harlot" (59–60), Swinburne agrees with her remark that "such a man as this king is . . . hardly 'man at all'" (58). He also objects to Tennyson's representation of Merlin. Instead of a magical masculinity, Merlin displays "the erotic fluctuations and vacillations of a dotard under the moral and physical manipulation of a prostitute" (60) – in other words, the triumph of a woman over a man and the upsetting of the proper prerogatives of the masculine. Quoting Alfred Austin's protest that Tennyson's "verse is devoted to the worship of 'woman, woman, woman, woman'" (61),[11] Swinburne scorns the domestication of Victorian poetry and calls for a remasculinization of verse through classical tragedy: "Adultery must be tragic and exceptional to afford stuff for art" (57).

Tristram of Lyonesse (1882) is Swinburne's version of heroic masculinity in the medievalizing mode. In the "Prelude: Tristram and Iseult," the narrator praises love for its ability to transcend physical passion, "the life of tears and fire," to achieve "The body spiritual of fire and light" (*ACS* IV, 6, 5). Not God but "Love," "One fiery raiment with all lives inwrought," is the origin of the universe, superseding the polarity of heaven/hell ("Prelude," IV, 5). In contrast to the "fool passion" in Arnold's "Tristram and Iseult" and especially to the prioritization of moral law over individual desire in Tennyson's *Idylls*, Swinburne's narrator celebrates the suffering and death of the lovers, Tristram and Iseult of Ireland, as a means to the end of eternal life. Not a moralistic domestic idyll "fit for the sole diet of girls," *Tristram of Lyonesse* is a sublime tragedy "fit for the sole sustenance of men."[12]

Whereas Tennyson uses a symbolic landscape to multiply ambiguities and ironies in the *Idylls*, Swinburne elaborates a symbolic seascape to emphasize the supremacy of desire in *Tristram of Lyonesse*. In Book I, "The Sailing of the Swallow," the lovers-to-be are surrounded by eroticized waves – "rosy and fiery" (IV, 26), the waters "Throb," their "center quiver[ing] with delight." The oxymoronic metaphor of "spirit in sense" elevates Tristram and Iseult's passion above ordinary lust. Book II, "The Queen's Pleasance," depicts female *jouissance* – Iseult of Ireland's "pleasure of desire" is likened to "a leaping fire" – but the representation of male pleasure is avoided as feminizing (IV, 44). Rather, Tristram incarnates the heroic ideal of the medieval warrior-knight: "Heart-hungry for the hot-mouthed feast of fight / And all athirst of mastery" (IV, 47). In Book III, "Tristram in Brittany," a series of metaphoric equivalences suggests that illicit love leads to death because moral laws attempt to deny individual desire. If Arnold's Tristram is unmanned by melancholy, Swinburne's hero overcomes it and escapes effeminization by stoically bearing his sorrow "With unbent head" (III, 265). He remains a martial hero, "as from fight / Crowned with hard conquest won by mastering might" (IV, 62). Swinburne ventriloquizes the feminine at length in Book V, "Iseult at Tintagel"; moreover, the discourse is cross-gendered. Like the rebellious Tannhäuser in Swinburne's "Laus Veneris" (1866), Iseult declares that she adores her lover more than she does Christ: " 'Shall I repent? / Nay . . . for herein I am blest, / That . . . I love him [Tristram] best – / More than mine own soul or thy love or thee" (IV, 78). Just as Tannhäuser's passionate and masochistic subjectivity opposes the Victorian ideal of manliness, so Iseult's powerful and non-conformist selfhood flouts the Victorian ideal of womanliness. Like both Sappho and Tannhäuser, Iseult parodies the language of Christianity by way of rejecting its morality and asserting free desire: "Blest am I beyond women even herein, / That beyond all women born is my sin, / And perfect my transgression."

Book VI, "Joyous Gard," revels in the lovers' "delight" (IV, 94) and reemphasizes the transcendent nature of love. The way that morality perverts desire – a central message in the first series of *Poems and Ballads* – emerges in the "passionate holiness" (IV, 107) of Iseult of Brittany. In her "righteousness of rage," she invokes the vengeful God of retribution whom Iseult of Ireland has rejected in Book V (IV, 108). While the women display a range of emotions, Tristram's continued questing and preoccupation with maintaining his martial "Fame" underscores his virility in Book VIII, "The Last Pilgrimage": "High-hearted with desire of happy fight / And strong in soul with merrier sense of might / . . . all his will was toward war" (IV, 115). Unlike Arnold's Tristram and Tennyson's Geraint, Swinburne's

Tristram is not weakened but strengthened by love, so that his body becomes splendidly perfect, as seen when he swims before battle: "each glad limb became / A note of rapture in the tune of life" (IV, 128). The sun outlines his body in a halo not of sanctity but of health and male vigor: he "felt the might / In all his limbs rejoice for strength" (IV, 128–29). Even in death, Swinburne's Tristram retains a heroic masculinity: in Book IX, "The Sailing of the Swan," he dies due equally to love for Iseult of Ireland and his war wounds. Again emphasizing the hero's virility and eschewing moralization, Swinburne's later contribution to Victorian versions of Arthurian legend, "The Tale of Balen" (1896), counters Tennyson's "Balin and Balan" (1885) by placing the knight's "wrath" and "pride" in the ennobling frame of tragedy, where they can be read as *hamartia* and *hubris* rather than deadly sins. Swinburne's elevation of Tristram and Iseult's illicit passion and Balen's character flaws through the genre of tragedy offers a revisionary portrayal of these heroes which corrects what he sees as Arnold's and Tennyson's inartistic because effeminate representations.

A recurrent topos in Victorian criticism is the need for the reinvigoration of poetry. Charles Kingsley calls for "martial song" about "the heroic past" that would convey "manful teaching" to counteract "the emasculating tendencies" of the nineteenth century.[13] Besides idealizing chivalric knights, Victorian men sought models for masculinity in the heroes of classical antiquity. More saliently virile in their exploits than the gentle courtly lovers of the medievalizing imagination, the heroes of classical Greek myth were especially appealing because they acted in a securely patriarchal world where women were relegated to the sidelines as mothers or nubile objects of exchange. Tennyson's, Arnold's, and Swinburne's different figures of male heroism reveal both how central the classical tradition is to Victorian culture and how contested and constructed the notion of masculinity is for these three poets.

Tennyson chooses Ulysses, but his rendition of an episode from Homer's epic in "The Lotos-Eaters" (1832) puts classical virility into question rather than simply confirming it. On the island of this "mild-eyed melancholy" (*AT* 27) people where the "languid air did swoon" (5), Ulysses's mariners are effeminized by pleasure and "half-dream" (101). Instead of "great deeds" (123), they embrace inertia: "'We have had enough of action, and of motion we'" (150). They abandon the Victorian standard of ascetic manhood with its duties to "wedded lives" (114) and the nation: "'Is there confusion in the little isle? / Let what is broken so remain'" (124–25). Contemporary critics took this poem as a sign of Tennyson's lack of "manly courage"; one warned that Tennyson "must not . . . eat of the lotos . . . in which we hear he takes more delight than becomes a man."[14] By way of remasculinizing his poetry after such comments, Tennyson writes "Ulysses" (1842), in which the speaker both invokes the ascetic norm of manhood and reinscribes sexual difference in terms of domestic ideology: "It little profits that an idle king, / By this still hearth . . . / Matched with an aged wife, I mete and dole / Unequal laws" (1–4). Renouncing rest at the end of his life, Ulysses vows "To follow knowledge like a sinking star, / Beyond the utmost bound of human thought" (31–32). Unlike the effeminately idle mariners in "The Lotos-Eaters" who sigh "Oh rest ye . . . we will not wander more" (173), Ulysses exemplifies the ideal of strenuous manliness in his vow "To strive, to seek, to find, and not to yield" (70). Tennyson's poem has been widely interpreted as a salvo in favor of British imperialism. Yet the goal of the questing envisioned by Ulysses himself involves less altruistic renunciation than personal pleasure. Confirming his patriarchal prerogatives by designating his son as the next ruler, Ulysses dubs himself "this gray spirit yearning in desire" (30) and describes voyaging as satisfaction: "I will drink / Life to the lees" (6–7). Is the "margin" which "fades / For ever and for ever when I move" the ever-elusive fiction of masculinity (20–21)?

Arnold's construction of an ideal of masculinity from classical culture is an ongoing agonistic project that informs both his poetry and his critical prose. In "Empedocles on Etna" (1852) he tries to inflect a Romantic male subjectivity, modeled after Byron's *Manfred* (1817), with a socially responsible one that corresponds to mid-Victorian ideas about manliness; these divergent masculinities are held together within a rationalizing frame of Greek philosophy. The eponymous hero is poet and philosopher, religious skeptic and humanitarian, tempestuously passionate and severely logical. On the one hand, Empedocles deconstructs Romantic masculinity: "Man with his lot . . . fights" (*MA* 153) because "he makes . . . *will* / The measure of his *rights*," ignoring the laws of "Nature" (154–55). On the other hand, Empedocles celebrates "That longing of our youth" that "Burns ever unconsumed" (369–70) and wishes to preserve "desire" (386) in all its fullness, rejecting "but *moderate* bliss" (391). He knows that the "wise man's plan" (267) in life is, as Carlyle urged, "To work" (269), but he cannot bring himself to renounce "Pleasure" and "dreams" (357). The "naked, eternally restless mind" (330) produced by this encounter of Romantic and mid-Victorian subjectivities produces an impasse which poetry, represented by the five intercalary lyrics about Greek myths composed by Callicles, cannot overcome. Anticipating Arnold's own renunciation of poetry in favor of critical prose, Empedocles lays aside his lyre and, unconsoled by Callicles's verses, chooses death as the only way to "cut his oscillations short" (233).

A controversy in which Arnold played poet and critic by turns ensued. "'Empedocles on Etna' is an utter mistake," declared one reviewer.[15] Like the rest of the 1852 poems, "Empedocles on Etna" shows Arnold "indulg[ing] to excess" in meditations that lead nowhere; it lacks "the severe manliness" of true poetry which requires "action in all its forms" (69–70). Taking his cue from such criticism, Arnold dropped "Empedocles on Etna" from *Poems* (1853) and undertook a remasculinization of his poetics. The famous "Preface" to his 1853 volume is a polemical essay that redefines the gender of the genre of poetry. Treating "Empedocles on Etna" as a failed poem, Arnold explains that he "intended to delineate the feelings" of its hero as he experiences the decadence of Greek philosophy in parallel to the "modern" situation which conduces to "the dialogue of the mind with itself."[16] Appealing to Aristotle's theory of mimesis, according to which action is more important than character, Arnold repudiates the effeminate emphasis on feelings found in Romantic texts and in his own poetry up through 1852.[17] "[S]uffering [which] finds no vent in action" (2) – such as Empedocles's – is "morbid" (3), Arnold concedes. What the mid-Victorian (male) reader wants is "incident" and a hero engaged in "resistance" to the forces of nature and society who by his efforts suggests "hope" (3). Action belongs to the public sphere of the masculine; feeling is effeminate in a man because it pertains to the private sphere of the feminine. Yet Arnold's play, *Merope* (1857), written to show how the model of classical tragedy could reinvigorate verse, met with a cool reception from Victorian critics. In contrast, Swinburne's first notoriety came from his oppositional version of classical tragedy, *Atalanta in Calydon* (1865), which radicalizes the fatality of desire and undercuts the Victorian ideal of manhood.

Swinburne reworks the mythology surrounding the classical god Apollo in oppositional directions that push at the boundaries of sexual difference while preserving his contrarious ideal of the virility of literature. Whereas in the first series of *Poems and Ballads* he exposes the links between Christian morality and sensual perversions, in *Songs Before Sunrise* (1871) Swinburne widens his critique by grafting a sado-erotic rhetoric on the discourse of the Christian tradition to deconstruct its main institutions: monarchy and the church. "Before a Crucifix," for example, exposes the abjection of both the "dead God" (*ACS* II, 86) and his worshippers: the "piteous" (II, 81) spectacle of Christ's "sacred body [which] hangs and bleeds" (II, 83) leads not to "freedom" and "less oppressions done" but to the people's continual suffering which mimes that of their masochistic icon Himself (II, 82). Christ-on-the-Cross is a disgusting fetish, "So when our souls look back to thee / They sicken, seeing against thy side, / . . . The leprous likeness of a bride, / Whose kissing lips through his lips grown /

Leave their God rotten to the bone" (II, 87). In contrast to the Christian God's abject masculinity stands the Hellenic god Apollo's splendid virility, figured throughout Swinburne's poetry in the 1870s and 1880s in Romantic metaphors of fire, light, dawn, and poetic "song." Swinburne draws on Carlyle's concept of the poet and the prophet as heroes. The poet's manhood is reinvigorated by republican vision in *Songs Before Sunrise*; he speaks as an oppositional sage who recognizes only the human imagination as "god." In "The Last Oracle" (from the second series of *Poems and Ballads* [1878]), the speaker receives the call of Apollo and confirmation of his own heroic status as poet-seer. Now worthy of joining the all-male group of singers apotheosized in "In the Bay" (1878), Swinburne's poetic persona attains union with the principle of poetic manhood, symbolized by Apollo, in "Thalassius" (1880).

The all-male literary tradition presided over by Apollo in "Thalassius" is inflected by the oscillations of gender identity undergone by the poetic persona in "On the Cliffs" (1880). Swinburne deploys classical Greek literature to burst the constraints of Victorian gender ideology, exploring the femininity within the masculinity of "song" or lyric poetry. Located "between" sea and land, day and night, mortal and divine, the speaker appropriates Sappho and Aeschylus, lyric and tragic poetry, the positions of both the transgressive feminine and the traditional masculine, by ventriloquizing each through fragmentary translations of their work at various points in his own poem. An alternation of Greek intertexts and Swinburneian intratexts (primarily "Anactoria") parallels an extensive series of metaphorical equivalences among Apollo (the principle of poetry), Sappho ("soul triune, woman and god and bird" [*ACS* III, 322]), the nightingale (heard singing on the cliffs by the sea at the time of the dramatic monologue), and the speaker himself (who claims kinship with the "bright born brethren" [III, 324] of birds as well as with Sappho).[18] "Because I have known thee always who thou art" (III, 318), he confides, "thy gods . . . be my gods, and their will / Made my song part of thy song" (III, 319). The speaker seeks the power which he believes that divinely poetic knowledge will yield in order to transcend suffering and death. As "Love's priestess, mad with pain and joy of song" (III, 318), Sappho has won immortality through her poetry, the "Lesbian word" (III, 318) whose subject is sublime perversion of the body. Through identification with her, the speaker declares at the end of "On the Cliffs," he has learned "Song, and the secrets of it, and their might" (III, 324).

But has he risked his masculinity in so closely merging with the feminine? Yes and no. Consider the several exchanges of power and desire in the poem. Heterosexual violence between Cassandra and Apollo, and between

Sappho and Apollo produces tragic and lyrical poetry, respectively. Death ensues for both women. The poetic persona feels and speaks through these feminine voices what he cannot articulate directly as a man without risking critical blame for effeminacy. At the same time, the Hellenic paradigm for prophetic and poetic creativity in "On the Cliffs" is grounded in a misogynistic homoeroticism: "The small dark body's Lesbian loveliness" (III, 324) merely serves as a vessel for "the fire eternal" of Apollo, and the male poet is most inspired when most femininely receptive to a stronger male force. The speaker ecstatically aspires to the Apollonian poetic "quire" (III, 314) of which the "strange manlike maiden" (III, 323) Sappho is an honorary member because she simulates masculinity as a lesbian. In both "Thalassius" and "On the Cliffs" Swinburne devises metaphor and revises myth in order to represent a range of Victorian masculinities, from the hegemonically virile to the dissidently homoerotic. What arises is not so much contradiction as continuum in the diverse ways that manliness is portrayed.

Emergent masculinities

This discussion has shown how several unconventional kinds of masculinity emerge from Tennyson's, Arnold's, and Swinburne's poetry. These male subjectivities issue from alternatives worked out of dominant and residual discourses by Tennyson and Arnold as well as the opposition posed to them by Swinburne. Such "emergent masculinities" tend to be uneven combinations of daringly new and comfortably familiar "meanings and values," "significances and experiences" (Williams, "Base and Superstructure," 41). Emergent masculinities operate within a dialectic of transgression and containment, as Jonathan Dollimore explains in *Sexual Dissidence: Augustine to Wilde, Freud to Foucault* (1991). The dominant Victorian concepts of manliness, including self-restraint and superiority to women, are constantly put under pressure from the representation of androgynous masculinities in Tennyson's poetry, feminized masculinities in Arnold's, and perverse masculinities in Swinburne's. In responding to these alternative and oppositional stances through a combination of resistance and accommodation, the hegemonic view of genders itself gradually shifts throughout the mid- and late nineteenth century.

An enduring critical controversy centers on Tennyson's extended lyric sequence, *In Memoriam*. Dramatic monologue, elegy, and theological *apologia*, this text has perplexed readers ever since its publication in 1850: Does the idealized close friendship between Tennyson and Hallam involve a proscribed male–male desire? Most Victorian reviewers lauded the poem:

"It is one of the most touching and exquisite monuments ever raised to a departed friend – the pure and unaffected expression of the truest and most perfect love".[19] A few raised alarm at "the tone of – may we say so? – amatory tenderness" which Tennyson adopted: "Surely this is a strange manner of address to a man."[20] Like other early and mid-Victorians, this reviewer judges poetry according to whether or not it upholds the presumably natural differences between masculinity and femininity, as elaborated in domestic ideology. Influenced by sexology and psychoanalysis, twentieth-century interpreters of *In Memoriam* have focused on the question of male–male desire in *In Memoriam*. Christopher Ricks asks "Is Tennyson's love for Hallam a homosexual love?" and answers with a resounding "no!"[21] In contrast, Christopher Craft argues that Tennyson's strategy of "recuperational homosexual desire" or legitimizing male–male intimacy in *In Memoriam* is the poet's challenging response to the "radically homophobic male homosociality" in Victorian culture.[22]

Consider the extended analogies in *In Memoriam*. Tennyson often figures his feelings toward his dead friend, Arthur Hallam, in terms of romantic love. In section VI, for example, he imagines himself as a woman who, happily awaiting her man's homecoming, is overcome by news of his death: "To her, perpetual maidenhood, / And unto me no second friend" (*AT* 43–44). In section VII, the speaker revisits Hallam's house, apostrophizing it like a forlorn lover: "Doors, where my heart was used to beat / So quickly, waiting for a hand" (3–4). The class difference between the speaker and Hallam is translated into an impossible love match in section LX: "He past; a soul of nobler tone: / My spirit loved and loves him yet / Like some poor girl whose heart is set / On one whose rank exceeds her own" (1–4). Tennyson also imagines himself and Hallam in a gamut of family roles. Physical grief overtakes the speaker in section XIII, where he compares himself to a bereaved husband with Hallam as his deceased wife: "Tears of the widower, when he . . . / . . . moves his doubtful arms, and feels / her place is empty" (1, 3–4). In section XCVII, the speaker represents himself with Hallam as "Two partners of a married life" (5). Taking the wife's part, he admires the husband's (Hallam's) "greatness" from afar: "I cannot understand: I love" (36). On the one hand, Tennyson reinscribes the dominant ideology of domesticity; on the other hand, he destabilizes the heterosocial contract by using familiar male–female analogues to represent male–male desire.

The major intertexts of the literary tradition to which *In Memoriam* alludes are similarly overdetermined, suggesting both conventional heterosexuality and dissident homoeroticism. Dante's *The Divine Comedy* provides a model for the poem's movement from funeral to marriage, sorrow to joy, and loss to gain. But notice how Tennyson revises Dante. By placing the poetic persona in the lover's position, Hallam in the position of Beatrice, and God at the summit of the triangulation, Tennyson homoeroticizes the spiritual mediation. The mystic marriage between Dante and Beatrice is transformed into one between Tennyson's persona and Hallam: "The dead man touched me . . . / [His] living soul was flashed on mine, / And mine in this [his] was wound" (XCV, 34, 36–37).[23] Although addressed as "the Spirit," Hallam continues to have a markedly physical presence: "Descend, and touch, and enter; hear / The wish too strong for words to name" (XCIII, 13–14). Is the penetration wished for here heavenly or carnal? The lyrical structure and equivocal mode of address throughout *In Memoriam* evoke another model, Shakespeare's sonnets: "I loved thee, Spirit, and love, nor can / The soul of Shakespeare love thee more" (LXI, 11–12). Victorian readers were discomfited by "the startling peculiarity of transferring every epithet of womanly endearment to a masculine friend."[24] A third discourse informing *In Memoriam* is the pastoral, which since the ancient Greek poet Theocritus has given voice to the possibilities of homoeroticism within the dominant heterosocial world. The speaker longingly recalls the university life he once shared with his friend in an idealized rural landscape: "And thou . . . / . . . towering sycamore; / How often . . . / My Arthur found your shadows fair" (LXXX, 3–6). Like his use of analogies, Tennyson deploys well known intertexts from the literary tradition in ways that are undecidably conventional and transgressive at the same time; consequently, Victorian as well as twentieth-century readers of *In Memoriam* disagree over its meanings.

A metonymic chain of beckoning hands links the speaker with Hallam and Christ. The "central warmth diffusing bliss" that Hallam once transmitted "In glance and smile, and clasp and kiss" is transformed into "the shining hand" with which Christ reaches out to the two men who unite "as a single soul" (LXXXIV, 6–7, 43–44). By metaphorical substitution, Hallam – the best friend on earth – typologically figures Christ, the redeeming Friend in heaven. Hallam's "manhood fused with female grace" (CIX, 17) reflects "The highest, holiest manhood" of Christ, founded on "Love" ("Prologue," 14, 1). The insistence on the bodily presence of Hallam–Christ puts into play a constant slippage between signifiers and signifieds. The speaker aims to sublimate his feelings for Hallam in worship of Christ: "Known and unknown, human and divine; / Sweet human hand and lips and eye; / Dear heavenly friend that canst not die, / Mine, mine, for ever, ever mine" (CXXIX, 5–8). The physical possessiveness expressed, though, does not imply completed transcendence. Charles Kingsley, one of the spokesmen for mid-Victorian "muscular Christianity," strains to legitimize the homoerotic overtones of *In Memoriam* by referring the bond between Tennyson and Hallam to the Biblical precedent of David and Jonathan.[25]

Like "Mariana" and *The Princess*, *In Memoriam* raises the question of the gender of poetry. Does the male poet who ventriloquizes women and privileges androgyny become feminized to the point of losing his manliness? "He loves to make parade of pain" (XXI, 10): the speaker displays his grief extravagantly, masochistically aligning himself with the feminine as excess. Compare the ideological effects of male masochism in "Laus Veneris" and *In Memoriam*. Whereas Swinburne sets his perverse anti-hero against the residual ideology of Christian chivalry and its Victorian twin, bourgeois morality, Tennyson shows the strenuous progress of the male subject as he passes through early homoerotic attachment – "Confusions of a wasted youth" ("Prologue," 42) – to mature heterosexual responsibilities: "For I myself . . . have grown / To something greater than before" ("Epilogue," 19–20). The Christological fantasy of his marriage with Hallam is counterbalanced by the familiar actuality of what was the planned marriage of Hallam to Tennyson's sister Emily. Hegemonic heterosexuality contains male–male desire as heterosocial marriage resanctions homosocial bonding. The female personifications of "Sorrow" and "Nature" onto which the speaker displaces his private emotions are superseded by "Wisdom" and virile action in the public sphere. Ultimately, the poet is remasculinized as a patriotic sage: "Ring out the old, ring in the new" (CVI, 5), he declares; "Ring in the valiant man and free, / . . . Ring in the Christ that is to be" (CVI, 29, 32). Hallam, "divinely gifted" (LXIV, 2), stands as a paragon of middle-class manhood: he "breaks his birth's invidious bar" (LXIV, 5) to rise above class; he "makes by force his merit known" and would, had he lived, have been the ideal statesman (LXIV, 9). Terry Eagleton reads *In Memoriam* as a "triumphant reaffirmation" of hegemonic values, but Alan Sinfield finds "the confusion of gender categories" in the poem . . . more difficult . . . for bourgeois hegemony to handle."[26] Tennyson interpellates or ideologically appeals to the dominant, heterosexual audience without entirely banishing the possibility of homoerotic desire.

Is the "pair of lovers together at night" in Arnold's famous dramatic monologue, "Dover Beach" (1851) a male–female couple, as Norman N. Holland assumes?[27] Or could the addressee "be the kind of man who was versed in the ancient Greek" plays of Sophocles alluded to in stanza three, as Joseph Bristow suggests?[28] The "melancholy" expressed here belongs to the alternative masculinity based on feminizing "gentleness" which characterizes the male speakers in the Switzerland cycle and "Tristram and

Iseult." Victorian critics objected to Arnold's "The Scholar-Gipsy" (1853) because its main figure rejects the manliness of work, preferring an aesthetically contemplative life. A tacit homoeroticism emerges when "The Scholar-Gipsy" and the elegy to Arthur Hugh Clough, "Thyrsis" (1866) are considered alongside *In Memoriam*. Arnold represents Victorian masculinity otherwise than according to the hegemonic model: Is his poetry compromised like Tennyson's or defiant like Swinburne's?

In the first series of *Poems and Ballads*, Swinburne defiantly explores the possibility of same-sex orientation. "Hermaphroditus" parodies the traditional portrait of a beautiful lady, deconstructing its dominant premise of sexual difference: "Choose of two loves and cleave to the best; / Two loves at either blossom of thy breast / Strive" (*ACS* I, 79). The statue of Hermaphroditus presents a troubling paradox: the male viewer sees one body but may feel two competing modes of desire, heteroerotic for its female contours and homoerotic for its male aspects. Swinburne's poem invites an indeterminate or undecidable response to an overdetermined or ambiguous situation. "Sex to sweet sex with lips and limbs is wed": the hermaphrodite evokes pleasure between an older and a younger man – "all thy boy's breath softened into sighs" (I, 81). The speaker remarks ironically on the limited perspective inscribed in standard love poetry which presupposes strictly male–female intimacies: "Love being blind [heterosexual], how should he know of this [male–male desire]?" The intertextual presence of Shakespeare's sonnets in both *In Memoriam* and "Hermaphroditus" points to an emergence of homoeroticism in Victorian poetry by mid-century. But in the former case proscribed relations between men are ultimately reoriented to support patriarchal hegemony, while in the latter case the transgressiveness of male–male desire remains, as Richard Dellamora suggests, "caught within the terms of its negation of an antithetically posed moral point of view."[29]

The gender identification of the male Victorian poet remained a critical issue for decades after Tennyson's "Mariana" appeared. The Fleshly School Controversy, initiated by the poet-critic Robert Buchanan in 1871, and involving primarily Swinburne and Dante Gabriel Rossetti, was one of the most contentious and influential of these debates.[30] "Fleshliness," according to Buchanan, consists in an "unwholesome" focus on the female body and passions; an insistence "that the body is greater than the soul" as a worthwhile theme for poetry; and a claim "that the poet, properly to develop his poetic faculty, must be an intellectual hermaphrodite."[31] Significantly, Buchanan blames Tennyson for providing a model of poetic aberrations in "Vivien" (1859), in which he "has concentrated all the epicene force" which the Fleshly School "wearisomely expanded," and especially in *Maud* (1855), whose "hysteric" speaker and "overloaded style" anticipate those of Swinburne (32). Tennyson, who has represented "that wonderful apotheosis of Masculine Chastity" (86) in King Arthur (in *Idylls of the King*), is equally capable of the kind of "effeminacy" that Buchanan finds characteristic of the Fleshly poets (70).[32]

This chapter has shown that Tennyson, Arnold, and Swinburne represent several contesting masculinities in their poetry. Alternative and oppositional masculinities are constructed in relation to the dominant domestic ideology. Medievalism and classicism provide residual ideologies of manliness and womanliness that can either support or interrogate the hegemonic ideal. Feminized masculinities and homoeroticism emerge from the very dominant and residual formations of manliness that sought to contain them.

NOTES

1 Leonore Davidoff and Catherine Hall, *Family Fortunes: Men and Women of the English Middle Class, 1750–1850* (Chicago, IL: Chicago University Press, 1987), 13.
2 Nancy Armstrong, *Desire and Domestic Fiction: A Political History of the Novel* (New York: Oxford University Press, 1987), 4.
3 Raymond Williams, "Base and Superstructure in Marxist Cultural Theory," in *Problems in Materialism and Culture* (London: Verso, 1980), 31–49; further page references appear in parentheses.
4 Antonio Gramsci, "Hegemony, Relations of Force, Historical Bloc," in *An Antonio Gramsci Reader: Selected Writings, 1916–1935*, ed. David Forgacs (New York: Schocken Books, 1988), 189–221.
5 A typical critic accuses Tennyson of "a want of all manliness" in topic and "an emasculate floridity in style," resulting in "effeminacies": "The Faults of Recent Poets: Poems by Alfred Tennyson," *New Monthly Magazine* 37 (1833), 74.
6 John Morley, "Review of Swinburne, *Poems and Ballads*," *Saturday Review*, 22 August 1866, 145–47, reprinted in *Swinburne: The Critical Heritage*, ed. Clyde K. Hyder (London: Routledge and Kegan Paul, 1970), 24.
7 John Morley, "Review of Swinburne, *Poems and Ballads*," 29.
8 Debra N. Mancoff surveys 1800s medievalism in *The Arthurian Revival in Victorian Art* (New York: Garland, 1990).
9 See Elliot L. Gilbert, "The Female King: Tennyson's Arthurian Apocalypse," *PMLA* 98 (1983), 863–78.
10 Swinburne, *Under the Microscope* (1872), in *Swinburne Replies*, ed. Clyde Kenneth Hyder (Syracuse, NY: Syracuse University Press, 1966), 56, 58; further page references appear in parentheses.
11 Alfred Austin, *The Poetry of the Period* (London: Richard Bentley, 1870; reprinted New York: Garland, 1986), 96.
12 Swinburne, *Notes on Poems and Reviews*, in *Swinburne Replies*, 32.
13 [Charles Kingsley,] "Review of Arnold's *Poems* of 1853," *Fraser's Magazine* 49 (1854), reprinted in Isobel Armstrong, *Victorian Scrutinies: Reviews of Poetry, 1830–1870* (London: Athlone Press, 1972), 174, 176.

14 Cited in Edgar F. Shannon, Jr., *Tennyson and the Reviewers: A Study of His Literary Reputation and of the Influence of the Critics upon His Poetry, 1827–1851* (Cambridge, MA: Harvard University Press, 1952), 88.

15 [G.D. Boyle,] "Review of *Empedocles on Etna, and Other Poems*," *North British Review* 9 (1853), 209–14, reprinted in *Matthew Arnold: The Poetry: The Critical Heritage*, ed. Carl Dawson (London: Routledge and Kegan Paul, 1973), 69; further page references in parentheses.

16 Arnold's "Preface to the First Edition of *Poems* (1853)," Arnold, *On the Classical Tradition*, ed. R.H. Super, *The Complete Works of Matthew Arnold*, 11 vols. (Ann Arbor, MI: University of Michigan Press, 1960–77), I, 1; further page references appear in parentheses.

17 Arnold is taking his distance from the Spasmodic School which, during the late 1840s and 1850s, divided critics between those who admired this kind of poetry's extremes of passion, as in "Empedocles on Etna," and those, like Charles Kingsley, who called the "spasmodic vogue" dangerously "effeminate": "Thoughts on Shelley and Byron," *Fraser's Magazine* 48 (1853), 568–76, reprinted in *Miscellanies* (London: John W. Parker, 1859), 318.

18 "Intertextuality" refers to the network of past and contemporaneous texts to which a given text may be related in several ways, including allusion, quotation, paraphrase, and revision. "Intratextuality" focuses on the relations among the texts of one single author's oeuvre, as Thaïs E. Morgan explains in "The Space of Intertextuality" in *Intertextuality and Contemporary American Fiction*, ed. Patrick O'Donnell and Robert Con Davis (Baltimore, MD: Johns Hopkins University Press, 1989), 239–79.

19 Anonymous, "Review of Tennyson, *In Memoriam*," *Tait's Magazine* n.s. 17 (1850), 499.

20 [Manley Hopkins?,] "The Poetry of Sorrow," *Times* [London] (November 1851), 8.

21 Christopher Ricks, *Tennyson* (London: Macmillan, 1972), 215, 217.

22 Christopher Craft, "'Descend, and Touch, and Enter': Tennyson's Strange Manner of Address," *Genders* 1 (1988), 88, 92.

23 The 1850 version of *In Memoriam* reads "His"/"his"; the 1872 revision, made in the homophobic context of the Fleshly School Controversy, reads "The"/"this."

24 [Hopkins?,] "The Poetry of Sorrow," 8.

25 [Charles Kingsley,] "Tennyson," *Fraser's Magazine* 42 (1850), 255. "Muscular Christianity" was an influential movement begun in the late 1850s by Charles Kingsley and others who advocated a remasculinization of religion, associating physical strength, Christian faith, and imperial supremacy.

26 Terry Eagleton, "Tennyson: Politics and Sexuality in *The Princess* and *In Memoriam*," in *1848: The Sociology of Literature*, ed. Francis Barker et al. (Colchester: Essex University Press, 1978), 85, 86; Alan Sinfield, *Alfred Tennyson* (Oxford: Basil Blackwell, 1986), 136.

27 Norman N. Holland presupposes an Oedipal situation behind "Dover Beach" in *The Dynamics of Literary Response* (New York: W.W. Norton, 1975), 119.

28 Joseph Bristow considers "the pronounced antagonism between same-sex affections and other-sex desires" in "'Love, let us be true to one another': Matthew Arnold, Arthur Hugh Clough, and 'our Aqueous Ages,'" *Literature and History* 4 (3rd series) (1995), 31.

29 Richard Dellamora places Swinburne's "poetic perversities" in relation to representations of alternative masculinities by Tennyson, Arnold, and Gerard Manley Hopkins in *Masculine Desire: The Sexual Politics of Victorian Aestheticism* (Chapel Hill, NC: University of North Carolina Press, 1990), 83.

30 Thaïs E. Morgan examines the representation of masculinities in this controversy in "Victorian Effeminacies," in *Victorian Sexual Dissidence*, ed. Richard Dellamora (Chicago, IL: University of Chicago Press, 1999), 109–25.

31 Robert Buchanan, *The Fleshly School of Poetry and Other Phenomena of the Day* (London: Strahan, 1872), reprinted in *The Victorian Muse: Selected Criticism and Parody of the Period*, eds. William E. Fredeman, Ira B. Nadel, and John F. Stasny (New York: Garland, 1986), 32.

32 Buchanan links the "Fleshly School" of the 1860s–early 1870s to the "Spasmodic School" of the late 1840s–1850s (15). Linda Dowling shows the importance of "classical republicanism" to the charge of "effeminacy" in *Hellenism and Homosexuality in Victorian Oxford* (Ithaca, NY: Cornell University Press, 1994), xv, 4–5.

11

KAREN ALKALAY-GUT

Aesthetic and Decadent poetry

When John Morley sharply criticized Algernon Charles Swinburne for "gloating" with "hot lustfulness" over "quivering flanks," "splendid supple thighs," "hot sweet throats," and "hotter hands than fire" throughout the first series of *Poems and Ballads* (1866),[1] the poet defended himself by asserting new criteria for art. Swinburne declared that he was not writing lyrics that expressed his own feelings or opinions. His work, he insisted, comprised dramatic monologues whose speakers should not be confused with himself: "the book is dramatic, many-faced, multifarious; and no utterance of enjoyment or despair, belief or unbelief, can properly be assumed as the assertion of its author's personal feeling or faith."[2] While some scholars have dismissed this defense as a marvelous ruse – one that allows Swinburne to deflect moral responsibility from his work by suggesting, "I'm not sick – it's those crazy characters of mine" – many Victorian readers reacted to this response by observing that the kind of mind that conceived of such personae could only be diseased. (Ralph Waldo Emerson, for one, condemned Swinburne as a "perfect leper and a mere sodomite."[3]) The polemic ignited by Swinburne's early poetry points to a crucial paradigm shift in how Victorian culture thought about literature. His defense involved a radical divergence from Matthew Arnold's influential demand that the best literary works should uphold a high moral seriousness that could both act as a modern substitute for religion and provide the basis of an improving education. "More and more mankind," Arnold writes in "The Study of Poetry" (1880), "will discover that we have to turn to poetry to interpret life for us, to console us, to sustain us."[4] Indeed, according to Arnold, "the matter and substance of the best poetry" embodies the "superior character of truth and seriousness."[5]

The powerful Arnoldian idea that art possessed a moral function – one that validated the genre of poetry in a period when society was driven to assign value through practical economics – in many ways harmonized with the prevailing Victorian belief that everything should have a calculable social purpose. Swinburne's conscious renunciation of Arnold's moral imperative in the name of art characterizes what would in the 1870s become known as the Aesthetic Movement, and which twentieth-century critics have labeled British aestheticism. By advancing the view that art has no obligations to anything but itself, poets like Swinburne could find themselves free to delve into unexplored topics, to plunge into their own uninhibited thoughts and feelings, and to venture into worlds liberated from moral censure. Aesthetic considerations could determine the course of the work, and actually lead the morally passive writer into the active world of the unconscious. As Swinburne gleefully pointed out in his poem "Félise" (1866), artistic imagination could transcend the limitations of banal reality and moral prescription by expanding its vision into a universe that was not the conventionally familiar one:

> For many loves are good to see;
>   Mutable loves, and loves perverse;
> But there is nothing, nor shall be,
>   So sweet, so wicked, but my verse
> Can dream of worse.   (ACS I, 193)

But while it seemed to emancipate poetry from the strict confines of morality, delighting in sexual transgression, this declaration of freedom also put the genre in a marginal position with regard to society, arguably diminishing the poet's cultural authority. If "Poets" were no longer the "unacknowledged legislators of the world" (as the radical Percy Bysshe Shelley had proclaimed much earlier in the century),[6] and if poets were not moral leaders as Arnold influentially declared, then poetry might be independent and free, but it was now also isolated, having no other relations and no significance except to aesthetics alone. Thus aestheticism's well-known battle-cry of "art for art's sake" – which Swinburne absorbed from French writers such as Théophile Gautier – had a dual effect, marginalizing art as it liberated it. Indeed, as aestheticism modulated into the movement that Arthur Symons would in 1893 name "Decadence,"[7] poets discovered that search for sensuous release from a moralistic world could prove estranging and frustrating, since they were increasingly disoriented and alienated both morally and aesthetically.

This chapter explores how a wide range of poets associated with both aestheticism and Decadents were enmeshed in a wide range of paradoxes as they sought to free themselves from the religious and social functions that had characterized art and elevated it above the world. Beginning with Dante Gabriel Rossetti's poetry, this discussion pays special attention to the emphasis that these poets often give to the developing importance of sexual desire as a means of resisting oppressive moral attitudes. Time and again, their work engages with the pleasures promised by what Ernest Dowson evokes as "wine and woman and song" (*ED* 110): a phrase that suggests that an intoxicated eroticism might provide the fundamental substance of a type of poetry that existed for its own sake. Yet this stress on sensuous pleasure in the name of an art emancipated from the customs and conventions of proper conduct had a diverse range of consequences. Each poetic example shows how and why "wine and woman and song" could drive aesthetic and Decadent writers toward various states of ecstasy and exhilaration as well as frustration, doom, and despair. Moreover, each poem discussed here shows both the growing needs for fulfillment through various types of sensuousness and sensuality and the increasing impossibility of such fulfillment.

II

Rossetti's work, like Swinburne's, provides some of the leading ideas about sensuous pleasure and sexual desire that shape aesthetic and Decadent poetry. In terms of form, "Jenny" (1870) is a poem of almost four hundred lines that belongs to the tradition of the Victorian dramatic monologue developed separately by Robert Browning and Alfred Tennyson in the 1830s. Particularly in Browning's use of this type of poem, it is not uncommon for a male speaker to address a female auditor, who is often otherwise occupied, asleep or dead, and because of this lack of response the persona frequently reveals more about his innermost psychology than he readily understands. Rossetti's "Jenny" follows in this poetic tradition but slightly changes the form by voicing the thoughts, rather than the dramatically spoken words, of a bookish young man who has been spending the night with the prostitute whose name titles the poem. In what might be termed an interior monologue, the speaker develops a number of contradictory ideas about both the individuality and the humanity of the kind of figure that some Victorian moralists described as "the great social evil." Since Jenny appears totally inert in her role as a sex worker (she falls asleep during the poem), he takes the opportunity to muse upon her beauty and to consider the social limitations and harsh pressures that she faces in everyday life. Rossetti's narrator at first seems a fairly typical product of middle-class society. He is an intellectual who claims to have found himself by accident in her rooms, and it is clear that he perceives himself as superior to her. After all, she is only a generic woman (it is no accident, as definitions in the *Oxford English Dictionary* make clear, that the name Jenny is often used to denote the female of the species, including asses). What is more, her interests – as the opening lines indicate with their grammatical parallels – are equally distributed between two objects, sex and money, by means of a single warm yet dispassionate verb: "Lazy, laughing, languid Jenny, / Fond of a kiss and fond of a guinea" (36). Even the alliteration of the first line serves to flatten out her personality, making her initially appear a mindlessly greedy voluptuary with no moral priorities whatsoever.

The male speaker feels superior to Jenny because of his artistic status as well and initially declares that his visit to her rooms is nothing more than a momentary lapse from his otherwise ascetic life of scholarship. This absence of sexual involvement allows him at times to perceive Jenny as an object of art, an aesthetic composition rather than a moral or sexual commodity. Early in the poem, he describes her sensual half-dressed state in painterly detail. Yet his reaction is not the obviously sensual one. On the contrary, her erotic attraction leads him immediately to meditate upon the unlikely subject of literature:

> Why, Jenny, as I watch you there, –
> For all your wealth of loosened hair,
> Your silk ungirdled and unlac'd
> And warm sweets open to the waist,
> All golden in the lamplight's gleam, –
> You know not what a book you seem.   (37)

As he watches Jenny drowse in the enhancing "golden" light, he interprets her meaning as if she were a "book": a subject to be discovered, learned, and understood. His sensitivity to beauty and art, together with his total subordination of moral and ethical issues, on occasion helps to deliver him from the moralistic conventions that condemn Jenny's life of prostitution. To be sure, by reading her body as a "book," the speaker may be thought to dehumanize her flesh from his superior scholarly position. But it is the freedom afforded by art, with its own rules of precise and objective observation, that leads him toward a much greater understanding of this most downtrodden and vilified type of humanity: "Our learned London children know, / Poor Jenny, all your pride and woe; / Have seen your lifted silken skirt / Advertise dainties through the dirt" (38). Paradoxically, his appreciation of art and his scholarly outlook challenge those Victorian commentators who abhor "the great social evil," and thus he produces an altogether higher conception of the motivations and limitations of the life of the prostitute. Certainly, he often images Jenny's body in negative terms – at one point he visualizes her "magic purse" (the genitals from which she makes her money) in grotesque language, as if she were a social parasite: "Grim web, how clogged with shrivelled flies" (42). (As Robin Sheets remarks, the "'grim web' conveys the sinister rapaciousness of Jenny's greed; the dead insects, the dirty profits."[8]) Yet, ultimately, the speaker's studied distance from his subject carefully and consciously makes him feel ashamed of his revulsion toward her body and releases him from any kind of romantic fantasy. In the end, he remains unwilling to "mock" her "to the last" (43), appreciating instead how and why she earns her living through sexual labor.

This absence of intimacy between the male viewer and the female object of desire is apparent in many of Swinburne's early poems. Since their publication, the contents of *Poems and Ballads* have been considered problematic because of their representation of perverse sexuality in prosodically assured forms that seem uninterested in any moral framework. Swinburne's reputation has often rested on two seemingly negative qualities: first, his incomparable ability to fashion mellifluous, if overextended, poems whose mesmerizing sounds frequently override sense; and second, his eagerness to voice shocking ideas about aspects of human behavior that can still repulse readers. Jerome J. McGann writes that Swinburne became "[n]otorious as a poet of frenzy and incoherence," not least because he was "the most complete of the nineteenth-century hellenes," whose pagan "revulsion from ordinary Christian standards was recognized and resented" in an often hostile press.[9]

These qualities are evident in "Dolores" (1866), a sacrilegious poem addressed to "Our Lady of Pain." In his initial description of this female figure, Swinburne's speaker paints a weirdly idealized portrait of an estranging, indifferent, and unloving woman. Focusing on the heavy eyelids that suggest self-absorption and world-weariness, the opening stanza begins by itemizing Dolores's physical features, giving the impression of a fragmented face, a series of details with no power. Thereafter, the concentration shifts to the overall effect of eyes, lips, and mouth, all of which express the suffering that Dolores imposes upon her subjects.

> Cold eyelids that hide like a jewel
>   Hard eyes that grow soft for an hour;
> The heavy white limbs, and the cruel
>   Red mouth like a venomous flower;
> When these are gone by with their glories,
>   What shall rest of thee then, what remain,
> O mystic and sombre Dolores,
>   Our Lady of Pain?   (*ACS* I, 154)

Swinburne represents Dolores's depths of pain and sorrow and her indifference to her worshippers as an affront to the forms of compassion and forgiveness associated with the Virgin Mary and reinforces this contrast in the 1866 pamphlet that he published defending his poetry, where he describes Dolores as "No Virgin, and unblessed of men."[10] This type of *femme fatale*, discussed in detail by Bram Dijkstra and many other critics,[11] manifests the male artist's hunger for total passionate immersion in a female being who exerts greater power than himself, thus releasing him from subjective agency and moral responsibility. Swinburne employs hypnotic rhythms and phrasal repetitions to dramatize this desire for loss of consciousness and loss of moral control, creating a situation in which there appears to be no alternative but submission to the overwhelming power of the senses. That is why Camille Paglia characterizes Swinburne's meters as "an automaton driven by a female robotlike despot."[12] But although it may appear that Swinburne willingly enslaves his art to an alternative god, whereby the rejection of one religion involves the instantiation of another, it should be emphasized that this enslavement is a voluntary and contractual one, and the slave is in fact the master of the situation.[13]

This contradictory structure reveals that it is misleading to charge Swinburne with writing simply for the sake of rebelliousness, as if he were an adolescent poking fun at Victorian morality. His work instead analyzes the bases of this morality and any of his other poems discloses the same kind of complexity. "The Leper" (1866), for example, takes the familiar medieval story of a clerk who has long been desperately in love with a disdainful lady:

> Mere scorn God knows she had of me,
>   A poor scribe, nowise great and fair,
> Who plucked his clerk's hood back to see
>   Her curled-up lips and amorous hair.   (*ACS* I, 119)

Surprisingly, in this dramatic monologue, the lovelorn clerk eventually wins the lady, and remains with her forever. But Swinburne has an altogether more perverse hitch on this classic tale. The lady has become disfigured by leprosy, and the enamored clerk continues to make love to her long after she becomes ill and dies, reiterating his romantic clichés about her hair and eyes over a rotting leprous corpse: "Yet am I glad to have her dead / Here in this wretched wattled house / Where I can kiss her eyes and head" (I, 119). "Nothing is better," he asserts in the opening of his poem, "Than love" (I, 119), and he repeats this statement as the details of his grotesque situation unfolds. A clear parody of courtly love, "The Leper" goes to excruciating lengths to identify the narcissistic nature of what is usually considered to be selfless and ennobling passion.

This pattern repeats throughout many of Swinburne's works in *Poems and Ballads*, including "Laus Veneris" (1866): Tannhäuser's dramatic monologue about his entrapment by Venus. In this story, immortalized in Richard Wagner's opera that Swinburne may have seen in Paris in 1861, the knight Tannhäuser complains bitterly of his sexual imprisonment by Venus, voicing his fears of her evil power while she (like Rossetti's Jenny) remains fast asleep, apparently unaware of his erotic torment. Referring to Venus impersonally as "it," he immediately betrays his abject condition. Focusing on the passionate mark that he has just made on her throat, he wrongly assumes that the fading love-bite signals that Venus is responding to him:

> Asleep or waking is it? for her neck,
> Kissed over close, wears yet a purple speck
>   Wherein the pained blood falters and goes out;
> Soft, and stung softly – fairer for a fleck.
>
> But though my lips shut sucking on the place,
> There is no vein at work upon her face;
>   Her eyelids are so peaceable, no doubt
> Deep sleep has warmed her blood through all its ways.
>
> (*ACS* I, 11)

Venus appears completely unaware of the role she is supposed to be playing. Indeed, she seems blameless of the accusations that he makes against her, accusations that construct her as a devouring goddess and inspire even greater desire on the part of Tannhäuser. The more he contemplates the rumors of her sexual powers and her control over men, the more he desires her. At the same time, the more he perceives her as evil, the more he apprehends his own life as virtuous. He has, after all, been a model knight, plundering and murdering in the name of God, and not like Venus, wasting his life in making love. In this manner, "Laus Veneris" lays bare some of the false pretenses of dialogue upon which the dramatic monologue is built, since this poetic form offers only one side of a conversation. Moreover, "Laus Veneris" suggests that the entire concept of evil is a projection of the self: an externalization of inner torments caused by the inculcation of twisted religious precepts. In this respect, "Laus Veneris" uses the poetic form to reveal questions about both the meaning of love and the meaning of morality. Therefore, even if Swinburne believed that art should exist for its own sake, he also had a marked interest in revealing the implications of this concept for contemporary moral attitudes.

Poems such as "The Leper" and "Laus Veneris" certainly indicate that aesthetic considerations, the nature of relationships, and questions about the perception of reality and morality were fundamental preoccupations of

Swinburne's ritualistic poetics. Yet it was left to George Meredith – who for a short time in 1862 lodged with both Rossetti and Swinburne – to explore these preoccupations in a palpably real world. In the impressive sonnet sequence "Modern Love" (1862), Meredith moves from the usual medieval settings or the sensational location of the fallen woman's rooms to deal with an everyday husband and wife. Because intimate relationships were to some extent replacing religion and social achievement as the source of happiness in literature at this time, one might reasonably expect from the title of this ambitious work that the topic would be the triumph of romantic success between men and women. But Meredith's poem recounts the story of a marriage that disintegrates, through no great fault of either the character or the class of the participants. Further, the sequence examines this fraught relationship from the protagonists' different points of view, implying that there is no objective standard against which the reader can judge this distinctly "modern" type of love. The opening sonnet presents the narrator's perspective, one that often feels very close to the husband's despairing outlook on his marriage:

> By this he knew she wept with waking eyes:
> That, at this hand's light quiver by her head,
> The strange low sobs that shook their common bed
> Were called into her with a sharp surprise,
> And strangled mute, like little gaping snakes,
> Dreadfully venomous to him. She lay
> Stone-still, and the long darkness flowed away
> With muffled pulses. Then, as midnight makes
> Her giant heart of Memory and Tears
> Drink the pale drug of silence, and so beat
> Sleep's heavy measure, they from head to feet
> Were moveless, looking through their dead black years,
> By vain regret scrawled over the blank wall.
> Like sculptured effigies they might be seen
> Upon their marriage-tomb, the sword between;
> Each wishing for the sword that severs all.   (GM 1–16)

From this first sensational episode, which takes place in the marriage bed when the husband recognizes in his wife's tears the failure of their union, until her suicide at the end of the sequence, the profound tension of love in the modern world – its arduous complexity, and the urgency of its success – is ruthlessly explored. The poetic means to analyze this "marriage-tomb" is an expanded sixteen-line sonnet: the additional two lines in themselves indicate that the conventional sonnet form has proved insufficient to represent "modern love." Unlike the traditional Petrarchan structure of many English sonnets, where a concluding sestet sets out to resolve both quatrains of the octave, Meredith's sixteen-line poem comprises four quatrains, in which the final one may or may not reach a point of resolution. Consequently, each of the expanded sonnets in "Modern Love" has no commitment to drawing the episodes in this deeply unhappy relationship to a neat conclusion.

Throughout Meredith's sonnet sequence, the underlying problem of "modern love" lies in the impossibility of expressing delicate emotions in an unfeeling post-Darwinian universe. Without an inherent connection to the Creator, human beings resemble sophisticated beasts. Indeed, their civilized behavior is merely a mask. In an extraordinary reversal of the English sonnet's traditional subject matter, Sonnet 30 begins: "What are we first? First animals" (1). The poem then traces the evolution of civilization, from basic appetite to pragmatic action, before turning to the emergence of ethical conduct. The poem comes to an abrupt close with an unexpected apostrophe: "Lady, this is my sonnet to your eyes" (16). This final line reduces the entire age-old romantic plot of adulterous love to the level of the jungle. If in tune with Darwin, Meredith's suggestion that men and women are "First animals" nevertheless conflicts with Victorian beliefs in the basic dignity of human life. But "Modern Love" neither celebrates lust nor moralizes about it. Instead, it strives to give serious attention to a topic that many of his contemporaries would dismiss as subject matter only fit for titillating erotica. As a result, we find Meredith's aesthetic poetry attempting to treat sensitive subject matter from an elegant and nonjudgmental distance.

But this is a masculine distance. Whenever Meredith, Rossetti, and Swinburne made women the central topics of their poetry, femininity remained the object of male scrutiny. It is not surprising, then, that the situation for women poets at this time was very different, not least because they were already at a distance, in many ways disenfranchised from the aesthetic world. Christina Rossetti's poetry countered this sense of exclusion in ingenious ways. In many of her early lyrics, she asserts a woman's individual identity by refusing to conform to the conventional rituals of courtship, engagement, and marriage. Although she shares with Dante Gabriel Rossetti and Swinburne a strong interest in cold, deathly, and silent femininity, she treats this figure from an opposing point of view. The first stanza of her much-anthologized "Song" (1862) should be seen in this way:

> When I am dead, my dearest,
>   Sing no sad songs for me;
> Plant thou no roses at my head,
>   Nor shady cypress tree:

> Be the green grass above me
>> With showers and dewdrops wet;
> And if thou wilt, remember,
>> And if thou wilt, forget.   (CR 1–8)

At first glance, the female speaker seems to accept a well-known Victorian stereotype of bourgeois femininity – romantically dead, aesthetically pleasing, and totally undemanding. But the potentially ironic tone quickly undermines this hackneyed image. By exerting control over her lover's reactions to her death, she expresses an independence and self-sufficiency that ultimately exclude him. Her identity remains intact whether he remembers her or not. Here Christina Rossetti's speaker distances herself from her already excluded existence as a woman. She does so by turning to what she implies is the freedom afforded by death. This is one of Rossetti's main techniques for refusing to adapt to the objectified position in which male aestheticism frequently tries to fix femininity.

In some respects, William Morris's representations of femininity mark a similar departure from Dante Gabriel Rossetti's and Swinburne's memorable icons of objectified womanhood. But where Christina Rossetti often links the integrity of her art with the liberating power of the afterlife, Morris attempts to bring aestheticism to all aspects of the everyday world. Architect, bookmaker, designer, painter, and poet: the multitalented Morris's intention from the mid-1850s onward was to return Victorian society to the pre-industrial beauty, individuality, and simplicity that he often associated with the Middle Ages. Assuredly, the sheer quantity of his works in different media is truly astounding. But his immense productivity is even more remarkable for its consistently high quality and complexity. This is a feature particularly evident in his poetry. Like Dante Gabriel Rossetti, with whom he worked closely, poetry was a prized activity for Morris, since it was untainted by any motive for profit. His poetry often deepens the sophistication evident in some of the powerful images of women that he depicted in many different paintings, stained glass, and tapestries.

Morris's portrait of Guenevere, King Arthur's adulterous queen, depicts a typically Pre-Raphaelite tragic and troubled beauty (see Figure 1). Yet it is only when we look at his dramatic monologue "The Defence of Guenevere" (1858) that we comprehend clearly why this female figure maintained such a strong hold over Morris's imagination. Certainly, Guenevere – to follow Morris' spelling of her name – was topical in the late 1850s. She came to public attention not just through Morris's art but also in the first volume of Tennyson's *Idylls of the King* (1859–85). Indeed, these adaptations of Arthurian legend provided Victorian readers with an image of an ideal kingdom that belonged to the distant past. At the same time, this legendary world could be used to explore urgent Victorian anxieties about sexual fidelity. In Arthurian legend, Guenevere's adultery plays a crucial role because she weakens the fraternal bonds between the Knights of the Round Table. Yet Morris has no interest in attacking Guenevere for threatening the potency of this brotherhood but is concerned instead with her ideas of truth and testimony.

Although Guenevere never has the opportunity to defend her adultery in the original Arthurian legends, she articulates a truly defiant voice in Morris's poem. In this dramatic monologue, she manages to divert the attention of her accusers just long enough for Lancelot to save her from execution, a heroic rescue totally unrelated to the verdict or justice of the trial. Guenevere develops an intricate pattern of contradictory explanations that have the texture of the densely woven decorative tapestries for which Morris became famous. In his painting of Guenevere, these distinctive tapestries adorn the bed, the furniture, and the walls, and are given as prominent coloring and detailing as the central character in the portrait. Drawing on the imagery of flowers, leaves, and stems, these designs adhere to John Ruskin's belief that art must be true to nature. Yet the fact that these realistic motifs run in repeated patterns suggests that artistic truth is relative not absolute, and that foregrounding some details over others is an arbitrary artistic decision.

It is the idea that truth is arbitrary that absorbs Guenevere's speech. Guenevere begins her formal defense by presenting an allegory in which a dying person simply addressed as "you" encounters an angel who presents him with two lengths of cloth, one long and blue, the other short and red. Told by the angel that "One of these cloths is heaven, and one is hell" (*WM* I, 1), the dying man is asked to choose between them. When the unnamed "you" selects the blue one, hoping to be saved, "you" discovers that the choice is wrong. The absolute values that formed the basis of that choice have proven fallacious. Yet if the values attached to the angel's cloths appear completely capricious, they do so with vital consequences. This is the familiar Pre-Raphaelite world that employs all kinds of traditional iconography only to erase any symbolic significance from such imagery. Guenevere, therefore, tells what appears to be a beautiful religious tale that sets up certain moral expectations but ultimately produces contradictory evidence. In this respect, it is significant that the poem begins *in medias res* with the disjunctive "But," which suggests that her words have been arbitrarily cut – rather like the repeated designs of Morris's well-known wallpapers – out of a much larger pattern: one whose meanings are less significant than the aesthetic pleasure they provide, and whose beginning and endings are more a function of the careful attention to the pattern and

Figure 1 William Morris, *Queen Guenevere* (1858), © Tate Gallery, London 1999.

design of the angel's cloths than the actions and events that comprise Guenevere's narrative.

Many of the preoccupations that I have so far identified with aesthetic poetry – its resistance to high moral seriousness, its nonsymbolic use of religious iconography, and its fascination with sensual experience – converge in Edward FitzGerald's elegant translation and adaptation of the Persian *Rubáiyát of Omar Khayyám*. Published anonymously in 1859, FitzGerald's volume was soon remaindered, and it might well have suffered the fate of many other scholarly works had it not been discovered by two of Rossetti's friends on a London bookstall. (The influence was immediate. Swinburne's "Laus Veneris" employs the *rubái* stanza.) To be sure, there are many questions about Omar Khayyám's intentions. In some ways, his poem can be read as an examination of mutability. But one thing is clear. As a devout Muslim he would not have openly advocated the kinds of hedonism that Rossetti, Swinburne, and many other English writers found in his work and developed in their own poetry. The following famous lines appear in various forms throughout late-nineteenth-century poetry:

> Here with a Loaf of Bread beneath the Bough,
> A Flask of Wine, a Book of Verse, and Thou
>   Beside me singing in the Wilderness –
> And Wilderness is Paradise enow.[14]

Given Omar Khayyám's religious beliefs, he would not have literally claimed that a "Flask of Wine" was the basis of "Paradise." Indeed, the poetic formula that we find here – wine, bread, and a beloved object of affection – probably echoes an atheistic version of Communion. But this formula became central to British aestheticism. Either in their poems or in their actual lives, writers belonging to this movement appealed to narcotics – such as absinthe, chloral hydrate, and wine – as a way of increasing sensation while dulling the moral pressures exerted by the everyday world. The conclusion of FitzGerald's stanza – "Wilderness is Paradise enow" – illustrates how aestheticism sought to substitute sensual fulfillment in the form of an artistically created situation for an absolute theological explanation of the world. True paradise is not alluring but a wilderness that can be transformed through artificial means to paradise is far more attractive. It is no accident that Darwin's theory of natural selection appeared in the same year as FitzGerald's *Rubáiyát*. Darwin's *Origin of Species* (1859) destroyed the absolute comfort of the Bible, contested the justification of the ways of God to humanity, and unsettled the concept of an afterlife. Art for its own sake seemed, for the moment, to hold the answer to human endeavor.

III

But, of course, it did not. Certainly, FitzGerald's transformation of "Wilderness" into "Paradise" made it seem as if poetry could make an intolerable Victorian world into one of beauty and pleasure. Yet the use of this same formula by a poet of the next generation reveals both its refinement and its limitation. Two poems by Ernest Dowson help to show the similarity and difference between FitzGerald's brand of desire and fulfillment and that of the Decadents. In his most famous poem, "Non Sum Qualis Eram Bonae sub Regno Cynarae" ('I am not what I once was in Cynara's day' [Horace, "Ode 4.1."] 1891) – later more commonly known as "Cynara" – the speaker spends the night with a prostitute while longing for his beloved, and claims this lack of fulfillment illustrates a contemporary version of devotion. He is true to the ideal beloved because he is not satisfied by the woman with whom he finds himself. "But I was desolate and sick of an old passion. / When I awoke and found the dawn was gray: / I have been faithful to thee, Cynara in my fashion" (*ED* 58). This idea of an ideal and thus impossible love forms the basis of what we might term the fashion of Decadence: a vague desire to feel some ideal love while wallowing in a degraded and unfulfilling environment. John R. Reed makes this crucial point about Decadence: "The central quality of Decadent style is implicit in the word's etymology. It involves a *falling away* from some established norm; it elaborates an existing tradition to the point of apparent dissolution."[15]

This double bind becomes apparent in Dowson's "Villanelle of the Poets' Road" (1899), in which ambivalence toward fulfillment is built into the structure of the poem:

> Wine and woman and song,
>   Three things garnish our way:
> Yet is day over long.
>
> Lest we do our youth wrong,
>   Gather them while we may:
> Wine and woman and song.
>
> Three things render us strong,
>   Vine leaves, kisses and bay;
> Yet is day over long.
>
> Unto us they belong,
>   Us the bitter and gay,
> Wine and woman and song.
>
> We, as we pass along,

> Are sad that they will not stay;
> Yet is day over long.
>
> Fruits and flowers among,
>   What is better than they:
> Wine and woman and song?
> Yet is day over long.   (*ED* 110)

Consciously revising a number of conventional tropes, Dowson's poem opens by giving a new twist to a much-used metaphor: the road of life. Although a road traditionally suggests linear progression, here it spirals around the cyclical form of the villanelle. Originating in sixteenth-century France, this particular genre was revived by Swinburne because of its obsessive repetitiousness. Consisting of nineteen lines (five tercets followed by a concluding quatrain), it derives its circularity from two related features: it uses two rhymes only; and it repeats its first and third lines in alternate stanzas. But its circularity does not make for static repetition. Lines 1, 6, 12, and 18, which delineate the pleasures of life, contrast with lines 3, 9, 15, and 19, which emphasize the insufficiency of these pleasures.

Thus the two likely purposes in life – pleasure and progress – cancel out each other, leaving the poetic voice in a state of frustrated weariness (like "passion" and "fashion" in "Cynara"). The first line, recalling FitzGerald's *Rubáiyát*, presents the favored nineteenth-century version of *carpe diem*. Yet the second line runs against the initial enthusiasm since "Wine and woman and song" are only "garnish." What is more, "Wine and woman and song" follow each other grammatically with neither subordination nor qualification. Where FitzGerald's rhyme scheme accentuates the pronoun "Thou" (making the "Book of Verse," the "Flask of Wine," and the "Loaf of Bread" lesser accompaniments to Omar Khayyám's lover), Dowson sandwiches the loved object between two equally significant nouns, linking all of them through the relativizing conjunction "and." Like the late-twentieth-century slogan "sex and drugs and rock and roll," the parataxis of "wine and woman and song" forms no hierarchy that can elevate any of the senses; it simply flattens them out. With no attainable goal in sight, therefore, the speaker must confront the difficulty of the burden of pleasure along the poets' "way."

The cyclical form of Dowson's poems suggests that once sensual pleasures have been experienced, they can only be numbingly repeated. This feature is evident in the phrase "gather them while we may," which recalls – only to contrast with – Robert Herrick's renowned (and, indeed, far more innocent) seventeenth-century enjoinder in his lyric "To the Virgins, to Make Much of Time" (1648): "Gather ye Rose-buds while ye may."[16]

Dowson transforms Herrick's ingenuous *carpe diem* into a hedonistic imperative that can only ruin the freshness of discovery and negate the ultimate value of pleasure in an ephemeral universe. This point becomes most salient in the final quatrain where the best that the world can offer – "fruits and flowers" – is questioned. Traditionally, the closing couplet of a villanelle aims to bind together the two lines that have been alternately repeated in the previous stanzas. But as a number of critics have noted, in Dowson's poem the last line returns to the opening tercet, implying that "day" is "over long" because everything that has been said amounts to a series of rhetorical embellishments and nothing more.[17] Dowson's negation of the possibility of pleasure is consciously aware of the contrast between himself and those Romantic and enthusiastic poets of the beginning of the nineteenth century. So it seems appropriate that Symons termed Dowson a "demoralised Keats."[18]

Before Dowson started publishing and before "Decadence" was named as such, the same experience that is resolved with artistic distance and the resignation of awareness was cause for great tragedy. Amy Levy, who died over a decade before Dowson's life came to an end, nevertheless is discussed after him here because her poetry often takes this type of demoralization, this idea that "day" is "over long," to its most bleak conclusion – suicide. Her profound disillusionment with the world is even more complex then Dowson's because she was female, lesbian, and Jewish, and therefore located triply outside even the marginalized group of Decadent outsiders. In particular, suicide is her most assertive poetic response to the perceived gap between expectation and achievement. In "Epitaph (On a Common-place Person who Died in Bed)" (1884), Levy offers this memorial to the inherent futility of human endeavor:

> He will never stretch out his hands in vain
> Groping and groping – never again.
> Never ask for bread, get a stone instead,
> Never pretend that the stone is bread;
> Nor sway and sway 'twixt the false and true,
> Weighing and noting the long hours through.
> Never ache and ache with the choked-up sighs;
> This is the end of him, here he lies. (*AL* 9–16)

Levy's "Epitaph" takes the logic of Dowson's villanelle to its terminal point in reality. Even if "day" is "over long" in "Villanelle of the Poets' Road," it remains possible to state that structure in a circular artistic pattern. But in "Epitaph" the battle against a world of earthly rewards ("bread") and absolute values ("false and true") has been given up once and for all.

This sentiment is partly visible even in the early poetry that Levy wrote while she was a student at Cambridge. In "Xantippe" (1881), she uses the dramatic monologue to explore what it meant for a woman intellectual to "ache and ache" for "bread," only to receive a "stone." The poem gives voice to Socrates's spouse: a figure reviled throughout history as the bane of the ancient philosopher's life. Drawing on Aristotle's *Ethics*, which calls on friendship as the means for mutual development, Xantippe recalls how she entered into marriage with the expectation that she would acquire philosophical wisdom, only to discover that Socrates was not in any respect a wise husband. Neither was he interested in making her a wise wife. Once "we were wedded" (*AL* 95), she declares, she learned "In sooth, a-many lessons; bitter ones" (96) that taught her "sorrow," not the kind of "love inspired" (97) that would reveal "Nature's divineness and her harmony" (103). Later in the poem, she realizes that Socrates would have been able to improve their marriage had he lived the philosophy that he preached:

> 'Twas only that the high philosopher,
> Pregnant with noble theories and great thoughts,
> Deigned not to stoop to touch so slight a thing
> As the fine fabric of a woman's brain –
> So subtle as a passionate woman's soul.
> I think, if he had stooped a little, and cared,
> I might have risen nearer to his height,
> And not lain shattered   (116–23)

This eloquent passage recalls a memorable moment in Browning's "My Last Duchess" (1842) where the ruthless Duke of Ferrara kills his wife rather than tell her what it is about her manner that "disgusts" him (*RB* 38)."I choose / Never to stoop" (42–43), the Duke remarks bluntly. This echo of Browning's poem indicates the larger project of "Xantippe" in revising poetic tradition. Although Dante Gabriel Rossetti built on Browning's dramatic monologues in an attempt to comprehend a woman's mind from a male viewpoint, Levy went a step further by employing a female persona to represent the misunderstood "passionate woman's soul" in history. But this is not her only achievement in contesting her poetic heritage. The title of her first full-length collection, *A Minor Poet and Other Verse* (1884), openly embraces the identity of the marginalized writer: one who, as Cynthia Scheinberg and Joseph Bristow point out,[19] opposes the anti-feminist, gentile, and heterosexual values central to the "major" canon favored by moralists such as Arnold.

Levy's lesbian contemporary Michael Field took an antithetical approach toward challenging some of the assumptions of the "major" poetic tradition, especially the conventions that male poets used to represent women's sexuality. Undefeated by the trials and tribulations that drove Levy to take her life in 1889, the aunt and niece (Katherine Bradley and Edith Cooper) who wrote jointly as Michael Field composed more than twenty volumes. Their work – which cannot be attributed to either Bradley or Cooper on an individual basis – certainly undermines the idea that poetry is the product of a single author. The mythical prophet Tiresias, who was both male and female, emerges as a significant figure in Field's writings. As Chris White observes: "Two women, writing under/through a man's name, operate as Tiresian poet, whose strength derives from femaleness and whose authority derives from the masculine Poet identity which can change the world." [20] By comparison, Yopie Prins has shown how in their volume titled *Long Ago* (1889) – which adapts the lesbian poet Sappho's fragments – Bradley and Cooper "develop a model of lyric authorship in which voice is the effect of an eroticized textual mediation between the two of them rather than the representation of an unmediated solitary utterance."[21] These insights throw important light on how Michael Field represents eroticism in one of the untitled lyrics collected in *Underneath the Bough* (1893):

> A Girl,
>   Her soul deep-wave pearl
> Dim, lucent of all lovely mysteries;
>   A face flowered for heart's ease,
>   A brow's grace soft as seas
>   Seen through faint forest-trees:
>   A mouth, the lips apart,
> Like aspen-leaflets trembling in the breeze
> From her tempestuous heart.
> Such: and our souls so knit,
> I leave a page half writ –
>   The work begun
> Will be to heaven's conception done,
>   If she come to it.[22]

It goes without saying that young women have often been the subjects of English lyrics. But here a sensuous girl remains central to the creation of this delicate poem: she is as much a participant in its "conception" as the "I" who waits for her to complete the "work begun." Importantly, these lines imply that lesbian desire can transcend the conventional antithesis between subject and object (speaker and beloved). Moreover, it is an author with a male name who mediates this passion, adding further intricacies to the poetic voice that admires the girl's "mouth, her lips apart."

In the poetry of the late 1880s and 1890s, the desire to resist conventional boundaries – whether of poetic form, sexual identity, or social mores

– appears everywhere. In part, this initiative can be traced back to many of Walter Pater's influential statements in the essays that he published from *Studies in the History of the Renaissance* (1873) onward. Pater, after all, remarked that "each art may be observed to pass into the condition of some other art . . . a partial alienation from its own limitations, through which the arts are able, not indeed to supply the place of each other, but reciprocally to lend each other new forces."[23] In his impressive poetry, Symons – more cosmopolitan, self-analytical, and traveled than most poets of this period – often explored the art-form of dance, the techniques of impressionist painting, and the tones of modern music. The transformation of life into art – indeed, the patterning of life through apparently spontaneous movement that Symons explores in his essay "The World as Ballet" (1907) – would soon become one of the hallmarks of literary Modernism. Like Dowson, Symons wished to accentuate sensuous pleasure. In the octave of his sonnet titled "The Opium Smoker" (1889), he both describes and imitates a drug-induced synesthesia:

> I am engulfed, and drown deliciously.
> Soft music like a perfume, and sweet light
> Golden with audible odours exquisite,
> Swathe me with the cerements for eternity.
> Time is no more. I pause and yet I flee   (*AS* I, 92)

The sestet, however, overturns these multifaceted pleasures. Quite unexpectedly, the last six lines itemize in cold and objective terms the reality that apparently remains insignificant to the oblivious addict:

> Also I have this garret which I rent,
> This bed of straw, and this that was a chair,
> This worn-out body like a tattered tent,
> This crust, of which the rats have eaten part,
> The pipe of opium; rage, remorse, despair;
> This soul at pawn and this delirious heart.

"The Opium Smoker" is a representative example of how in his poetry Symons compares and contrasts two significant elements: cultivated neurosis and careful observation. In his noteworthy essay, "A Prelude to Life" (1905), he writes:

If there ever was a religion of the eyes, I have devoutly practised that religion. I noted every face that passed me on the pavement; I looked into the omnibuses, the cabs, always with the same eager hope of seeing some beautiful or interesting person, some gracious movement, a delicate expression, which would be gone if I did not catch it as it went. The search without an aim grew almost a torture to me . . . I grasped at all these sights with the same futile energy as a dog that I once saw standing in an Irish stream, and snapping at the bubbles that ran continually past him on the water. Life ran past me continually, and I tried to make all its bubbles my own.   (*AS* V, 32)

This passage makes it clear that observation is a necessary yet taxing activity for the Decadent poet. Since this type of writer no longer possesses a clearly defined hierarchy of values, everything before him ("This garret," "This bed of straw," "This worn-out body," and so forth) holds equal worth. Consequently, the amount of data to be processed and set in order can prove exhausting – artistically, morally, physically, and spiritually.

Symons, then, faced a contradiction. He knew that there were so many things to be experienced and yet so few guidelines to make sense of those experiences that the imperative to capture (so to speak) the "bubbles" in a poem was ultimately doomed to failure. It is no wonder that love, perhaps more than anything else, is destined for ruin, as the neurotic sonnet "Nerves" (1897) reveals:

> The modern malady of love is nerves.
> Love, once a simple madness, now observes
> The stages of his passionate disease,
> And is twice sorrowful because he sees
> Inch by inch entering, the fatal knife.
> O health of simple minds, give me your life,
> And let me, for one midnight, cease to hear
> The clock for ever ticking in my ear,
> The clock that tells the minutes in my brain.
> It is not love, nor love's despair, this pain
> That shoots a witless, keener pang across
> The simple agony of love and loss.
> Nerves, nerves! O folly of a child who dreams
> Of heaven, and, waking in the darkness, screams.   (*AS* I, 228)

In formal terms, this appears a fairly traditional poem. Appropriately enough, the conventional topic of love takes shape in the Shakespearean sonnet that devotes one quatrain to spatial and another to temporal concerns. But as each line unfolds, the poetic voice reveals that the kind of amatory "madness" that Shakespeare celebrated is now literally "diseased." Part of love's "malady" results from the relentless passing of time that does not lead toward any goal, judgment, or satisfaction. Every experience, therefore, undergoes a dulling repetition, resulting in feelings of disappointment, incompleteness, and loss. Unlike Dowson, however, Symons's lack of fulfillment ends not in weariness but terror. The final line refers to a well-known phrase from Tennyson's *In Memoriam* (1850) where Tennyson wishes to believe in a divinely ordered universe but remains confused and frightened like "an infant crying in the night" (*AT* LIV, 19). Yet where Tennyson's poem moves toward a position where it is possible to imagine that God finally cares for humanity, in "Nerves" Symons's lover is left like a child screaming at the thought that there is no "heaven" that will save him from his "agony of love and loss."

In his groundbreaking essay "The Decadent Movement in Literature" (1893), Symons critically reflects on many of the characteristic features that we can see in poems such as "The Opium Smoker" and "Nerves." "Decadent" writing, he claims, involves "an intense self-consciousness," "a restless curiosity in research," an "over-subtilizing refinement upon refinement," and a "spiritual and moral perversity."[24] Each of these qualities underlines the assumption that "Decadence" marks a falling away from a classical period of artistic perfection, a period in which was simple, sane, and proportionate. Although his discussion of Decadence mainly concentrates on the works of French poets such as Paul Verlaine, Symons identifies two English writers as representatives of this movement: the critic Pater; and the poet William Ernest Henley. In many respects, Henley seems an unusual choice, since he is remembered today for the one poem that is supposed to embody Victorian strength of character. Initially, the poem best known as "Invictus" (1875) but later retitled "Echoes, IV" looks like an incantatory profession of faith in one's power to overcome the doom and gloom that confronted Decadent writers like Symons:

> Out of the night that covers me,
>   Black as the Pit from pole to pole,
> I thank whatever gods may be
>   For my unconquerable soul.
>
> In the fell clutch of circumstance
>   I have not winced nor cried aloud
> Under the bludgeonings of chance
>   My head is bloody, but unbowed.
>
> Beyond this place of wrath and tears
>   Looms but the Horror of the shade,
> And yet the menace of the years
>   Finds, and shall find, me unafraid.
>
> It matters not how strait the gate,
>   How charged with punishments the scroll,
> I am the master of my fate:
>   I am the captain of my soul.[25]

Perhaps surprisingly, this apparent embodiment of fearless Victorian values bears strong similarities to the prevailing ideas that informed Symons's view of Decadence in the 1890s. The darkness of nature coupled with the lack of divine responsibility; the progressively menacing external world; the existential situation in which the individual rather than some divine power has control over his response: all of these elements point to the despondent vision that enervated many of Henley's Decadent contemporaries such as Dowson and Levy.

Symons's evaluation of Henley's poetry assesses a range of qualities evident in the poetic diary titled "In Hospital" (written between 1872 and 1875). Like "Invictus," "In Hospital" was composed around the time when the famous doctor Joseph Lister succeeded in saving Henley, who had already had a leg surgically removed, from a further amputation. This moving series of poems records both the professional activities of the hospital and the poet's unflinching reactions to them. Symons's remarks on Henley's work are worth reading because they reveal how broad the definition of Decadence could be:

> The ache and throb of the body in its long nights on a tumbled bed, and as it lies on the operating-table awaiting "the thick, sweet mystery of chloroform," are brought home to us as nothing else I know in poetry has ever brought the physical sensations . . . [I]n certain fragments, he has come nearer than any other English singer to what I have called the achievement of Verlaine and the ideal of the Decadence: to be a disembodied voice, and yet the voice of a human soul.[26]

The vivid image of the aching and throbbing body awaiting surgery in some respects anticipates how in 1917 T.S. Eliot's J. Alfred Prufrock imaged the sky "like a patient etherised upon a table."[27] Consequently, the marked sense of mental and physical alienation that characterizes "In Hospital" may well appear proto-Modernist, signaling a new development in literature. But Henley's readers in the 1890s were more likely to view such Decadence as the deterioration of humanity, where all that is left are numbing "physical sensations" and a "disembodied voice" to articulate them.

Given his reputation, Oscar Wilde would at first seem a far more familiar Decadent than Henley ever was. And, indeed, their approaches to life and literature could not be more different. Even though W.B. Yeats would class Wilde among the many 1890s poets who belonged to a "tragic generation,"[28] it was the case that Wilde sometimes saw in the relativity of truth the possibility of creativity, rather than doom and destruction. If nothing is definitively true, he felt, then everything is possible: a point that his essays such as "The Decay of Lying" (1889) and "The Critic As Artist" (1890) take to its logical and liberating conclusion. In fact, one might argue that in this respect Wilde's innovative criticism consciously started to revise some of the precepts of Decadence in the name of the movement that would become known as Modernism. His poetry, however, is not quite so confident. In "Hélas!" the sonnet that he placed at the opening of *Poems* (1881), the poetic voice at first exhibits a longing for the passive and yet intense sensuous experience advocated by Pater. In many respects, the poem echoes some of the more famous statements in Pater's "Conclusion" to *Studies in the History of the Renaissance*: "A counted number of pulses only is given to us of a variegated, dramatic life. How may we see in them all that is to be seen in them by the finest senses? How shall we pass most swiftly from point to point, and be present always at the focus where the greatest number of vital forces unite in their purest energy?"[29] Wilde's poem opens by figuring this desire to explore the Paterian "finest senses" through an image familiar to readers of Samuel Taylor Coleridge's poetry – namely, the aeolian harp: "To drift with every passion till my soul / Is a stringed lute on which all winds can play" (*OW* 1–2). But by the end of the poem, the poetic voice recalls the vengeful deity of the Hebrew Scriptures. Echoing the Book of Samuel, where Jonathan breaks the holy fast and is punished by death, Wilde seems to invoke his own punishment for indulging in "every passion" (1): "I did but touch the honey of romance – / And must I lose a soul's inheritance?" (13–14).

In his last poem, *The Ballad of Reading Gaol* (1898), written after he was released from two years of hard labor in solitary confinement for committing acts of "gross indecency," Wilde's solution is no longer to explore Pater's "finest senses" but to uphold the values of human sympathy. Broken by the hypocritical society that first offered him fame and fortune and then brutally withdrew the smallest tokens of humanity during his 1895 trials, Wilde's long poem concentrates on the urgent need for prison reform. He dedicated *The Ballad of Reading Gaol* to a fellow prisoner, Charles Thomas Wooldridge, who had been hanged for murdering his spouse. The poem recounts the events that led to Wooldridge's execution and the reactions of the prisoner to his fate. A trooper in the Royal Guards, Wooldridge slit his spouse's throat three times with a razor. Since this was obviously a premeditated crime, he was sentenced to death on 7 July 1896. This was the second occasion that the scaffold at Reading Gaol had been used since it was installed eighteen years before. If in some respects realistic, Wilde's poem nonetheless invokes right from the start familiar aesthetic and Decadent motifs. Its subject, of course, is death, and it draws on the iconography of "wine and woman and song":

> He did not wear his scarlet coat,
>   For blood and wine are red,
> And blood and wine were on his hands
>   When they found him with the dead,

> The poor dead woman whom he loved,
> And murdered in her bed. (*OW* 1–6)

Here the death of the unnamed woman not only differs from the events described in newspaper reports but also involves a careful stylization. The solider removes the uniform that would mechanize and negate the individual passion central to this murder; he kills her in a romanticized environment; and he mixes blood and wine as if partaking in a ritual communion. To connect his uniform with the blood and wine, we are led to believe that Wooldridge was a redcoat (although his military unit wore blue). Moreover, the ballad combines wine and women in a manner that even Wilde's contemporaries thought was artificial. English soldiers were known to drink beer or gin, not red wine. But here the recollection of "wine and woman and song" attempts to make a real murder part of an identifiable literary tradition. As more detailed readings of the poem suggest, we might begin to wonder if Wilde's *Ballad* – with its focus on the mental and physical torture of human beings – is condemning aestheticism rather than murder as a crime.[30]

Wilde's Irish contemporary, Yeats, escaped the fate of the "tragic generation" because he outlived them all. But his early poetry bears resemblances to many of the characteristics we have seen in aesthetic and Decadent poetry. "He Wishes for the Cloths of Heaven" (1899), for example, evokes the kind of passivity and self-degradation that we discover in Dowson's villanelle. In the opening lines, its pattern of imagery also recalls the rich colors and textures of Dante Gabriel Rossetti's and Morris's works:

> Had I the heavens' embroidered cloths,
> Enwrought with golden and silver light,
> The blue and the dim and the dark cloths
> Of night and light and the half-light,
> I would spread the cloths under your feet:
> But I, being poor, have only my dreams;
> I have spread my dreams under your feet;
> Tread softly because you tread on my dreams. (*WBY* 1–8)

The artificiality of "heavens' embroidered cloths" envelops the first five lines in a pseudo-medieval world of courtly love. But the last three lines move into an entirely different dimension. To be sure, the identifiably Pre-Raphaelite environment of "golden and silver light" seems lush and attractive. But Yeats's speaker claims to be "poor," having only the world of the self and its aspirations. No less Romantic than the various "cloths," the unadorned world of "dreams" is presented as a more real, if vulnerable, poetic offering. There is also an obligation placed on the silent woman of

Victorian poetry to be responsive to his vulnerability, despite its artificiality. Later in his poetry, Yeats rejects "embroideries" (2) altogether, claiming that there is "more enterprise / In walking naked" ("A Coat" [1914], *WBY* 9–10). In many respects, this appeal to "naked[ness]" – where poetry no longer has any need for ornate decoration – may well sound one of the keynotes of literary Modernism: the avant-garde movement with which Yeats's work is usually associated, and which often sought to strip poetry bare of rhetorical superfluities. But if we agree that a "naked" aesthetic announces the "enterprise" of Modernism, then we must understand that such "enterprise" was deeply embedded in the "night and light and half-light" of aestheticism and Decadence. Indeed, the word "naked" – for all its Modernist "enterprise" – reminds us of those frustrated passions and yearned-for sensations that absorbed two generations of Victorian poets, from Dante Gabriel Rossetti to Wilde, in "wine and woman and song."

NOTES

1 John Morley, "Mr Swinburne's New Poems," *Saturday Review*, 4 August 1866, 145.

2 Swinburne, *Notes on Poems and Reviews* (London: John Camden Hotten, 1866), reprinted in Swinburne, *Swinburne Replies: Notes on Poems and Reviews, Under the Microscope, Dedicatory Epistle*, ed. Clyde Kenneth Hyder (Syracuse, NY: Syracuse University Press, 1966), 18.

3 Emerson's words are recorded in an interview that appeared in *Frank Leslie's Illustrated Newspaper*, 3 January 1874, and reprinted in Clyde K. Hyder, "Emerson on Swinburne: A Sensational Interview," *Modern Language Notes* 48 (1933), 180.

4 Matthew Arnold "The Study of Poetry," in Arnold, *English Literature and Irish Politics*, ed. R.H. Super, *The Complete Prose Works Of Matthew Arnold*, 11 vols. (Ann Arbor, MI: University of Michigan Press, 1960–77), IX, 161.

5 Arnold, "The Study of Poetry," 171.

6 Percy Bysshe Shelley, "A Defence of Poetry, or Remarks Suggested by an Essay Entitled 'Four Ages of Poetry,'" in Shelley, *Shelley's Poetry and Prose*, ed. Donald H. Reiman and Sharon B. Powers (New York: W.W. Norton, 1977), 508. Shelley's essay first appeared in *Ollier's Literary Miscellany* 1 (1820).

7 Arthur Symons, "The Decadent Movement in Literature," *Harper's New Monthly Magazine* 87 (1893), 858.

8 Robin Sheets, "Pornography and Art: The Case of 'Jenny,'" *Critical Inquiry* 14 (1988), 323.

9 Jerome J. McGann, *Swinburne: An Experiment in Criticism* (Chicago, IL: University of Chicago Press: Chicago, 1972), 34, 35. McGann's experimental study offers a unique approach to understanding Victorian poetry; he orchestrates his argument through dialogues spoken by six characters who are based on noted late-Victorian and early-twentieth-century critics who wrote at length about Swinburne.

10 Swinburne, *Swinburne Replies*, 23.

11 Bram Djikstra, *Idols of Perversity Fantasies of Feminine Evil in Fin-de-Siècle Culture* (New York: Oxford University Press, 1986).

12 Camille Paglia, "Nature, Sex, and Decadence," in *Pre-Raphaelite Poets*, ed. Harold Bloom (New York: Chelsea House, 1986), 226.

13 As Gilles Deleuze has pointed out, the sadistic antagonist of Leopold von Sacher-Masoch's *Venus in Furs* (1870), the prototypical dominatrix, is also described as the creation of the masochist-narrator, a goddess invented to provide intensity, purpose, and meaning to life: see "Coldness and Cruelty," in *Masochism*, trans. Jean McNeil (New York: Zone, 1989).

14 Omar Khayyám, *Rubáiyat of Omar Khayyám: The Astronomer-Poet of Persia, Translated into English Verse*, trans. Edward FitzGerald (London: Bernard Quaritch, 1859), 3.

15 John R. Reed, *Decadent Style* (Athens, OH: Ohio University Press, 1985), 10.

16 Robert Herrick, "To the Virgins, to Make Much of Time," in *The Poetical Works of Robert Herrick*, ed. L.C. Martin (Oxford: Clarendon Press, 1956), 84.

17 See Chris Snodgrass, "Aesthetic Memory's Cul-de-sac: The Art of Ernest Dowson," *English Literature in Transition, 1880–1920* 35 (1992), 26–53, and John R. Reed, "Bedlamite and Pierrot: Ernest Dowson's Esthetic of Futility," *ELH* 35 (1968), 94–113.

18 Arthur Symons, "Ernest Dowson," in *The Poems of Ernest Dowson* (London: John Lane, The Bodley Head, 1905), x.

19 Cynthia Scheinberg, "Canonizing the Jew: Amy Levy's Challenge to Victorian Poetic Identity," *Victorian Studies* 39 (1996), 175–99, and Joseph Bristow, "'All out of Tune in this World's Instrument': The 'Minor' Poetry of Amy Levy," *Journal of Victorian Culture* 5 (1999), 118–45.

20 Chris White, "Michael Field: Tiresian Poet," in *Victorian Women Poets: A Critical Reader*, ed. Angela Leighton (Oxford: Blackwell, 1996), 148–61.

21 Yopie Prins, *Victorian Sappho* (Princeton, NJ: Princeton University Press, 1999), 76.

22 Michael Field, *Underneath the Bough: A Book of Verses* (London: George Bell, 1893), 68–69.

23 Walter Pater, *The Renaissance: Studies in Art and Poetry – The 1893 Text*, ed. Donald L. Hill (Berkeley, CA: University of California Press, 1980), 105. Pater's study was first published as *Studies in the History of Renaissance* (London: Macmillan, 1873).

24 Symons, "The Decadent Movement in Literature," 858–59.

25 W.E. Henley, "Echoes, IV: To R.T.H.B.," in Henley, *Poems* (London: David Nutt, 1898), 119.

26 Symons, "The Decadent Movement in Literature," 867. In a contemporaneous essay on Henley, Symons observed: "Here is poetry made out of personal sensations, poetry which is half physiological, poetry which is pathology – and yet essential poetry" ("Mr. Henley's Poetry," *Fortnightly Review* 58 [1892], 186).

27 T.S. Eliot, "The Love Song of J. Alfred Prufrock," in Eliot, *The Complete Poems and Plays, 1909–1950* (New York: Harcourt Brace, 1952), 3.

28 See W.B. Yeats, "The Tragic Generation," in Yeats, *Autobiographies*, ed.

William H. O'Donnell and Douglas N. Archibald, *The Collected Works of W.B. Yeats*, 14 vols. (New York: Scribner, 1999), 219–66.

29 Pater, *The Renaissance: Studies in Art and Poetry*, 188.

30 See, for example, Leonard Nathan, "The Ballads of Reading Gaol: At the Limits of the Lyric," in *Critical Essays on Oscar Wilde*, ed. Regenia Gagnier, (New York: G.K. Hall, 1991) 213–22, and Karen Alkalay-Gut "The Thing He Loves: Murder as an Aesthetic Experience in 'The Ballad of Reading Gaol,'" *Victorian Poetry* 35 (1997), 349–66.

12

TRICIA LOOTENS

Victorian poetry and patriotism

I

For literary critics who anticipated or experienced the devastation of the First World War, there was something peculiarly "Victorian" – and peculiarly suspect – about patriotic poetry. By 1910, even Hugh Walker, who had devoted several pages of *The Greater Victorian Poets* (1895) to praise Alfred Tennyson's patriotic writing, judged Victoria's former Poet Laureate as "too prone to echo back the thoughts of his own time and country"[1] – and thus, suggestively, as an ideological ally of Germany. "Patriotism is good," wrote Walker, "but it is not a pure good when there goes with it a hard, unsympathetic tone of mind towards other races; and in Tennyson we hear rather too much of 'the blind hysterics of the Celt,' and 'the red fool-fury of the Seine.' He lived under the sway of the Teutonic idea, and already the Teutonic idea is discredited."[2]

"An Englishman taking himself seriously," G.K. Chesterton wrote of Tennyson in 1913, was "an awful sight."[3] Such claims were not entirely tongue-in-cheek, as Virginia Woolf's *To the Lighthouse* (1927) underscores. In Woolf's novel, as Mr. Ramsay begins to declaim Tennyson's famous "Charge of the Light Brigade" (1854) in a voice "between a croak and a song," what was "ridiculous" suddenly becomes "alarming." Shouting "Boldly we rode and well" (*AT* 23), Ramsay charges his guest Lily Briscoe, nearly overturning her easel – and with it, the art that stands at the novel's center.[4] Written in the shadow of another war against Germany, Woolf's anti-war meditation *Three Guineas* (1938) would explicitly connect "the tyrannies and servilities" of the nineteenth-century "private house" to those of Hitler or Mussolini, envisioning a female anti-war Outsiders' Society whose members refuse allegiance to masculinist militarist nation-states. "As a woman," the society's imaginary representative says, "I have no country."[5]

Given the urgency of such early-twentieth-century efforts to discredit the dangerous heritage of Victorian patriotism, it may be no wonder that patriotic writing should have been one of the last Victorian poetic genres to be recuperated for extensive scholarly study. Such relative neglect has been in some respects ironic. For as Eric Hobsbawm and others have pointed out, although right-wing nationalism, militant masculinism, and "state patriotism" assuredly dominated patriotic thinking at the end of the nineteenth century, earlier Victorian writers who called for national unity were likely to do so in the name of "liberal and radical movements."[6] In 1843, for example, the poem "A Patriot's Grave" celebrated Irish rebellion against England,[7] while "God's Englishman the bold," in radical poet Ebenezer Jones's "A Coming Cry" (1843), was prepared to "make thrones totter" rather than enter a government-run workhouse.[8] Indeed, the strong currents of republican fervor within the work of Jones, Elizabeth Barrett Browning, Algernon Charles Swinburne, and James Thomson ("B.V.") – to name only a few – still remain an underresearched area of inquiry. Marked by "an internationalist pacifism, a deep-rooted suspicion of the state, and the invocation of a tradition of English freedom," the eighteenth-century legacy of what Hugh Cunningham terms "radical patriotism" lived on, through the end of the nineteenth century and beyond.[9]

Even if this were not the case, however, Victorian patriotic poetry would be crucial to the study of nineteenth-century poetic culture. For as Benedict Anderson has memorably pointed out, to call upon the name of any nation is to evoke an "imagined community"[10]; and Victorian poetry is inextricably linked to the project of imagining such a community. Calling upon visions of "natural" identities of blood, bone, skin, and soil, and grounding such identities in dreams of home, Victorian patriotic poetry sought to translate "natal" loyalties into a larger love of country. Both "love" and "country" remained contested terms, however; and the volatile project of imagining nationhood crystallized and fractured deep cultural longings. Often, the counterpart of calls for unity revealed itself as fear of division; and where Victorian celebrations of the "land of one's birth" resonated most loudly, they often spoke to terror of bodily engulfment or of alienation and exile.

II

No nineteenth-century British poet was more devoted to such paradoxes – or more notorious for popular patriotic writing – than Felicia Dorothea Browne Hemans. Author of the unforgettable opening line, "The boy stood on the burning deck" (*FH* IV, 157), Hemans was born in 1793 and came of age, like early Victorian patriotic writing itself, during the Napoleonic

Wars. Indeed, "Casabianca" (1826), whose first few words are quoted above, commemorates the 1798 Battle of the Nile. On Hemans's deathbed in 1835, two years before Victoria's accession to the throne, Hemans expressed regret that she had failed to compose "some more noble and complete work . . . which might permanently take its place as the work of a British poetess."[11] Her sorrow was understandable. Taken as a whole, Hemans's poetry failed to propose any "complete" account of patriotism itself, much less attain the epic national status for which she clearly longed. Yet in its very conflicts and instability, Hemans's work resonated throughout the century. Perceived threats to one's country; symbolic or actual separation from that country: these have often been the catalysts for powerful strains of patriotic poetry. They also mark the unraveling points of a patriotic tradition torn between celebration of England, Ireland, Scotland, Great Britain, and the imagined "Greater Britain" of empire, as well as between radically different understandings of the British "people." Hemans's immensely popular poetry was instrumental in the linking of such concerns to specific formulations of home, homesickness, and exile; to meditations on the national and/or spiritual – as opposed to strategic – value of wartime sacrifice and suffering; and to claims for nationhood as a unifying means of engaging the symbolic and literal relations between land, gender, and class.

"Females are forbidden to interfere in politics," the young Felicia Dorothea Browne acknowledged in an 1808 letter[12]; and from the moment her first book, *Poems*, appeared that same year, she sought to formulate a feminine patriotic poetry that would be, as much as possible, rooted in the domestic sphere. No single text more powerfully illustrates the under-pinnings of such domestic patriotism than G.W.F. Hegel's *Phenomenology of Spirit* (1807). Here Hemans's German contemporary reads the Greek tragedy *Antigone* as dramatizing the true relations between the domestic and the public spheres. When Sophocles's heroine Antigone defies her king's law in the attempt to give her brother's body decent burial, Hegel argues, she undertakes more than a "simple movement of individualized pathos."[13] She asserts a power that governs both divine law and the community's "autonomous individuation into families": the power of femininity. If the masculine state is to survive, Hegel emphasizes, then it must suspend such divine familial law. For the state "engenders itself through what it oppresses and through what is at the same time essential to it": in other words, the divine law of femininity. Since the state thus "retains its existence only through the disruption of familial happiness and through the dissolution of self-awareness within the general," it must claim living soldiers as its own; and it must also create "in femininity altogether its internal enemy." Yet it dare not fully disregard feminine law. It must, for example, return the bodies of dead soldiers to their families – and hence to that divine eternal "element" in which the historical state ultimately moves.

In Hemans's writing as in Hegel's, women both mourn and accept the waging of war: the technically useless but symbolically essential pouring-out of women's metaphoric heart's blood thus becomes a precise counter-part (and at points a subversive counter) to the spilling of soldiers' lifeblood on the battlefield. Soldiers die in military exile, redeemed by the "The Spells of Home" (1828; *FH* V, 295–96); women themselves live and die in spiritual exile within "The Homes of England" (1828; *FH* V, 228–29).

Cease your proud "swelling / Into rich floods of joy," pleads the presumably feminine speaker of Hemans's "Triumphant Music" (1830; *FH* VI, 134). Songs of triumph should sound for the national, military figures of a "young chieftain dying" under a "freed country's banner"; "a martyr, leading / Unto victorious death serenely on" (VI, 135); or a "patriot by his rescued altars bleeding" – not for "one whose heart is beating / Against life's narrow bound, in conflict vain!" (VI, 135). With "no crown of victory to inherit," the speaker's spirit protests, it is "but pain, / To mount so high, yet find on high no dwelling":

> For power, for joy, high hope, and rapturous greeting,
> Thou wak'st lone thirst – be hush'd, exulting strain!
>
> Be hush'd, or breathe of grief! – of exile yearnings
> Under the willows of the stranger-shore.   (VI, 135)

Thus, "with her domestic affection devoted to healing others," Hemans's ideal female patriot must, in Susan J. Wolfson's words, "accept her own depletion."[14] Here, as elsewhere – as Anne K. Mellor observes – Hemans's poetry "exhausts the very ideology it espouses."[15]

Such a paradigm was always unstable, however. Some of Hemans's poems glorify female figures who defy the masculine authority of the state or kill and die for the united honor of nation and family, for example. In Jerome J. McGann's words, even apparently conventional patriotic favor-ites such as Hemans's "The Homes of England" "understand that they are haunted by death and insubstantialities."[16] This is certainly true of "Casabianca," where divine and mortal laws fuse to detonate both a battleship and a family. Here Hemans stages the moment when "A creature of heroic blood," young Casabianca, destroys his family's future as he saves its honor. He will not leave his post until released by the man who is both his admiral and his father; and that man lies dead beneath the burning deck. Read literally, this is a horrifying scene, not only because the child's last moments are so agonizing but also because his death seems so useless.

Yet, as Hemans's consistent reference to "father" underscores, one precedent for Casabianca's anguish at the Battle of the Nile may lie in Christ's suffering at Gethsemane. "My father! must I stay?" (IV, 158). Alive, the boy is subject to a rule whose combined familial and governmental force is at once miraculous and harrowing. Dead, he is a burnt sacrifice. When the final stanza announces that the "noblest thing which perish'd there / Was that young faithful heart!" (IV, 158), Casabianca's death emerges, perhaps not entirely persuasively, as the greatest of many noble gifts of sacramental military faith.

Significantly, the hero of "Casabianca" is French. In dozens of "national lyrics" and battle-songs on behalf of an amazing range of countries, Hemans celebrated an internationalist patriotism rooted in what William Hazlitt called a universal "law of our rational and moral nature."[17] Yet she also supported what Marlon B. Ross has termed "the romance of Wordsworthian organicism," with its project of consolidating national identity.[18] Logically, such versions of patriotism were irreconcilable; metaphorically, they met in the trope of the heroic soldier's grave. For even as the return of soldiers' bodies to their families reconciles Hegelian divine and human law, so the organic return of those bodies to the soil creates rational grounds for attachment to specific portions of the earth. "Wave may not foam, nor wild wind sweep, / Where rest not England's dead" (*FH* V, 129): the claim, from Hemans's "England's Dead" (1823), consecrates far-flung burials for reverence whose sources are at once intimate and imperial. In great part through Hemans, Victorian patriotic writing thus came to be intimately linked to longings for home; and home came to be linked to far-flung places of mourning and exile. British soldiers' graves were destined to be crucial sites for struggle over national identity, through the First World War and beyond; and poetry was crucial to such struggles.

III

For Victorians, then, patriotic poetry was not always what Peter Brooker and Peter Widdowson have termed "literature for England."[19] This point is most striking with respect to mid-century women poets, among whom no British struggle provoked such ambitious patriotic poetry as did the Risorgimento, the struggle for Italian national unification. Here, as elsewhere, the Napoleonic Wars are central: for it was in 1807, five years after Napoleon banished the famous French intellectual Germaine de Staël from Paris, that she published *Corinne, or, Italy*. Near the novel's opening, Corinne is crowned at the Roman Capitol as an inspired "priestess" of Italian national "genius."[20] Many critics have addressed the extent to which de Staël's myth of the doomed poetic heir to Sappho haunted aspiring women poets for the remainder of the century. What remains to be fully explored is how thoroughly Corinne and her successors are shaped by fantasies of female patriotic authority.

"Daughter of th' Italian heaven!" begins Hemans's famous poem "Corinne at the Capitol" (1830; *FH* VI, 87). The apostrophe is ironic: for though Corinne may "be" Italy, she is also the biological daughter of a less than celestial English aristocrat. Indeed, in cutting short its own dazzling account of Corinne's poetic and patriotic triumph, Hemans's poem merely anticipates the moment at which de Staël dramatizes Corinne's secret, fatal national vulnerability. Transfixed by the bleak gaze of a Scotsman, de Staël's Corinne interrupts herself, transforming a joyous improvization on the glories of Italy into a meditation on death and mourning. The shift is symbolic: for Corinne, this man's consistent Britishness will prove as deadly as his wavering adoration. When de Staël's betrayed poet sings her last song, toward the novel's close, it will be a farewell to "lovely" Italy, "the liberal nation that does not banish women from its temple."[21]

In *Corinne* whereas Italy is the land of feminine genius, Britain is that of domesticity. And thus when Hemans interrupts Corinne's "burning words of song" (VI, 89) to lecture what Nanora Sweet terms Italy's "woman laureate"[22] on the superiority of the "humblest hearth," her strictures against joyful public confidence may well reveal their author's own patriotic project. "Felicia Hemans, or England": the imagined title, which allows no triumphant music, requires only the crown of household love.

Can a British woman write patriotic songs of triumph? She can, *Corinne* teaches, if she writes of Italy. While Hemans's "Corinne" sought to domesticate and thus anglicize feminine patriotic poetry, works by other British women poets wholeheartedly embraced the early-nineteenth-century "Romance of Italy." As a feminized and alluring, if often ultimately inaccessible, Western European cultural homeland, "Italy" could shift from what Sandra M. Gilbert calls a potential "political state to a female state of mind"[23]; as a political state, it could provide inspiration for reimagining England and Englishness.[24]

None of these possibilities was lost on Elizabeth Barrett Browning. From "The Battle of Marathon" (1820), the poem that she published at fourteen, to her final preface for *Poems before Congress* (1861), which insisted that "if patriotism be a virtue indeed, it cannot mean an exclusive devotion to our country's interests" (*EBB* III, 215), Barrett Browning wrote as a Christian female patriotic poet. After her marriage to Robert Browning in 1846, England's "Queen of Song" lived in ambivalent, partially self-imposed, exile in Italy; and as Barrett Browning's later poetry gained in political explicitness, her criticisms of British policies became increasingly harsh. Many English poets, among them Swinburne and Harriet Eleanor Hamilton King, wrote passionate Risorgimento poetry; but for no other Victorian poet, perhaps, did the Risorgimento unite deeper, more immediate concerns.

"I heard last night a little child go singing / 'Neath Casa Guidi windows, by the church, / *Oh bella libertà, O bella!*" begins *Casa Guidi Windows* (1851; *EBB* 1–2), Barrett Browning's longest, most ambitious political poem. Birdlike in its pure exaltation, this triumphant music floats in through the windows of the Brownings' home in Florence, Casa Guidi, and echoes throughout the poem, seeming to voice not only "the heart of Italy" (I. 8) but also the joyous beauty of simple national song (I. 155). In her meditation on the Florentines' exuberant 1847 welcome of Duke Leopold I, whose liberalization of Tuscan laws seemed to open way for Italy's constitutional unification, the explicitly English speaker follows Corinne in positioning herself as reverent heir to Italy's older singers. Such writers have troped Italy as a victimized or fallen woman – a Cybele, a Niobe, or a Juliet, laid "corpse-like on a bier" (I. 34). If Italy *is* a Juliet now, however, she has risen: her tomb is "as void" as "all images / Men set between themselves and actual wrong" (I. 43–44). The time for mourning is over. "Of such songs enough . . . !" (I. 40–41). Poets should now sing with those who "are awake"; and England should seize its chance to unite "good and glory" (I. 156) in the Italian cause, hastening the time when "Drums and battle-cries, / Go out in music of the morning-star" (I. 726–27).

Juliet's resurrection is a bad omen, however. By Part II of *Casa Guidi Windows*, the speaker's poetic revolution seems to have failed, along with the early Risorgimento. Once more the Duke returns to Florence – this time under protection of the city's Austrian occupiers. Remembering the child's song, the speaker laments, "Alas, poor people, of an unfledged will, / Most fitly expressed by such a callow voice!" (II. 270–71). What she had taken for Italy's national song was "just the trilling on an opera-stage, / Of 'libertà' to bravos – (a fair word, / Yet too allied to inarticulate rage / And breathless sobs, for singing)" (I. 226–29). "Great nations have great shames" (I. 648) moreover; and England has added to its own by failing to come to Italy's aid. What remains, for England as for Italy, is a counterfeit peace whose reality is "treason, stiff with doom, – / . . . gagged despair, and inarticulate wrong" (I. 414–15; see also I. 374–84). "Still, graves, when Italy is talked upon" (I. 724), the speaker mourns. "Still Niobe!" (I. 726). Has Italy won "Nothing but death-songs?" (I. 728–30).

Despite such defeat, however, "Life throbs in noble Piedmont!" (I. 731). Carnal and female, the Italian landscape has been sown with patriots' graves as with dragons' teeth: "These Dead be seeds of life, and shall encumber / The sad heart of the land, until it loose / The clammy clods and let out the Spring-growth / In beatific green through every bruise" (I. 663–66). Charles Albert of Piedmont, whose abdication opened the way for Italy's reunification under his son Victor Emmanuel II, lies in such uneasy soil; so, too, does the hastily buried Anita Garibaldi, who "outfaced the whistling shot and hissing waves," at the side of her husband, the nationalist leader Giuseppe Garibaldi, "until she felt her little babe unborn, / Recoil, within her" (I. 678–81). The "hope and omen" of the original child's song are thus vindicated; and as *Casa Guidi Windows* closes, the "brave blue English eyes" (I. 738) of the speaker's own "young Florentine" (I. 747) – her Italian-born son – prophesy that "elemental / New springs of life are gushing everywhere" (I. 761–62). The "earth's alive, and gentle or ungentle / Motions within her, signify but growth! – / The ground swells greenest o'er the labouring moles" (I. 765–67). With this shocking equation of a swelling, moving, and pregnant body, soon to gush new life, and the unquiet Italian earth, under which patriots rest and moles tunnel, Barrett Browning literalizes and nationalizes "Mother Earth," even as she radically transforms Hemans's association of soldiers' graves with feminine divine law.

As the Risorgimento's ultimate success became clear, Barrett Browning returned to what Flavia Alaya calls the "revolutionary archetype" of an Italy at once "mother and child," delivered "out of her own flesh."[25] In the politically problematic "Napoleon III in Italy" (1860), for example, patriots "feel the underground heave and strain" (*EBB* 149) as Italy "rises up at the shout of her sons, / At the trumpet of France, / And lives anew" (129–31). It is in the posthumous volume *Last Poems* (1862), however, that Barrett Browning most powerfully revisits her carnal vision of the birth of nations. Like so much patriotic poetry, "Mother and Poet" is an occasional piece: at its center stand the wartime deaths of both sons of the Italian nationalist poet Laura Savio. Torn between maternal sorrow and national triumph, Barrett Browning's Savio is a far cry from Hemans's innocent victims of the masculine state. "*I* made them indeed / Speak plain the word *country*" (*EBB* 21–22), Savio mourns: "*I* taught them, no doubt, / That a country's a thing men should die for at need" (22–23). Granted, Savio, too, now lives in exile on earth: pointing "above the star pricked by the last peak of snow," she cries, "My Italy's THERE, with my brave civic Pair" (88–89). She will write no triumphant music, no "great song for Italy free" (4):

> Forgive me. Some women bear children in strength,
> And bite back the cry of their pain in self-scorn;

> But the birth-pangs of nations will wring us at length
> Into wail such as this – and we sit on forlorn
> When the man-child is born. (91–95)

Yet though this mother and poet has been wrung into "wail," she still speaks with a patriotic voice: her cry does not condemn the natural unavoidable process that has given birth to her (masculine) nation, even as it killed her sons.

IV

As a young man, Tennyson shared some of Barrett Browning's idealistic internationalism: he not only wrote sonnets protesting Russian oppression of Hungary and Poland ("Sonnet" and "Poland" [both 1832]) but also participated in an abortive rebellion in Spain. By 1850, however, when Tennyson accepted the position of Poet Laureate, there could be no doubt that his patriotism was passionately English. Officially, Tennyson's first major poem as Laureate was the dignified "Ode on the Death of the Duke of Wellington" (1852), which casts England as "the eye, the soul / Of Europe" (AT 160–61), promising that if God and "Statesmen" guard against "brute control" (which John Lucas identifies as "mass democracy"[26]), the British model of "sober freedom" and "loyal passion for our temperate kings" will "help to save mankind." Unofficially, however, Tennyson preceded his ode to the Napoleonic War hero with a very different sort of patriotic writing: a spate of vehement – not to say frenzied – anonymous or pseudonymous periodical poetry calling British citizens to arm against a possible French invasion (see, for example, "The Penny-Wise," "Britons, Guard Your Own," and "Hands All Round" [all 1852]). The juxtaposition is suggestive, given Tennyson's next – thoroughly controversial – major work, *Maud* (1855). Called by Tennyson a "monodrama," and at one point subtitled "The Madness," *Maud* plays out a succession of extreme, passionate states of mind. Set adrift in a terrifying mid-Victorian crisis of class, national, and gender identities, and tormented by fear of madness as well as by thwarted patriotic ambitions and erotic desires, the speaker of *Maud* is deeply unstable; and so, too, as many recent critics insist, are the formal and ideological structures of *Maud* itself.[27] As Linda M. Shires suggests, Tennyson's poem "tells a tale against itself."[28]

"I hate the dreadful hollow" (AT I. 1). With these words, *Maud* evokes a feminized, terrifyingly familial, English landscape whose "lips" (I. 2) or "red-ribbed ledges drip with a silent horror of blood" (I. 3). Here, wrecked by the failure of a "vast speculation" (I. 9), the speaker's father died, "mangled, and flattened, and crushed" (I. 7); here the orphaned son fears he too may someday "creep" to commit suicide (I. 54). Condemned to class exile within England, he haunts his "own dark garden," which rings with the "shipwrecking roar" (I. 98) of the sea and "the scream of a maddened beach" (I. 99), and a woodland "world of plunder and prey" (I. 125). Although he traces his immediate suffering to a "wretched swindler's lie" (I. 56) by his cousin Maud's father, he associates such betrayal with a larger, brutal, and commercial "Civil war" (I. 27) that has corrupted all England and even threatens Europe. As passive Great Britain has fallen prey to "lust of gain" (I. 23), Russia has been left free to wreak its "rod" on Poland and Hungary (I. 147). At first, however, when the speaker cries for "loud war" (I. 47), it is merely as an open honorable substitute for vile underhanded "Civil war." "Shall I weep if a Poland fall?" (I. 147), he asks. "Shall I shriek if a Hungary fail?" No: "*I* have not made the world, and He that made it will guide" (I. 149).

This situation soon changes. For at the center of the speaker's consciousness, in a space both symbolically charged and vacant of individual presence, emerges Maud herself, a figure whose very name means battle, might, and strife. Suddenly, as he is out walking, the speaker hears

> A voice by the cedar tree
> In the meadow under the Hall!
> She is singing an air that is known to me,
> A passionate ballad gallant and gay,
> A martial song like a trumpet's call!   (I. 162–66)

The voice is, of course, that of "Maud with her exquisite face, / And wild voice pealing up to the sunny sky / And feet like sunny gems on an English green" (I. 173–75). "Singing of Death, and of Honour that cannot die," Maud is in fact the poem's first patriotic singer (I. 177). What sings itself, through her, is the combined folk and chivalric tradition from which the future author of *Idylls of the King* (1859–85) was to draw his most ambitious attempts to link England's idealized past to its future. Ringing out over a pastoral green, from the lips of an artlessly aristocratic lady, this already "known" ballad momentarily allows the speaker to listen as if he were a patriot of another time – an era, presumably, in which mid-Victorian peace societies, supported by Manchester School industrialists who opposed war because it blocked free trade, did not send "huckster" pacifists to "preach our poor little army down / And play the game of despot kings" (I. 367–68), and in which military authority did not take the form of "a lord, a captain, a padded shape, / A bought commission, a waxen face" (I. 358–59). Hearing Maud's song, the speaker "could weep for a time so sordid and mean, / And myself so languid and base" (I. 178–79); remembering it, he longs for "a man to arise in me, / That the man I am may cease to be!" (I. 396–97). He longs, too, for a "still, strong man in a blatant land . . . / One who can rule and dare not lie"; "Whatever they call him, what care I? / Aristocrat, democrat, autocrat –" or perhaps Laureate? (I. 392–95). Moved, the speaker learns to hope; and he woos Maud in a newly courtly springtime pastoral landscape to which Tennyson devotes some of his lushest, most sensual, and most famous lyricism.

Maud herself is less a living woman than a form for the speaker's projections and desires. Significantly, one of those desires is for salvation, "Perhaps from madness, perhaps from crime, / Perhaps from a selfish grave" (I. 558–59). Before long, however, crime arrives; and soon after, madness. Surprised into a duel with Maud's "dandy-despot" (I. 231) politician brother, the speaker hears her living voice emerge over the grounds of the Hall for the last time:

> Then glided out of the joyous wood
> The ghastly Wraith of one that I know;
> And there rang on a sudden a passionate cry,
> A cry for a brother's blood:
> It will ring in my heart and my ears, till I die, till I die.   (II. 31–35)

Like the "Echo" at the blood-rimmed "dreadful hollow" of the poem's opening, which answers only "Death" (I. 4), Maud's voice resonates with the remembered shriek of the speaker's own violently widowed mother. "Would there be sorrow for *me*?" (I. 57), the speaker had asked, contemplating his mother's loss and his own mortality before Maud's first arrival. Now, it seems, he cannot hope even to avoid a "selfish grave"; for Maud's cry, which might once have marked a patriot's reunion with darkness, femininity, and divine law, reverberates through a newly abject, horrifying English landscape on which he himself has spilled the blood of vile civil strife. No wonder, in his subsequent madness, he wonders "why have they not buried me deep enough?" (II. 334); no wonder he dreams, as an exile in Brittany, of the dead Maud, singing "as of old" (II. 184) – only to hear her ballad broken by "a passionate cry" (II. 187) that "there is someone dying or dead" (II. 188), and a "sullen thunder" (II. 189). "An old song," presumably Maud's ballad of chivalrous death in battle, "vexes" his "ear"; but it is no longer his own: "that of" the Biblical killer Lamech "is mine" (II. 95–96).

In the poem's third and final section, the speaker seems to emerge from his madness. He has been inspired, he says, by a dream of Maud dividing "from the band of the blest" (III. 10) to speak "of a hope for the world in the coming wars" and to promise "I tarry for thee" (III. 11–12). In this longed-for restoration of patriotic authority as elsewhere, however, *Maud* tells a tale against itself. For since Maud's "ghastly Wraith" appeared after the duel, it has not left. "A disease, a hard mechanic ghost / That never came from on high / Nor ever arose from below" (II. 82–84), this "shadow" (II. 151) or "deathlike type of pain" (II. 198) has in fact become the speaker's "spectral bride" (II. 318). "Silence, beautiful voice!" (I. 180), he had thought upon first hearing Maud's passionate ballad, thus echoing Hemans's "Triumphant Music" in his yearning (and perhaps feminized) alienation from patriotic song. Now he has his silence: "not beautiful now, not even kind" (II. 204), the phantom never leaves, and "she never speaks her mind" (II. 305). He has heard Maud singing, and she will not sing to him. She is, in fact, "ever the one thing silent here" (II. 306). Is she a speechless unappeased "internal enemy"? Does she foreshadow Woolf's imaginary "daughters of educated men" in *Three Guineas*, who pledge themselves "not to incite their brothers to fight, or to dissuade them, but to maintain an attitude of complete indifference"?[29] She is surely no vessel or catalyst for patriotic feeling.

Eventually, the speaker decides that it is "time" (III. 30) for "that old hysterical mock-disease" to "die" (III. 33). Cleaving to a "cause I felt to be pure and true" (III. 31), he enlists for the Crimean War; and as he mixes his "breath / With a loyal people shouting a battle cry" (III. 34–35), he watches Maud's "dreary phantom arise and fly / Far into the North, and battle, and seas of death" (III. 36–37). "Let it go or stay," he proclaims (III. 38). The English "have proved we have hearts in a cause, we are noble still" (III. 55); and he himself has "awaked, as it seems, to the better mind" of a truer patriot (III. 56). "It is better to fight for the good than to rail at the ill" (III. 57); better (and easier, perhaps) to fight a Russian "giant liar" (III. 45) than dishonest "Jack on his ale-house bench" (I. 110). For the Poet Laureate of the 1850s, perhaps, as for his speaker, war offers an opportunity to cease "rail[ing]" against the liars at home.

"I have felt with my native land, I am one with my kind / I embrace the purpose of God, and the doom assigned" (III. 58–59): thus the poem ends. This would be a rousing conclusion, could one forget its speaker and his situation. For if "sentimental love" of a rural "mother-country" is "central" to late-nineteenth-century "expressions of Englishness," as Brooker and Widdowson assert,[30] then perverse fascination with gothic maternal visions of England's soil seems no less central to what Herbert F. Tucker calls the "cultural entombment" celebrated at the close of the poem.[31] What might it mean to "feel with" a "native land" whose literal manifestations include the gaping, womb-like "blood-red" hollow – or even Maud's lush garden, under which the speaker has imagined his own sentient and thwarted dust blossoming "in purple and red" (I. 923)? In a poem permeated by drowning imagery, moreover, the speaker is now sailing toward the "blood-red blossom of war" (III. 53) – preceded by the diseased mechanical phantom of Maud, the patriotic anti-Muse.

The Crimean War (1854–56), which appears to the speaker of *Maud* as a cause to hold "good" and "true," scarcely delivered on such promises. Undertaken in opposition to Russian incursions upon the vulnerable – and corrupt – Ottoman Empire, the Crimean War may have been unnecessary; and it has won fame primarily through exposés of military incompetence. It was, however, Victorian Britain's only major European war; and for many nineteenth-century writers, hatred of the Russian Czar (which moved not only Tennyson but also the likes of Karl Marx), ensured sympathy for Britain's and France's claims to altruistic protection of Turkey. For these and other reasons, the Crimean War powerfully affected Victorian poetry. No Crimean writing, however, achieved anything like the fame of another of Tennyson's poems, "The Charge of the Light Brigade."

"It is not a poem on which I pique myself," Tennyson noted[32]; yet echoing what must have been thousands of parlor performances, the Laureate's own sonorous voice can still be heard, preserved by one of the earliest poetic recording sessions, intoning, "Half a league, half a league, half a league onward" (1). In the drama of Tennyson's "Charge," the fate of Hemans's "Casabianca" plays out on a grand scale: senseless sacrifice had perhaps never been so successfully celebrated. "Their's not to reason why, / Their's but to do and die" (14–15): this line's repellent resonance with the phrase "only following orders" is partly, if only partly, anachronistic. Not all orders are alike, after all; and the idealized Victorian soldier's "trade" was, as John Ruskin stressed, "not slaying, but being slain."[33] "Who fears to die?" (*AT* 1) is the question that opens Tennyson's "English Warsong" (1830), one of the young poet's earliest efforts at patriotic verse. Still, as Tennyson's own "Epilogue" to the much later poem "The Charge of the Heavy Brigade at Balaclava" (1885) makes clear, many of the Laureate's own contemporaries challenged his poetry's bloodthirstiness. "Who loves War for War's own sake" (*AT* 29), his defensive "POET" tells one such critic – a young woman suitably named "IRENE" (which means peace) – "Is fool, or crazed, or worse" (30). Yet even if "that realm were in the wrong / For which her warriors bleed, / It still were right to crown with song / The warrior's noble deed" (33–36).

The coda of Tennyson's "Epilogue" is styled a plea of "the Singer for his Art" (*AT* 77). Suggestively, as Tennyson's speaker defends patriotic poetry to lovers of peace, he also defends poetic composition as patriotic action:

"The song that nerves a nation's heart, / Is in itself a deed" (79–80). Whatever his later doubts about "The Charge of the Light Brigade," Tennyson seems to have seen the poem as such a deed: he had it printed on fly-leaves and sent to the soldiers of the Crimean military hospital at Scutari.[34] Termed, in M. van Wyk Smith's words, "probably the last great battle-piece that could be written in English,"[35] Tennyson's poem stands at a watershed partly of its own making. "Some one had blundered" (12): the phrase (mis)remembered from a London *Times* account of the Crimean War disaster Tennyson immortalized, resonated within and beyond a British public newly critical of heavily aristocratic military leadership. In omitting all but three poems of their Crimean *War Lyrics* (1855) from their *Collected Poems* (1897), for example, poets Louisa and Arabella Shore explained that "we have learned to regard the Crimean War, in spite of the heroism of our soldiers, not as a just cause and a glorious achievement so much as a deplorable blunder."[36] Socially high-ranking but generally inexperienced soldiers comprised the Light Brigade. As McGann has demonstrated, by focusing on the heroism of elite units "The Charge of the Light Brigade" actually celebrates that "historically threatened class," the aristocracy.[37] Nonetheless, Tennyson's blunt acknowledgment of high-level military incompetence presages a shift in the subjective position of the patriotic poetry of war. By the time of the second Anglo-Boer War (1899–1902), when literate armed forces and new journalistic technologies intersected with larger changes in the discourse of realism, this shift would be decisive. Henceforth, much of the patriotic poetry of war would be spoken through, if not always by, soldiers.[38] No writer would be more crucial to such a shift than the man whom W.D. Howells would call the "laureate" of "larger England" – Rudyard Kipling.[39]

V

"Kipling *is* a jingo imperialist," George Orwell wrote in 1942. "He *is* morally insensitive and aesthetically disgusting. It is better to start by admitting that, and then to try to find out why he still survives while the refined people who have sniggered at him seem to wear so badly."[40] Orwell's project remains irresistible; for no other late-Victorian poet's patriotic writing has demonstrated such vitality, while provoking (and earning) such hostility, even from some of its most sympathetic critics. What frequently renders Kipling's patriotic poetry compelling is its radical instability – an instability grounded in questions of affiliation and exile.

J.M.S. Tompkins points out that Kipling called England "the most interesting foreign country I have ever been in"; but, she adds, "he also called it 'inalienably mine.'"[41] Like England's official Laureate, the Anglo-Indian Kipling hoped to write the "song that nerves a nation's heart." Where Tennyson traced the chivalric patriotic ballad of *Maud* to a great hall, however, Kipling sought inspiration from imperial barrack-rooms and urban music-halls. In place of the pure tones of Tennyson's aristocratic maiden, he often set the voices of working-class soldiers whose rowdy slang is often not even entirely English in origin. Suggestively, the poem Kipling considered his best is a national hymn.[42] "Recessional" (1897), which commemorates the Diamond Jubilee (England's celebration of Victoria's sixty-year reign), appeared only after the festivities had ended. The poem's tone is one of anticipatory elegiac. "Far-called, our navies melt away" (*RK* 327), begins the fourth stanza; and though the literal reference is to the departure of colonial and imperial celebrants, another application is irresistible: "Lo, all our pomp of yesterday / Is one with Nineveh and Tyre!" The poem becomes, in fact, less a culmination of the Jubilee than a prayer for divine forgiveness of such jubilation:

> For heathen heart that puts her trust
>   In reeking tube and iron shard,
> All valiant dust that builds on dust,
>   And guarding, calls not Thee to guard,
> For frantic boast and foolish word –
> Thy mercy on Thy People, Lord! (327)

By 1901, "Recessional" had entered not only the *Oxford Book of English Verse* but also the hymnbook of the Church of England.[43] Not coincidentally, as Ann Parry notes, it was also performed by some 10,000 British soldiers in a Boer War victory ceremony outside the Parliament of the Transvaal.[44] For in its very humility, this is still triumphant music. A recessional, after all, is sung after holy services; and in warning of Britain's spiritual (and hence national) dangers, Kipling's national hymn addresses a God prepared to give "His" British "People" dominion, over not only "palm and pine" but also "lesser breeds without the Law."

Of "The Absent-Minded Beggar" (1899), in contrast, Parry reports that Kipling "wryly observed that were it not suicide he would have shot the man who wrote it."[45] First published in the "independent and imperial" *Daily Mail*, and later set to music by Arthur Sullivan, "The Absent-Minded Beggar" annexed the power of the music hall to the ends of military charity. Printed on everything from tobacco jars to souvenir triptychs, the poem netted £250,000 for soldiers' widows and orphans within months.[46] As with "Recessional," the title says a great deal. "Absent-minded" Tommy Atkins, the stereotypic comic Cockney soldier, has run off and left "a lot of little things behind him" (*RK* 457) – including his home, and perhaps his wife, children, or sweetheart. "His weaknesses are great – / But we and Paul must take him as we find him." Like Paulus Kruger, the Boer leader, English civilians will find Atkins at the ready: for he has absented his mind – and body – from home to do his "country's work." Thus literalizing "absent-minded," Kipling narrows the meaning of "beggar." Atkins may merit the affectionate label of "poor beggar" but he seeks no hand-outs: "There are families by the thousands, far too proud to beg or speak" (*RK* 458), who will "live on half o' nothing, paid 'em punctual once a week, / 'Cause the man that earns the wage is ordered out."

So loyal is Atkins, Kipling suggests, that he may even "forget" if England sends his "kiddies" to the workhouse while he fights (458). The claim underscores Isobel Armstrong's assertion that Kipling's poetry "portrays, exploits and glories in a working-class solidarity which consents to an ideology it may not analyse."[47] "Jingoism" is the word often used for such writing, of course; and the term, whose roots lie in music-hall militarism, is indispensable. Yet the roots of jingoism's belief in the manly redemptive power of national bloodletting lie not only in the music hall but also in the philosophy of a Hegel or the prophetic eloquence of a Victorian sage such as Thomas Carlyle or Ruskin. Moreover, with his aggressive mockery of civilian fondness for patriotic song, and his implicit condemnation of an "absent-minded" state, the poem's speaker is no mere jingoist. "When you've shouted 'Rule Britannia,'" he begins; "When you've sung 'God Save the Queen,' / When you've finished killing Kruger with your mouth, / Will you kindly drop a shilling in my little tambourine / For a gentleman in khaki ordered South?" (457). The question resonates with the request of Kipling's shambling, desperate former Crimean soldiers in the bitter "Last of the Light Brigade" (1891) who visit the Laureate to say, "You wrote we were heroes once, sir. Please, write we are starving now" (201). Given Kipling's history of scathing exposés of civilian exploitation and mistreatment of common British soldiers, the challenge to civilians to pay "for your credit's sake" was serious indeed ("The Absent-Minded Beggar" [457]).

Who has the "credit" to speak – or sing – as a British patriot? Never fully answered, the question shapes Kipling's poetry. In early Kipling poems such as "The English Flag" (1891) or "Christmas in India" (1892), as in Hemans, homesickness is an imperial duty: the British earn imperial land through patriotic exile. In the poetry of the late-Victorian Kipling, however, the professional imperial soldier often has no home – unless it is in the homosocial company of his military peers. Ultimately, those peers may even include the former enemy.

Celebration of bonds between warriors is as old as English literature; and popular Victorian poetry took particular pleasure in dramatizing such ties within the context of doomed imperial heroism. In Francis H. Doyle's widely circulated "The Red Thread of Honour" (1844), for example, "wild" Muslim robbers accord dead Englishmen a ritual symbol of courage denied even to their own greatest warriors,[48] while in Henry Newbolt's "Guides at Cabul, 1879," Afghani soldiers fight on even after their British "masters" have been killed.[49] From this latter poem it is a short step to Kipling's "Ballad of East and West" (1899) whose opening and closing stanza has entered popular culture in suggestively repressed form. "*O East is East, and West is West,*" the stanza begins, "*and never the twain shall meet*" (*RK* 233). But then it continues:

> *Till Earth and Sky stand presently at God's great Judgment Seat;*
> *But there is neither East nor West, Border, nor Breed, nor Birth,*
> *When two strong men stand face to face, though they come from the*
>   *ends of the earth!* (233)

In the body of the poem, the courage of a British colonel's son inspires Kamal (a daring Indian border thief) to send his own son to serve under the Briton "who leads a troop" of "Guides" (236). East and West are essentially alien; Englishmen are models to the world; the British are born to rule; strong men are essentially alike. Such paradoxical assumptions structure Kipling's poetry, two of whose most famous lines have become "Take up the White Man's burden" ("The White Man's Burden" [1899; *RK* 321]), and "You're a better man than I am, Gunga Din" ("Gunga Din" [1899; *RK* 406]).

"The 'eathen in 'is blindness bows down to wood and stone," begins Kipling's "The 'Eathen" (1896; *RK* 449): "'E don't obey no orders unless they is 'is own; / 'E keeps 'is side-arms awful: 'e leaves 'em all about, / An' then comes up the Regiment an' pokes the 'eathen out" (449). The joke is most obviously on the naive narrator, a former "'eathen" from what became known in the 1890s as "Darkest London," to whom military discipline has offered a sort of salvation. On another level, however, in this speaker's world as in much of Kipling's writing, to be a British civilian is to be "a 'eathen." Thus Kipling lends unpredictable form to the late-Victorian civic religion of the nation state.

"Me that 'ave been what I've been," begins "Chant-Pagan" (1903; *RK* 453). "Me that 'ave gone where I've gone – / Me that 'ave seen what I've seen – / 'Ow can I ever take on / With awful old England again?" The poem ends:

> *I know of a sun an' a wind,*
> An' some plains and a mountain be'ind,

An' some graves by a barb-wire fence,
An' a Dutchman I've fought 'oo might give
Me a job were I ever inclined
To look in an' offsaddle an' live
Where there's neither a road nor a tree –
But only my Maker an' me,
And I think it will kill me or cure,
So I think I will go there an' see.
                            Me!   (461)

Home is where the graves are; and the graves in question are those of one's comrades. The speaker of "Chant-Pagan" turns to his former enemy, in imagination, as one who has "gone where he's gone" and "seen what he's seen." Drawn, too, by the "silence, the shine, an' the size" of South Africa's "'igh, inexpressible skies" (459), Kipling's speaker strikes at the heart of English pastoralism: he can no longer bear a native land in which "something" seems to have "gone small" (460).

"Chant-Pagan" speaks directly to the paradox of Kipling's "Greater Britain." "A smell came out over the sea –" reads an uncollected 1891 essay that Kipling wrote on returning to India. It was the "smell of damp earth, coconut oil, ginger, onions and mankind. It spoke with a strong voice, recalling many things; but the most curious revelation to one man was the sudden knowledge that under these skies lay home."[50] Once the "Native-Born" heard such voices ("The Native-Born" [1894]); once their dead lay in the cemeteries of Lahore or the karoo; once they came to think (or perhaps even learned to think), as some did, in a language other than English – on what grounds could they claim to speak as British patriots? Blood was the only answer. Indeed, as Stephen D. Arata has argued, on such grounds, colonials might even claim superior patriotic authority, as the hardiest of all British stock.[51] And thus, for all Kipling's internationalist identification with "strong men," to do one's patriotic duty to Greater Britain was to glorify the mastery of the British "white men." The strong Eastern robber's son must enlist under the Western colonel's son; that "better man," the Indian water-bearer Gunga Din, must submit to being "belted," "flayed" (406), and yet praised as "white, clear white, inside" (405).

Kipling's belief in war as source of unity, like his belief in a Greater Britain, was thus both fueled and riven by his own war with civilian middle-class Englishness. The great spokesman for British xenophobia, he was himself irretrievably alien, passionately and powerfully drawn to aliens. In the end, as the increasing vehemence of Kipling's post-Victorian poetry may suggest, neither the claims of blood nor the spilling of blood could keep even the poet's own literary dreams of a British warrior-empire alive.

VI

"The voice of the hooligan": the phrase, famously applied to the works of Rudyard Kipling, by Robert Buchanan's scathing 1899 review, might more accurately describe those of Kipling's great admirer W.E. Henley.[52] To read Henley is to recognize why early-twentieth-century critics often found not only Kipling but also Tennyson hard to take. For though Henley's "dismal," "teeming," or thoroughly abstract imperial "junior Englands" (*WEH*, 236, 231, 237) are as far from the "'igh inexpressible skies" of Kipling's karoo as his callous soldiers are from Kipling's absent-minded beggar, Henley's patriotic poetry distills the warmongering, xenophobia, and misogyny of its models, even as it annexes their righteous rhetorical energy.

No work is more important to this project than an 1890 poem dedicated to Kipling, "The Song of the Sword." Created by God, before Adam and Eve, and "Edged to annihilate, / Hilted with government," Henley's Sword calls men to "Follow, O, follow me, / Till the waste places / All the gray globe over / Ooze" with the "sweetness" of blood, then "Give back in beauty / The dread and the anguish / They had of me visitant" (*WEH* 33–34). In "Pro Rege Nostro," perhaps the most popular poem of Henley's Boer War volume *For England's Sake* (1900), what Richard LeGallienne calls Henley's "sword-evangel"[53] becomes explicitly British: here the nation is not only the "Mother of Ships" and the "Chosen daughter of the Lord" but also the divine "Spouse-in-Chief of the ancient Sword" (*WEH* 231). At her best, Henley's nation is the "Mother of mothering girls and governing men" ("Envoy" *WEH* 242), an "everlasting Mother" who demands "the lust and the pain of battle," so that "the One Race might starkly spread" ("Last Post" *WEH* 239). At her worst, she excels even the corrupting female peacetime corporeality of *Maud*. Tennyson's drunken Peace may lounge "slurring the days gone by" his "Mammomite mother" may kill her child for money (*AT* I. 33, 45); but in Henley's "Epilogue" England itself "hangs," "in a dream / Of money and love and sport," "at the paps / Of well-being, and so / Goes fattening, mellowing, dozing, rotting down / Into a rich deliquium of decay" (*WEH* 240–41). "War, the Red Angel" alone can save such a nation (241).

Henley actively promoted the association of his own vein of violent abstract nation-state erotics with Hemans, Kipling, Tennyson, and other Victorian poets well into the twentieth century. His anthology, *Lyra*

Heroica: A Book of Verse for Boys (1891) – which opens with a notorious warmongering passage from *Maud* – was reprinted as late as 1927; it may stand for a whole series of such works, whose underlying anxieties about what Anita Hemphill McCormick terms "manliness in decline" may have helped shape many twentieth-century readers' first, disturbing, exposure to poetry.[54]

VII

As the century's end brought forth a surge of vehement, often abstract, imperial patriotic poetry, it also gave rise to what Thomas Hardy termed "works that breathe a more quiet and philosophic spirit."[55] Of these, Hardy's own sequence of "War Poems" (1899–1901) counts among the best known. In a career whose writing on issues of war and nation stretches from early Wessex Poems on the Napoleonic Wars (such as "Valenciennes" and "Leipzig" [both 1898]) through the Napoleonic epic *The Dynasts* (1904–08), to the post-First World War weariness of "Christmas: 1924," "War Poems" comprise what Kathryn R. King and William W. Morgan have called Hardy's "first significant public poems."[56] Both through their deliberately – even aggressively – modest tone and their evocation of speakers' relationships to tangible, sensuously experienced national landscapes, his "War Poems" counter the bombast of "Greater England" jingoism.

"How long, O striving Teutons, Slavs, and Gaels, / Must your wroth reasoning trade on lives like these, / That are as puppets in a playing hand?" (*TH* 8–10). When shall "patriotism, grown Godlike, scorn to stand / Bondslave to realms, but circle earth and seas?" (13–14). These questions, whose "seeming words" (7) are beaten out by the "late long tramp of mounting men" (6) in "Departure," echo through Hardy's poetic sequence. Still "Bondslave to realms" (14), the state patriotism of "War Poems" inspires military sacrifices that bear only the most ironic or equivocal relations to glory.

Located, through a parenthetical dateline, on the "Southampton Docks: October 1899," the sonnet "Embarcation" opens the roughly chronological sequence by rehearsing – and reversing – conventional patriotic glorification of Britain's military past:

> Here, where Vespasian's legions struck the sands,
> And Cerdic with his Saxons entered in,
> And Henry's army leapt afloat to win
> Convincing triumphs over neighbour lands,

Vaster battalions press for further strands,
To argue in the selfsame bloody mode
Which this late age of thought, and pact, and code,
Still fails to mend. (*TH* 1–8)

England's own shore thus stands as a reminder not only of Roman and Saxon invasions but also of "Convincing triumphs" that led England to ultimate defeat (in this case, the 1415 Battle of Agincourt). To embark on a war is merely to "argue in the selfsame bloody mode" that has betrayed centuries of Britons and their opponents alike; and as succeeding poems emphasize, patriotic song is part of that mode. In "The Colonel's Soliloquy," an aging soldier embarks to the tune of "The Girl I've Left behind Me" (21), painfully aware that the no longer resilient "girl" he leaves behind is "a grandmother" (35). In "The Going of the Battery," which is subtitled "Wives' Lament," Hardy offers a bleak counterpoint to "The Charge of the Light Brigade": "Rain came down drenchingly; but we unblenchingly / Trudged on beside them through mirk and through mire" (*TH* 5–6). At first grimly echoing both the heroic progress and the meter of Tennyson's poem, Hardy's patriotic heroines falter on the words "All we loved" (19); and though they resume Tennyson's martial cadences only a few lines later, the lapse underscores the vulnerability of these women's courage.

As the sequence progresses, patriotic domestication of graves, too, takes on newly somber meanings. "A Christmas Ghost-Story," whose title conjures up visions of cozy holiday hearths, presents a "mouldering soldier" (*TH* 2), his "gray bones" "Awry and doubled up" (3) in a South African grave, while his exiled and "puzzled phantom" (4) moans nightly to "clear Canopus": "I would know / By whom and when the All-Earth-Gladdening Law / Of Peace, brought in by that Man Crucified, / Was ruled to be inept, and set aside?" (5–8). The next poem, "Drummer Hodge," begins: "They throw in Drummer Hodge to rest, / Uncoffined – just as found" (*TH* 1–2). Who are "they"? We do not know; and indeed, of the dead soldier himself, we know only his position as a drummer and his origins as a rural laborer – a generic "Hodge." What we can be sure, however, is that no reverent patriot will seek out this nameless man's unmarked grave on a "kopje-crest" (3). Far from his "Wessex home" (8), he must sink under "Strange stars" (12) into an alien landscape whose "meaning" (9) he "never knew" (7). Early in the First World War, Rupert Brooke's "The Soldier" (1914) would still be able to call upon Hemans's and Kipling's consolations: "If I should die, think only this of me, / That there's some corner of a foreign field, / That is for ever England."[57] With "Drummer Hodge," however, Hardy sounded the knell of a poetic tradition. It only remained for First World War poets such as Siegfried Sassoon or Wilfred Owen to strike the death blows.

Though many aspects of Victorian patriotic poetry fell (and were pushed) into discredit during and after the First World War, as Hardy's later poems bitterly attest, the glorification of war did not. The final poem of Hardy's sequence, "The Sick Battle-God" has thus been understandably criticized for its optimistic assertion that the "Battle-god is god no more" (*TH* 44). Hardy's poetry stands, nonetheless, as an impressive patriotic refusal to invoke that god's "fearsome aid" through "rune and rhyme" (8). Late in the sequence, as the lone meditative speaker of "The Souls of the Slain" watches over the Bill of Portland, the moth-like spirits of soldiers arrive in direct flight from South Africa, hoping to "feast" on their "fame" (36). Met by a "senior soul-flame" (32), they learn that their "kin linger less" (39) on their "glory and war-mightiness" (40) than on their "Deeds of home" (63). Those souls "whose record was lovely and true" (82) rejoice a "thousand times more" (78) in "hearts" that have kept them "green for old kindness" (77) than in military glory; they speed home. The others, who had counted on heroism in battle to outshine domestic "bitter traditions" (83), fly seaward – and plunge "to the fathomless regions / Of myriads forgot" (89–90).

In "The Souls of the Slain," the line between "lovely" and "bitter" bonds to one's homeland emerges clearly. Within Victorian patriotic poetry as a whole, however, expressions of love for the imagined community of Britain or "Greater Britain" cannot help but resonate with cries for oppressive "unity" or praise of brutal militarism, any more than they can avoid echoing laments of national – and personal – loss, division, or exile. Chesterton's and Woolf's generation may thus have been both right and wrong in its attempts to discredit such writing. At present, Victorian patriotic fervor in its diverse forms deserves closer scrutiny, not least because – even in its most reactionary moments – it strives so openly to unite developing conceptions of subjective identity, at its most intimate, private, and inescapable, with shifting definitions of the powers and duties of public political subjects. Crucial in nineteenth-century terms, that project still speaks to the readers of nations whose own "bitter" and "lovely" imagined communities remain under dispute.

NOTES

Thanks to Sandy Hughes for her assistance in locating sources for this chapter.
1 Hugh Walker, *The Greater Victorian Poets* (London: Swan Sonnenschein, 1895), 134.
2 Hugh Walker, *The Literature of the Victorian Era* (Cambridge: Cambridge

University Press, 1910), 409. Walker quotes Tennyson, *In Memoriam*, CIX, 16 and CXXVII, 7.

3 G.K. Chesterton, *The Victorian Age in Literature* (1913; London: Thornton Butterworth, 1931), 163.

4 Virginia Woolf, *To the Lighthouse* (New York: Harcourt Brace, 1955), 28–30. The line is actually "Boldly they rode."

5 Virginia Woolf, *Three Guineas* (New York: Harcourt Brace, 1938), 142, 109.

6 Eric Hobsbawm, *The Age of Empire, 1875–1914* (New York: Vintage, 1987), 143.

7 [Anonymous,] "The Patriot's Grave," *The Northern Star*, 9 September 1843, reprinted in *An Anthology of Chartist Poetry*, ed. Peter Scheckner (London: Associated University Presses, 1989), 72.

8 Ebenezer Jones, "A Coming Cry," in Jones, *Studies of Sensation and Event; Poems* (London: Charles Fox, 1843), 164–66.

9 Hugh Cunningham, "The Language of Patriotism, 1750–1914," *History Workshop Journal* 12 (1981), 27.

10 Benedict Anderson, *Imagined Communities: Reflections on the Origin and Spread of Nationalism*, revised edition (London: Verso, 1991).

11 Henry Fothergill Chorley, *Memorials of Mrs. Hemans*, 2 vols. (London: Saunders and Otley, 1836), II, 213.

12 Felicia Hemans, "Letter" [to her "dearest aunt"], 19 December 1808, in Chorley, *Memorials of Mrs Hemans*, I, 25.

13 Georg Wilhelm Friedrich Hegel, *Phänomenologie des Geistes*, ed. Wolfgang Bonsiepen and Reinhard Heede, *Gesammelte Werke*, 21 vols. (Hamburg: Meiner, 1990), IX, 258–59; translated by Tricia Lootens in "Hemans and Home: Victorianism, Feminine 'Internal Enemies,' and the Domestication of National Identity," *PMLA* 109 (1994), 242.

14 Susan J. Wolfson, "'Domestic Affections' and 'The Spear of Minerva': Felicia Hemans and the Dilemma of Gender," in *Re-Visioning Romanticism*, ed. Carol Shiner Wilson and Joel Haefner (Philadelphia, PA: University of Pennsylvania Press, 1994), 143.

15 Anne K. Mellor, *Romanticism and Gender* (New York: Routledge, 1993), 142.

16 Jerome J. McGann, "Literary History, Romanticism, and Felicia Hemans," in *Re-Visioning Romanticism*, 220.

17 William Hazlitt, "On Patriotism: A Fragment," in Hazlitt, *The Round Table: Characters of Shakespear's Plays* (1817; New York: Dutton, 1969), 67.

18 Marlon B. Ross, "Romancing the Nation-State: The Poetics of Romantic Nationalism," in *Macropolitics of Nineteenth-Century Literature*, ed. Jonathan Arac and Harriet Ritvo (Philadelphia, PA: University of Pennsylvania Press, 1991), 65.

19 Peter Brooker and Peter Widdowson, "A Literature for England," in *Englishness: Politics and Culture, 1880–1920*, eds. Robert Colls and Philip Dodd (London: Croom Helm, 1986), 116–63.

20 Germaine de Staël, *Corinne, or, Italy*, trans. Avriel Goldberger (New Brunswick, NJ: Rutgers University Press, 1987), 21–22.

21 De Staël, *Corinne*, 416–17.

22 Nanora Sweet, "'Lorenzo's' Liverpool and 'Corinne's' Coppet: The Italianate

Salon and Romantic Education," in *Lessons of Romanticism*, ed. Thomas Pfau and Robert F. Gleckner (Durham, NC: Duke University Press, 1998), 251.

23 Sandra M. Gilbert, "From *Patria* to *Matria*: Elizabeth Barrett Browning's Risorgimento," *PMLA* 99 (1984), 195.

24 See Maura O'Connor, *The Romance of Italy and the Political Imagination* (New York: St. Martin's Press, 1998).

25 Flavia Alaya, "The Ring, the Rescue, and the Risorgimento: Reunifying the Brownings' Italy," *Browning Institute Studies* 6 (1978), 16.

26 John Lucas, *England and Englishness* (London: Hogarth Press, 1990), 188

27 Isobel Armstrong *Victorian Poetry: Poetry, Politics, Poetics* (London: Routledge, 1993), 268–83; Joseph Bristow, "Nation, Class, and Gender: Tennyson's *Maud* and War," in *Tennyson*, ed. Rebecca Stott (Harlow: Addison Wesley Longman, 1997), 127–47; and Herbert F. Tucker, "*Maud* and the Doom of Culture," in *Critical Essays on Alfred Lord Tennyson*, ed. Tucker (New York: G.K. Hall, 1993), 174–94.

28 Linda M. Shires, "*Maud*, Masculinity and Poetic Identity," *Criticism* 29 (1987), 269.

29 Woolf, *Three Guineas*, 107.

30 Brooker and Widdowson, "A Literature for England," 117.

31 Tucker, "*Maud* and the Doom of Culture," 191.

32 Alfred Tennyson, "To F.G. Tuckerman," 1855, in Hallam Tennyson, *Alfred, Lord Tennyson: A Memoir*, 2 vols. (London: Macmillan, 1905), I, 409–10.

33 John Ruskin, "The Roots of Honor," in Ruskin, *Unto this Last*, in *The Works of John Ruskin*, ed. E.T. Cook and Alexander Wedderburn, 39 vols. (London: George Allen, 1903–12), XVII, 36–37.

34 Susan Shatto, *Tennyson's "Maud": A Definitive Edition* (London: Athlone, 1986), 25–27.

35 M. van Wyk Smith, *Drummer Hodge: The Poetry of the Anglo-Boer War (1899–1902)* (Oxford: Clarendon Press, 1978), 12.

36 Arabella and Louisa Shore, *Poems by A. and L.* (London: Grant Richards, 1897), 335.

37 Jerome J. McGann, *The Beauty of Inflections: Literary Investigations in Historical Method and Theory* (Oxford: Clarendon Press, 1985), 187, 190–202.

38 Van Wyk Smith, *Drummer Hodge*, 3–5, 11–14.

39 W.D. Howells, "Review of Rudyard Kipling," *The Seven Seas*, *McClure's Magazine* 8 (1897), 453–55, reprinted in *Kipling: The Critical Heritage*, ed. Roger Lancelyn Green (London: Routledge and Kegan Paul, 1971), 195.

40 George Orwell, "Rudyard Kipling," *Critical Essays* (London: Secker and Warburg, 1961), 112.

41 J.M.S. Tompkins, "The Variety of Kipling," *Kipling Journal* 56 (1983), 23.

42 James Morris, *Pax Brittanica* (New York: Harcourt, 1968), 351.

43 Helmut Papajewski, "Kipling's 'Recessional,'" *Germanisch-Romanische Monatsschrift* 21 (1971), 46–47.

44 Ann Parry, *The Poetry of Rudyard Kipling* (Buckingham: Open University Press, 1992), 79.

45 Parry, *The Poetry of Rudyard Kipling*, 79.

46 Parry, *The Poetry of Rudyard Kipling*, 91–93.

47 Armstrong, *Victorian Poetry*, 482.

48 Francis H. Doyle, "The Red Thread of Honour," in *War Songs of Britain*, ed. Harold E. Butler (London: Archibald Constable, 1903), 193–97.

49 Henry Newbolt, "The Guides at Cabul, 1879," in *Poetry of Empire*, ed. John and Jean Lang (London: T.C. & E.C. Jack, 1910), 346–48.

50 M. Enamul Karim, "Kipling's Personal Vision of India in an Uncollected Article 'Home,'" *Journal of Commonwealth Literature* 8 (1978), 20.

51 Stephen D. Arata, "A Universal Foreignness: Kipling in the Fin-de-Siècle," *ELT* 36 (1993), 11–18.

52 Robert Buchanan, "The Voice of the Hooligan," in *Kipling: the Critical Heritage*, ed. Green, 233–49.

53 Richard LeGallienne, "W.E. Henley," in LeGallienne, *Retrospective Reviews* (London: John Lane, 1896), 98.

54 Anita Hemphill McCormick, "Ancestral Voices Prophesying War: Manliness in Decline in Henley's *Lyra Heroica*," *Nineteenth-Century Contexts* 13 (1989), 211–25.

55 Thomas Hardy, *The Life and Work of Thomas Hardy*, ed. Michael Millgate (Athens, GA: University of Georgia Press, 1985), 334, cited in Kathryn R. King and William W. Morgan, "Hardy and the Boer War: The Public Poet in Spite of Himself," *Victorian Poetry* 17 (1979), 70.

56 King and Morgan, "Hardy and the Boer War," 71.

57 Rupert Brooke, "The Soldier," in Brooke, *1914 and Other Poems* (London: Sidgwick and Jackson, 1915), 15.

13

JOHN LUCAS

Voices of authority, voices of subversion: poetry in the late nineteenth century

I

With the publication of *Poems* in 1842 Alfred Tennyson became not only famous but also Poet Laureate in waiting. One poem in particular, "Locksley Hall" (which he wrote in 1837–38), with its eager readiness to imagine a future bright for "the Federation of the world" (*AT* 128), endorsed the new industrial age as one of heady promise. "Let the great world," says his speaker, "spin for ever down the ringing grooves of change" (182). Although, as critics have often pointed out, the image that Tennyson chose to embody this change was inaccurate – train wheels did not run in "grooves" – the ardor with which he looked to the beaconing distance seemed very much of a piece with the spirit of the age. As Thomas Carlyle might well have observed, such ardor was only too plainly – and betrayingly – a "sign of the times."[1]

Almost half a century later in 1886, the aged Tennyson, who had been Poet Laureate since 1850, decided to write a progress report on that early optimistic vision. Had the intervening years lived up to his expectations? The short answer is no. "Locksley Hall Sixty Years After" comments bleakly on the state of the nation as it appeared to Tennyson in the mid-1880s. The future that once flared so vigorously has turned into an ashy present. Thanks to the malign influence of France, mass democracy has become a terrible threat to order and to peace: "France had shown a light to all men, preached a Gospel, all men's good; / Celtic Demos rose a Demon, shrieked and slaked the light with blood" (89–90). And where in 1842 he heralded "the Parliament of man" (128), imminent anarchy looms: "madness . . . massacre . . . Jacobinism and Jacquerie" (157) abound because men, "yelling with the yelling street," threaten to "Set the feet above the brain and swear the brain is in the feet" (135–36). In all likelihood, this "yelling" mob will "Break the State, the Church, the Throne, and roll their ruins down the slope" (138). Celtic Demos,

Jacobinism, Jacquerie: the names are meant to chill the blood. The Irish, those unruly Celts, were becoming increasingly violent in their demands for Home Rule. (In 1882 the so-called Phoenix Park murders occurred in Dublin where the Secretary to Ireland Lord Frederick Cavendish and the Under-Secretary T.H. Burke were assassinated by militants.) Jacobins were the most radical element of the French Revolution of 1789, and "Jacquerie" was the term given to French peasants who rebelled against the nobility in 1358. In 1886 rebellion was again in the air, spread by the modern contagion of city life (although agricultural depression was also a feature of the decade).

The city in particular not only permits but also makes an inescapable hell-on-earth. In a similar vein, science – which in "Locksley Hall" looked as if it was the promised redeemer – has turned into the false Messiah:

> Is it well that while we range with Science, glorying in the Time,
> City children soak and blacken soul and sense in city slime?

> There among the glooming alleys Progress halts on palsied feet,
> Crime and hunger cast our maidens by the thousand on the street.

> There the Master scrimps his haggard sempstress of her daily bread,
> There a single sordid attic holds the living and the dead.

> There the smouldering fire of fever creeps across the rotted floor,
> And the crowded couch of incest in the warrens of the poor.   (217–24)

Tennyson's cast of mind, which is essentially that of a fatalistic Tory, makes sure that his preference is for country ways: "Plowmen, Shepherds, have I found, and more than once, and still could find, / Sons of God, and kings of men in utter nobleness of mind" (121–22). It is equally inevitable that he should regard contemporary mores revealed in the estates of art and letters with abhorrence:

> Authors – essayist, atheist, novelist, realist, rhymester, play your part,
> Paint the mortal shame of nature with the living hues of Art.

> Rip your brothers' vices open, strip your own foul passion bare;
> Down with Reticence, down with Reverence – forward – naked – let them stare.

> Feed the budding rose of boyhood with the drainage of your sewer;
> Send the drain into the fountain, lest the stream should issue pure.

> Set the maiden fancies wallowing in the trough of Zolaism, –
> Forward, forward, ay and backward, downward too into the abysm.
>
>   (139–46)

This attack on what would soon become known as "the Decadence" might on the face of it seem more of the moment than Tennyson's discovery of urban misery. Thomas Hood's "Song of the Shirt," that famously pathetic cry of protest on behalf of exploited sempstresses, had after all been published in the Christmas 1843 number of *Punch*. Throughout the middle years of the century, writers had been preoccupied to the point of obsession with the horrors of urban life. One thinks of the start of Charles Dickens's *Bleak House* (1853–53) where choking "[s]moke lowering down from chimney-pots, making a soft black drizzle" produces "a general infection of ill-temper" in the heaving crowds of London.[2] But Tennyson's tactic is from his point of view sound enough. In a society where so many human beings are brutalized, how can any responsible person want "Demos" to take control? For "Demos" is precisely composed of individuals who have been brutalized – whether by economic circumstance or the depravities of art.

It is important, therefore, to recall that Tennyson was writing "Locksley Hall, Sixty Years After" at a time when other writers were becoming anxious – even appalled – at the prospect of mass democracy turning "the Parliament of Man" into licensed bedlam. George Gissing's novel *Demos* appeared in 1886, as did Henry James's *The Princess Casamassima* and W.H. Mallock's *The Old Order Changes* (the last paying conscious homage to Tennyson in its title). All of these narratives brood over what they see as the stirrings of "Demos": what James, in the 1908 preface to his novel, retrospectively perceived to have been "go[ing] on irreconcilably, subversively, beneath the vast smug surface" of English social life.[3] Likewise, these fictions take seriously the threat of future anarchy: the collapse of "The State, the Church, the Throne." Each narrative responds to actual events of that year when the streets of London were regularly filled with marches led by the unemployed – and by campaigners agitating for economic and political reform.

Throughout the 1870s and 1880s, moreover, innovative forms of art, fiction, and poetry were often subject to censure. In 1885, for example, George Moore produced his pamphlet *Literature at Nurse, or Circulating Morals* to protest the suppression of his Zolaesque novel, *A Mummer's Wife* (1885), after Mudie's circulating library banned it. Moore, who had spent some time in Paris, became convinced that the hope for the future of fiction lay in Émile Zola's naturalist narratives. In his preface to *Thérèse Raquin* (1867), Zola defined his modern fictional method as one in which "l'analyse scientifique" ('scientific analysis') produced "pièces d'anatomie nues et vivante" ('bare, live anatomical pieces').[4] This scientific approach struck his detractors as an excuse for laying bare sordid aspects of human behavior, particularly sexual behavior. Behind this controversy there swells the brouhaha first heard in Robert Buchanan's denunciation of Dante Gabriel Rossetti as the leader of a so-called "Fleshly School of Poetry" in

1871. Buchanan's condemnation of what he termed Rossetti's offensive "fleshly" poetry was followed some six years later by John Ruskin's accusation that the American painter James McNeill Whistler was "throwing a point of paint in the public's face."[5] (Whistler sued for libel, receiving the belittling sum of a farthing's damages.) The assault on contentious works of art continued in Mallock's "A Familiar Colloquy," which the *Nineteenth Century* published in 1878. In this absurd though nasty piece, Mallock goes on the attack against French writer Théophile Gautier's *Mademoiselle de Maupin* (1835), requiring one of the speakers in this "colloquy" to call the novel – notorious for its depiction of lesbian desire – "the foulest and filthiest book that ever man put pen to. It is the glorification of nameless and shameless vice." In response, another of Mallock's interlocutors remarks that her brother "horsewhipped a man" because he lent it to her sister. [6] Such fierce criticism makes it plain that "Locksley Hall Sixty Years After" is very much the poem of a Laureate. It is a poem that addresses the state of the nation.

II

Tennyson died in 1892. Who was to succeed him as Poet Laureate? The question was often enough asked in the following years because, contrary to custom, this post remained vacant until New Year's Day, 1896, when it was announced that his successor was to be Alfred Austin. The prolonged agonizing about this choice of Laureate has been well documented by Norton B. Crowell.[7] There is no need for a lengthy discussion of Austin's poetry. It was execrable. But, then, whoever made a case for earlier Laureates like Laurence Eusden (1688–1730), say, or Henry Pye (1745–1813)? During the eighteenth century the Laureateship was not of much concern. During the nineteenth century, however, it most certainly was. We need, therefore, to ask why Austin was allowed to succeed to a post that Tennyson had filled with such colossal distinction.

The very fact that Tennyson made the Laureateship so visible, giving it real luster, created an obvious difficulty. Who next to choose? His great contemporaries were all dead. Matthew Arnold passed away in 1888. In the following year, Robert Browning died (although, since he retained his Republicanism to the last, his death probably came as a relief to the appointees). And what about George Meredith, the poet whose controversial volume *Modern Love and Other Poems* (in which the title poem explores a disintegrating marriage) established his reputation in 1862? He was still alive and still publishing but not a poet to compare with Tennyson. Who, then, could measure up to Tennyson's stature? There were, as it happened, two poets whose claims as poets were strong. Other considerations, however, made them unthinkable.

According to Edmund Gosse, it was "reported that Queen Victoria, discussing the matter" of Tennyson's successor with Gladstone, "said, 'I am told that Mr. Swinburne is the best poet of my dominions.'"[8] So he was. Yet Swinburne was hardly likely to find favor as a candidate for the vacant post. He was a known Republican, an atheist, and his early *Poems and Ballads* (1866), which had brought him to fame, had also by their sexual transgressiveness earned him lasting notoriety. What, then, of William Morris as a suitable candidate? By the time of Tennyson's death Morris had come to be seen as a poet of genuine stature. But he was also a proclaimed Marxist and active in support of exactly those forces that for Tennyson posed threats to "the State, the Church, the Throne."

Whether Tennyson had Morris in his sights when he wrote "Locksley Hall Sixty Years After" I rather doubt. But he probably intended his readers to think of Swinburne as implicated in that list of "Authors – essayist, atheist, novelist, realist, rhymester" who would play their part in painting "the mortal shame of nature with the living hues of Art." Indeed, by paying tribute to the abilities of those poets whom he detests – for how else can we read the phrase "living hues of Art"? – Tennyson is candidly admitting that it is their artistic powers that make them so dangerous. It scarcely matters whether he is overestimating the political and social influence of such powers. The crucial point is Tennyson's determination to block the way to the Laureateship of those authors whom he has in mind. We must then reflect on why, since only a "rhymester" could become Laureate, Swinburne must surely have been the writer with whom Tennyson was most concerned. We might even read Tennyson's list of "Authors" as quite specifically identifying Swinburne: he was, after all, an essayist and novelist as well as poet.[9]

"Locksley Hall Sixty Years After" was written in the months that followed the unlooked-for death of Tennyson's son, Lionel, on 25 April 1886. Robert Bernard Martin quotes Tennyson's disclaimer that "*there is not one touch of biography*" in the poem "*from beginning to end.*" But Martin rightly adds: "the assertion is surely disingenuous, for the emotions are biographically his even if the events of the poem are not."[10] These emotions include not only the facts of aging and death but also Tennyson's scornful attitude to what Charles Tennyson calls the poet's "fierce disillusion" with the age. It seemed, he says, "a deliberate repudiation of all the social and economic progress of the last half-century. Mr Gladstone felt it deeply and took up the challenge with an elaborately deferential article in *The Nineteenth Century* for January, 1887."[11] Martin suggests that Gladstone may have been prompted to write the article because he saw in the poem's attack on the age "in part an attack on himself." Consequently, "the article becomes an externalization of the usually unspoken antagonism that the two men felt" (560).

This antagonism is well documented. Yet it was Gladstone who in 1884 had offered Tennyson his peerage. Given the differences between them the gesture can be read as one of great magnanimity. But it can also be interpreted in a more ambiguous way: since you have your peerage, you can give up the Laureateship. Martin hints that this was a possible motive behind Gladstone's offer:

> On the occasion of great anniversaries and honours, old men in the public eye are showered with good wishes, as Tennyson had been, but in between them there is occasionally a feeling that they have been around too long. As Gladstone had once had to listen to Tennyson bringing the Queen's proposal for his retirement from public life, now Tennyson in his turn had to put up with the younger poets who felt that he had long since written his best and that there was little more to expect of him. Lewis Morris, who had wanted to speak for the other poets of England in congratulating Tennyson on his peerage, now said that it was the duty of the "Commander in Chief" to step down in favour of the "subaltern," as Morris had his eye on the post of Laureate, regarding himself as Tennyson's natural heir even if no one else did so. When Morris spread rumours that Tennyson was on the verge of retirement, Hallam wrote to Theodore Watts to assure him that his father had "not really the slightest intention of resigning until he feels that he can no longer do the work. It was by the personal wish of the Prince Consort & the Queen that he accepted the Laureateship: & he has had too much from HM, to think of resigning except into her own hands & with her full concurrence." As a snub to Morris's hopes he added that it was probable that the Laureateship would be abolished on the death of Tennyson. (561)

Although Martin does not give chapter and verse for his suspicions that the Welsh poet Lewis Morris was maneuvering to succeed to the Laureateship Morris assumed would soon be vacant, there seems no reason to doubt that younger contemporaries were indeed jostling to knock the aged eagle from his perch. And Lewis Morris by no means lacked supporters. When his *Ode of Life* appeared in 1880, the left-leaning *Westminster Review* claimed that it ought to prove the most popular of Morris's works: "People flock to hear Mr Stopford Brooke, or Dean Stanley, or the Bishop of Manchester preach, but in this book they will hear a voice more eloquent than theirs, dealing with the most important subjects that can ever occupy the thoughts of man."[12] Similarly, the *Nineteenth Century* praised "the high devout purpose and wide human sympathy [that] ennoble all the writer's work."[13]

Both the *Westminster Review* and *Nineteenth Century* are weighty authorities. Besides, the terms in which these noted journals praise Morris make it clear why Morris would have thought himself a suitable candidate for the Laureateship. Morris, it will be evident, was a public poet, one who took on the big subjects – life, death, and most points in between – and who came up with unexceptional answers to problems preoccupying late-nineteenth-century thought. He was basically High Church, monarchist, and Tory. His credentials for the post of Laureate were therefore impeccable. True, he was an uninspiring poet but that need not have counted against him. It certainly did not count against Austin.

Nor would it have counted against William Watson, another frontrunner and one who, like Morris, was eager to become Laureate. Watson came to notice in 1885 when he published a series of sonnets in the *National Review*. According to James G. Nelson, in these sonnets (called "Ver Tenebrosum") Watson "for the first time decks himself in the robes of the poet-prophet and lashes out at his country's unjust actions in the Soudan and against its weak, indecisive response to Russia's hostile moves in Afghanistan."[14] As an upholder of Tory values, the *National Review* would have been pleased with a sonnet on the Liberal Gladstone – betrayer of Khartoum and General Gordon, or so right-wing opinion had it – that begins:

> A skilful leech, so long as we were whole:
> Who scann'd the nation's every outward part
> But ah! misheard the beating of its heart.
> Sire of huge sorrows, yet erect of soul.
> Swift rider with calamity for goal,
> Who, overtasking his equestrian art,
> Unstall'd a steed full willing for the start,
> But wondrous hard to curb or to control.[15]

We have seen how Gladstone was drawn into replying to "Locksley Hall Sixty Years Later." But as far as I know he kept silent about Watson's public rebuke. Attacks on Gladstone's perfectly sensible policy over the Sudan were widespread. If Gladstone read Watson's poem, he may have felt that the phrase stating that he was "erect of soul" made up for the rest. More likely, as an accomplished man of letters, Gladstone would have felt that he had not much to fear from someone who began by describing him as a leech with powers of farsightedness, then turned him into a horseman aiming for calamity who ended up by missing it. (Surely this was the opposite of what Watson intended to say.) Nelson honorably quotes W.B. Yeats's dismissal of Watson's sonnets as fatally dependent on Milton and Wordsworth and as "in no way new or personal," in hope of rebutting the charge (51).[16] "Watson was a fiercely patriotic man," Nelson says, who "demanded the highest conduct of his nation" (51). Maybe. But it is difficult to avoid the feeling that Watson's inept sonnets are written with an eye to the main chance. He is putting himself on show as Tory, patriot, and by implication monarchist. (By 1885, Queen Victoria's dislike of Gladstone was common knowledge, and any threat to the empire was anathema to her.) Watson is therefore to be seen as the acceptable face of poetry.

The face was on show again in 1890. In that year Watson published his edition of Austin's *English Lyrics*. His preface to that volume makes plain his intention to put considerable distance between himself and other contemporary poets:

> Unless immemorial principles of right taste and judgment are to be annulled, life, substance, reason, and reality, with a just balance of sense and sound, are what future generations will look for in our singers. And surely if poetry is not to sink altogether under the lethargy of an emasculate euphuism, and finally to die surfeited with unwholesome sweetmeats, crushed under a load of redundant ornament, and smothered in artificial rose-leaves, the strenuous and virile temper which animates this volume must come to be more and more the temper of English song?[17]

The originator of this "emasculate euphuism" – its unmanly rhetoric – is apparently the Romantic radical Percy Bysshe Shelley, deceased for over sixty years. Among Shelley's unnatural progeny are, of course, Swinburne and his followers: Oscar Wilde, Arthur Symons, Ernest Dowson, and other writers whose names, rightly or wrongly, would be associated with "the Decadence" represented in the short-lived but controversial *Yellow Book* (1894–97). It is well known that, with the arrest of Wilde in April 1895, Watson – together with other reactionary authors – sent a telegram to John Lane (the publisher of the *Yellow Book),* who was then in New York City. The telegram urged Lane to dismiss Aubrey Beardsley, notorious for his sexually provocative illustrations, from his post as the journal's art editor. Watson, according to Nelson, "like so many Victorians, had merely tolerated the *fin-de-siècle* artists and poseurs, and had only waited for the right moment to act" (111). But Watson's very public behavior would have been further evidence of his acceptability to the powers-that-were, and it was surely in this spirit that he meant to be taken. The announcement of Alfred Austin as Poet Laureate must therefore have hurt.

Crowell takes for granted the Marquess of Salisbury's cynicism in appointing Austin. Apparently, Prime Minister Salisbury told Sir Algernon West that Austin was given the Laureateship "[f]or the best possible reason, because he wanted it" (*Alfred Austin*, 157). But so did Lewis Morris, so did Watson, and for that matter so did Sir Edwin Arnold, whose *The Light of*

Asia was for a time widely admired after its publication in 1879. Unfortunately for Edwin Arnold, as Crowell says, the poem was felt "in orthodox circles, to be too sympathetic toward Buddhism" (148). More importantly, neither he nor the other possible candidates had given such service to the Tory party as had Austin, who founded the *National Review* and remained generally untiring in what Crowell calls his "sycophantic bootlicking" (155). Crowell quotes Meredith's observation that "it will suit little Alfred to hymn the babies of the house of Hanover" (155).[18] The soubriquet stuck. The Laureateship had passed from Alfred the Great to Alfred the Little.

III

So far we have seen that at the end of the nineteenth century poetry was important to many people in England because its practitioners were expected to uphold orthodox views. The idea of "England" is crucial here. The other constituent parts of the United Kingdom do not come into this particular concept of nation. Although Nick Russel gives the subtitle "Britain's Laureates" to his study *Poets by Appointment*, he begins his introduction by remarking: "Before Charles II's time a number of English kings had singled out the occasional contemporary poet for royal favours" (1). The selection of Laureates had at first been by English kings, and later by Lord Chamberlains and Prime Ministers, officials of state who saw themselves speaking for England rather than for the United Kingdom as a whole. Ramsay MacDonald, the first Labour Prime Minister in a position to appoint a Laureate, chose John Masefield in 1930. Russel suggests that MacDonald's preferred choice was A.E. Housman (author of *A Shropshire Lad* [1896]), while King George V plumped for the jingoistic Rudyard Kipling (who made his name as a poet with *Barrack-Room Ballads* [1892]), although there was good reason to believe that each writer would have declined the position (7). Masefield was an acceptable compromise. The Scottish MacDonald would never have thought of offering the post to a fellow Scotsman. As to a sister Scotswoman or, for that matter, an Englishwoman, it remained unthinkable.

At the end of the nineteenth century, when poetry was a national issue, the appointment of the Laureate mattered far more than ever before. That poetry was an issue for England becomes clear as soon as we consider how the state honored certain poets – Sir Lewis Morris, Sir Edwin Arnold, above all Lord Tennyson (Watson received his knighthood in 1917) – when for novelists such public recognition was out of the question. Imagine Lord Dickens or Sir Thomas Hardy. Whoever spoke for poetry in an official capacity had obviously to speak for ideologically official England: Anglican, monarchical, and evidently Tory, or at least acquiescent and deferential to the imperialism that underpinned official England.

That Swinburne and William Morris were ruled out of consideration is not, therefore, to be wondered at. For official England felt itself under threat from "Demos." This is why Watson and his reactionary contemporaries made such great play of both their patriotism and their "strenuous and virile" muse. If Republicanism appeared a French disease, so too did those tendencies that threaten all that is manly: Gautier, Zola, and other "unwholesome sweetmeats." This, without question, is the language of anti-Decadence, of an especially repellent strain of posturing that finds expression in the imperialist 1890s poetry of W.E. Henley and Sir Henry Newbolt[19] and then feeds into much patriotic verse written at the outbreak of the Great War in 1914. I do not intend to say more about this development beyond remarking that it provides one more manifestation of the place that poetry occupied in the public eye. At this time, the poetry favored by the state operates as a form of official utterance for imperialist "healthy" England, and the major enemy within is precisely that "Decadent," urban, and degenerative spirit – as its opponents were prompt to label it – about which I now want to comment.

We have seen how Watson thought that Shelley started the rot. And certainly Shelley, atheist, Republican, ardent believer in sexual equality, came to be regarded in the later years of the nineteenth century as a dangerous force. Hence Matthew Arnold's famous recoil from the account of Shelley's life provided by Edward Dowden in 1886.[20] Anyone familiar with this period recalls Arnold's shocked expostulation, "What a set! What a world."[21] Fewer perhaps remember that this essay is so taken up with that "set" and that "world" that he is left at the very end to remark: "Of his poetry I have not space now to speak" (XI, 327). The implication, however, is unmistakable. Given the life, what hope for the art?

Arnold's unstated belief in the inextricable connection between poet and work was upheld by many nineteenth-century male writers, perhaps most memorably by Carlyle where he comments that Goethe's poetry expressed "no separate faculty, no mental handicraft; but the voice of the whole harmonious manhood." "[N]ay," Carlyle added, "it is the very harmony, the living and life-giving harmony of that rich manhood which forms his poetry" ("Goethe" [1828], XXVI, 208). By the time Arnold pronounced judgment on Shelley's life, harmonious manhood had come to seem the last thing that more recent poets were interested in upholding. Hence, perhaps, Arnold's tone of studied sorrow. Very probably, Arnold lamented how Shelley's "set" betrayed the cherished values of "sweetness and light" that Arnold associated with the "faith and tradition of Oxford." Oxford's "beauty and sweetness," he claimed, were "essential characteristics of a complete human perfection."[22] As R.H. Super remarks: "There was much about Shelley's life . . . that was close to Arnold." Arnold's father "went up to Oxford as an undergraduate the year after Shelley." Moreover, the "senior dons at Oriel [College] when Arnold was a young member of Common Room in the late forties were Shelley's contemporaries. And so Arnold turned with some eagerness" to Dowden's biography.[23]

Swinburne, too, was an Oxford poet, as was his devotee Wilde, who studied at Magdalen College in the years following the immediate stir caused by Robert Buchanan's 1871 attack on Rossetti, Swinburne, and their circle. This circle, according to Buchanan, formed "a solemn league and covenant to extol fleshliness as the distinct and supreme end of poetic and pictorial art."[24] Buchanan's article, which first appeared in the *Contemporary Review*, was expanded into a pamphlet the following year. Rossetti replied to Buchanan, as did Swinburne.[25] Buchanan came back at Swinburne,[26] and then in 1875 a book-length poem called *Jonas Fisher* was published anonymously. Swinburne attributed this crude caricature of the fleshly school to Buchanan, although the author was in fact James Carnegie. In his response to what he assumed was Buchanan's work, Swinburne called Buchanan the "'multifaced' idyllist of the gutter,"[27] and an enraged Buchanan sued Swinburne for £5,000 damages. Buchanan won the case, although he had to make do with only £150 as well as much adverse publicity.

Richard Ellmann does not mention the trial in his definitive biography of Wilde. This omission is odd because Wilde must have seen the entire episode as proof positive that true art was the enemy of bourgeois morality. It was, of course, the first of those public confrontations that might be called art versus the public – Whistler versus Ruskin, George Moore versus Mudie's – that would culminate in Wilde's own trials twenty years later. It is not that in 1875 Wilde could have anticipated this outcome. But as a confirmed admirer of both Swinburne's *Poems and Ballads* and *Songs Before Sunrise* (1871), he undoubtedly regarded the poet's opponents as precisely those advocates of conventionality that it was the artist's duty to scorn in the sacred cause of aestheticism.[28] Nor was aestheticism alone the issue. If *Poems and Ballads* celebrates what John Morley in 1866 condemned as "libidinous song,"[29] *Songs Before Sunrise* just as ardently extols both atheism and Republicanism. "Hymn of Man," for example, announces exultantly: "Thou art smitten, thou God, thou art smitten; thy death is upon thee, O Lord. / And the love-song of earth as thou diest resounds through the winds of her wings – / Glory to Man in the highest! for Man is the master of things" (*ACS* II, 104). And in "A Marching Song"

Swinburne contentiously describes "royalties rust-eaten" as "fanged meridian vermin" and "Blind flesh-flies" (*ACS* II, 154–55).

The year 1871, the year when *Songs Before Sunrise* appeared, was the year of the Paris Commune and its vicious suppression. It was also the year when Gerard Manley Hopkins sent Robert Bridges his famous "red" letter, in which he told Bridges that his awareness of the plight of so many people, and of their inevitably violent response to material inequality, had made him a Communist.[30] It may well have been in that same year that another Oxford undergraduate, W.H. Mallock, encountered Swinburne. In his *Memoirs of Life and Literature*, Mallock recalls the impact that *Poems and Ballads* made on him and his contemporaries in 1866. Mallock was then still a pupil at a private school. Four years later he began life as a student at Oxford and soon afterward met Swinburne in Benjamin Jowett's rooms at Balliol College. Jowett, whom Mallock never really liked, was at that time probably the most famous of Oxford's dons: a classical scholar, a leading light in the Broad Church, and an inveterate university schemer. But he tolerated Swinburne. And here, therefore, Mallock first met "the veritable genius who had made the English language a new instrument of passion." An increasingly drunk Swinburne, so Mallock recalls, recited among much else some lines by Sydney Dobell, about a girl bathing: "She with her body bright sprinkles the waters white, / Which flee from her fair form and flee in vain." Swinburne, says Mallock, was "almost shouting these words when another sound became audible – that of an opening door, followed by Jowett's voice, which said in high-pitched syllables: "You'd both better go to bed now."[31]

A few days later Mallock met Swinburne again, this time at a luncheon party hosted by a group of the poet's undergraduate admirers:

[Swinburne,] as I presently gathered, was about to begin an account of an historical drama by himself, which existed in his memory only – a sort of parody of what Victor Hugo might have written had he dramatized English events at the opening of the reign of Queen Victoria. The first act, he said, showed England on the verge of a revolution, which was due to the frightful orgies of the Queen at "Buckingham's Palace." The Queen, with unblushing effrontery, had taken to herself a lover, in the person of Lord John Russell, who had for his rival "Sir Peel" . . . In a later act it appeared that the Queen and Lord John Russell had between them given the world a daughter, who, having been left to her own devices, or, in other words, to the streets, reappears as "Miss Kitty," and is accorded some respectable rank. Under these conditions she becomes the object of much princely devotion; but the moral hypocrisy of England has branded her as a public scandal. With regard to her so-called depravities nobody entertains a doubt, but one princely admirer, of broader mind than the rest, declares that in spite of these she is really the embodiment of everything that is divine in woman. "She may," he says, "have done everything which might have made a Messalina blush, but whenever she looked at the sky, she murmured "God," and whenever she looked at a flower she murmured "mother."   (74–76)

Not long after these meetings, Mallock produced his first published work, *Everyman His Own Poet, or The Inspired Singer's Recipe Book*, in which would-be poets are told how to concoct poems in the manner of contemporary masters. The recipe for making an epic poem by Tennyson recommends taking "one blameless prig": "Set him upright in the middle of a round table, and place beside him a beautiful wife, who cannot abide prigs. Add to these, one marred goodly man; and tie the three together in a bundle with a link or two of Destiny."[32] Here Mallock would have expected his readers to recognize a parodic account of the main theme of Tennyson's Arthurian *Idylls of the King* (1859–85). Swinburne comes under the recipe for patriotic poems, though not patriotic fervor for England. Among the ingredients for Swinburne are a love of France and a detestation of the British monarchy.

Mallock's comments elucidate why Arnold, when delivering his lecture on Shelley, would have been well aware that the "beautiful *and ineffectual angel*," as he called him,[33] had in fact been effective (or so it could be held) in recruiting later poets to his multiple causes of atheism, Republicanism, and sexual liberation. The line from Shelley to Swinburne looked to run both clear and strong, and for that reason alone it is not at all surprising that orthodox opinion should have ruled Swinburne out from consideration for the Laureateship.

But there may be more to it than that. By the beginning of the 1890s the so-called "fleshly" school of aestheticism was modulating into "the Decadence," a still greater threat to all that was "strenuous and virile." By then Swinburne was himself *hors de combat*. As Ian Fletcher puts it: "In 1879, by arrangement with his parents, he was taken into care by the critic and poet Theodore Watts-Dunton and the quality of his poetry declined gradually over the next thirty years of staid domesticity."[34] Yet Swinburne's earlier life, notably his frequent drunkenness and regular visits to flagellation brothels, was hardly a secret. Although it would be absurd to suggest that admirers thought the young Swinburne's behavior was necessary to the creation of poetry, it is not absurd to claim that during the 1890s the poet was widely perceived to be a special type of human being.

One version of this type can be found Yeats's famous definition of the "tragic generation" of poets who sacrificed their lives to and for their art. Included in this grouping is Ernest Dowson, whose life of "dissipation and drink" was likely to see him spend the night "upon a sixpenny bed in a doss house."[35] Equally important here was the inebriate Lionel Johnson. "[W]hat he drank," Yeats writes, "would certainly be too much for that of most of the men I knew" (379). Another, equally famous, version is the degenerate. In early 1895 Max Nordau's *Degeneration* was published in England in a translation made from the original German edition of 1892; this study was widely reviewed and debated, particularly Nordau's belief in the inescapable "incapacity for inaction" and "predilection for inane reverie" that characterize "degenerates."[36] Such individuals are the products of industrialized societies, specifically cities. They suffer from decayed brain centers, they therefore lack all discipline, and so they produce the "senseless stammering and babbling of deranged minds": the "convulsions and spasms of exhaustion" (43).

For Nordau, morality in literature is essential to its worth: "The work of art is not its own aim, but it has a specially organic, and a social task. It is subject to the moral law; it must obey this; it has claim to esteem only if it is morally beautiful and ideal" (336). We can get a fairly exact measure of what Nordau has in mind if we put his claims for art's subjection to "moral law" against the dicta that constitute the "Preface" that Wilde added to the second edition of his novel *The Picture of Dorian Gray* (1891). The following statements summarize Wilde's opposing position: "There is no such thing as a moral or an immoral book. Books are well written, or badly written. That is all"; "No artist has ethical sympathies. An ethical sympathy in an artist is an unpardonable mannerism of style"; "Vice and virtue are to the artist materials for an art"; "We can forgive a man for making a useful thing as long as he does not admire it. The only excuse for making a useless thing is that one admires it intensely"; "All art is quite useless."[37] Wilde is very obviously "degeneration" made flesh, which is precisely how Nordau regards him: "[w]hen . . . an Oscar Wilde goes about in 'aesthetic costume' among gazing Philistines, exciting either their ridicule or their wrath, it is no indication of independence of character, but rather from a purely anti-socialistic, ego-maniacal recklessness and hysterical longing to make a sensation" (319). Although Wilde's only known comment on Nordau came after his release from imprisonment – "I quite agree with Dr. Nordau's assertion that all men of genius are insane," he told Chris Healy in September 1897, "but Dr Nordau forgets that all sane people are idiots"[38] – it is difficult to imagine that Nordau's book would have had no impact on those people who, in whatever capacity, attended the trials that eventually sentenced Wilde for committing acts of "gross indecency."

The connection between genius and insanity is age-old. But Nordau felt that he was entitled to emphasize it because of the work of Cesare Lombroso, whose *Genius and Insanity* – first published in Italy as *Genio e*

Follio (1863) and translated into English in 1891 – was, as George L. Mosse observes, "one of the principal sources of inspiration for Degeneration."[39] Mosse usefully remarks that at the heart of Lombroso's argument is the belief that "a man's mode of feeling and his conduct of life are determined by his physical constitution which is reflected in his bodily structure . . . The human being was conceived as a unity – both in himself and with his environment – on the basis of physical, determinate factors" (xx). The qualities that Watson claimed were "strenuous and virile" support the kind of sanity that in Lombroso's view resists all of the factors of modern life that make for degenerate types. Building on Lombroso's work, Nordau insists that degeneration is both a feature and consequence of the modern city – a place whose "atmosphere" is "charged with organic detritus" (35).

IV

But during the later years of the nineteenth century it is of course the city that becomes the focus for much imaginative writing, including poetry. Fletcher makes this point extremely well in his discussion of lyric poets of the century's last two decades: "The idiom is nocturnal . . . shifting colours and lights, ladies of pleasure, music halls, the Café Royal. The influence comes from Whistler and [Walter] Sickert rather than from the French Impressionist painters, but the poets themselves write as if they were all eye, abstaining at their best from moral comment . . . Any attempt to sense the city as a total organism or to search for some transcendental significance is now simply abandoned" (xix–xx). Fletcher rightly wishes to contrast this fin-de-siècle response to the city with that of James Thomson ("B.V."), whose urban epic *The City of Dreadful Night* (1874) voices a more considered, thoroughgoing pessimism – if not nihilism – in the way that it registers alienation as the condition of city living.

That this was indeed how the city felt to many writers, and had indeed done so from the late eighteenth century on, has often been noted. What is new in Thomson's remarkable poem is its sense of the city as fit image of a purposeless universe. In the 1790s, William Blake had radical politics and his own version of God to oppose to the horrors of man-made London. By comparison, Wordsworth had God and the natural world. Dickens, far and away the greatest of all writers about the city, had a sense of community – community endlessly defeated, it is true, but just as endlessly reasserting itself. Yet for Thomson "the bitter old and wrinkled truth" is one "Stripped naked of all vesture that beguiles, / False dreams, false hopes, false masks and modes of youth."[40] Although Thomson represents "The City of

Dreadful Night" as a phantasm, there can be no doubt that it is meant to express a deep truth that, as Fletcher says, "promises no transcendence" because "the alienation of the speaker is final" (xix).

Yet we need to understand that, powerful though Thomson's poem is, it can hardly be taken as in any sense a realistic study. In his 1910 monograph on Thomson, Betram Dobell remarks:

> Thomson does not often attempt the dramatic presentation of the world outside: he prefers rather to study the workings of his own mind than to observe the evolutions of the great drama of humanity. His own thoughts and emotions were almost exclusively the subjects of his writings. Perhaps his works, while gaining in intensity from this cause, lost something in breadth of sympathy and in sanity of outlook upon life.[41]

The last sentence may nod toward the then current orthodoxy about the bonds that tie genius to insanity, but it inevitably owes something to Dobell's unstated awareness of Thomson's life of drug dependency, leading to the belief that his death from alcoholic poisoning was in fact suicide. John Stokes has written instructively of suicide in the 1890s, and although Stokes does not mention him, Thomson can surely be regarded as a forerunner of the Decadent hero, one "exceptionally sensitive to the world around him."[42] Stokes quotes Arthur Symons's remarks on how Dowson possessed a "swift, disastrous and suicidal energy of genius."[43] Stokes also notes how Holbrook Jackson, in his influential *The Eighteen Nineties* (1913), marveled at the many characteristic figures of the 1890s – Aubrey Beardsley, Dowson, and Lionel Johnson, among others – who died young.

Other poets had already died: the "fleshly" Rossetti in 1882, the free-thinking Thomson also in 1882, and the Anglo-Jewish feminist Amy Levy in 1889. All of these writers can be thought of as caught up and perhaps trapped by that developing belief in the artist as wounded by his or her art so that artistic utterance was the display of temperament. Levy's poetry is a good example of this "wounded" temperament. Her London, however, appears not as a city of dreadful night but one of dreadful day. Here, for example, is the opening stanza of "London Poets":

> They trod the streets and squares where now I tread,
> With weary hearts, a little while ago;
> When, thin and grey, the melancholy snow
> Clung to the leafless branches overhead;
> Or when the smoke-veiled sky grew stormy-red
> In autumn; with a re-arisen woe
> Wrestled, what time the passionate spring winds blow. (*AL* 389)

In these lines, there is no Romantic consolation of the seasons – no hope, no anticipation: nothing but the torpor induced by despair. While it would be unfair to suggest that all of Levy's poetry operates in this mode, it is certainly the case that most of it does.

This despondent tone may be a matter of gender. Women probably found London an even more alienating place to be than did most male poets. Ella Hepworth Dixon's *The Story of a Modern Woman* (1894), for instance, ends with its protagonist Mary Erle, a would-be writer, gazing down on London at sunset: "Standing alone, there on the heights, she made a feint as if to grasp the city spread out before her, but the movement ended in a vain gesture, and the radiance of her face was blotted out as she began to plod homewards in the twilight of the suburban road."[44] Bohemian women such as Nancy Cunard, Nina Hammett, as well as a number of artists – including Kathleen Hales, Evelyn Gibbs, and Elizabeth Vellácott – will erupt into London nightlife two decades later. In the 1890s women more typically returned home in the evening, although "home" might mean the bleak solitariness of lodgings. But for male writers of the city during this decade, the idiom was, as Fletcher observes, "nocturnal." And the night-time city, it hardly needs saying, is a place released from and licensed to withstand the bourgeois assumptions of what is "strenuous and virile."

As a consequence, some male poets identified with the energies of women who themselves were released from bourgeois assumptions. Hence Symons's "Nora on the Pavement," which celebrates a free spirit, "innocently spendthrift of herself" (*AS* I, 83) (Since the first performance in England in 1889 of Henrik Ibsen's *A Doll's House*, "Nora" had become a name synonymous with the rejection of conventional mores.) The poem ends:

> It is the soul of Nora,
> Living at last, and giving forth to the night,
> Bird-like, the burden of its own delight,
> All its desire, and all the joy of living,
> In that blithe madness in the soul of Nora.   (*AS* I, 84)

The poem comes from Symons's *London Nights*, published in 1896. Linda Dowling remarks that Symons found "London charged with 'romance' not least because it was the thrilling venue for his own sexual adventures; his poetic speakers see London's 'villainous music-halls' and 'little rooms' brimming with a special, if factitiously lurid glamour."[45] And she usefully draws attention to his claim, made in 1892 in the course of a review of Henley's poems, that the personal note in poetry – "personal romance, the romance of oneself"[46] – provided a fresh subject for poets faced with the exhaustion of traditional themes.

That the "romance of oneself" is the subject seems to have been widely accepted among members of Symons's coterie, with the result that, even when the apparent matter is derived from night-time London, the focus is really on the poet-creator. As Dowling observes, Herbert Horne transmutes a slum girl into an image of pastoral delight:

> She laughs through a summer of curls;
> She moves in a garden of grace:
> Her glance is a treasure of pearls,
> How saved from the deeps of her face!
>
> And the magical reach of her thigh
> Is the measure, with which God began
> To build up the peace of the sky,
> And fashion the pleasures of man.[47]

"A blithe rhythm out of Herrick," Dowling says, transforms this girl's life into "urban pastoral."[48] But is it straight out of Robert Herrick's seventeenth-century lyrics? Surely the early Swinburne is nearer to hand. The three-stress (predominantly anapestic) line is one that Swinburne made very much his own, most famously perhaps in those lines that T. S. Eliot would mock in 1920:

> Before the beginning of years
>   There came to the making of man
> Time, with a gift of tears;
>   Grief, with a glass that ran
>   (*Atalanta in Calydon*; *ACS* IV, 258)[49]

Eliot was no doubt right to deride the chorus from Swinburne's verse-drama *Atalanta in Calydon* (1865), which is styled on Aeschylus's tragedies, that contains these lines. As Eliot says, this passage "has not even the significance of commonplace" (148). And for good measure he adds that, although the Chorus appears to be making "a tremendous statement, like statements made in our dreams," it is the case that "when we wake up we find that the 'glass that ran' would do far better for time than for grief, and that the gift of tears would be as appropriately bestowed by grief as by time" (148–49). True, all true. Yet there is something slightly odd in the fact that Eliot's essay, written in 1920, when he was already brooding over the poem which would become *The Waste Land* (1922), has nothing to say about Swinburne's subject matter, above all Swinburne's readiness to handle sexual transgressiveness. Eliot appears to be solely concerned with the sound of Swinburne's words. But appearances, of course, can be deceptive. Swinburne's poetry, Eliot says, is "not morbid, it is not erotic, it is not destructive. These are adjectives which can be applied to the material, the human feelings, which in Swinburne's case do not exist" (149). Eliot, in my view, is working his way toward deciding what will make for a poetry of erotic morbid human feelings – the feelings of, say, Tiresias's words, or those of the city director's wife, or those of the typist and the clerk in *The Waste Land*.

And then we have to notice that *The Waste Land*, that definitive city poem as it has seemed to some critics, is very much absorbed with a subject whose roots are at least partly to be located in the night soil of the fin de siècle. And what nourishes that soil? The answer is Swinburne's poetry. As Fletcher observes: "The Victorian world in Swinburne's eyes was unable to resolve the antinomies that haunted it: the public world of bourgeois culture and repressive Christianity . . . The contradiction is only to be addressed in the closed world of pornography (to which Swinburne made his own contribution) or the counter-culture of free thinking and action" (xl). No wonder Eliot should wish to cover over Swinburne's readiness to expose such instabilities – instabilities that *The Waste Land* testifies to and yet by which it is betrayed. More to the point of the present chapter, it is no wonder that Swinburne could not be made Poet Laureate. For a little while longer, Alfred the Little would have to protect England from the growing threat to bourgeois culture. Austin's first publication as Laureate was *England's Darling* (1896), a verse-drama recounting how Alfred the Great saved England from Danish invasion. It ends with the rhetorical question "For why on English soil should foe's foot stand?"[50] But the enemy was already within.

NOTES

1   Carlyle's "Signs of the Times" first appeared in the *Edinburgh Review* 49 (1829), 439–59. In this essay, he famously defined the coming age as the "the Mechanical Age" (442), reprinted in *The Works of Thomas Carlyle*, 30 vols. (London: Chapman and Hall, 1896–99), XXVII, 59; further volume and page references appear in parentheses.
2   Charles Dickens, *Bleak House*, ed. George Ford and Sylvère Monod (New York: W.W. Norton, 1977), 5.
3   Henry James, *The Princess Casamassima*, New York edition, 26 vols. (New York: Scribner's, 1908), V, xxii.
4   Émile Zola, "Preface de la deuxième edition," in Zola, *La Confession de Claude et Thérèse Raquin*, Les Romans d'Émile Zola, 24 vols. (Lausanne: Éditions Recontre, 1960), XXI, 214.
5   The libel was made in John Ruskin, "Letter 79" (18 June 1877), *Fors Claveriga*, vol. 7, reprinted in *The Complete Works of John Ruskin*, ed. E.T. Cook and Alexander Wedderburn, 39 vols. (London: George Allen, 1907), XXIX, 160. Whistler began libel proceedings in November that year, and exactly twelve months later the case came to court.

6 W.H. Mallock, "A Familiar Colloquy," *Nineteenth Century* 4 (1885), 298. For more on Mallock's article, see John Lucas, "Tilting at the Moderns," in Lucas, *Romantic to Modern Literature* (Brighton: Harvester Press, 1982), 167–87. For the context of George Moore's pamphlet, see *George Moore: Literature at Nurse*, ed. Pierre Coustillas (Hassocks: Harvester Press, 1976), 9–24.

7 Norton B. Crowell, *Alfred Austin: Victorian* (London: Weidenfeld and Nicolson, 1955), 19–26; further page references appear in parentheses.

8 Edmund Gosse, *The Life of A.C. Swinburne* (New York: Macmillan, 1917), 276.

9 In the *Tatler* of 1877 Swinburne published a novel, *A Year's Letters*, under the name of "Mrs Horace Manners," although his authorship was an open secret. (When the novel was reprinted as *Love's Cross-Currents: A Year's Letters* [London: Chatto and Windus, 1905], it bore Swinburne's own name.) *Essays and Studies* (London Chatto and Windus, 1875) appeared under Swinburne's name.

10 Robert Bernard Martin, *Tennyson: The Unquiet Heart* (London: Oxford University Press and Faber and Faber, 1980), 559; further page references appear in parentheses.

11 Charles Tennyson, *Alfred Tennyson* (London: Macmillan, 1949), 494.

12 [J.R. Wise,] "Review of Lewis Morris, *The Ode of Life*," *Westminster Review* [American Edition], 114 (1880), 144.

13 [Anonymous,] "Review of Lewis Morris, *The Ode of Life*," *Nineteenth Century*, 6 (1880), 337.

14 James G. Nelson, *Sir William Watson* (New York: Twayne, 1966), 50; further page references appear in parentheses.

15 Watson, "Gladstone, 1885 (During the Soudanese War)," in *The Poems of Sir William Watson, 1878–1935* (London: Harrap, 1936), 27. Watson's "Ver Tenebrosum: Sonnets of March and April 1885" appeared in the *National Review* 5 (1885), 484–89.

16 Yeats's definitive remarks were made in the course of his essay "A Scholar Poet," *Providence Sunday Journal*, 15 June 1890, reprinted in Yeats, *Letters to the New Island*, ed. George Bornstein and Hugh Witemeyer, *The Collected Works of W.B. Yeats*, 12 vols. (New York: Macmillan, 1989), VII, 104. In 1892 Gladstone awarded Watson £200 from the Royal Bounty Fund. This was a magnanimous gesture, perhaps, but then Gladstone was a magnanimous man. (It is of course possible to read the gesture as implying thus far and no further. If so, Watson refused to understand the implication of Gladstone's gesture, for in the same year he produced a patriotic poem "England My Mother," intended no doubt to strengthen his claim to the Laureateship; see *The Poems of Sir William Watson*, 78–82.)

17 William Watson, "Preface," in Alfred Austin, *English Lyrics*, ed. Watson (London: Macmillan, 1890), xxiii.

18 Meredith's remark appears in Michael Field, *Works and Days, from the Journals of Michael Field*, ed. T. Sturge Moore (London: John Murray, 1932), 97.

19 See, for example, W.E. Henley, *The Song of the Sword and Other Verses* (London: David Nutt, 1898), and Henry Newbolt, *Admirals All and Other Verses* (London: John Lane, 1892).

20 Dowden's *Life of Percy Bysshe Shelley*, 2 vols. (London: Kegan Paul, Trench, 1886), while intending to be fully supportive of Shelley, had the opposite effect on many readers, who were or who claimed to be shocked by its many revelations about the irregularity of Shelley's life, especially the poet's love affairs, his two marriages, and his passionate avowal of the rights of free love.

21 Matthew Arnold, "Shelley," *Nineteenth Century* 23 (1888), 23–39, reprinted in Arnold, *The Last Word*, ed. R.H. Super, *The Complete Prose Works of Matthew Arnold*, 11 vols. (Ann Arbor, MI: University of Michigan Press, 1960–1977), XI, 320; further volume and page references appear in parentheses.

22 Matthew Arnold, *Culture and Anarchy: An Essay in Political and Social Criticism*, in *The Complete Prose Works of Matthew Arnold*, V, 106.

23 R.H. Super, in Arnold, *Culture and Anarchy*, 471.

24 "Thomas Maitland" [Robert Buchanan] "The Fleshly School of Poetry," *Contemporary Review* 18 (1871), 335. "Thomas Maitland" was the pseudonym attached to Buchanan's essay.

25 Dante Gabriel Rossetti replied to Buchanan's "The Fleshly School of Poetry," in "The Stealthy School of Criticism," *Athenaeum*, 16 December 1871, 792–94. Swinburne responded at length to Buchanan's pamphlet *The Fleshly School of Poetry and Other Phenomena of the Day* (London: Strahan, 1872) in *Under the Microscope* (London: Hotten, 1872).

26 Buchanan, "The Monkey and the Microscope," *St. Paul's Magazine* 9 (1872), 240.

27 "Thomas Maitland" [Algernon Charles Swinburne], "The Devil's Due," *Examiner*, 11 December 1875, 1388.

28 Richard Ellmann writes of Wilde as an undergraduate torn between Walter Pater, the apostle of aestheticism who taught at Brasenose College, Oxford, and John Ruskin, the most eminent nineteenth-century art critic. Wilde was certainly influenced by Ruskin, for a short time at least; he even helped dig the planned road to Ferry Hinksey near Oxford. But Wilde's leaning toward Pater's aestheticism becomes more pronounced as his Oxford career develops; see Ellmann, *Oscar Wilde* (London: Hamish Hamilton, 1987), 47–52.

29 [John Morley,] "Mr Swinburne's New Poems," *Saturday Review* 22 (1866), 145.

30 In his famous "red" letter of 2 August 1871, Gerard Manley Hopkins informed Robert Bridges: "Horrible to say, in a manner I am a Communist . . . England has grown hugely wealthy but this wealth has not reached the working classes . . . The more I look the more black and deservedly black the future looks." *The Letters of Gerard Manley Hopkins to Robert Bridges*, ed. Claude Colleer Abbott (London: Oxford University Press, 1935), 27–28.

31 W.H. Mallock, *Memoirs of Life and Literature* (New York: Harper and Brothers, 1920), 73; further page references appear in parentheses.

32 W.H. Mallock, *Every Man His Own Poet, or the Inspired Singer's Recipe Book*, second edition (London: Simkin, Marshall, 1877), reprinted in *Victorian Poets after 1850*, *Dictionary of Literary Biography*, eds. William E. Fredeman and Ira B. Nadel, 200 vols. to date (Detroit, MI: Gale Research Company, 1985), XXXV, 298.

33 Arnold, "Shelley," in *The Last Word*, 327. Here Arnold is quoting from his

earlier essay "Byron" that first appeared in *Macmillan's Magazine* 43 (1880–81), 367–77, reprinted in Arnold, *English Literature and Irish Politics*, ed. R.H. Super, *The Complete Prose Works of Matthew Arnold*, XI, 237; further page reference appears in parentheses.

34 *British Poetry and Prose, 1870–1905*, ed. Ian Fletcher (Oxford: Oxford University Press, 1987), 486–87; further page references appear in parentheses.

35 W.B. Yeats, *Autobiographies: Reveries over Childhood and Youth and The Trembling of the Veil* (London: Macmillan, 1926), 373; further page reference appears in parentheses.

36 Max Nordau, *Degeneration*, trans. anonymous (Lincoln, NE: University of Nebraska Press, 1968), 21; further page references appear in parentheses. This edition reprints the English-language translation published by D. Appleton in New York in 1895.

37 Oscar Wilde, *The Picture of Dorian Gray*, ed. Donald L. Lawler, Norton Critical Edition (New York: W.W. Norton, 1988), 3–4.

38 Chris Healy, *To-Day*, 8 October 1902, cited in Ellmann, *Oscar Wilde*, 550.

39 Mosse, "Introduction," in Nordau, *Degeneration*, xx; further page reference appears in parentheses.

40 James Thomson, "The City of Dreadful Night," in Thomson, *The City of Dreadful Night and Other Poems* (London: Reeves and Turner, 1880), 2. Thomson's poem first appeared in the Republican *National Reformer* during March–May 1874.

41 Bertram Dobell, *The Laureate of Pessimism: A Sketch of the Life and Character of James Thomson ("B.V.")* (London: Bertram Dobell, 1910), 58. This passage has some similarities with remarks that Dobell made in his lengthy memoir of Thomson that prefaces *The Poetical Works of James Thomson*, ed. Dobell, 2 vols. (London: Reeves and Turner, 1895), I, ix–xcii.

42 John Stokes, *In the Nineties* (Hemel Hempstead: Harvester Wheatsheaf, 1989), 118; further page reference appears in parentheses.

43 Arthur Symons, "A Literary Censure: A Book of Verses," *Savoy* 4 (1896), 91–93.

44 Ella Hepworth Dixon, *The Story of a Modern Woman*, ed. Kate Flint (London: Merlin Press, 1990), 271.

45 Linda Dowling, *Language and Decadence in the Victorian Fin de Siècle* (Princeton, NJ: Princeton University Press, 1986), 219.

46 Symons, "Mr Henley's Poetry," *Fortnightly Review* 52 (1892), 188.

47 Herbert Horne, "Paradise Walk," in Horne, *Diversi Colores* (London: Privately Printed, 1891), 23, cited in Dowling, *Language and Decadence in the Victorian Fin de Siècle*, 222.

48 Dowling, *Language and Decadence in the Victorian Fin de Siècle*, 222.

49 Eliot cites these lines in "Swinburne as Poet," in Eliot, *The Sacred Wood: Essays in Poetry and Criticism* (London: Methuen, 1928), 148; further page references appear in parentheses. Eliot's essay was first published in *Athenaeum*, 16 January 1920, 72–73 and revised for the first edition of *The Sacred Wood* (London: Methuen, 1920).

50 Austin, *England's Darling* (London: Macmillan, 1896), 94.

GLOSSARY

accentual-syllabic verse Sometimes called "stress-and-syllable" verse, it counts a repeated number of stresses and the syllables between them. Combining the "stress" model of Old English and the "syllable" model of Old French, "accentual-syllabic verse" has been the predominant meter of English poetry since the time of Chaucer.

anapest A metrical foot comprising two unstressed syllables followed by a stressed syllable (i.e. x x /).

apostrophe A figure of speech that addresses an absent or dead person or an animate object as if he, she, or it were alive or present.

caesura A gap in the continuity of a line that is subject to a metrical rule; it can be used to create emphasis.

dactyl A metrical foot comprising a stressed syllable followed by two unstressed syllables (i.e. / x x).

dimiter A metrical line of two feet.

end-stopped This is where a line of poetry comes to an end with the completion of a syntactical unit.

enjambment Sometimes called a "run-on," enjambment is where one line of poetry flows into the next. Strictly speaking, enjambment denotes where there is a difference between the metrical completion of a line and the continuing movement of a syntactical unit from one line to another.

hexameter A metrical line of six feet.

iamb A metrical foot comprising a unstressed syllable followed by a stressed syllable (i.e. x /); the most common metrical foot in English poetry.

intertextuality This concept suggests that all texts are inescapably enmeshed with many other different texts that circulate within a culture. In other words, all texts are bearers of a multiplicity of intertexts by way of allusion, sources of influence, and levels of discourse.

intratextuality The interrelations between the texts contained within an author's canon of work.

pathetic fallacy A term coined by John Ruskin in *Modern Painters* VIII (1856) that describes the ways that poets attribute human feelings to the natural world; it is close in sense to the term anthropomorphism.

pentameter A metrical line of five feet. Iambic pentameter is the most common meter in English poetry.

prosody The study of structures of verse, namely meter, rhyme, and stanza.

pyrrhic   A metrical foot comprising two unstressed syllables (i.e. x x).

quantitative verse   Classical verse adopts quantitative prosody, so-called because it depends on the duration of each syllable; such prosody is based upon a contrast between long and short syllables.

spondee   A metrical foot comprising two stressed syllables (i.e. / /).

tetrameter   A metrical line of four feet.

trimeter   A metrical line of three feet.

trochee   A metrical foot comprising a stressed syllable followed by an unstressed syllable (i.e. / x).

GUIDE TO FURTHER READING

Anthologies of Victorian poetry

Armstrong, Isobel and Joseph Bristow with Cath Sharrock, eds., *Nineteenth-Century Women Poets: An Oxford Anthology* (Oxford: Clarendon Press, 1996).

Collins, Thomas J. and Vivienne J. Rundle, eds., *The Broadview Anthology of Victorian Poetry and Poetic Theory* (Peterborough, Ontario: Broadview Press, 1999). The most comprehensive anthology currently available.

Karlin, Daniel, ed., *The Penguin Book of Victorian Verse* (Harmondsworth: Penguin Books, 1997).

Leighton, Angela and Margaret Reynolds, eds., *Victorian Women Poets: An Anthology* (Oxford: Basil Blackwell, 1995).

Maidment, Brian, ed., *The Poorhouse Fugitives: Self-Taught Poets and Poetry in Victorian Britain* (Manchester: Carcanet, 1987).

Victorian criticism of poetry

Armstrong, Isobel, *Victorian Scrutinies: Reviews of Poetry, 1830–1870* (London: Athlone, 1972).

Beckson, Karl, ed., *Oscar Wilde: The Critical Heritage* (London: Routledge and Kegan Paul, 1970).

Bristow, Joseph, ed., *The Victorian Poet: Poetics and Persona* (Beckenham: Croom Helm, 1987).

Cox, R.G., ed., *Thomas Hardy: The Critical Heritage* (London: Routledge and Kegan Paul, 1970).

Dawson, Carl, ed., *Matthew Arnold, the Poetry: The Critical Heritage* (London: Routledge and Kegan Paul, 1973).

Faulkner, Peter, ed., *William Morris: The Critical Heritage* (London: Routledge and Kegan Paul, 1973).

Green, Roger Lancelyn, ed., *Kipling: The Critical Heritage* (London: Routledge and Kegan Paul, 1971).

Hyder, Clyde K., ed., *Swinburne: The Critical Heritage* (London: Routledge and Kegan Paul, 1970).

Jump, John D., ed., *Tennyson: The Critical Heritage* (London: Routledge and Kegan Paul, 1967).

Litzinger, Boyd and Donald Smalley, eds., *Browning: The Critical Heritage* (London: Routledge and Kegan Paul, 1970).
Roberts, Gerald, ed., *Gerard Manley Hopkins: The Critical Heritage* (London: Routledge and Kegan Paul, 1987).
Thorpe, Michael, ed., *Clough: The Critical Heritage* (London: Routledge and Kegan Paul, 1972).
Williams, Ioan, ed., *Meredith: The Critical Heritage* (London: Routledge and Kegan Paul, 1971).

MODERN CRITICISM OF VICTORIAN POETRY

General studies

Armstrong, Isobel and Virginia Blain, eds., *Women's Poetry, Late Romantic to Late Victorian: Gender and Genre, 1830–1900* (New York: St. Martin's Press, 1999).
Armstrong, Isobel, *Victorian Poetry: Poetry, Politics, Poetics* (London: Routledge, 1993). Comprehensive study that includes detailed readings of poems by broad range of poets.
Campbell, Matthew, *Rhythm and Will in Victorian Poetry* (Cambridge: Cambridge University Press, 1999). Chapters explore the works of Robert Browning, Hopkins, and Tennyson.
Christ, Carol T., *Victorian and Modern Poetics* (Chicago, IL: University of Chicago Press, 1984). Clarifies connections and distinctions between Victorian and Modernist poetic methods.
Dellamora, Richard, *Masculine Desire: The Sexual Politics of Victorian Aestheticism* (Chapel Hill, NC: University of North Carolina Press, 1990). Includes chapters on Hopkins, Swinburne, and Tennyson.
Edmond, Rod, *Affairs of the Hearth: Victorian Poetry and Domestic Narrative* (London: Routledge, 1988). Includes studies of Elizabeth Barrett Browning, Clough, Meredith, Christina Rossetti, and Tennyson.
Elfenbein, Andrew, *Byron and the Victorians* (Cambridge: Cambridge University Press, 1995). Study of intertextual relations between an influential Romantic poet and his Victorian successors.
Faas, Ekbert, *Retreat into the Mind: Victorian Poetry and the Rise of Psychiatry* (Princeton, NJ: Princeton University Press, 1988). An inclusive study that concentrates attention on the dramatic monologue.
Griffiths, Eric, *The Printed Voice of Victorian Poetry* (Oxford: Oxford University Press, 1989). Includes chapters on Robert Browning, Hopkins, and Tennyson.
Harrison, Antony H., *Victorian Poets and the Politics of Culture: Discourse and Ideology* (Charlottesville, VA: University Press of Virginia, 1998). Includes studies of Arnold, Robert Browning, Christina Rossetti, and Tennyson.
Harrison, Antony H., *Victorian Poets and Romantic Poems: Intertextuality and Ideology* (Charlottesville, VA: University Press of Virginia, 1990). Features chapters on relations between Romantic poets and Arnold, Robert Browning, Morris, Christina Rossetti, Dante Gabriel Rossetti, Swinburne, and Tennyson.

Janowitz, Anne, *Lyric and Labour in the Romantic Tradition* (Cambridge: Cambridge University Press, 1998). Includes studies of Chartist, Republican, and socialist poets such as Ernest Jones, W.J. Linton, and Morris.

Leighton, Angela, ed., *Victorian Women Poets: A Critical Reader* (Oxford: Basil Blackwell, 1996). Contains studies of Hemans, Elizabeth Barrett Browning, Emily Brontë, George Eliot, Procter, Christina Rossetti, Michael Field, Rosamund Marriott Watson (Graham R. Tomson), and M.E. Coleridge.

Leighton, Angela, *Victorian Women Poets: Writing against the Heart* (Charlottesville, VA: University Press of Virginia, 1992). Includes chapters on Hemans, L.E.L., Elizabeth Barrett Browning, Christina Rossetti, Webster, Michael Field, Alice Meynell, and Charlotte Mew.

Lootens, Tricia, *Lost Saints: Silence, Gender, and Victorian Literary Canonization* (Charlottesville, VA: University Press of Virginia, 1996). Features studies of Elizabeth Barrett Browning and Christina Rossetti.

Lucas, John, *England and Englishness* (London: Hogarth Press, 1990). Includes discussions of Arnold, Robert Browning, Clough, and Tennyson.

McSweeney, Kerry, *Supreme Attachments: Studies in Victorian Love Poetry* (Aldershot: Ashgate, 1998). Includes studies of Robert Browning, Clough, Hardy, Meredith, Dante Gabriel Rossetti, Patmore, and Tennyson

Mellor, Anne K., *Romanticism and Gender* (New York: Routledge, 1993). Includes discussions of Hemans and L.E.L.

Mermin, Dorothy, *The Audience in the Poem: Five Victorian Poets* (New Brunswick, NJ: Rutgers University Press, 1983). Focuses on speakers and auditors in the works of Arnold, Robert Browning, Clough, Meredith, and Tennyson.

Prins, Yopie, *Victorian Sappho* (Princeton, NJ: Princeton University Press, 1999). Contains chapters on Michael Field and Swinburne.

Psomiades, Kathy Alexis, *Beauty's Body: Femininity and Representation in British Aestheticism* (Stanford, CA: Stanford University Press, 1997). Includes analyses of Tennyson, Dante Gabriel Rossetti, and Swinburne.

Shaw, W. David, *The Lucid Veil: Poetic Truth in the Victorian Age* (London: Athlone Press, 1987). Links poetry to major philosophical debates of the era.

Shaw, W. David, "Lyric Displacement in the Victorian Monologue: Naturalizing the Vocative," *Nineteenth-Century Literature* 52 (1997), 302–25.

Slinn, E. Warwick, *The Discourse of Self in Victorian Poetry* (Charlottesville, VA: University Press of Virginia, 1991). Contains chapters on Robert Browning, Clough, and Tennyson.

Sussman, Herbert L., *Victorian Masculinities: Manhood and Masculine Poetics in Early Victorian Literature and Art* (Cambridge: Cambridge University Press, 1995). Includes studies of the Pre-Raphaelites and Robert Browning.

Tennyson, G.B., *Victorian Devotional Poetry: The Tractarian Mode* (Berkeley, CA: University of California Press, 1981). Elucidates the works of John Keble, among other religious writers.

Thesing, William B., *The London Muse: Victorian Poetic Responses to the City* (Athens, GA: University of Georgia Press, 1982). Wide-ranging book that includes analyses of Morris and Tennyson, among many other poets.

Tucker, Herbert F., "Of Monuments and Moments: Spacetime in Nineteenth-Century Poetry," *Modern Language Quarterly* 58 (1997), 269–97.

INDIVIDUAL POETS

Arnold

Culler, A. Dwight, *Imaginative Reason: The Poetry of Matthew Arnold* (New Haven, CT: Yale University Press, 1966).

Hamilton, Ian, *A Gift Imprisoned: The Poetic Life of Matthew Arnold* (London: Bloomsbury, 1998).

Honan, Park, *Matthew Arnold: A Life* (New York: McGraw-Hill, 1981).

Murray, Nicholas, *A Life of Matthew Arnold* (London: Hodder and Stoughton, 1996).

Riede, David G., *Matthew Arnold and the Betrayal of Language* (Charlottesville, VA: University Press of Virginia, 1988).

Elizabeth Barrett Browning

Forster, Margaret, *Elizabeth Barrett Browning: The Lives and Loves of a Poet* (New York: St. Martin's Press, 1988). Biography that pays little close attention to the poetry.

Leighton, Angela, *Elizabeth Barrett Browning* (Bloomington, IN: Indiana University Press, 1986).

Lewis, Linda M., *Elizabeth Barrett Browning's Spiritual Progress: Face to Face with God* (Columbia, MI, 1998).

Mermin, Dorothy, *Elizabeth Barrett Browning: The Origins of a New Poetry* (Chicago, IL: University of Chicago Press, 1989).

Stone, Marjorie, *Elizabeth Barrett Browning* (New York: St. Martin's Press, 1995).

Robert Browning

Bloom, Harold, ed., *Robert Browning: A Collection of Critical Essays* (Englewood Cliffs, NJ: Prentice-Hall, 1980).

Bristow, Joseph, *Robert Browning* (New York: St. Martin's Press, 1991).

Gibson, Mary Ellis, ed., *Critical Essays on Robert Browning* (New York: G.K. Hall, 1992). Collection of recent criticism.

Gibson, Mary Ellis, *History and the Prism of Art: Browning's Poetic Experiments* (Columbus, OH: Ohio State University Press, 1987).

Karlin, Daniel, *Browning's Hatreds* (Oxford: Oxford University Press, 1995).

Karlin, Daniel and John Woolford, *Robert Browning* (Harlow: Longman, 1996).

Slinn, E. Warwick, *Browning and the Fictions of Identity* (Basingstoke: Macmillan, 1982).

Shaw, W. David, *The Dialectical Temper: The Rhetorical Art of Robert Browning* (Ithaca, NY: Cornell University Press, 1968).

Tucker, Herbert F., *Browning's Beginnings: The Art of Disclosure* (Minneapolis, MN: University of Minnesota Press, 1980). Covers the early poetry.

Tucker, Herbert F., "Epiphany and Browning: Character Made Manifest," *PMLA* 107 (1992), 1208–21.

Tucker, Herbert F., "Wanted Dead of Alive: Browning's Historicism," *Victorian Studies* 38 (1994), 25–39.

Arthur Hugh Clough

Biswas, Robindra Kumar, *Arthur Hugh Clough: Towards a Reconsideration* (Oxford: Clarendon Press, 1972).

Gatrell, Simon, "Histories de Voyages: The Italian Poems of Arthur Hugh Clough," in *Creditable Warriors, 1830–1876*, ed. Gatrell, English Literature and Wider World, vol. 3 (London: Ashfield, 1990), 159–72.

Greenberger, Evelyn Barish, *Arthur Hugh Clough: The Growth of a Poet's Mind* (Cambridge, MA: Harvard University Press, 1970).

Phelan, Joseph Patrick, "Radical Metre: The English Hexameter of Clough's *Bothie of Toper-na-Fuosich*," *Review of English Studies* 50 (1999), 166–87.

Tinko, Michael, *Innocent Victorian: The Satiric Poetry of Arthur Hugh Clough* (Athens, OH: Ohio University Press, 1966).

Thomas Hardy

Gibson, James, "Thomas Hardy's Poetry: Poetic Apprehension and Poetic Method," in *Celebrating Thomas Hardy: Insights and Appreciations*, ed. Charles P. Pettit (Basingstoke: Macmillan, 1996).

Green, Brian, *Hardy's Lyrics: Pearls of Pity* (Basingstoke: Macmillan, 1996).

Knoepflmacher, U.C., "Hardy Ruins: Female Spaces and Male Designs," *PMLA* 105 (1990), 1055–70.

Orel, Harold., ed., *Critical Essays on Thomas Hardy's Poetry* (New York: G.K. Hall, 1995). Collection of recent criticism.

Taylor, Dennis, *Hardy's Metres and Victorian Prosody* (Oxford: Clarendon Press, 1988).

Taylor, Dennis, *Hardy's Poetry, 1860–1928*, second edition (Basingstoke: Macmillan, 1989).

Felicia Hemans

Clarke, Norma, *Ambitious Heights: Writing, Friendship, and Love – The Jewsbury Sisters, Felicia Hemans and Jane Carlyle* (London: Routledge, 1990).

Lootens, Tricia, "Hemans and Home: Victorianism, Feminine 'Internal Enemies,' and the Domestication of National Identity," *PMLA* 109 (1994), 238–63.

Sweet, Nanora, "History, Imperialism, and the Aesthetics of the Beautiful: Hemans and the Post-Napoleonic Moment," in *At the Limits of Romanticism: Essays in Cultural, Feminist, and Materialist Criticism*, ed. Mary A. Favret and Nicola J. Watson (Bloomington, IN: Indiana University Press, 1994), 170–84.

Wolfson, Susan J., " 'Domestic Affections' and 'The Spear of Minerva': Felicia Hemans and the Dilemma of Gender," in *Re-Visioning Romanticism: British Women Writers, 1776–1837*, ed. Carol Shiner Wilson and Joel Haefner (Philadelphia, PA: University of Pennsylvania Press, 1994), 128–66.

Gerard Manley Hopkins

Beer, Gillian, "Helmholtz, Tyndall, Gerard Manley Hopkins: Leaps of the Prepared Imagination," *Comparative Criticism* 13 (1991), 117–45.

Bristow, Joseph, "'Churlsgrace': Gerard Manley Hopkins and the Working-Class Male Body," *ELH* 59 (1992), 693–711.

Brown, Daniel, *Hopkins's Idealism: Philosophy, Physics, Poetry* (Oxford: Clarendon Press, 1997).

Fennell, Francis L., ed., *Rereading Hopkins: Selected New Essays* (Victoria, British Columbia: University of Victoria, 1996).

Harris, Daniel A., *Inspirations Unbidden: The "Terrible" Sonnets of Gerard Manley Hopkins* (Berkeley, CA: University of California Press, 1982).

Hollahan, Eugene, ed., *Gerard Manley Hopkins and Critical Discourse* (New York: AMS Press, 1993). Collection of recent criticism.

Martin, Robert Bernard, *Gerard Manley Hopkins: A Very Private Life* (London: HarperCollins, 1991).

Sprinker, Michael, *A Counterpoint of Dissonance: The Aesthetics and Poetry of Gerard Manley Hopkins* (Baltimore, MD: The Johns Hopkins University Press, 1980).

White, Norman, *Hopkins: A Literary Biography* (Oxford: Clarendon Press, 1992).

Zaniello, Tom, *Hopkins in the Age of Darwin* (Iowa City, IA: University of Iowa Press, 1988).

Rudyard Kipling

Keating, Peter, *Kipling the Poet* (London: Secker and Warburg, 1994).

Orel, Harold, ed., *Critical Essays on Rudyard Kipling* (New York: G.K. Hall, 1994). Includes three essays on Kipling's poetry.

Parry, Ann, *The Poetry of Rudyard Kipling* (Buckingham: Open University Press, 1992).

L.E.L (Letitia Elizabeth Landon)

Stephenson, Glennis, *Letitia Landon: The Woman behind L.E.L.* (Manchester: Manchester University Press, 1995).

Amy Levy

Bristow, Joseph, "'All out of Tune in this World's Instrument': The 'Minor' Poetry of Amy Levy," *Journal of Victorian Culture* 5 (1999), 76–103.

Scheinberg, Cynthia, "Canonizing the Jew: Amy Levy's Challenge to Victorian Poetic Identity," *Victorian Studies* 39 (1996), 173–200.

William Morris

Boos, Florence S., "The Argument of *The Earthly Paradise*," *Victorian Poetry* 23 (1985), 75–92.

Boos, Florence S., "Sexual Polarities in *The Defence of Guenevere*," *Browning Institute Studies* 13 (1985), 181–200.

Boos, Florence S. and Carole G. Silver, eds., *Socialism and the Literary Artistry of William Morris* (Columbia, MI: University of Missouri Press, 1990).

Riede, David G., "Morris, Modernism, and Romance," *ELH* 51 (1984), 85–106.

Shaw, W. David, "Arthurian Ghosts: The Phantom Art of 'The Defence of Guenevere,'" *Victorian Poetry* 34 (1996), 299–312.

Smith, Lindsay, *Victorian Photography, Painting and Poetry: The Enigma of Visibility in Ruskin, Morris and the Pre-Raphaelites* (Cambridge: Cambridge University Press, 1995).

Tompkins, J.M.S., *William Morris: An Approach to the Poetry* (London: Cecil Woolf, 1987).

Christina Rossetti

Arseneau, Mary, Antony H. Harrison, and Lorraine Janzen Kooistra, eds., *The Culture of Christina Rossetti: Female Poetics and Victorian Contexts* (Athens, GA: Ohio University Press, 1999).

Harrison, Antony H., *Christina Rossetti in Context* (Chapel Hill, NC: University of North Carolina Press, 1988).

Jones, Kathleen, *"Learning Not to Be First": The Life of Christina Rossetti* (New York: St. Martin's Press, 1991).

Kent, David A., ed., *The Achievement of Christina Rossetti* (Ithaca, NY: Cornell University Press, 1987).

Marsh, Jan, *Christina Rossetti: A Literary Biography* (London: Jonathan Cape, 1994).

Rosenblum, Dolores, *Christina Rossetti: the Poetry of Endurance* (Carbondale, IL: Southern Illinois University Press, 1986).

Dante Gabriel Rossetti

Anderson, Amanda S., "D.G. Rossetti's 'Jenny': Agency, Intersubjectivity, and the Prostitute," *Genders* 4 (1989), 103–21.

Harris, Daniel A., "D.G. Rossetti's 'Jenny': Sex, Money, and the Interior Monologue," *Victorian Poetry* 22 (1984), 197–215.

McGann, Jerome J., "Dante Gabriel Rossetti and the Betrayal of Truth," *Victorian Poetry* 26 (1988), 339–61.

Riede, David G., *Dante Gabriel Rossetti and the Limits of Victorian Vision* (Ithaca, NY: Cornell University Press, 1983).

Riede, David G., *Dante Gabriel Rossetti Revisited* (New York: Twayne, 1992).

Sheets, Robin, "Pornography and Art: The Case of 'Jenny,'" *Critical Inquiry* 14 (1988), 315–34.

Algernon Charles Swinburne

Clements, Patricia, *Baudelaire and the English Tradition* (Princeton, NJ: Princeton University Press, 1985). Includes a detailed study of Swinburne.

Harrison, Antony H., *Swinburne's Medievalism: A Study in Victorian Love Poetry* (Baton Rouge, LA: Louisiana State University Press, 1988).

Louis, Margot K., *Swinburne and His Gods* (Montreal: McGill-Queen's University Press, 1990).

McGann, Jerome J., *Swinburne: An Experiment in Criticism* (Chicago, IL: University of Chicago Press, 1972).

Morgan, Thaïs E., "Male Lesbian Bodies: The Construction of Alternative Masculinities in Courbet, Baudelaire, and Swinburne," *Genders* 15 (1992), 37–57.

Morgan, Thaïs E., "Swinburne's Dramatic Monologues: Sex and Ideology," *Victorian Poetry* 22 (1984), 175–95.

Rooksby, Rikky, *A.C. Swinburne: A Poet's Life* (Aldershot: Scolar Press, 1997).

Rooksby, Rikky and Nicholas Shrimpton, eds., *The Whole Music of Passion: New
Essays on Swinburne* (Aldershot: Scolar Press, 1993).

Alfred Tennyson

Culler, A. Dwight, *The Poetry of Tennyson* (New Haven, CT: Yale University Press,
1977).

Hair, Donald S., *Tennyson's Language* (Toronto: University of Toronto Press,
1991).

Hughes, Linda K., *The Manyfaced Glass: Tennyson's Dramatic Monologues*
(Athens, OH: Ohio University Press, 1987).

Jordan, Elaine, *Alfred Tennyson* (Cambridge: Cambridge University Press, 1998).

Joseph, Gerhard, *Tennyson and the Text: The Weaver's Shuttle* (Cambridge: Cambridge University Press, 1992). Post-structuralist study.

Martin, Robert Bernard, *Tennyson: The Unquiet Heart* (Oxford: Clarendon Press,
1980). Standard biography.

Ricks, Christopher, *Tennyson* (London: Macmillan, 1972).

Rowlinson, Matthew, *Tennyson's Fixations: Psychoanalysis and the Topics of the
Early Poetry* (Charlottesville, VA: University Press of Virginia, 1994).

Shaw, Marion, *Alfred Lord Tennyson* (Hemel Hempstead: Harvester Wheatsheaf,
1988). Feminist study.

Shaw, W. David, *Tennyson's Style* (Ithaca, NY: Cornell University Press, 1976).

Sinfield, Alan, *Alfred Tennyson* (Oxford: Basil Blackwell, 1986). Materialist study.

Stott, Rebecca, ed., *Alfred Tennyson: A Critical Reader* (Harlow: Addison Wesley
Longman, 1997). Collection of recent criticism.

Tucker, Herbert F., ed., *Critical Essays on Alfred Lord Tennyson* (New York: G.K.
Hall, 1993). Collection of recent criticism.

Tucker, Herbert F., *Tennyson and the Doom of Romanticism* (Cambridge, MA:
Harvard University Press, 1988). Focuses on Tennyson's writings up to and
including *Maud*.

Oscar Wilde

Alkalay-Gut, Karen, "The Thing He Loves: Murder as an Aesthetic Experience in
'The Ballad of Reading Gaol,'" *Victorian Poetry* 35 (1997), 349–66.

Buckley, Jerome H., "Echo and Artifice: The Poetry of Oscar Wilde," *Victorian
Poetry* 28 (1990), 19–31.

Gagnier, Regenia, *Idylls of the Marketplace: Oscar Wilde and the Victorian Public*
(Stanford, CA: Stanford University Press, 1986). Includes discussion of "The
Ballad of Reading Gaol."

Nathan, Leonard, "The Ballads of Reading Gaol: At the Limits of Lyric," in *Critical
Essays on Oscar Wilde*, ed. Regenia Gagnier (New York: G.K. Hall, 1991),
213–22.

INDEX